HERSTORY

Based on the information in these commonly-used high school texts, one might summarize the history and contributions of the American woman as follows: Women arrived in 1619 . . . They held the Seneca Falls Convention on Women's Rights in 1848. During the rest of the nineteenth century, they participated in reform movements, chiefly temperance, and were exploited in factories. In 1920 they were given the vote. They joined the armed forces for the first time during the second World War and thereafter have enjoyed the good life in America. Add the names of the women who are invariably mentioned: Harriet Beecher Stowe, Jane Addams, Dorothea Dix, and Frances Perkins, with perhaps Susan B. Anthony, Elizabeth Cady Stanton and, almost as frequently, Carrie Nation, and you have the basic "text."

—Janice Law Trecker, "Women in U.S. History High School Textbooks," *Social Education*, March 1971

HERSTORY

*A
WOMAN'S
VIEW
OF
AMERICAN
HISTORY*

JUNE SOCHEN

*Alfred Publishing Co., Inc.
New York*

Grateful acknowledgment is made for use of the following:

As Time Goes By / page 353
© 1931 Harms, Inc.
Copyright Renewed, All Rights Reserved
Used by permission of Warner Bros. Music

Ivory and Horn / page 379
from *Manhattan Pastures*
© 1963 by Yale University Press

Library of Congress Catalog Card Number: 74-80471

ISBN: 0-88284-017-7 (hard cover)
ISBN: 0-88284-018-5 (soft cover)

Printed in the United States of America

This book has been set at Precision Typographers by Pat-
ricia Pelton and Susan Mayer on the V.I.P. in Caledonia
type with Bulmer display. Mechanicals were prepared by
Patricia McLaughlin. The picture research was done by
Donna Dennis and Iris Manus. Mary Elinore Smith edited
the manuscript. The cover design is the work of Loretta
Trezzo. Printing was done by Noble Offset Printers in
New York.

Alfred Publishing Co.
75 Channel Drive, Port Washington, New York, 11050

Dedication

*To my mother and father, who brought me up
to be a* person, *not a gender.*

Preface

*H*erstory: A Woman's View of American History is both an ambitious and a modest effort to present the woman's side of the American past. It is ambitious because it contains, within one volume, a lot of forgotten material about half of the human beings who lived in and built the United States of America. It is modest because it imposes so many restrictions, limitations, and boundaries upon the material. *Herstory* does not pretend to deal with all or most of the important women and women's accomplishments any more than a book by a male historian "covers" all of male-oriented American history. It is presumptuous for any historian, male or female, to pretend comprehensiveness in any single volume.

Herstory hopes to point some new roads for future readers, researchers, and writers to travel. The future possibilities in woman's herstory are rich and endless. My discussion concentrates upon two broad areas: upon the *ideology* held concerning women, children, blacks, American Indians, and foreigners —that is, all non-white American males; and upon the *reality* of their lives. At times, *Herstory* sweeps across the human landscape with bold, broad strokes, and at other times it narrows the subject matter and focuses upon specific women in specific places at specific times.

Among my particular concerns in the following pages is the similar treatment that WASMs (white Anglo-Saxon males) gave to all human beings other than themselves, as well as to the environment. There are more similarities than differences between the white male attitude toward women, Indians, black slaves, forests, and wildlife than historians have realized. Thus, the

Preface

following chapters, though largely concerned with women's lives and thoughts, also include material about these other less privileged humans and about the preyed-upon environment. This combination of themes may disconcert some, startle others, and confuse a few. The intention, however, is to point out the multiple examples of WASM consistency, in attitude and behavior, toward recurrent problems in the American past.

Though organized chronologically and thus traditionally, *Herstory* does not recount presidential administrative actions in predictable fashion, nor does it review political or military activities. Rather, it surveys each major period in light of the life stories, experiences, and thoughts of some of its forgotten Americans. Women, constituting a majority of Americans, have been the most ignored and therefore receive the most attention in this book.

I would like to thank Bill Knowles, my editor, and Iris and Morty Manus, my publishers, for their encouragement and thoughtful comments during the preparation of this book. Mary Elinore Smith, my copy editor, has also been enormously helpful. Two of my colleagues at Northeastern Illinois University, Professors Gregory Singleton and Duke Frederick, were helpful in their comments on early drafts of *Herstory;* and I acknowledge my gratitude to them. Ultimately, of course, the perspective and analysis revealed in the following pages reflect my own biases, interests, and values, for which I assume full responsibility.

June Sochen
Northeastern Illinois University

Contents

Contents

Contents

xiii

HERSTORY

CHAPTER ONE

Introduction

Today we make the machine the standard for everything. Among the most admired, the most successful, the most envied men are those who in manner resemble machines: men who are efficient, punctual, serious, standardized . . . who can harness the power of nature and turn it into wealth. We think like the Sioux, only we think about different things. We imitate the machine. He imitated the buffalo.

 —Stanley Vestal, *Sitting Bull: Champion of the Sioux*

More than 100,000 small farmers are going out of business every year. Only 2.88 million farm operators remain, of whom 1.5 million earn less than poverty-level incomes. As the exodus grows, hundreds of once flourishing small towns are shriveling and dying.

 —James M. Pierce, *The Condition of Farm Workers and Small Farmers in 1971*, Report to the National Board of National Sharecroppers Fund

Gentle, withdrawing, but withdrawing permanently, she backed out of people's lives, turning aside from offers of friendship, from urgency, intensity, the admiration of men who did not know her at all. She liked all these people well enough, she just did not want to be close to them.

 —Joyce Carol Oates, *Bodies*

And so, in the administration of a State neither a woman as a woman nor a man as a man has any special function, but the gifts of nature are equally diffused in both sexes, all the pursuits of men are the pursuits of women also, and in all of them woman is only a lesser man.

 —Plato, *The Republic*, Book V

1

Point of View

Writers of American history rarely dwell on the forgotten victims of white American "progress." Losers have no place in official history, only victors. American Indians, women, black Americans, marginal farmers and children, collectively, constitute a large and significant group of hidden Americans who have largely been ignored by historians. When these losers gained the courage to express their discontent, their voices were unheeded, their pleas heartlessly denied. This aspect of American history has been muted and, whenever possible, omitted. Most American historians prefer to view the story of our country as one of progress and uplift—is it by chance that they are white males?

The history of the United States is a grand success story from one point of view and a grand failure from another. It is a story of the growth, expansion, and development of a continent—and at the same time the story of the destruction of the native American Indian population and the despoliation of the natural landscape. It is the story of material accumulation and human impoverishment. It is the rhetoric of freedom and the reality of repressing women, blacks, and American Indians. The Europeans who were transplanted to these shores believed they had to tame and conquer all natural and human obstacles. The forests had to be cut down, the Indians chased away or killed, and the wilderness transformed into villages.

The abundance of wildlife on vast stretches of land amazed and impressed all early explorers of these shores. Truly, this was the land of milk and honey promised by the Lord. Those who migrated here considered themselves chosen people who de-

3

served the riches they gained through their hard work and suffering.

In less than four hundred years, a continent of endless forests and prairies was transformed into a nation with the most advanced technological society in human history. This is one kind of success story—a materialistic success story of man-made products prevailing over the natural environment—of highways, cars, computers, and spaceships. This concept of success, or "progress," was made by men, white men, *for* white men. Surely the white men believed that they brought happiness and prosperity to their women and children as well. But the active doing, the measurable accomplishments, were male determined and male evaluated. There was little flexibility or choice for the ignored Americans; neither women, children, black slaves, nor Indians participated in deciding their fate.

I call this book a "feminist-humanist" commentary on American history. Why feminist-humanist? As a woman historian, I have come to the conclusion that the historians (mostly male) who have written about the growth of this country do not view women as equal partners with men in the experience of building America. As a feminist who values all humanity, I think everyone who lived here should be included in any description of America's past. Women, children, blacks, and American Indians all worked, fought, loved, and hated alongside WASMs (white Anglo-Saxon males), the power-holders of the country. Their story requires inclusion in any re-creation of the past. They were never invisible or dispensable. No day passed without their critically needed participation.

There has always existed a minority of women, like a minority of black Americans and American Indians, who did not sit still, who did not accept society's strictures upon them. These people deserve a place in the history books, as do the ordinary undistinguished souls in each period: their everyday life and ideas, their attitudes toward child-raising, their favorite novels and movies. All human actions, admittedly, are not of equal worth; all human thought is not of equal validity. Evaluations and distinctions must be made in historical, as well as all other kinds of writing. But the student and general reader of history should be aware of both elite and popular ideas, and become acquainted with the lot of so-called common people.

Whose history am I reading? Who is writing it? What has

been included and what excluded? On what basis? *Herstory* reveals my perspective from the outset. Most historians strive for objectivity, which I reject as an unattainable and undesirable posture. I want to look at American history from the point of view of an educated woman, of a humanist, and of a historian trained in intellectual and cultural history. I want to question established views and introduce new ones. I am a loving critic of American capitalism, a serious questioner of the gap between American ideals and American reality, and a complete believer in the right of each human being to grow up without artificial and institutional restrictions. Of course, all of us are born with limitations inherited from our parents and ancestors, and we must all develop within these limitations. But throughout human history significant, often excruciating, cultural inhibitions have been placed upon human development as well. The institution of slavery precluded the natural growth of all black people, and the institution of the family prevented the development of women in other than wifely and maternal roles.

POPULAR MYTH: Women are the weaker sex.

CONTRARY EVIDENCE: American Indian women dried surplus meat, harvested wild rice, tanned buffalo hides, made tepees, cut wood with two- or three-pound hatchets, packed the horses' loads during a move, bore children, cooked, sewed, and cleaned.

POPULAR MYTH: American Indian women were promiscuous.

CONTRARY EVIDENCE (from Robert Beverly, *The History and Present State of Virginia*, 1705):

. . . the young Indian Women are said to prostitute their bodies for *wampom* peak, runtees, beads, and other such like fineries; yet I never could find any ground for the accusation, and believe it only to be an unjust scandal upon them. This I know, that if ever they have a child while they are single, it is such a disgrace to them, that they never after get husbands.

5

An Indian squaw's destiny. (Culver)

There are a variety of ways for humans to organize a society. If the human group in question held a feminist-equalitarian philosophy, they would develop equalitarian practices. If, on the other hand, they held an elite view of humanity—that is, the right of the few to dominate the many, they would develop a set of practices to implement that philosophy. Indeed, elitism has been a dominant world-view since the earliest civilizations. The United States has developed a third form of society: Americans have preached equalitarianism and practiced elitism. The colonists who wrote the Declaration of Independence never meant to include all humans in their definition of humanity. Women have always been treated as less than men, and American Indians and black Americans have been ruthlessly destroyed or exploited.

The ideas imposed upon Americans and other Western men and women by their religions have largely predetermined their life plan. The biblical view of Eve as man's first temptress, the

6

concept of children as miniature savages needing discipline, and the belief in sin and sinfulness have shaped Western thought and behavior in significant ways. The whole course of American history offers countless illustrations of people behaving according to attitudes inculcated in childhood; of people upholding the virtues of capitalism during a depression; and of people believing that each and every one of them could succeed according to the Horatio Alger formula. One example of success has buoyed the spirits and sustained the commitments of thousands.

Ideas are indeed powerful. The old ideas about women's roles persist in the last third of the twentieth century, when technology has made it eminently easy for women to control reproduction, leave the home, and pursue a wide variety of human activities. The gap, really a chasm, between the American ideals of equality, liberty, and happiness for all and the reality of gross institutional discrimination, of intolerance, of violence, and of cruelty has never been fully or even partially explored in standard accounts of American history.

This book is a modest, highly selective interpretation of American history. It is by no means a comprehensive study. All writers have their own perspectives, biases, and values. They include some things and leave out others. I shall try to present some well-known Americans in a new light and introduce my readers to certain other Americans who have not been given their rightful places in the records of America. Some of the ground retraced will be familiar, some unfamiliar. Using the feminist perspective, I will try to ask new questions about old material and restate certain eternal questions in new ways.

Obviously, not all deserving members of the forgotten groups—all notable women, all articulate blacks, and all courageous Indian spokesmen—can be included. Not only have I been restricted by the typical historical inhibition of being unable to include people whose records have not been preserved, but also by the limits of my own research and knowledge.

Power Positions

One of the old but essential historical questions that can be reexamined from a feminist perspective is that of power and politics.

Introduction

In 1970, Kate Millett called her study of how women are viewed in Western literature *Sexual Politics*. In so doing, she illuminated the relationship between sex and power in our culture. The image is a rich and multi-layered one: women use their sex to achieve whatever power they exert over the men in their lives because it is their only weapon. Males, who hold the power positions sexually, politically, economically, and culturally, have always decided everything. Any position of power assumes a hierarchy for all who participate, with some on top and some below. Men have always been on top, and women have always been dominated, sexually and in every other way. Men conferred status, power, and prestige upon their women and in a male-determined world, they still decided who should hold power.

Decision-makers may have disguised their power in sweet-sounding rhetoric, and power-holders have often preferred to wield influence behind the scenes rather than in public. In the early days of this country, each male Puritan minister would decide what moral and religious policies should govern his congregation. Then and now congressmen have made their "deals" before entering the legislative halls. The gift and talent of the powerful is to make the powerless accept their fate as just and proper. Only when the powerless rise to question the established order and mobilize to change it, can there be meaningful change. Otherwise, both the powerful and the powerless accept the terms of the arrangement, or at least do not oppose it strenuously.

From this point of view, women have been a powerless group throughout American history. Their exploitation was sometimes expressed in song.

FRONTIER SONGS ABOUT WOMEN

Took in some washin', made a dollar or two,
He comes and steals it, I don't know what to do.

—I Wish I Was a Single Girl Again

The grave will decay you and turn you to dust,
There's not one boy in fifty that a poor girl can trust.

—Foggy Dew

Dishes to wash and spring to go,
Now I am married, I've everything to do.
When I was single, marryin' was my crave,
Now I'm married, I've troubles to my grave.

—*Single Girl*

The heart is the fortune of all womankind,
They're always controlled, they're always confined,
Controlled by their family until they are wives,
Then slaves to their husbands the rest of their lives.

—*The Wagoner's Lad*

Because they knew little about the human body and how conception occurred, pioneer women and city women alike had many children. Dependent upon their husbands economically and psychically, they were without the will or the wherewithal to survive independently in the world. So they accepted the

While the colonial men at Cape Cod (background) practice shooting, the women carry on the essential domestic chores of the community. (Culver)

male view that maternity was their greatest experience and their major reason for living. Maternity, after all, was a biological reality that occurred to adult women frequently. Women defined themselves, as men defined them, in terms of their role as wife and mother. Women never became people, separate from this rigid definition. Some, of course, did not accept their cultural fate. Some women questioned their powerlessness; some rebelled and railed against it; and some quietly despaired.

Because women were powerless, they empathized with other powerless groups in the society: the Indians, the black slaves, the children, the orphans, the insane, and the criminal. It is no accident that women have been a vital part of every major American reform movement. They knew what powerlessness was, and working for deprived groups gave them a sense of power over their own lives that they had never known before. In helping others, they also helped themselves. This revelation occurred to individual women throughout American history. Helping to rid the world of drunkards gave women a measure of self-confidence and meaningful activity that some transferred to their personal lives. Temperance reform led a few women into feminist reform. But even the multitudes of women reformers who never became feminists learned a valuable lesson: they discovered they could be effective human beings in a role other than the wifely and maternal one.

Women's Unique Dilemma

Women hold an unusual place in the story of any country. As sociologist Alice Rossi has pointed out, they live in intimate relations with their oppressors and find it extraordinarily difficult to disassociate themselves from the males in their lives. How can a mother rebel against her husband and children? How can a young woman defy her father? A shipload of colonists may well perceive themselves as a cohesive group separate from Mother England, and slaves may view all white people as their enslavers, but women have an entirely different problem: they have always had strong ties with the power-holders who have enforced their state of powerlessness. In this paradox lies the critical reason for the woman's long period of submission to male domination.

A further dilemma emerges: women, growing up within the same culture, share the value system of their brothers, fathers, and husbands. They imitate their mothers and repeat the maternal life cycle. They share, then, in shaping and determining their own futures. In this sense, women cannot be described merely as victims; they are active participators in deciding their own destinies. Most men and women never question the validity of the culture's edicts; most never quarrel with the social roles they play. Only a few in each generation step out of the socially approved forms of behavior, evaluate them critically, and carve their own definitions of human conduct. Only a few criticize social institutions and attempt to change them.

POPULAR MYTH: All women stick together.

CONTRARY EVIDENCE (from Mrs. Gilbert E. Jones, an opponent of the right of women to vote, speaking in 1910):

Women are not well trained and often very deficient and unskilled in most of their occupations. They are generally only supplementary workers and drop their work when they marry. When married, and home and children are to be cared for, they are handicapped way beyond their strength. Married women should be kept out of industry, rather than urged into it, as scientists, physicians, and sociologists all state that as women enter into competitive industrial life with men, just so does the death rate of little children increase and the birth rate decrease.

The family structure, for example, emerges as the most durable and stable of social institutions. The way it is organized in the United States effectively demonstrates the Western commitment to male dominance. Girls obey their fathers and learn the lessons of domesticity from their mothers, always within the framework of the family. The family is viewed as all-important and the woman is expected to sacrifice her personal wishes to the good of its members. The father is the wage earner, and the mother is the homebody who cooks, cleans, cares for the children, and is a symbol of morality and decency to her children. But women never wrote the rules that regulate family life. Obedience and submission within a family tradition that lauded the sacredness of motherhood—this has been the consistent

A colonial wife's sphere. (Culver)

message instilled into the female of the species. The male sex has always represented power and authority, and doubters of both sexes have been severely treated.

Social control has always been a powerful instrument to preserve the status quo. Small, cohesive communities in agricultural America enforced the social code and tolerated little deviation from it. Both sexes accepted the validity of the system, and in that sense women participated in their own enslavement. But they had little choice. Since they married young and became mothers quickly, biology seemed to determine their cultural destiny. Women who tried to experiment with other life roles found that when their childbearing days were over, few opportunities were available to them. In their quest for fulfillment they often created their own activities outside the home; they organized volunteer organizations to aid the needy in their communities and provided a variety of social services.

Why has women's work in charitable and social organizations never received the attention it deserves in history books? True, women did much to humanize their society, but males never valued that type of work and so never recognized it as worthy. Conquering the frontier and killing Indians was the male defini-

12

tion of accomplishment. What a culture deems important, what it remembers and records in its history books, is a revealing indication of the value system of that culture. Women have always contributed to the well-being of their society. They have made the home an attractive refuge from the marketplace, and they have also worked to ease all people's burdens. Until the twentieth century, it was usually women's groups, not government, that attended to the sick, the orphaned, the widowed, and the insane, another significant fact worthy of discussion. On the other hand, few farms and factories operated without women's labor. Women have always contributed to the building of America, though their accomplishments have been largely ignored.

Men and Women

The American woman's life cannot be described in a vacuum; her fate has been tied to the fate of man. Thus, this book also considers how male Americans have earned a living and how they have viewed the economic system. The male American genius for creating wealth, for inventing new forms of labor and for turning adversity into advantage relates to the woman's story of America. How both sexes have viewed the environment has also influenced their lives and decided their fates. The natural riches of the land have yielded an abundance of food, resulting in surpluses previously unknown in human history. Yet at the same time the American farmer has experienced much hardship, and people have starved, and continue to starve, in the richest country in the world.

The economic wealth of this country has not been equitably distributed, since our economy has always rested firmly on the sacred principle of private enterprise and the profit system. At least in theory, the person who succeeds, through his own efforts, is entitled to his rewards without the interference of governmental agencies or social concerns. In practice, of course, laissez-faire—that is, the hands-off policy of government toward economic interests—has never been practiced. Throughout our history, the government has aided, often vigorously, business interests. Labor unions, on the other hand, have not always been as kindly treated.

Introduction

Our economic myths have had a life of their own. Americans have always been told that the farmer is the backbone of the country, that every individual can "make it" if he tries hard enough, and that the poor are poor because of their own deficiencies. Despite long and persistent commitment to these myths, economic reality in this country has always been otherwise: the myth has never accurately described the reality. True, in every age there have been persons, often the exceptions, who actually exemplified a myth to the eager many who wanted to believe in it. Yet for every Horatio Alger hero, there were scores of hard-working people who never enjoyed spectacular success. For every rich farmer, there were hundreds who barely eked a living out of the land. For every landowner, there were thousands of black sharecroppers; and for every industrialist, there were thousands of sweating workers. Work and virtue, however, continue to be linked in the public mind. Many Americans still believe that God rewards the hard workers and punishes the unworthy. Social welfare programs continue to fight an uphill battle against this view.

Moreover, economic progress has never been continuous. Depressions have come in the wake of prosperity; busts have usually followed booms. People have known as many hard times as easy ones, but still—and this is truly one of the remarkable facts about Americans—they have continued to have faith in their country and hope for its future. The remembrance of past good times has always carried them through present bad times and back to the good again. Depressions have been followed by booms, and Americans, eternal optimists, believed each depression would be the last.

Tied in with the economic growth and traumas of America is the financial relationship between the government and the people. Where is the government to get the money to provide services to its citizens? How extensive should these services be? People have always hated to pay taxes. They have always had to be convinced that they were getting something worthwhile for their money. Thus, the "askers" have always had to create elaborate rationales for their request. Public education would benefit business, public sewage would reduce disease, and public highways would help everyone. In every case, the taxpayer has become convinced that the benefits would outweigh temporary hardships.

14

The American Dream is another important component of American history. It has provided the substance for many Americans' individual dreams. The belief in each person's worth, in his ability to succeed according to the formula of hard work plus virtuous behavior plus self-reliance, has motivated many generations of Americans. Belief in work and its importance, belief in material success, and belief in equal opportunity for everyone have all provided the underpinnings for our society. On the basis of these beliefs, laws have been passed and programs instituted.

As industrialization created new ways of acquiring wealth and huge, unprecedented fortunes, Americans came to admire the luxury, the ornamentation, and the reckless excesses of the affluent few. Indulging in a paradox, one of many, they managed to believe simultaneously in hard work and in conspicuous consumption. They admired frugality out of pragmatic necessity, all the while longing for the wealth that would free them of the need for self-discipline and unceasing labor.

Women have played an important role in this dimension of life. The wives of the rich, as the economist Thorstein Veblen observed in the 1890s, served as status symbols. Their bejeweled bodies, expensive velvet wraps, and pale complexions all testified to their husbands' economic success. Middle-class women, anxiously watching the beautifully gowned style-setters of the upper class, tried desperately to imitate them and dreamed of the day when they too could ride around in shiny carriages and give up any and all forms of work. Thus women, like men, became captives of the materialistic American Dream. They too thought in terms of economic success—not their own, but their husbands'. A woman would enjoy the fruits of her husband's labor while reflecting, and reveling in, his glory.

Because people's beliefs, whether consciously articulated or unconsciously harbored, largely determine how they behave, it is just as important to know about the thoughts and values of Americans as about their country's economics and politics. American history textbooks have concentrated upon the deeds of the few, with little attention to the attitudes of the many. For example, an attitude in early America that one seldom associates with Puritan New England concerned bundling. Bundling was an accepted custom in the 1600s and 1700s. On cold nights, a courting couple would lie in bed together with their clothes on. Thus they could keep warm and save fuel, at the same time enjoying each other's company in cramped quarters where there was little privacy. But as time went on, some Puritan ministers came to believe that bundling had immoral implications. As a counter-argument, the Reverend Samuel Peters of Connecticut related this story:

> In 1776, a clergyman from one of the polite towns went into the country, and preached against the unchristian custom of young men and maidens lying together on a bed. He was no sooner out of the church than attacked by a shoal of good old women with "Sir, do you think we and our daughters are naughty, because we allow of bundling?"
>
> "You lead yourselves into temptation by it."
>
> They all replied at once, "Sir, have you been told thus, or has experience taught it you?"
>
> The Levite began to lift up his eyes, and to consider of his situation, and bowing, said, "I have been told so."
>
> The ladies, *una voce* [with one voice], bawled out. "Your informants, sir, we conclude, are those city ladies who prefer a sofa to a bed. We advise you to alter your sermon by substituting the word 'sofa' for 'bundling,' and on your return home preach it to them, for experience has told us that city folks send more children into the country without fathers or mothers to own them than are born among us. Therefore, you see, a sofa is more dangerous than a bed."
>
> The poor priest, seemingly convinced of his blunder, . . . confessed his error, begged pardon, and promised never more to preach against bundling, or to think amiss of the custom. The ladies generously forgave him, and went away.

The Power of a Culture

Each generation of Americans has contributed to the preserving, adapting, or changing of its culture. The process is dynamic. Some people will behave according to old cultural precepts while vigorously declaring their adherence to new ones. Others will proclaim their allegiance to old ideas while behaving in new ways. In the last third of the twentieth century, many women still claim that their major role is that of wife and mother, yet spend several hours each day outside the home. Others will insist that they are modern, "liberated" women, but never explore the full meaning of that claim.

Every human being has a different way of looking at the world, depending on his/her particular background, inherited potential, and unique personality. At the same time, because so many experiences are shared, any given individual will see the world as do others with the same religious, educational, or ethnic background. No person is alone, nor does he/she see the world from a lonely eminence. In every age, however, certain unusually gifted Americans—women and men, black and white—broke with cultural traditions and created their own interpretation of life. Their rebellion required great acts of courage, as did their efforts to win supporters for their new views of life's possibilities.

Many less gifted ones, too, tried to throw off the bonds of tradition and "make it" on their own. Whether or not they succeeded depended on a multitude of variables and not a little serendipity. In 1757, a bored young boy on a farm might run away to the city at the age of seventeen, apprentice himself to a blacksmith, and begin a new life, unshackled by rural tradition. A bored old man on a farm would probably do no more than sigh, resign himself to his fate, and return to his plowing. For women and blacks, awareness of their cultural constraints could only prove painful, since any prospect of changing their life appeared dim at best. On the other hand, there are always those fortunate people who enjoy their cultural position and are supremely fitted for it. Craftsmen who love their craft, farmers who love farming, mothers who love bringing up children, teachers who love teaching—all these have found a lifework in which their talents help to fill important social needs.

How much freedom of choice can any culture allow without threat to its survival, its self-perpetuation? Or, how much change can any community tolerate and still remain viable? Critics in each age, liberals and conservatives alike, have asked and answered these questions. But regardless of their answers, for over three hundred years something called the American culture has taken root, grown, changed—and persisted. There *is* an American culture, with a definable value system, a style of living, and a world-view. The way it looks at women, children, blacks, Indians, and the environment—this is all of a piece. *Herstory* hopes to reveal some of the cultural views of Americans while telling a small part of the story of women and other powerless people.

CHAPTER TWO

Spokes on the Wheel of Western Culture
1600–1775

> Woman is the gate of the devil, the path of wickedness, the sting of the serpent, in a word a perilous object.
>
> —St. Jerome

> Woman was created to be man's helpmate, but her unique role is in conception ... since for other purposes men would be better assisted by other men.
>
> —St. Thomas Aquinas

*T*he European explorers and the English settlers who came to North America brought with them a culture, a way of life they had learned and accepted in their homelands. They worked to adapt that way of life to a new physical environment and, with amazing doggedness, they succeeded. In the course of adaptation, a new American culture gradually emerged, though still indelibly imprinted with English and European ideas.

Adventurers—All White, All Male

From the outset, the rules of living were determined by men. Exploring, with its adventure, risk, and excitement, belonged to them alone. Women were too delicate, too closely tied to the home, to go off seeking new lands and new experiences. So from the beginning, Spaniards, Frenchmen, and Englishmen set forth

19

in small ships to explore the New World while their women-folk stayed behind. The female population of the newly discovered territories, of course, became fair game for the sex-starved explorers.

Pueblo Indian women, Aztec women, and Mayan women became the prey of the Spanish adventurers. Giovanni da Verrazano, a Florentine navigator who sailed for France, kept a record of his explorations in the New World in 1524. He told about going ashore somewhere in Virginia or Maryland with his men and being greeted by an old woman, a lovely young girl, and a few children. The explorers proceeded to lure the innocent children and to kidnap one of them. They tried to capture the beautiful squaw, but her screams drove them away.

Englishmen, too, coming ashore on the Eastern coast of this country (on land that would later be named Virginia, after their virgin queen) found the native Indian women attractive objects for their lust. But unlike the Spaniards, who often married Indian women, these Englishmen sought wives from their homeland. One source in the early 1600s noted that any single woman who traveled to Virginia would "have the best luck as in any place in

Wives for the settlers at Jamestown. (N.Y. Public Library)

the World, . . . for they are no sooner on shore than they are courted into . . . matrimony."

The first successful English settlers came to Jamestown, Virginia in 1607—120 bachelors. Their leader, Captain John Smith, kept sending propaganda pamphlets back to England, encouraging more and more people, including women, to cross the ocean to the new land. He did not want Virginia to remain a solitary outpost of the British empire; he wanted it to become a major settlement, a permanent new homeland for Englishmen in search of opportunity and adventure. Smith, a known braggart and liar, was captured by Chief Powhatan in 1607 while exploring the Chickahominy River. According to his later account, he was saved from death by the eleven-year-old daughter of the chief, Pocahontas, who took an instant liking to him. Other accounts claim that Smith's promise of guns to the Indians saved him from death. In any case, the beautiful Pocahontas married another Englishman, John Rolfe, seven years later. She went to England with her husband and was presented at court. She died of smallpox in 1617 at the tender age of twenty-one.

In 1630, the Puritans landed in Massachusetts Bay with almost a thousand men and women. These people planned on staying; they came in families, with all their worldly possessions. They planned on building their homes, establishing their church and the laws, and creating the New Jerusalem in the wilderness of the new land. Their relationship with the natives was to be that of master to servant, Christian to primitive. They were not equals and were never to consider such an outrageous possibility.

The transplanted Englishmen who invaded the Eastern coast of the continent—and those who explored its diverse landscape for many generations—assumed that the vast stretches of untouched land belonged to no one and were, in fact, only waiting for them. Some, seeing the widely scattered Indian villages, did pause to consider who owned the natural riches of the continent, but most of them blithely assumed that this virgin territory was available to anyone. Imagine the frontiersman's sense of power and excitement as he began clearing a plot for his farm and building a home out of the hewed timber! The fertility of the land, the wildlife, and the freshwater streams existed, it seemed to him, for his special use. And use them he did.

The settlers in both Virginia and Massachusetts agreed that

their communities would be run by men—white men. Women, children, Indians, and (later) blacks would not, and should not, be considered a part of the ruling or participating class. When Virginia's House of Burgesses, the first representative political body on the continent, was created in 1619, it provided that all *men* over seventeen could vote to elect their officials. In Massachusetts, women did not sign the Mayflower Compact in 1620, nor did they gain political rights in the Bay Colony. The basic cultural, political, and economic patterns that were to govern all future generations were thus firmly set in the 1600s. Politics was the man's business; his was the power to run the affairs of the colony. Women, like children, should be seen and not heard, be respectful to their fathers and husbands and dutiful in all domestic chores.

Adam's Rib

The Puritan New Englanders and the Anglican Virginians shared the same biblical philosophy about woman. Created out of Adam's rib, she had a definite and special function to perform on earth: to be helpmate, wife, and mother unto the nation; be cooperative, submissive to the wishes of her father, brother, and husband, and respectful of God's laws; teach customs and rituals, care for the children, and preserve the home. This was biblically ordained. The role of all good Christians was to obey and fulfill the sacred laws. Women were not expected to participate in government or religious affairs. Their proper "sphere," a word much used in the seventeenth (and subsequent) centuries, was the home—not the marketplace, the church pulpit, the courtroom, or the voting place. Women also had a dangerous side, which had to be carefully watched and controlled: their sexuality. This was the power which, in the form of Eve, tempted and lured innocent Adam out of the Garden of Eden and introduced sin into the world. Woman as temptress, warned the New England and Virginia ministers, was a constant evil to watch for and prevent from expression.

Woman's nature, therefore, had its positive and negative sides. She was capable of motherhood (which, too, had its negative side when it was expressed out of wedlock), nurturing her young, and creating a comfortable domestic environment. In-

22

deed, the mothering role of woman was predominant. Ignorant of effective birth control methods, seventeenth-century women bore many children: to fructify and multiply, after all, was a biblical injunction, despite a high rate of infant and maternal mortality. (Midwives and doctors took few sanitary precautions, and infections and fatal fevers were common.) Many a colonial woman could bear seven children at two-year intervals. For on virgin soil, with seemingly infinite acres of land to be cultivated, large families were not only desirable but necessary. Although the woman's condition was a difficult one in frontier America, she shared with her man the biblical explanation of her fate, and both men and women agreed that the traditional biblical view of women was the godly and humanly proper one. So no serious doubts about woman's role occurred as a result of the move from the Old World to the New.

Just as ideas about woman's role were gained from reading the Bible, so too were ideas in many other areas of life. The Bible—primarily the Old Testament for the Puritans—was the major source of authority in all human affairs. The early settlers saw themselves as God-fearing, devout people. Indeed, the Puritans and Pilgrims left the Old World because they wanted to be able to practice their religion according to their own beliefs. The early Virginians, though still loyal to the established Anglican Church of England, shared with their northern neighbors a commitment to Christianity. Stories from the Bible were told to children at the fireside, formed the substance of the Sunday sermons, and provided guidelines for all adults. The seventeenth-century settlers established a good many of the early institutions precisely to fulfill religious tenets. Schools, for instance, were quickly set up in New England so that children—that is, boy children—could learn to read the Bible. Literacy was highly valued because it was essential to a knowledge of God's truth.

Western culture has always allowed women to express their dependent nature within the framework of religious practice. Consequently, they have been Christianity's most devout practitioners and its most respectful followers—and understandably so. Life on this earth has usually been difficult for women, especially in early America. They had to bear and rear children, milk the cows, tend the vegetable patch, sow the wheat, feed the chickens, cook the food, spin the yarn and make the clothes, clean the house, nurse the babies, and care for the husband and

23

the older children. No one's life was easy in colonial America, but the woman's was more than doubly hard because of the demands of her three roles—maternal, domestic, and agricultural. In this setting, the Christian religion provided an outlet, a release for women's emotional frustrations, grievances, and longings. Prayer, sacrifice, disciplined behavior, all part of the ritualistic religious scene, satisfied many of their needs. Since the next world offered them far better prospects than the present one, they were comforted by the promise of salvation. The figure of Christ, whose virtues were largely the feminine ones of humility, love, and cooperation, also consoled them.

Women have always attended religious services and church meetings in greater numbers than men and with greater frequency, from colonial times to this day. Colonial women could not and did not lead the services (the ministers were men except in such liberal Protestant churches as the Quakers), but they gladly participated in them and in all social activities attached to the church. In fact, the church had another important function for women: it allowed them sociability. They could gather together for a church bazaar to help the orphans and the poor of the community, or for a supper to raise money for a new church building. There, in a socially approved setting, women could gossip, talk about their worries and their pleasures, enjoy the sisterhood of other women, and be temporarily freed from their daily responsibilities.

The Puritan and the American Indian

To the Puritans, who were the major group of settlers in the New England area in the seventeenth century, God's will prevailed in all areas of life. No event occurred without his knowledge and possible intervention. No earthquake, no drought, no personal tragedy, and no success was unknown to him, and all human actions could be interpreted in religious terms. Thus, when the Puritans looked at the native American Indian, they searched for biblical explanations for his behavior. Being devout Christians but also believing that their religion was the only true one, the Puritans saw the Indian as a son of Satan, a barbarian, and a heathen. Cotton Mather (1663–1728), the son and grandson of Puritan ministers and natural heir to a leadership position in the

24

Puritan hierarchy, believed that the Indians had been tricked by the Devil "in hopes that the Gospel of Jesus Christ wouldn't come here, to destroy or disturb his Absolute Empire." Since Mather believed in the greater power of the Lord over that of Satan, he favored converting the Indians to Christianity, though they often rejected conversion. In *Magnalia Christi Americana*, Mather's major work, he described what happened to one Indian tribe that repudiated Christianity:

> The Nation of the Narragansetts was one of the most populous among the Indians, and once filled this mighty wilderness. Unto that woeful nation the gospel of our Lord Jesus Christ was freely tendered; but they, with much affront and contempt, rejected it. . . . The glorious Lord Jesus Christ, whom they had slighted, was with our army. . . . Their city was laid in ashes. Above twenty of their chief captains were killed; a proportionable desolation cut off the inferiour savages, mortal sickness, and horrid famine pursu'd the remainders of 'em so that we can hardly tell where any of 'em are left alive upon the face of the earth.

Since the beginnings of Christianity, non-Christians have been persecuted in its name, and the New England Puritans continued that tradition. They fought the Indians not only out of pragmatic necessity but out of religious conviction: that their religion and culture were superior to the red man's and that Jesus Christ supported their ventures. As always, there were dissenters from the majority view—some few who opposed the Christians' treatment of the Indians. Among them were John Eliot of Massachusetts (1604–1690) and Roger Williams of Rhode Island (1603–1683). Eliot, who translated the Bible into Algonquin, set up churches for the Indians and helped build the first Indian seminary on the Harvard College campus in 1655. He even told the Indians that they were the true Christians and that the white men perverted the truths of Christianity.

Roger Williams, who lived among the Narragansett Indians for many years and studied Indian culture and language, believed that the white settlers should pay the Indians for their land. He observed that all these natives had "a savor of civility and courtesy even amongst themselves and towards strangers." Williams was one of the few Puritan ministers who, believing there were many paths to godliness, thought the Indians' religion could lead them to salvation just as well as Christianity

Spokes on the Wheel of Western Culture 1600–1775

A New Settler's View of His Indian Neighbors

The manner of the Indians treating their young children is very strange, for instead of keeping them warm, at their first entry into the world, and wrapping them up, with I don't know how many cloths, according to our own fond custom; the first thing they do, is to dip the child over the head and ears in cold water, and then to bind it naked to a convenient board, having a hole fitly placed for evacuation; but they always put cotton, wool, fur, or other soft thing, for the body to rest easy on, between the child and the board. In this posture they keep it several months, till the bones begin to harden, the joints to knit, and the limbs to grow strong; and then they let it loose from the board, suffering it to crawl about, except when they are feeding, or playing with it.

While the child is thus at the board, they either lay it flat on its back, or set it leaning on one end, or else hang it up by a string fastened to the upper end of the board for that purpose. The child and board being all this while carried about together. As our women undress their children to clean them and shift their linen, so they do theirs to wash and grease them.

The method the women have of carrying their children after they are suffered to crawl about, is very particular; they carry them at their backs in summer, taking one leg of the child under their arm, and the counter-arm of the child in their hand over their shoulder; the other leg hanging down, and the child all the while holding fast with its other hand; but in winter they carry them in the hollow of their match-coat at their back, leaving nothing but the child's head out. . . .

Intermarriage had been indeed the method proposed very often by the Indians in the beginning, urging it frequently as a certain rule, that the English were not their friends, if they refused it. And I can't but think it would have been happy for that country, had they embraced this proposal: for, the jealousy of the Indians, which I take to be the cause of most of the rapines and murders they committed, would by this means have been altogether prevented . . . the colony, instead of all these losses of men on both sides, would have been increasing in children to its advantage . . . and, in all likelihood, many, if not most, of the Indians would have been converted to Christianity by this kind method.

—Robert Beverly, *The History and Present State of Virginia* (1705).

26

Roger Williams sheltered by the Narragansetts. (Culver)

could. This was an heretical view, not only unpopular but unacceptable.

Roger Williams carried his critical questioning of the Puritan establishment into other areas as well. He told the Puritans that ". . . the people (the origin of all free power and government) are not invested with power from Christ Jesus to rule . . . wife or church." He raised the extraordinary possibility that all people were qualified to determine governmental actions and that women were able to rule themselves. There was only one way for the Puritans to deal with a man who spoke for Indians' rights, women's rights, and all people's rights: exile him.

To true believers, according to Puritanism, there was only one truth, theirs; the churches of England and Rome were corrupt, but their Congregational church system was pure. Considering toleration of others a dangerous proposition, the Puritans consistently persecuted not only Indians but Quakers, Jews, blacks, and any other non-Puritan groups that had the misfortune to arrive on the shores of Massachusetts. Their eventual acceptance of religious toleration, of allowing different religions the right to be practiced, came grudgingly and pragmatically. The zealots never approved of it, but practical necessity—that is, the need for additional population—demanded concessions and compromises. Additionally, as fewer and fewer descendants of Puritans adhered strictly to the faith, it became increasingly difficult to force conformity, even within the fold.

The Puritan view of Indians as sons of Satan could, and would, be transferred to black slaves, Catholics, Jews, and other heretics. But the Puritans found themselves under attack from two fronts, internal and external. Their own children strayed from the paths of virtue, unwilling to toe the strict religious line, and the constant stream of newcomers to the colony came from different backgrounds than theirs. The Puritans found they could impose their authority neither upon their own families nor upon the strangers in their midst. They had forcibly eliminated the Indian from consideration but could not fight all the others. Indeed, their Christian orientation, which, combined with their ethnocentric view that white and English was right, made it possible for them to kill Indians but compelled them to find another way of dealing with white English dissenters. Then, too, there was a practical deterrent: the new pioneers had the same military knowledge and equipment as they themselves had. While the Indians were seriously disadvantaged, with only tomahawks, bows, arrows, and spears, the new settlers shared the Puritans' knowledge of guns and of English means of defense.

Respect for different religions, cultures, and points of view, then, has not been easily acquired by Americans. Although many new colonies in the seventeenth century had laws guaranteeing religious toleration, there were always serious tensions between the established community and the "different" newcomers. Catholics were not greeted hospitably upon their arrival in most colonies; neither were Jews. People whose religion strongly resembled the Puritan and Anglican brand of Protestantism were more easily integrated into the fold; others were often badly treated. Quakers, the most uncompromising of the Protestant sects, found Protestant America inhospitable, at times openly hostile. (Ann Burden, a Quaker, arrived in Boston in July 1656 to settle the estate of her deceased husband, who had been a citizen of Boston. But a Puritan law forbade Quakers from entering the Commonwealth of Massachusetts. As a result, Ann Burden's goods were confiscated and shipped to Barbados for sale there. Mrs. Burden left Boston by the same ship on which she had come.)

Thus the Puritan and Anglican settlers' attitudes toward, and treatment of, American Indians were a piece with their attitudes and behavior toward all outsiders. Differentness was cause for suspicion, not respect. One result of this fear of difference, which has survived for three centuries, is emphasis on conformity. Americans, the ultimate conformists, are required to dress alike, eat the same breakfast cereals, and live in the same kinds of houses so that no one will be different enough to pose a threat to his neighbors. This pervasive attitude of the twentieth century was born in the seventeenth.

The continuously arriving new colonists from England and the European continent, along with the restless settlers of New England, clashed with the Indians on every frontier. Carolinians enslaved those who invaded their lands, and British redcoats killed Indian raiders on the border of western Pennsylvania. Finally, after years of local bloodshed, the Indians organized to defend themselves against the white men. The tribes in the Ohio Valley formed a confederacy and in 1763, the last year of the French and Indian War, staged their most ambitious and massive assault upon the colonists. Led by Pontiac, chief of the Ottawas, they attacked every western fort except Detroit and Pittsburgh. From Niagara to Virginia, hundreds of frontier families were killed. Eventually, however, the Indians were defeated by the colonists.

This was the last major Indian battle east of the Mississippi. But the outcome proved nothing. The Indians were pushed farther westward, true, yet this hardly provided a peaceful, long-range solution to the conflict between the two peoples. Would they always meet as enemies? Could they ever co-exist as friends? Neither the British empire nor the colonists offered any enlightened answer to this question in the eighteenth century—or in any subsequent century, for that matter. The white men's belief in their innate superiority, which entitled them to all the land on the new continent, made a constant series of violent clashes inevitable.

Godliness and Slavery

Although there were few black people in seventeenth-century New England, the Puritans viewed them as they viewed the rest of the world. Africans, brought here in chains, were barbarians, uncivilized, and un-Christian, much like their Indian counter-

The arrival of African slaves. (Brown Bros.)

parts on this continent. Slavery, according to the Puritan theologians, was approved by the Bible; it was the duty of God-fearing people to convert the heathens to Christianity if possible, but their basic servitude was not against the Lord's will. Cotton Mather established a night school to educate black slaves in Boston while keeping a slave in his house for ten years.

In New England, black slaves often became household help, skilled workers, and farmhands. Unlike blacks in the South, they were never the major labor force of the area because the agricultural economy depended on small farms, not great plantations. Black male slaves learned to be carpenters, goldsmiths, cabinet-makers, and shipbuilders, while the black women worked as housemaids and laundresses. Some were allowed to buy their freedom, learn to read and write, and become church members. But the basic attitude of the Puritans toward blacks did not waver: like the Indians, blacks were inferior, sons of Satan, and not entitled to the same human rights as white men. The easily identifiable color of the Africans, of course, stamped their differentness indelibly. No black slave could escape his color—at least not among the early generations, before sufficient mixing of the races permitted light-skinned mulattoes to pass into the white population.

Early in its history, New England established laws to insure the perpetual servitude of the African immigrants. A Rhode Island statute in the early 1650s stated the case simply: "It is a common course practiced amongst Englishmen to buy Negers, to that end they may have them for service or slaves forever." Armed with both the Bible and the confidence that Western civilization was superior to all others, Puritan New Englanders and Anglican Southerners instituted slavery of blacks. Their consciences were clear because there was ample historical precedent in the Bible and Western culture for superior peoples to enslave inferior ones.

As is usually the case, a few courageous critics were willing to question and challenge the majority's view. In 1701, Samuel Sewall (1652–1730), a judge of the Massachusetts supreme court for thirty-six years, published "The Selling of Joseph," a serious critique of slavery. Although Sewall was a respected member of the community, his brave attack on the institution did not lead to mass rejection of slavery.

At the close of the seventeenth century, the number of African slaves was increasing in the South and would continue to do so dramatically into the next century. The number of slaves in New England, however, did not increase as significantly. Many obtained their freedom, and a substantial free black population developed in the Northern colonies. Moreover, white immigration to the New England and Middle colonies offset the increase in the black population; yet in the Southern colonies, the influx of new black slaves far outweighed any additional white immigration.

The following passage from Harriet Brent Jacobs' *Incidents in the Life of a Slave-Girl, Written by Herself* is about a black woman slave in New England.

> I have mentioned my great-aunt, who was a slave in Dr. Flint's family. . . . This aunt had been married at twenty years of age; that is, as far as slaves *can* marry. She had the consent of her master and mistress, and a clergyman performed the ceremony. . . . She had always slept on the floor in the entry, near Mrs. Flint's chamber door, that she might be within call. When she was married, she was told she might have the small room in an outhouse. Her mother and her husband furnished it. He was a seafaring man, and was allowed to sleep there when he was at home. But on the wedding evening, the bride was ordered to her old post on the entry floor.
>
> Mrs. Flint, at that time, had no children; but she was expecting to be a mother, and if she should want a drink of water in the night, what could she do without her slave to bring it?
>
> —Reprinted in Gerda Lerner, *Black Women in White America*, 1973.

While all this was going on, attitudes changed slowly, if at all. The landscape of America changed swiftly and social and economic realities also changed, but people's views remained the same. As white Americans learned to adapt many long-held attitudes to their new environments and institutions, their deep conviction that black men and red men were inferior did not waver, and neither did their belief in women's role.

Other Influences

Not only the religion of the early pioneers but also their family structure and their legal system came directly from England.

32

Permeating these and other significant aspects of Western culture was the commitment to private property, to the capitalistic system, and above all, to individualism. On the frontier, one's very survival depended on individual responsibility—"Every man for himself." Each person was responsible for his/her own welfare, his/her own success on this earth, his/her own salvation. Men carved clearings out of the wilderness, built homes with their own hands, and farmed the land with the aid of their families. Private property, rather than communally owned property, became the rule. Private profit, rather than public sharing, became the economic motif.

Every one of the idea systems brought from the Old World was based upon male dominance, which was often heightened by conditions in the New World. As a result, male attitudes toward women, children, and the family persisted from one generation to the next. Building, farming, trading, and negotiating were all viewed as masculine activities. Men alone engaged in capitalism, in seeking profit, and in operating the marketplace.

The white man believed in his right to rule the home as well as his right to determine where he and his family would settle. He was the authority figure, and the entire natural environment, together with all non-whites and all white females, was subject to his will. He demanded obedience and punished disobedience. Fortunately, he could call on the Bible for support—along with the traditional capitalistic reliance on such "male" traits as competitiveness, high risk-taking, and profit-seeking. Disobedience could lead only to the breakdown of the family as an institution—which in turn could lead to social anarchy. Both ideologically and practically, then, the patriarchal system required complete obedience in order to function effectively.

Babes in America

Children were viewed as miniature adults, but adults who needed taming and civilizing and in whose hearts the war between the Devil and the Lord was waged most vividly and continuously. Since Satan and primitivism dominated them, they were particularly susceptible to waywardness and temptation, and their natural inclinations needed to be restrained. Discipline

33

had to be maintained, through whippings or the threat thereof, and punishment was essential to produce obedient, God-fearing young people.

Seventeenth- and eighteenth-century parents knew little about the stages of human growth: childhood, adolescence, and young adulthood, each with its own characteristics and problems. Indeed, at that time almost nothing was known about the physiology and psychology of human development. Therefore English child-raising manuals, the major source of wisdom for parents, offered little help.

Early Americans expected six- and seven-year-old children to participate in work around the farm, do their household chores, and obey their parents' directives. If there was a school nearby, boy children were sent off at the age of eight or so to learn reading, writing, and arithmetic. Such knowledge was all they needed; it would enable them to read the Bible, keep ledgers and records, and count. Often the girls were not educated at all. If they were, their education usually took place after the boys' school hours. Why so? Well, imagine a typical farm family in which Lucy, aged eight, is the eldest of five children. She rises before the sun, dresses quickly in the dark, and quietly goes out to the barn to milk the cows. Her mother and father are already up. Father is readying the horse for the day's plowing, while mother cooks the breakfast bacon over the open fire. After milking the cows, Lucy feeds the chickens, dresses the younger children, and then helps her mother sew some trousers for her brother. Her day is full of chores, leaving no time for school.

Except in well-to-do families, the child's education was limited to a few years of elementary learning. The New England primer, first compiled in 1683, set the tone for all education—one of its primary lessons was: "In Adam's fall, we sinned all." Given the fact that free schooling for farmers' children did not exist in England or Europe at that time, even this much public education was a major departure from traditional practice.

The Dutiful Child's Promises

I will fear God, and honour the King.
I will honor my Father & Mother.
I will obey my superiors.

34

I will submit to my elders.
I will love my friends.
I will hate no man.
I will forgive my enemies, and pray to God
        for them.
I will as much as in me lies keep all God's
        Holy Commandments.
I will learn my catechism.
I will keep the Lord's Day Holy.
I will reverence God's sanctuary,
    For our God is a consuming Fire.

   —The New England Primer

The Puritans believed that boys had to be able to read the Bible—most other learning could be acquired from helping their father or becoming apprentices to craftsmen. Girls, on the other hand, could learn what they needed to know from their mothers: how to sew, cook, and behave. In the eighteenth century, families that could afford the niceties of life sent their daughters to "finishing" schools which taught etiquette and French. The purpose of these schools was to "finish" a young woman—that is, prepare her for a suitable marriage to a prosperous man.

Every child, according to child-care experts of the time, should be toilet-trained at around the age of one. But mothers found it hard to achieve this goal—they were much too busy. Often a woman would have a child every two years, nurse it for a year or so, wean it, and within a few months conceive another child. Although bottle-feeding began in the eighteenth century, breast-feeding continued to be regarded as the most practical and healthy way to nourish babies.

In contrast to the strict discipline imposed on older children, babies up to three years of age were often indulged and permitted a wide latitude of behavior. Yet childhood was short-lived; children learned early in life to be self-sufficient, to perform tasks, and to become independent. Unlike twentieth-century children in this country, who remain financially and emotionally dependent on their parents until the end of their teen years, children of the seventeenth century often left home as apprentices at the age of ten, struck out on their own at the age of fifteen, and married in their early twenties.

35

The Life Cycle

Marrying young, the couples began immediately to have large families. Women who survived their childbearing years might live into their sixties. But if a woman died in childbirth, her husband usually remarried quickly and continued to expand his family. Widows, too, did not remain widowed for long. Remarriage was the order of the day, for both ideological and practical reasons. In the first place, marriage was considered the natural and proper state of being for everybody. Then, too, widows, inexperienced in independent living, felt they needed protection in the male-oriented society. Widowers, for their part, wanted heirs to their property, as well as extra hands to help them with their work. Single persons were eyed with suspicion by both sexes. Women feared the males' lecherous advances, while men believed that bachelors encouraged licentiousness in the community. (Envy and resentment of their state of freedom probably played a part too.) So both sexes discouraged bachelorhood. Since the family was a holy structure that had to include all people, those who lived alone were viewed with wariness.

Spinsterhood was regarded as a fate almost as bad as death. An unmarried woman had to rely on her parents, brother, or married sister for her home and sustenance. Even though many spinsters raised their sisters' and brothers' children, taught school, and spun yarn endlessly (hence the term "spinster"), they were totally dependent on the good will and economic fortune of others. They might have earned their keep, and more, but in the eyes of society they were tolerated rejects.

In the colonial period, especially the seventeenth and early eighteenth centuries, there were few spinsters. As men almost invariably outnumbered women in any community, women were at a premium and were quickly married. But around 1800, the ratio of women to men was reversed, especially in New England, and the "extra" women suffered the ignominy of the minority. Marriage still remained the primary goal of all young girls. The society did not change its attitude to accommodate the new reality—more unmarried adult women.

Early American society, like subsequent American societies, never considered women as being in any way the equals of men. A woman could not prepare for a career or a life of independence as a man could. Rather than provide for other life options, young

36

women were taught that marriage was the only worthwhile kind of life. Those who failed to marry were pitied and regarded as doomed. Although both married and unmarried women performed many different functions in the life of the community, the only role that counted was that of wife and mother. A woman could be a midwife, a tavern-keeper, a barrister, a writer, or a teacher, but her primary identification was as the wife of Mr. So-and-So and the mother of X, Y, and Z.

Women always worked in the fields and, when industrialization came, in the factories. They also worked in shops, but usually to help out their husbands or fathers or because they were widowed. No woman who wanted to be considered sane and respectable ever admitted that she worked outside the home because she wanted to or because she gained professional satisfaction from her work. Woman's role was limited and clearly defined: she was wife, mother, and helper to her man. The idea of her wanting an independent life and identity was unheard of and would have been completely unacceptable.

When a disturbed husband came to Cotton Mather and asked him what could be done with a wife who took no interest in her home or in caring for her children, Mather shook his head in agitation. A disobedient and uninterested wife, he told the man, was a curse, one of the most disturbing misfortunes that could happen to a husband. Mather offered little hope, but counseled more prayer and stricter discipline. Just as a rebellious child should be punished and further restrained, so a rebellious wife should be subjugated to the authority of her husband. Such a wife had to learn, Mather reminded the unhappy man, that her husband was her master and that she was subject to his will. After all, according to the colonial common law system, the children belonged to him, the property belonged to him, and so did the wife. This reflected the edict of Blackstone, the English jurist: a woman and a man became one when they married—and the one was the husband. Married women were invisible in the eyes of the law.

The family unit, as we know it today, already existed in Boston, Charleston, and Cambridge, in villages, and on farms. Often grandparents, aunts and uncles, and cousins would live in or near the home of the nuclear family. Hence colonial families were characterized by a mingling of different age groups. Children could confide in their grandparents, in cousins of various

37

ages, in bachelor uncles and spinster aunts. They could be disciplined and chastised by several authority figures other than their parents, and could learn things from them. Generally they felt at ease with both old and young. In such small communities, everybody knew everybody, including each other's personal and family history. Few secrets were possible in the closely knit communities of colonial America.

Recreation was communal too, of course. Boys and girls played ball games, tag, hide-and-seek, and went on hayrides. Women had sewing bees, quilting parties, and church bazaars. Men, in the company of their friends, played cards, smoked, and drank, especially on the frontier. Everyone sang.

How will you come to the weddin'—
My dear old buffalo boy?

I guess I come in my ox cart—
That is if the weather be good.

Why don't you come in your buggy—
My dear old buffalo boy?

'Cause an ox won't fit in my buggy—
Not even if the weather be good.

Who you gonna bring to the weddin'—
My dear old buffalo boy?

I guess I bring my children—
That is if the weather be good.

I didn't know you had children—
My dear old buffalo boy!

Oh yes, I have five children—
Maybe six if the weather be good.

Well, there ain't gonna be no weddin'—
Not even if the weather be good?
Not even if the weather be good!

—*Buffalo Boy*, a folk song

The church was the setting for most of the cultural offerings, at which ministers lectured on all matters and local writers read

38

from their work. Sociability, particularly the art of conversation, was encouraged. Huddled together in a frontier settlement, surrounded by unknown Indian tribes, the pioneers practiced togetherness. They cooperated in building each other's homes, in harvesting the crops, and in sharing amusements. To be a loner, to enjoy solitude, was considered queer and unnatural, because any deviation from the socially approved ways was looked upon with suspicion and sometimes open hostility. For the most part, people in the seventeenth century had few luxuries or frivolities. They were too busy surviving in a wilderness, coping with an unfriendly soil and unfriendly Indians, and resisting the Devil's temptations. Middle-class city folk one hundred years later began enjoying the benefits of materialism and sophisticated culture, but for farmers during the first two hundred years of settlement, life was reduced to basic essentials.

The main literary resource of book-reading colonists was the sermons and diaries of Puritan leaders—along with volumes of simple, unaffected prose and poetry that glorified God and the education of man to His purpose. The histories of William Bradford, the Pilgrim leader, and John Winthrop, the second governor of Massachusetts Bay Colony, were read, as were the sermons of Thomas Hooker and Cotton Mather. Though Anne Bradstreet was a woman, her poetry was acceptable because it was written in the proper form and dealt with approved subjects.

> If ever two were one, then surely we;
> If ever man were loved by wife, then thee;
> If ever wife was happy in a man,
> Compare with me, ye women, if you can.
> I prize thy love more than whole mines of gold,
> Or all the riches that the East doth hold.
> My love is such that rivers cannot quench,
> Nor aught but love from thee give recompense.
> Thy love is such I can no way repay;
> The heavens reward thee manifold, I pray.
> Then while we live in love let's so persevere.
> That when we live no more we may live ever.
>
> —Anne Bradstreet, *To My Dear and Loving Husband,* 1678

Stories of Indian captivity were early best-sellers, most of them written by women. Mary Rowlandson's account of her capture by Indians during King Philip's War was one of the most popular, going into a second edition in 1682. Its title—*The Sovereignty and Goodness of God, Together with the Faithfulness of His Promises Displayed; Being a Narrative of the Captivity and Restoration of Mrs. Mary Rolandson*—gave readers a suggestion of the drama and excitement its pages contained.

Farms and Cities

The eighteenth century saw an amazing growth in city populations. By 1775, Philadelphia, New York, Boston, and Charleston each boasted more than 20,000 people—8 per cent of all Americans. Living on the Atlantic seaboard, they enjoyed opportunities not open to inland settlers. They could mingle with foreigners, read newspapers imported from England, and buy goods brought over from Europe.

Meanwhile, the westward movement continued, steadily converting forests into farmlands. Explorers tracked and charted new rivers, and were followed by land-seeking pioneers from the East Coast and Europe. Even poor farmers could afford to pay a dollar an acre for a sixty-acre parcel of land. If a farmer wanted less land, he could buy from one of the speculators who purchased large parcels, divided them into small units, and sold these at higher prices.

Small wonder that, while this was going on, the idea of the superiority of farm life gained tremendous currency and force. Early promoters of agriculture, some of them poets, reminded people that the yeoman farmer was the backbone of the country. His wheat provided bread for city folk, and he himself, besides performing vitally essential services for his fellowmen, came to symbolize the virtues of the simple life. Hence the popular stereotype of city versus country—the city with its alluring images of corruption and temptation, the country with its honest, wholesome pleasures.

Agriculture absorbed the time, attention, and energy of 92 per cent of eighteenth-century Americans. Their working hours were long and hard; their daily routine was determined by the seasons of the year and the particular crops being raised. Rural life might have been praised by gentlemen farmers such as Thomas Jefferson, but in reality it was monotonous, difficult, and lonely. Most white farmers, Northern and Southern, worked their own modest parcels of land with the help of their wives, children, and a hired hand. There were few who, like William Byrd of Virginia, owned thousands of acres, few who maintained manorial estates in upper New York, and few who had large landholdings in the West.

The church, as we have seen, provided farm families with social contacts and entertainment as well as religious comfort. In many communities, the religious message was less important than the social opportunities available at the church. People regularly endured the weekly sermons in order to enjoy the bazaars, dances, and suppers. Traveling lecturers often used the pulpit to acquaint the farmers with some of the new thinking in literature and politics. Politicians, too, orated before the country folk during preelection periods, ignoring them the rest of the year.

Another community meeting ground was the main street of the village, visited weekly by the farmers and their families. The general store displayed the latest wares, and the women gathered there to shop and gossip. In the farm communities and in the cities as well, it became the custom for the women to do the buying for their families.

Out of necessity the agricultural society was a mobile one. When a farmer found his soil depleted, he and his family packed up and moved westward in a covered wagon. For a pregnant woman who had to sit day after day on a hard clapboard seat, bumping across unknown territory, the experience was hardly pleasurable and often dangerous. Accustomed to the stable life of a farm community, these pioneer wives often found the wilderness terrifying and frustrating, but they endured and indeed prevailed. They worked shoulder to shoulder with their husbands, loyally trying to make the new home, the new venture, a success. Their diaries, letters, and memoirs attest to their courage and patience as they managed to live through the cold winters in log cabins with poor insulation, no windows, and rough floor coverings. They gave birth without benefit of medical attention, and they farmed, cooked, cleaned, and raised their children to carry on the same kind of life. Examples from later periods illustrate frontier conditions:

It is a dark, sloppy, muddy, disagreeable day and I have been working hard, washing dishes, looking into closets, and seeing a great

41

deal of the dark side of domestic life. . . . I am sick of the smell of sour milk, and sour meat, and sour everything, and then the clothes *will* not dry, and no wet thing does, and everything smells moldy; and altogether I feel as if I never wanted to eat again.

—Harriet Beecher Stowe, in a letter to her husband
Calvin in the late 1830s.

My wife had a good wheel, and knowed exactly how to use it. She was also a good weaver, as most of the Irish are, whether men or women; and being very industrious with her wheel, she had, in little or no time, a fine web of cloth, ready to make up; and she was good at that too, and at almost any thing that a woman could do.

—Davy Crockett, *Autobiography*

Mrs. Eliza Farnham of Illinois asked a farmer why he married his wife. He replied because of her size: "I reckon women are some like horses and oxen, the biggest one can do the most work, and that's what I want one for."

Like most men, my dear father should never have married. . . . Thus when he took up his claim of three hundred and sixty acres of land in the wilderness of northern Michigan, and sent my mother and five young children to live there alone until he could join us eighteen months later, he gave no thought to the manner in which we were to make the struggle and survive the hardships before us. He had furnished us the land and the four walls of a log cabin.

—Anna Howard Shaw, *The Story of a Pioneer*

James Roberton, an English traveler, met an emigrant family on a train at Niagara Falls, New York, in 1854. He asked the young wife how she felt about leaving her home and friends. She smiled faintly and replied, "Wherever he goes, that is my home."

In 1821, Elizabeth Clemmons, age eleven, migrated with her parents from North Carolina to Pike County, Illinois. She later wrote:
"Wolves and panthers were destructive to our stock. I have carried a gun on more than one occasion to assist the killing of wolves that were after our stock. I was chased by a panther nearly a mile, taking refuge in an old cabin. When just having closed the door, it sprang upon the roof and I had to remain there all night."

This was the life style of the majority of pioneer women and, by extension, of all adults. Mothers trained their daughters in domesticity, raised their sons to imitate their fathers, and perpetuated the role differences that have persisted to this day.

By 1800, values, behavior, and life styles, though always varying in response to changing conditions, still followed the basic patterns laid down in the first two hundred years of white settlement. The landscape might change, and the people's ways of earning a living might change, but attitudes toward women, toward non-whites, and toward strangers remained unchanged. True, paradoxes arose to accommodate new realities. The myth of woman's fragility flourished even as women went to work in factories. White men declaimed pompously about human rights while enslaving black people. And respect for property ownership became a major value while Indians were being deprived of their land.

Suggestions for Further Reading

Antinomianism in the Colony of Massachusetts Bay, 1636–1638. Prince Society Publications, XXI (1894). A record of Anne Hutchinson's trial.

Arthur W. Calhoun. *A Social History of the American Family.* 3 vols. Rev. ed. (New York, 1960).

John Demos. *A Little Commonwealth: Family Life in Plymouth Colony* (New York, 1970).

Duke Frederick, William L. Howenstine, and June Sochen. *Destroy to Create* (Hinsdale, Ill., 1972).

Philip J. Greven, Jr. *Four Generations: Population, Lord and Family in Colonial Andover, Massachusetts* (Ithaca, N.Y., 1970).

Aileen S. Kraditor, editor. *Up from the Pedestal: Selected Writings in the History of American Feminism* (Chicago, 1968).

Cotton Mather. *Magnalia Christi Americana.* Various editions.

Edmund S. Morgan. *The Puritan Family: Essays on Religion and Domestic Relations in Seventeenth Century New England.* Rev. ed. (New York, 1966).

Edmund S. Morgan. *Virginians at Home: Family Life in the Eighteenth Century* (Chapel Hill, N.C., 1952).

CHAPTER THREE

The Defiant Ones
1600—1775

She [Anne Hutchinson] advanced doctrines and opinions which involved the colony in disputes and contentions. . . .

— Trial record, *Trial of Anne Hutchinson*

In short, the way to wealth, if you desire it, is as plain as the way to market. It depends chiefly on two words, industry and frugality; that is, waste neither time nor money, but make the best use of both.

— Benjamin Franklin, 1748

*I*n every century and in every culture, there are individuals who deviate from the majority. Why do some people march to their own tunes while the majority dance to another melody? Why did Anne Hutchinson interpret religious truths differently from the ministers? Why did she insist upon the rightness of her views after the clergy expressed their disapproval? What was it about Ben Franklin that made him the extraordinary success that he was? Deviants from the norm—and Franklin is a case in point—need not be critics of their culture. They need only behave exceptionally, carve out their own destinies, and impress society with their unique differences. They offer later generations instructive insights on dominant cultural values and minority views, as well as the consequences of deviant behavior.

The quantity and the nature of individual deviation vary greatly. Women have deviated from cultural norms far less than men, since their traditional roles have consumed most of their time and energy and since, in their case, the strictures against nonconformity have been overpoweringly great. In the early days of America it was truly the exceptional woman who walked her own path and scorned the opinion of others. However, as the lives of women changed in the United States, particularly in the eighteenth and nineteenth centuries, more and more women boldly proclaimed their displeasure with existing values, more and more women articulated their criticisms and their suggestions for change. And as a middle class developed in colonial and industrial America, more and more women had the leisure and the education to question society's statements about their sex.

Let us take a brief look at some individuals who deviated from the culture's values in the seventeenth and eighteenth centuries. Then we shall have a backdrop for future discussions of society's rebels.

To differ from the majority requires courage, self-confidence, and inner strength. For Anne Hutchinson, this seemed to be the natural way; for Ben Franklin, it also appeared natural. Sometimes the deviant achieved a place of importance in his/her culture (witness Franklin); most often, he/she was rejected by his/her peers. Often the deviant was punished, exiled, or killed. Women accused of witchcraft in Puritan New England lost their lives, and Anne Hutchinson ended hers in exile. The majority rarely tolerates its critics, though their presence is necessary for a vital and changing society. Deviants and deviations are undesired but essential in every generation.

Bewitched

Puritan New England believed in the Devil, witches, and spirits. Witches, especially, plagued the minds and imaginations of many Puritans. People believed that witches lived within the hearts of women. For since women were Eve's descendants and possessed the power of temptation, they could use that power to ensnare men, to sway them from the path of virtue, and to instill their victims with evil thoughts. Minister Cotton Mather believed that the Devil was his particular enemy. Since he had devoted his life to battling Satan, the Devil reciprocated by tempting him to sin constantly. He was convinced that women were often used to flirt with him and lead him into the path to Hell. In his diary for February 1702, Mather reported:

There is a young gentlewoman of incomparable accomplishments
. . . she first addresses me with diverse letters, and then makes me a
visit at my house; wherein she gives me to understand, that she has
long had a more than ordinary value for my ministry; and that since
my present condition has given her more of liberty to think of me,
she must confess herself charmed with my person, to such a degree,
that she could not but break in upon me, with her most importunate
requests, that I would make her mine; and that the highest consideration she had in it, was her eternal salvation, for if she were mine,
she could not but hope the effect of it would be, that she should also
be Christ's.

Mather resisted her overtures, he said, by fasting, praying,
and beseeching the gentlewoman to restrain herself. Eventually,
she stopped her advances, Mather married, and the Lord won
another victory.

Puritan ministers continually warned their congregations of

Bridget Bishop, convicted witch, is executed
at Salem, 1692. (Brown Bros.)

the danger of witches and deviltry and punished any women accused of witchcraft. But in 1692, an outburst of witchlike activities occurred in Salem, Massachusetts, that led to a major witchcraft trial and the execution of twenty women. In that year, young girls began barking like dogs, men pointed accusing fingers at women who had cursed them, and the community experienced a fit of mass hysteria that lasted eight months. Cotton Mather observed the trials of the accused women; he concluded that the unfortunate were possessed of the Devil, and the witch women, the Devil's agents, required severe punishment. The evidence he heard was emotionally charged. A farmer swore that a witch predicted he would never own more than two cows and her prophecy came true. Another witch had stolen into the bed of an unsuspecting male (so he testified) and left only after he had bitten her finger down to the bone. Lengthy court trials followed the accusations. Some of the accused were found guilty and lost their lives, while many were proved innocent. The executions ended the controversy, and the community calmed down.

Witches, of course, were women who deviated from the proper Puritan mode of behavior. The first three women accused of witchcraft, for example, were nonconformists. Tituba, a black slave brought to Massachusetts from Barbados, boasted of her knowledge of magic and voodoo. Sarah Good was a leathery-faced old woman who wandered around Salem Village, often neglecting her own children and cursing anyone who refused her a handout. And Sarah Osborne had shocked the town when a man moved into her house some months before they were married. As deviants, they all had to be punished. Puritanism was a closed system. Since the nature of woman made her susceptible to emotions, to waywardness, and to sin, it appeared logical and natural that she would be involved in any devilish activities.

The type of nonconformity that appears in any society is influenced by the rules and strictures of that society. In a religious atmosphere, deviants appear as sinners possessed by the Lord's rival. In a secular society, the deviants take on a greater variety of poses. Analysts of the Salem witch trials have varied in their interpretations of the phenomenon. Some have pointed out that many of the accusers were impressionable adolescent girls who had been cooped up in their houses all winter and required some emotional release. Others have noted that the Puritans were frustrated and disturbed as a group, because of the political difficulties they experienced in efforts to gain a renewal of their charter with England. Still others have pointed to witchcraft as the only way dissidents could express themselves in a church-state system.

Whatever the reason or reasons, the witchcraft phenomenon showed how close was the connection between medieval Christianity and the New England community of Puritans. How little change in thought and attitude had occurred in so many centuries! The late seventeenth-century Puritans in New England still believed in witches and identified the Devil with women, as did their Christian ancestors. Both sexes could vent their particular frustrations upon the unfortunate few women in their community who appeared different, strange, and/or eccentric.

A Woman Rebels

Women were always followers, never leaders—that was the accepted pattern. Puritan ministers were invariably men, and college educated; many of the first-generation colonial ministers held degrees from Cambridge University in England. Women, of course, were not allowed at Cambridge and never studied theology formally, since their minds were not considered suited to absorbing such heady stuff. Thus, they could never be qualified to preach, to teach the Bible's truths, and to lead a congregation. Given this set of taboos, it is no wonder that the actions of Anne Hutchinson (1591–1643) caused such an uproar. She had come to Massachusetts in 1634 because her favorite minister, John Cotton, had migrated there. Being a strong-minded woman, she had uprooted her family and followed him to the New World.

But Anne Hutchinson was also a sensitive, serious thinker about religious matters, and she discovered, as time went by, that many of the Puritan ministers said things that she questioned. While she herself professed the Covenant of Grace, that is, the belief in faith as the basic link between God and people, they— some of them—preached the Covenant of Works—a belief in salvation based upon good deeds. To Anne Hutchinson, the mysterious power of God's grace, felt inwardly by a person, superseded good works as the basis of salvation.

She began holding separate meetings, attended by about

eighty people, mostly women, at which she would discuss the Sunday sermon. At one meeting, she boldly claimed that only John Cotton and John Wainwright were proper ministers, because they were the only ones who preached the Covenant of Grace. The other ministers in the community were startled and outraged. What would happen if other women questioned their views and challenged their power?

Although Anne Hutchinson was always respectful, she did claim that her insights and her intuitions were also sources of God's truth. Book learning might be important, she reasoned, but listening to your own heart's meanings was crucial. "I think the soul to be nothing but light," she declared. More and more women came to listen to Mrs. Hutchinson's views, and more and more ministers grew uncomfortable. Sincerely intentioned, she still challenged the established church in two key ways: she argued that God's truth could be known and arrived at by other than learned, rational analyses of the Bible, and she insisted that persons other than ordained ministers could know the truth.

For her efforts, Anne Hutchinson was brought to trial in 1637, found guilty of heresy, and banished with her family from the colony. The trial record stated:

> Mrs. Hutchinson, the wife of Mr. William Hutchinson, being convicted for traducing the ministers and their ministry in the country, she declared voluntarily her revelations, and that she should be delivered . . . and thereupon was banished. . . .

She and her family were later killed in an Indian uprising, thereby confirming the Puritan leaders' view that she was sinful and that God's will would be done. Anne Hutchinson was guilty, in their eyes, not only for the above-stated reasons but because she was a woman. Of course, men could not question the established truth either; witness the same banishment pronounced upon Roger Williams. But women, possessors of emotion and sinfulness, should surely remember their proper sphere and not venture forth into the holy world of theological analysis. They were expected to attend church regularly, raise their children to

Anne Hutchinson interprets the
minister's sermon. (N.Y. Public Library)

be God fearing, and observe the Sabbath day, but they were not expected to question the meaning of the Sunday sermon or presume to understand God's—and man's—ways. Their dependency status was confirmed in religious as well as secular terms.

Benjamin Franklin: White Male Hero

In many ways the epitome of the new American was Benjamin Franklin, an eighteenth-century man who inspired thousands of his own generation, as well as subsequent ones, to imitate his behavior. Expressing a paradox in inimitable American fashion, people interpreted Franklin's unusual achievements in many fields as those of a "common man," a model for all young men to emulate. His example, however, did not apply to young women.

Franklin represented the male definition of success in a growing, mercantile society. Born on January 17, 1706, in Boston, he was the tenth and youngest son of a candlemaker named Josiah Franklin. He lived long enough to span most of the eighteenth century, and his accomplishments made him a living legend. His writings, too, contributed to his reputation and helped shape the way future generations would look upon him. In his memoirs, in the practical wisdom of *Poor Richard's Almanac*, and in numerous political essays, Benjamin Franklin established himself as a major interpreter of eighteenth-century everyday life in the colonies.

With a minimal formal education, Franklin became an apprentice printer to his brother James at the age of twelve. Later he ran away, first to New York and then on to Philadelphia at the age of seventeen. Within a year, he had proved himself to be such a good printer that the governor of Pennsylvania agreed to pay for young Franklin's passage to London to buy printing equipment. But the governor reneged on the agreement and Franklin was left in London without funds. Undaunted, he found work as a printer, wrote a pamphlet on the necessity of liberty, and became friendly with many of London's leading intellectuals. Already, Benjamin Franklin was revealing traits that would serve him well throughout his life: self-confidence and courage.

Returning to Philadelphia in 1726, Franklin established himself as a printer of note. By 1730, he had his own newspaper and had become the official printer for the colonial government of Pennsylvania. Obviously, he already understood the relationship between business and politics and, by acquainting himself with government officials, could obtain favored business deals with them. A practical man above all else, Franklin never acted illegally, but he believed in cultivating valuable acquaintances, people who could be beneficial to his future. Along with his business enterprises, he followed a variety of other interests as well. He had a keen mind, a natural curiosity, and a sharp wit. Socially responsible and interested in human progress, he wanted his adopted city, Philadelphia, to develop a vibrant cultural life.

A natural leader, Benjamin Franklin organized the first subscription library in America, the American Philosophical Society, and the first fire-fighting company. By 1748, when he was only forty-two years old, he was a well-known member of his community and rich enough to retire, though retaining a financial interest in his printing business. The publication of *Poor Richard's Almanac* every year since 1732 had endeared him to ordinary people throughout the colonies who read his practical words of advice avidly. When Franklin told his readers to live frugally, they knew he had once lived by that advice. "Remember," Franklin wrote, "that Time is Money. He that can earn Ten Shillings a Day by his Labour, and goes abroad, or sits idle one half of that Day, tho' he spends but Sixpence during his Diversion or Idleness, ought not to reckon That the only Expence; he has really spent or rather thrown away Five Shillings besides." Take advantage of all opportunities, Franklin counseled his readers, and never waste precious time.

Franklin's far-ranging mind led him to original research into electricity and the lightning rod. He corresponded with leading scientists in England and encouraged his fellow colonists to conduct scientific experiments. He supported medical research and urged smallpox inoculation when many colonists were wary of it. In addition to his cultural and business accomplishments, he became an outstanding colonial political leader. In 1757 he went to England to represent Pennsylvania citizens in their dispute with their governor, and during the next twenty years he became the colonial agent in England for Georgia, New Jersey, and Massachusetts. While maintaining cordial ties with the British government, he criticized Parliament for its Stamp Act and all subsequent examples of repressive legislation upon the colonies. Indeed he had been an early critic of Britain's restraint-of-trade policies.

Franklin returned to the colonies just after the battles of Lexington and Concord. Elected to the Second Continental Congress, he sat on the committee that drafted the Declaration of Independence. Then, within the year, he returned to Europe, this time to France to negotiate an alliance with the French King, Louis XVI. He remained in Europe and participated in the peace negotiations with King George III. When he returned to this country in 1785, he was seventy-nine years old, had spent the better part of thirty years abroad, and had established himself as a witty, charming American. With the possible exception of Thomas Jefferson, who also spent time in France during this period, no other American achieved such renown and respect both among his own people and in Europe. In 1787, when the new United States of America called a Constitutional Convention to reshape the existing Articles of Confederation, Benjamin Franklin was a delegate. Thereafter his health steadily declined, and he retired to write his memoirs. He died on April 17, 1790, at the age of eighty-four.

The remarkable career of Benjamin Franklin cannot be underrated. However, a reading of his life and actions from the feminist perspective can be very instructive. Though he always acknowledged the help of the Lord and of his wife, most of his words and all his deeds suggested that a *man,* any man, could shape his own destiny. His Puritan background may have taught him that self-help was essential to godliness (though it was no guarantee), but he adapted that view to mean that self-help was the foundation of earthly success—the only kind of success worth having anyway.

How could a colonial woman apply any of the lessons that Franklin taught? Could a twelve-year-old girl leave her home, run away to another city, and begin life anew? Not if she did not want to become a prostitute or a slave in some domineering person's kitchen forever. Did hard work bring women material success? Rarely. How could women gain the self-confidence that seemed to radiate from Franklin's being? How could an unescorted young woman secure an honest apprenticeship in a growing profession such as printing, when women printers were few (usually the widows of printers), were actively discouraged from venturing out of the home, and were timid and unsure of their own capabilities? Women never spoke before male audiences in the eighteenth century and would have been politely escorted out of any legislative hall in which they attempted to do so.

Franklin's words of wisdom were directed exclusively toward men. Time was not money for women. They were not paid for their work in the home. Their numerous hours over the washboard, the ironing board, and the kitchen stove were not counted up and paid for. Nor could women enter politics as a way to success, since they could not vote, could not participate in legislative discussions, and were not encouraged to read political materials. The Declaration of Independence was written by white men for white men. Women were not consulted in the writing of that document or, for that matter, in any debate over political or economic matters. Women, like blacks and children, were seen and not heard. Franklin's model, of an active individual carving out his own fortune, applied only to men. Women had no way of becoming the determiners of their own destiny in the way Franklin described. The American model for success was a male model. Men were the adventurers and the doers; women were the preservers of the homefires—the observers of life's great events, not the makers of them. In a letter to a young man, Franklin displays his attitude towards marriage and the other woman:

June 25, 1745

My dear Friend,

I know of no Medicine fit to diminish the violent natural Inclinations you mention; and if I did, I think I should not communicate it to you. Marriage is the proper Remedy. It is the most natural State of Man, and therefore the State in which you are most likely to find solid Happiness. Your Reasons against entring into it at present, appear to me not well-founded. The circumstantial Advantages you have in View by postponing it, are not only undertain, but they are small in comparison with that of the Thing itself, the being *married and settled*. It is the Man and Woman united that make the compleat human Being. Separate, she wants his Force of Body and Strength of Reason; he, her Softness, Sensibility and acute Discernment. Together they are more likely to succeed in the World. A single Man has not nearly the Value he would have in that State of Union. He is an incomplete Animal. He resembles the odd Half of a Pair of Scissars. If you get a prudent healthy Wife, your Industry in your Profession, with her good Oeconomy, will be a Fortune sufficient.

But if you will take this Counsel, and persist in thinking a Commerce with the Sex inevitable, then I repeat my former Advice, that in all your Amours you should *prefer old Women to young ones*. You call this a Paradox, and demand my Reasons. They are these:

1. Because as they have more Knowledge of the World and their Minds are better stor'd with Observations, their Conversation is more improving and more lastingly agreable.

2. Because when Women cease to be handsome, they study to be good. To maintain their Influence over Men, they supply the Diminution of Beauty by an Augmentation of Utility. They learn to do a 1000 Services small and great, and are the most tender and useful of all Friends when you are sick. Thus they continue amiable. And hence there is hardly such a thing to be found as an old Woman who is not a good Woman.

3. Because there is no hazard of Children, which irregularly produc'd may be attended with much Inconvenience.

4. Because thro' more Experience, they are more prudent and discreet in conducting an Intrigue to prevent Suspicion. The Commerce with them is therefore with regard to your Reputation. And with regard to theirs, if the Affair should happen to be known, considerable People might be rather inclin'd to excuse an old Woman who would kindly take care of a young Man, form his Manners by her good Counsels, and prevent his ruining his Health and Fortune among mercenary Prostitutes.

5. Because in every Animal that walks upright, the Deficiency of the Fluids that fill the Muscles appears first in the highest Part: The Face first grows lank and wrinkled; then the Neck; then the Breast and Arms; the lower Parts continuing to the last as plump as ever: So that covering all above with a Basket, and regarding only what is below the Girdle, it is impossible of two Women to know an old from a young one. And as in the dark all Cats are grey, the Pleasure of corporal Enjoyment with an old Woman is at least equal, and frequently superior, every Knack being by Practice capable of Improvement.

6. Because the Sin is less. The debauching of a Virgin may be her Ruin, and make her for Life unhappy.

7. Because the Compunction is less. The having made a young

56

Girl *miserable* may give you frequent bitter Reflections; none of which can attend the making an old Woman *happy*.

8thly and Lastly. They are *so grateful!!*

Thus much for my paradox. But still I advise you to marry directly; being sincerely

Your affectionate Friend.

—Benjamin Franklin, *Advice to a Young Man on Taking a Mistress*

Female Ben Franklins

There were a few female equivalents of Benjamin Franklin, though they never received the public recognition that Mr. Franklin did. Some women entered business and made a success of it. Hector Crèvecoeur, an astute commentator on American life in the eighteenth century, noted many wealthy Nantucket women who became entrepreneurs while their husbands were away at sea. One woman traded pins and needles, taught school, and eventually built up such a large trade that she had representatives in London. Other women learned the printing business and became publishers; still others conducted dress manufacturing establishments as well as retail stores. But businesswomen never extended their influence into politics, nor were they given the same respect in the community as businessmen. A wealthy male merchant could hold positions in the city council, the church, and other community organizations. A wealthy businesswoman could never play a part in the influential, powerful institutions of her city.

Because women were excluded from the centers of power, they often created their own groups and conferred status upon their own activities. New York City women merchants organized themselves and appealed to the councils of government on their own behalf (to little avail). Prayer meetings led by women were attended by as many as fifty women at a time. Women writers also became an early and well-established group of wage earners, as we shall see in a later chapter. Some ambitious women appeared in law courts and some widows wrote marriage contracts for themselves when they remarried. But the essential commitment of women was always to home and hearth.

The Defiant Ones 1600–1775

The law itself reflected the Puritan-WASM disregard for woman's rights. Married women could not own property in their own name and could not enter into contractual relationships. (Widows and single women could do so, however.) A conversation, held in the next century, illustrates married women's property rights:

> One Christmas morning I went into the office to show them, among other of my presents, a new coral necklace and bracelets. They all admired the jewelry and then began to tease me with hypothetical cases of future ownership. "Now," said Henry Bayard, "if in due time you should be my wife, those ornaments would be mine; I could take them and lock them up, and you could never wear them except with my permission. I could even exchange them for a box of cigars, and you could watch them evaporate in smoke."
>
> —Elizabeth Cady Stanton, *Eighty Years and More*

Occasionally a married businesswoman sued in the equity courts to gain just treatment, but most wives found themselves invisible in the eyes of the law: neither their children nor their personal possessions legally belonged to them. And not until the 1840s did the laws begin to change. Eighteenth-century married women—that is, the overwhelming majority of adult women —were discriminated against by the law, government, and the business world.

Because of the labor shortage, some ambitious, energetic women found it possible to enter business and the professions. Able hands were needed to deliver babies, tend shops, keep records, and manage taverns. Though the number of women in these "unwomanly" jobs was never very high, their presence was usually justified by economic and practical necessity. Most men did not relinquish their belief that woman's place was in the home. They simply suspended it when expediency demanded her presence in the marketplace.

Both sexes admired Benjamin Franklin and other males who successfully made their own destinies, but both also assumed that the business and diplomatic worlds were male spheres of action—arenas which only an exceptional woman (and very infrequently) could enter.

58

Southern Differences

Most aspects of English Protestant culture took on a different texture in the South—the South became a regional deviation from the colonial norm. Slavery, with its continued increase throughout the eighteenth century, influenced man-woman and black-white relations in such a way as to make the Southern culture quite different from that of the North. Individual effort and achievement, for example, could never be a motivating doctrine for slaves or for most small white farmers in the South. Group effort was needed to produce and harvest the tobacco, rice, cotton, and indigo that became the major exports of the area. These products came mainly from large plantations. Small white farmers managed to grow enough food for themselves, with little left over to sell. But even they, the poor white farmers, gained comfort and pride from the fact they were not at the bottom of the socioeconomic scale; beneath them was another group of Southerners—the slaves.

Most white Southerners did not own slaves, but their conspicuous existence provided a constant reference point by which whites could measure their own meager accomplishments. No matter how poverty-stricken a man was, he could never be as low as a slave.

The Southern whites who owned large plantations and managed to free themselves and their wives from manual labor adopted the elaborate manners and rituals of aristocrats, "ladies and gentlemen." In reality, the plantation owner and his wife spent many hours a day supervising their slaves and other workers—the owner on the land, the wife indoors overseeing the household staff. The Southern landowner's goal, a negative one and rarely attained, was leisure—to work as little as possible. Slaves had to work, as did the majority of poor white farmers and their wives. Even the rich had to work part of each day, but they had time to enjoy sporting events, dances, and elaborate dinners. But Southern ladies of the cultivated class prided themselves upon their hospitality and good manners. One traveler noted in her diary:

> "The mothers took the care of the girls, they were trained up under them and not only instructed in the family duties necessary to the

59

sex, but in these accomplishments and genteel manners that are still so visible amongst them, and this descended from mother to daughter."

One way the Southerner measured his success was by the complexion of the woman of the house: the paler she was, the more genteel. A black woman worked as a slave. A sun-tanned woman worked in the fields. But a pale woman did not have to work outside and therefore could stay in the house, shielded from the brutal heat of the midday sun. Yet this ideal of the pale-skinned white woman was seldom achieved, since the overwhelming majority of women in the agricultural South did work outdoors.

Black women were most tragically exploited. Sexually used and abused by white men, they had no legal recourse because in the eyes of the law they did not exist. And they could not betray their white masters for fear of death, whippings, or being sold. Their lives and those of their children depended on their masters' generosity. Black men were not allowed to maintain a stable, monogamous family life, with a wife and children, because white owners often used them as studs to keep the slave population growing. A feminist of that time wrote the following about women slaves:

> There is another class of women in this country to whom I cannot refer without feelings of the deepest shame and sorrow. I allude to our female slaves. Our southern cities are whelmed beneath a tide of pollution; the virtue of female slaves is wholly at the mercy of irresponsible tyrants, and women are bought and sold in our slave markets to gratify the brutal lust of those who bear the name of Christians. In our slave States, if amid all her degradation and ignorance a woman desires to preserve her virtue unsullied, she is either bribed or whipped into compliance; or if she dares resist her seducer, her life by the laws of some of the slave states may be, and has actually been, sacrificed to the fury of disappointed passion. Where such laws do not exist, the power which is necessarily vested in the master over his property leaves the defenseless slave entirely at his mercy, and the sufferings of some females on this account, both physical and mental, are intense. . . .
>
> . . . Nor does the colored woman suffer alone: The moral purity of the white woman is deeply contaminated. In the daily habit of seeing

the virtue of her enslaved sister sacrificed without hesitancy or re-
morse, she looks upon the crimes of seduction and illicit intercourse
without horror, and although not personally involved in the guilt,
she loses that value for innocence in her own as well as the other sex
which is one of the strongest safeguards to virtue. She lives in
habitual intercourse with men whom she knows to be polluted by
licentiousness, and often is she compelled to witness in her own
domestic circle those disgusting and heart-sickening jealousies and
strifes which disgraced and distracted the family of Abraham. In
addition to all this, the female slaves suffer every species of degradation and cruelty which the most wanton barbarity can inflict; they
are indecently divested of their clothing, sometimes tied up and
severely whipped, sometimes prostrated on the earth while their
naked bodies are torn by the scorpion lash.

—Sarah Grimké, *Letters on the Equality of the Sexes*

William Faulkner's twentieth-century novels portray vividly
and profoundly how the experience of slavery affected every
generation of Southerners. The white upper-class woman silently accepted her privileged status in the home, knowing that
her husband shared his affections with a slave girl. The rise of a
significant mulatto population in this country is one result of
such sexual mating between black women and white men.
Another is the complex set of sexual fantasies developed by
white men about black men and women—for example, the notion
that blacks, being dark and swarthy, represented pure passion
and animal sexuality. In the psychoanalytic terms of the twentieth century, white men projected their own repressed desires
upon blacks. They imagined that black men lusted constantly
after white women, and thereby disguised their own lust for
black women. For many decades, white men would punish, in
severe and brutal ways, any black man who indicated the sligh-
test sexual interest in a white woman.

White women who yearned for sexual expression also had
repressed wishes about black men. If a woman's dream became a
reality and she was caught in a compromising position with a
black man, she would scream "Rape!" and the man would be
promptly castrated and lynched. The bestial state of slavery prevented any viable human interaction between the races, and
these sexual overtones and undertones made their relationships

with one another almost inhuman. Their close physical proximity, moreover, served to increase tensions and to remind both races of their intolerable position.

White Northerners never experienced this same cultural tension, since slaves were not an essential part of daily life in the North. For one thing, they were far fewer in number. In 1790, when Virginia had 292,000 black slaves, Pennsylvania had 3,707 and New York 21,193.

Because slaves were vitally necessary to the whole Southern way of life, any criticism of the status quo was severely punished. The Grimké sisters of South Carolina left the South in the 1820s because they could not preach abolition while living among slave-holders and sympathizers. As slavery grew, as the intricate human relationships based upon it were deepened and intensified, supporters of the system became louder and more vigorous. It is not by accident that no major social reform movement ever began in the South. A society founded on the inhuman institution of slavery could not consider human reform without facing its own contradictions. The defenders of slavery, always protesting too loudly, betraying greater defensiveness as the years passed, for 250 years taught their children to treat all blacks as inferior, to call every fifty-year-old black man "Boy," and to fear their own passion because blacks were "primitives."

The daily lives of white women, white men, black women, and black men were all tainted by slavery, as were all the institutions of Southern society. Some perceptive white women saw the connections. Mary Chesnut, the wife of a slaveowner, kept a diary and recorded her feelings: "There is no slave, after all, like a wife. You know how women sell themselves and are sold in marriage, from queens downward. Poor women, poor slaves."

Thus two very different cultures developed in this country—one in the North and Middle West and the other in the South. The egalitarian myth that hard work always brought success was strictly a Northern myth. Indeed, the oft-articulated but impractical American ideal of equality for all, of progress and material advancement, has always been unbelieved and unarticulated in the South. Change became the North's byword; tradition controlled the South.

The South's agricultural economy, carried on by black slaves and a homogeneous white population, created its unique culture—a culture that placed high value on personal contacts, family ties, local traditions, and closeness to the land. Southern culture perpetuated a belief in hierarchy and racism. Women were locked into their wife-mother roles to an even greater extent than in the North. Some Northern women broke out of their narrow role definitions; only a very few did so in the South.

Southern blacks developed a positive culture of their own, partly as a defense against their white masters. They integrated Christianity with African folklore, practical necessity with philosophical resignation, cunning with discretion, and humor with patience. The great spirituals that emerged from the souls of black people reflect their constant desire for freedom, their identification with the enslaved Hebrews of biblical times, and the repeated theme of helplessness and despondency. "Sometimes I Feel Like a Motherless Child" surely captures the dominant, and understandable, feelings of blacks who were brought to this continent against their will and enslaved and brutalized by supposedly God-fearing people. Another song "Follow the Drinking Gourd" spoke covertly of freedom.

> Follow the drinking gourd,
> Follow the drinking gourd,
> For the old man is awaiting
> For to carry you to freedom
> If you follow the drinking gourd.
>
> Well the river bank makes a mighty good road,
> The dead trees will show you the way.
> On the left foot, peg foot, traveling on,
> Follow the drinking gourd.
>
> When the sun comes up, and the first quail calls,
> Follow the drinking gourd,
> For the old man is a-waiting for to carry you
> > to freedom
> If you follow the drinking gourd.

A social class system also arose within the black population. Just as whites had their classes based upon family background, wealth, and breeding, so black slaves made distinctions between different types of workers. House servants were more highly respected than field hands. Skilled craftsmen, of whom there were many, received more deference, both from whites and blacks, than did cotton-pickers. Indeed, able slaves were often given positions of responsibility by their white masters. Black men built the cabins and the plantations, shoed the horses, cultivated the fields, managed business enterprises, supervised fellow blacks in farm work, traveled down the rivers of the South to sell timber in New Orleans, and performed a wide range of activities. Yet, however important their jobs were, they were still black men in a white world, even the fortunate few who were freed by their masters. White people labeled the whole race inferior, and discriminated equally against the free blacks and slaves, the literate and illiterate, the skilled and unskilled.

In all power relationships, blacks (like women) were utterly dependent on white men. If they attempted to rebel against their masters, they were doomed. The few slave rebellions that occurred, particularly in the 1830s, were quickly squelched. Outwardly, therefore, blacks were forced to remain quiet and seemingly acquiescent. Inwardly, they had to repress their resentment and/or channel it into socially approved behavior. Many chose religion as their only solace, believing that God would reward his children—if not on this earth, then in eternity. Black ministers emphasized the trials and sufferings of the Old Testament Hebrews and reminded their congregations that the Lord worked in mysterious ways.

By the early 1800s, there were so many black people in the South (more blacks than whites in many Deep South counties) that to white Southerners any social change, even if desired, seemed impossible. What would happen to all the slaves if they were freed? Who would care for them? Obviously, the argument went, they could not care for themselves, being ignorant, lazy, and inexperienced in solving their own problems. Thus, by using a circular kind of reasoning, white Southerners successfully convinced themselves that slavery as an institution was essential to everyone's welfare. The slaves remained ignorant because whites kept them ignorant; but since they were untutored and ill prepared to operate in white society, they could not be freed.

A Forbidden Subject

One of the least discussed subjects in all Western culture was sex. Using the Bible as their source of truth, the Puritans and

Church of England Anglicans believed that sexual relations were essential for procreation and for good health but that sexual *pleasure* had to be minimized. The ministers encouraged early marriages, recognizing that preoccupation with sex could divert people from God's ways and also that sexual gratification was a basic human need. At the same time, they zealously preached about human sinfulness, often linking it to Eve's provocation of Adam. Woman, according to their view, knows of man's need for her and uses her sexual attractiveness to fulfill his physical urges, thus gaining some control over him.

This association of women with sexual temptation, which would persist in America for many generations, was as old as Christianity. From St. Paul on, Christian interpreters of the Old and New Testament warned men to beware of the snares of women. To medieval Catholics, the nun and the monk were ideal human beings—asexual creatures who repressed their natural instincts. Puritan leaders, as we have seen, did advocate normal sexual relations when these were sanctioned by marriage. How else could their people survive? Wives had to procreate, bear children who could help their father till the soil and would later have children of their own. In colonial America, women were at a premium. They were expected to marry and to be faithful to their husbands. And similar fidelity was demanded of their husbands. Premarital sex, on the other hand, was overlooked, penalized only by the hasty marriages to which it often led.

On cold New England nights, entertainment was sparse and sexual feelings strong. Young farm boys and girls "bundled" in one bed and explored their sexual natures together. The result was often a quick marriage to accommodate the soon-to-arrive product of their union. But if a woman was unlucky enough to become pregnant by a cad who refused to marry her or ran away, she bore the shame and guilt alone. Society disapproved her, censured her, shunned her. She, not the man, showed evidence of the encounter, so the punishment was reserved for her. Following Eve's example, she had lured an innocent male (the argument went); therefore she had to pay the price.

As historian John Demos' study of Plymouth Colony suggested, there were many instances of single people being fined for engaging in sexual intercourse (the evidence being the pregnancy of the girl). A betrothed couple—that is, a couple who signed a marriage contract,—were likely to have sexual

65

relations and the birth of a "premature" baby resulted in a fine
—though lighter than one imposed on a single girl.

Medical science afforded no enlightenment regarding the
woman's physiology. Doctors did not know when it was that a
woman could conceive during her monthly cycle, and were forbidden to examine women's bodies. The midwives, who attended women during childbirth, skillfully handled the
mechanics of their job but knew nothing of physiology. Doctors
and midwives never practiced sanitation when dealing with patients, and there were no hospitals. Women delivered their
babies at home and often returned to their household chores
within a day or two. Indian women were known to go into the
fields hours after delivering a baby. In any case, a woman's destiny seemed closely tied to her biology.

Because farming villages were small, everyone knew about
everyone else's activities. When a reckless Sarah Osborne tried
to live with a man, without the benefit of marriage, she was
ostracized. On the surface, Christian society preserved its religious, moral veneer. Bold men and women did not live together
openly and publicly reject marriage. No one proclaimed their
individual right to privacy and sexual freedom. There is no record in Massachusetts, or anywhere else, of a woman defying the
society by living alone, having children by a variety of men, and
ignoring society's codes. Village life forbade such conduct.
Closeness made it impossible without discovery.

Wives and daughters of merchants who lived in the village
visited one another's homes, gossiped idly, volunteered to sew
clothes for the poor, baked cakes for the church bazaar, and attended the latest lecture on moral philosophy. Young girls
looked forward to the day when they too had a home of their own
and participated in the same social activities as their mothers.
Conformity dominated and deviants paid a high price for their
deviations.

In Contrast

Of some interest in comparison with the rigid code of colonial
society was the native American Indians' attitude toward marriage and divorce. Virginian Robert Beverly observed:

> The Indians have their solemnities of Marriage, and esteem the vows made at that time, as most sacred and inviolable. Notwithstanding they allow both the man and the wife to part upon disagreement; yet so great is the disreputation of divorce, that married people, to avoid the character of inconstant and ungenerous, very rarely let their quarrels proceed to a separation. However, when it does so happen, they reckon all the ties of matrimony dissolved, and each hath the liberty of marrying another.

The Indians' approach to marriage and divorce seemed natural and enlightened indeed in contrast with the Puritans' marriage laws. While the Puritans viewed everything within a strict framework of principle, the Indians appeared far more practical. Note their approach to the custody of children:

> In these separations, the children go, according to the affection of the parent, with the one or the other; for children are not reckoned a charge among them, but rather riches, according to the blessing of the Old Testament; and if they happen to differ about dividing their children, their method is then, to part them equally, allowing the man the first choice.

Suggestions for Further Reading

Carl Bridenbaugh. *Cities in Revolt, 1743–1776* (New York, 1955).

Carl Bridenbaugh. *Cities in the Wilderness, 1625–1742* (New York, 1938; paperback).

Elizabeth A. Dexter. *Colonial Women of Affairs: Women in Business and Professions in America before 1776* (Boston, 1931).

Benjamin Franklin. *Autobiography and Other Writings* (New York, 1951).

Winthrop D. Jordan. *White over Black: American Attitudes Toward the Negro, 1550–1812* (Chapel Hill, N.C., 1968).

Leo Kanowitz. *Women and the Law* (Albuquerque, N.M., 1969).

Perry Miller, editor. *The American Puritans: Their Prose and Poetry* (New York, 1956; paperback).

Perry Miller. *The New England Mind: The Seventeenth Century* (Boston, 1951; paperback).

Julia Cherry Spruill. *Women's Life and Work in the Southern Colonies* (Chapel Hill, N.C., 1938).

Theodore D. Weld, editor. *American Slavery As It Is: Testimony of a Thousand Witnesses* (New York, 1839).

Louis B. Wright. *The Cultural Life of the American Colonies* (New York, 1957).

CHAPTER FOUR

Independence for Whom?
1775–1800

Should you, my lord, while you peruse my song,
Wonder from whence my love of *Freedom* sprung,
Whence flow these wishes for the common good,
By feeling hearts alone best understood,
I, young in life, by seeming cruel fate
Was snatch'd from *Afric's* fancy'd happy seat:
What pangs excruciating must molest,
What sorrows labour in my parent's breast?
Steel'd was that soul and by no misery mov'd
That from a father seiz'd his babe belov'd
Such, such my case. And can I then but pray
Others may never feel tyrannic sway?

> —Phillis Wheatley, *To the Right Honorable William,
> Earl of Dartmouth, His Majesty's Principal Secretary
> of State for North America* (1773)

If you happen to have any learning keep it a profound secret, especially from the men, who generally look with a jealous and malignant eye on a woman of great parts and a cultivated understanding.

> —Dr. Gregory, *A Father's Legacy to his Daughters* (1775)

*T*he foregoing quotations reflect very different world-views. Black poetess Phillis Wheatley had experienced slavery and wrote of black people's wish for freedom. Dr. Gregory, a Presbyterian minister, reminded his motherless daughters in a most popular "advice" book that woman's primary occupation was snaring a husband. Phillis Wheatley yearned for the colonies' freedom from Great Britain as she had yearned for freedom from slavery; Dr. Gregory deplored the concept of freedom as applied to women's role in society. Perhaps Dr. Gregory

69

would have agreed with Miss Wheatley that freedom for the colonies was desirable. But he surely would not have carried her quest for freedom to its logical conclusion—the quest for all human freedom. True to the paradoxical nature of human beings, Dr. Gregory believed in freedom for America but not for women.

Phillis Wheatley's love of freedom, she explained, came from her experience of slavery; adversity created the wish to be free. She knew that one-third of the slave cargo brought to America were women, whose sufferings on ship and after were described by an observer:

> I saw pregnant women give birth to babies while chained to corpses which our drunken overseers had not removed. . . .

> One day at Bonny I saw a middle-aged stout woman, who had been brought down from a fair that preceding day, chained to the post of a black trader's door, in a state of furious insanity.

Similarly, the white colonists' fight for independence from Great Britain came from the experience of self-rule. The British practice of benign neglect had ended in the 1760s, and the colonists found themselves subject to new rules and regulations from the English Parliament. Nearly half the colonial population found the new restrictions intolerable and agreed with the American radicals that separation was essential. But the separatists' view of independence never included a belief in liberating women, slaves, Indians, small farmers, and property-less workers. The separatists used a popular eighteenth-century concept to justify their advocacy of colonial independence: natural rights. They argued, with Jefferson's Declaration of Independence as the best example, that "all men are created equal" and that they are "endowed with certain unalienable rights." No other political document had claimed such an audacious assumption.

By claiming natural rights to be the basis as well as the justification for revolution, the revolutionary leaders laid the foundation for all future demands for social change by deprived groups. Slaves seeking their freedom and women asking for their rights have usually relied on the Declaration of Independence. How could a people who asserted that all human beings born (or naturalized) in the United States had natural rights to life, liberty, and the pursuit of happiness deny those basic rights to a

70

Poet Phillis Wheatley. (Brown Bros.)

segment of their population? Later, in 1848, at Seneca Falls, New York, feminist Elizabeth Cady Stanton drafted a declaration of women's rights, the Declaration of Sentiments and Resolutions, that was modeled after the 1776 Declaration. Seekers of independence here and abroad have continued to refer to the eloquent phrases and philosophy of that document. [See Appendix I for complete Declaration.]

> *Resolved, therefore,* That, being invested by the Creator with the same capabilities, and the same consciousness of responsibility for their exercise, it is demonstrably the right and duty of woman, equally with man, to promote every righteous cause by every righteous means; and especially in regard to the great subjects of morals and religion, it is self-evidently her right to participate with her brother in teaching them, both in private and in public, by writing and by speaking, by any instrumentalities proper to be used, and in any assemblies proper to be held; and this being a self-evident truth growing out of the divinely implanted principles of human nature, any custom or authority adverse to it, whether modern or wearing the hoary sanction of antiquity, is to be regarded as a self-evident falsehood, and at war with mankind.

The natural rights theory is all-sweeping; it denies exceptions and exclusions. If rights are natural to all human beings, then no restrictions should be placed upon them. The simplicity and beauty of this concept appealed to Jefferson, and has continued to appeal to multitudes of deprived people. Indeed, the natural rights theory fits in neatly with the American view of individualism. It assumes that each person, equipped with certain basic rights, begins life on an equal footing with every other person. Whether or not he succeeds depends on his ability and personality. Each person, according to this doctrine, determines his fate while pursuing his personal happiness. No artificial boundaries exist to prevent his reaching that goal. The unsuccessful fail because of personal flaws and inadequacies. The successful achieve their ends through hard work, self-reliance, and determination.

The colonial revolutionaries assumed that neither the government, nor the churches, nor the commercial interests would obstruct the free expression of each American's natural rights. Political, religious, and economic power would be diffused among the people, and all Americans could cultivate their natural inclinations. They believed naively that free men, with options open, would wisely choose a representative government, membership in an established church, and an upright family life. Few natural rights advocates seriously entertained the notion that some individuals might interpret the right to liberty as their right to live in a polygamous, godless community; that some women might want to live independently, outside the family structure; and that the theory applied to black slaves.

Human Rights for Whom?

Thomas Jefferson did not entertain the thought that women, blacks, and Indians were nature's creatures and therefore entitled to the same privileges and rights as those granted to white men. When the daughter of General Schuyler wrote Jefferson to ask about the new federal Constitution, he answered that she should not agitate herself, for ". . . the tender breasts of ladies were not formed for political convulsion." Indeed, he did not really believe that all men are created equal in any meaningful sense. Aristocrats in Virginia, inheritors of thousand-acre estates, surely began life with advantages unknown to male children born on a thirty-acre farm in Pennsylvania or Georgia. Illiterate men, propertyless men, and itinerant workers surely did not face life with the same opportunities as educated property-holders. In many places, property qualifications determined which men could vote and which ones could hold public office. Massachusetts landowners held power over landless merchants. Rich men enjoyed special treatment before the law not given to poor men. Thus, even within the community of men, as Jefferson well knew, there was no practice of equality.

Abigail Adams (1744–1818), wife of John Adams and a contemporary of Jefferson, questioned the legitimacy of the Declaration as well as the general limitations placed upon women in the 1770s. She wrote to her husband on March 31, 1777, while he was in Philadelphia attending the meetings of the Second Continental Congress, and asked him whether women would be included in the deliberations.

> I long to hear that you have declared an independency, and by the way, in the new code of laws which I suppose it will be necessary

for you to make, I desire you would remember the ladies and be more generous and favorable to them than were your ancestors. Do not put such unlimited power into the hands of husbands. Remember all men would be tyrants if they could. If particular care and attention are not paid to the ladies we are determined to foment a rebellion, and will not hold ourselves bound to obey any laws in which we have no voice or representation.

The final sentence carried a threat that Mrs. Adams, unfortunately, never acted upon. Her husband answered hastily and unsatisfactorily, but a month later, when discussing the voting privilege of propertyless men, Adams stated:

Why exclude Women? . . . Whence arises the right of the men to govern women without their consent? Because they are unacquainted with public affairs? Is it not equally true that men in general who are wholly destitute of property are also too little acquainted with public affairs? . . . Women have as good judgments, as independent minds, as those men who are destitute of property.

Despite the excellent sentiment, John Adams ended up supporting the franchise only for propertied men, denying it to all women as well as men without property.

While courting Abigail, John had been delighted and impressed with the intelligence and wit of his future bride. But in one letter to her, dated May 7, 1764, he teased her by cataloguing her "faults":

In the first place, then, give me leave to say, you have been extremely negligent, in attending so little to cards. You have very little inclination, to that noble and elegant diversion, and whenever you have taken a hand you have held it but awkwardly and played it, with a very uncourtly, and indifferent, air. . . .

. . . you could never yet be prevailed on to learn to sing. This I take very soberly to be an imperfection of the most moment of any. . . .

Another fault, which seems to have been obstinately persisted in, after frequent remonstrances, advices and admonitions of your

Abigail Adams asked John
some hard questions. (Brown Bros.)

friends, is that of sitting with the legs across. This ruins the figure and the air, this injures the health. And springs I fear from the former source—too much thinking. These things ought not to be!

Mercy Otis Warren (1728–1814), a friend of the Adamses, a playwright, and an historian, tried to add her voice to Abigail Adams' in favor of women's rights. Mrs. Warren was self-educated and could command respect in all learned circles. But John Adams' avowed admiration for both women still did not make him a vigorous advocate of women's rights. Gaining adherents for colonial independence took priority in his mind.

Mrs. Adams and Mrs. Warren were intelligent, sensitive women. Other women, too, hearing the popular cry of equality for all, wondered why they were denied that equality, but most of them did not record their questions for posterity. An exception was the Englishwoman Mary Wollstonecraft (1759–1797), who wrote an essay in 1786 called "Thoughts on the Education of Daughters." The French Revolution of 1789 inspired her to write a larger work, a ringing critique of Western society's treatment of women that was read widely in America. This book, *Vindication of the Rights of Women* (1792), applied the natural rights theory to women. Challenging the institution of marriage, she asked, in dramatic and cogent tones: Were not women human beings with natural rights? Did not marriage impinge upon their natural development?

> To render women truly useful members of . . . society, I argue that they should be led, by having their understandings cultivated on a large scale, to acquire a rational affection for their country, founded on knowledge, because it is obvious that we are little interested about what we do not understand. And to render this general knowledge of due importance, I have endeavored to show that private duties are never properly fulfilled unless the understanding enlarges the heart and that public virtue is only an aggregate of private. . . .

> The affection of husbands and wives cannot be pure when they have so few sentiments in common and when so little confidence is established at home as must be the case when their pursuits are so different. That intimacy from which tenderness should flow will not, cannot subsist between the vicious.

Many male philosophers received bad grades in Mary Wollstonecraft's analysis. She found Dr. Gregory's advice to his

Mary Wollstonecraft—
her words inspired other women.
(N.Y. Public Library)

daughter, quoted at the opening of this chapter, particularly offensive. "Liberty is the mother of virtues; and if women be by their very constitution slaves . . . they must ever languish like exotics, and be reckoned beautiful flaws in nature." Women, she argued, required the same education and the same life opportunities as men, or they would indeed be "flaws in nature." Men encouraged women's dependency and built a whole system upon it.

In her book, the first great feminist document, Mary Wollstonecraft reminded her readers that

> Women may have different duties to fulfill; but they are *human* duties, and the principles that regulate the discharge of them must be the same.

She insisted that marriage could, and should, be based only upon mutual regard, and that a one-sided love-obedience relationship could not produce a desirable marriage. She subjected the law, education, and marriage to her scrutiny and concluded that all these man-made institutions were unjust to women. All needed serious changes before women could take their rightful place in human society.

By 1800, more and more white women were becoming aware

of the chasm that existed between the rhetoric of marriage and its reality. Up to that time, it could have been argued that marriage, despite its flaws, actually was the inevitable destiny of all women. There were few spinsters in colonial America because of a continuing shortage of women. After 1800, however, the shortage turned into a surplus, and the number of spinsters, especially in New England, increased substantially. So many young single men moved westward that a girl bent on marriage would do well to go to the frontier, where men continued to outnumber women during most of the nineteenth century.

Many women chose to remain single rather than go west or marry one of the newly arriving immigrant males from the continent. What did society do to acknowledge the existence of these spinsters, a new social type? It did nothing. The rhetoric of marriage as holy matrimony, the only proper state for womankind, continued to be articulated.

Thus the problem became even more complex. Not only did the marriage reformers receive little attention, but anyone who pointed out the inconsistency between the concept of marriage and its practical reality received none at all. Woman's role remained unchanged. The spinster was an uncomfortable anomaly in a society that continued to praise wifehood and motherhood as the only viable occupation for a woman.

Spinsters usually lived with a member of the family. They learned to be patient, long-suffering, and tolerant of society's many abuses, including acrimony toward themselves. While some surely wasted away in despair over their unhappy state, many filled their lives with useful, constructive work. Often they became the dispensers of charity, the organizers of church activities, and the leaders of reform groups. Without a home and family of their own, they performed valuable services to their communities. But still they remained set apart, unappreciated, their contributions unacknowledged. Young girls were told by their mothers that the reason spinsters ran orphanages was that they had nothing else to do with their time!

American literature abounds in characterizations of spinsters as loveless and resigned. Being unmarried, they were to be pitied because they lacked a husband and children. The warm relationships they formed with other women were always interpreted as substitute behavior, since no relationship could be as deeply rewarding as that between a husband and a wife.

Typical of Western stereotyped thinking is Americans' narrow definition of love. They have always believed that there is only one proper type of adult love: the love of a man-husband for a woman-wife. Female love for other females, like that of males for males, is forbidden; so is woman's love for a man outside marriage. The Platonic love of an unmarried woman for a married man, or vice versa, was long frowned upon and probably still is in most communities. Further, the only acceptable fruits of love, according to the Christian tradition, were children; thus, sanctioned love resulted in offspring and a family. If an unmarried woman had illegitimate children, she was censured and branded by the community. If a woman had no husband and no children, her life was regarded as empty and unfulfilled. The spinster fitted only one image—that of the unfortunate, left-out person.

Thomas Paine—Feminist Advocate

Even the radical political theorists of the day—though they challenged Britain's right to rule and promoted the truly revolutionary idea that the people should participate in their government—did not extend their radicalism to the realm of women and the family. Thomas Paine (1737–1809), known for his famous essay on freedom, was the exceptional male radical of the period. In 1775 he wrote two brief pieces on the subject of women for the *Pennsylvania Magazine* which he called: "Reflections on Unhappy Marriages" and "An Occasional Letter on the Female Sex." Both challenged traditional views. Himself a victim of two unhappy marriages, Paine questioned the possibility of attaining marital happiness. In his letter on women, he criticized all cultures' restraints upon women that prevented the development of their natural inclinations and talents. If a woman were to defend the cause of her sex, she might address men in the following manner:

> How great is your injustice? If we have an equal right with you to virtue, why should we not have an equal right to praise? The public esteem ought to wait upon merit. Our duties are different from yours, but they are not therefore less difficult to fulfil, or of less consequence to society. . . . Permit our names to be sometimes

79

pronounced beyond the narrow circle in which we live. Permit friendship, or at least love, to inscribe its emblem on the tomb where our ashes repose; and deny us not that public esteem which, after the esteem of one's self, is the sweetest reward of well doing.

—Thomas Paine, *An Occasional Letter on the Female Sex*

Sure of each other by the nuptial band, they no longer take any pains to be mutually agreeable; careless if they displease; and yet angry if reproached; with so little relish for each other's company that anybody's else is welcome, and more entertaining. Their union thus broke, they pursue separate pleasures; never meet but to wrangle, or part but to find comfort in other society.

—Thomas Paine, *Reflections on Unhappy Marriages*

Paine's remarks never received the attention or acclaim of his famous *Common Sense.* Rather, most Americans, radicals and conservatives alike, shared Benjamin Franklin's view that marriage was an institution completely in harmony with natural laws: the man was its natural head, and the woman obediently followed his lead. Hence there was no need to change the institution. But who decided whether any social institution was natural or unnatural? Clearly, the men. If the institution of marriage suited their needs, then it was natural, God given; if it did not, it was unnatural. No one asked women whether marriage was natural and God-given for them, whether their needs were filled by marriage, or whether any changes were needed to make marriage more responsive to their wishes.

A woman "belonged" to the man in her life, bore and raised his children, and required the institution of marriage in order to do so. Society needed such predictable behavior from women, so that life could go on in an orderly fashion and communities be run efficiently. Women who aspired to careers outside the home had to be discouraged. Women who found marriage inhibiting and destructive had to be restrained. Marriage was a natural institution, just as human rights were "natural" for men. This was the dominant view of the eighteenth century.

In a sense, Paine's essay on marriage was far more revolutionary than his essay on political independence. Similarly, Mary

Wollstonecraft's essay on women's rights was far more radical than Jefferson's Declaration of Independence. Thomas Paine and Mary Wollstonecraft both questioned one of the most sacred institutions in Western society, marriage. They argued that half of the human race, women, required rights not previously granted to them and that patterns of behavior based upon those rights required major alterations in human society. But the natural rights doctrine espoused by Jefferson was set forth to justify an already changed situation in the colonies of the New World. The American colonists were already independent, to a degree. They practiced self-government before 1776; they managed their own political and economic lives before 1776. They wrote the Declaration of Independence and waged a war to retain what Britain was trying to take away from them—not to achieve a new, untried state of being.

In contrast, Mary Wollstonecraft wanted something that had not existed before. She wanted to change human patterns—to alter, in significant and dramatic ways, the family and marriage institutions of Western society. If her ideas had been implemented, the family and marriage would have been considerably different, and the two sexes would have had different roles. Children might have been raised by non-family members in what we now call an extended family. Women might have become engineers, and men, perhaps, domestic caretakers in the home. All the traditional definitions of womanly and manly would have been reevaluated and possibly redefined. The single-family home might have been replaced by collective dormitories, where fathers might care for the children while mothers worked. Both sexes might work on alternating half-day schedules. The possibilities of diverse human arrangements are unending, as couples are only starting to discover today.

Mary Wollstonecraft's *Vindication of the Rights of Women,* as well as Paine's essay on marriage, were truly revolutionary—far too revolutionary for their time. While the American colonists wanted political freedom from a repressive mother country, a freedom they had been experiencing for over one hundred years, they did not want to change family and marriage arrangements. They mouthed the words "natural rights," "freedom," and "independence" but did not apply them to the most important human institution of their society.

81

Women's Fashions: Symbol of Servitude

In more ways than one, fashion and style have always limited the American woman's freedom. In colonial days, European capitals, and later New York and Boston, determined fashion trends for women. Styles in dress had little to do with the natural contours of the female body. Modesty demanded that women wear long skirts, under which they wore multiple petticoats. To show off a slender waist above all the petticoats, a woman would lace herself into an extremely tight whaleboned corset that could shrink her twenty-four-inch waist to a petite seventeen inches. Even as eighteenth-century women accepted the taste-makers' edict that they hide their natural form, they still managed to display it.

The purpose of wearing fashionable dress, of course, was identical with the ultimate goal of every female on earth: to attract and capture a potential husband. Yet by accepting male-determined fashions, middle- and upper-class women implicitly agreed that their alluringly ornamented bodies were their only available means of gaining their life objective. For this, they could, and did, endure any physical discomfort, any painful contortion. A fashionably dressed woman, they knew, had an advantage over all other women in the marriage market.

> . . . Woman in all ages and countries has been the scoff and the jest of her lordly master. If she attempted, like him, to improve her mind, she was ridiculed as pedantic and driven from the temple of science and literature by coarse attacks and vulgar sarcasms. If she yielded to the pressure of circumstances and sought relief from the monotony of existence by resorting to the theatre and the ball-room, by ornamenting her person with flowers and with jewels while her mind was empty and her heart desolate, she was still the mark at which wit and satire and cruelty levelled their arrows.
>
> "Woman," says Adam Clarke, "has been invidiously defined, *an animal of dress*. How long will they permit themselves to be thus degraded?" I have been an attentive observer of my sex, and I am constrained to believe that the passion for dress which so generally characterizes them is one cause why there is so little of that solid improvement and weight of character which might be acquired under almost any circumstances if the mind were not occupied by the love of admiration and the desire to gratify personal vanity.
>
> —Sarah Grimké, *Letters on the Equality of the Sexes*

Women's Fashions: Symbol of Servitude

In their slavish imitation of styles not of their own making, women often suffered real physical ailments from the rigorous demands of fashion. Curvature of the spine and broken ribs were two common female afflictions in the eighteenth and nineteenth centuries. When dress reformer Amelia Bloomer in the 1850s rebelled against the absurd outfits of her contemporaries and invented the bloomer-trouser (a baggy trouser covered by a short skirt), she was literally laughed off the streets. She could not walk anywhere without being jeered at. Yet on rainy, muddy days, when long, full petticoats could be dirtied during the briefest stroll, Amelia Bloomer's costume would have been much more comfortable and practical. But women did not follow her lead. Trousers for women did not become an accepted style of dress until the mid-twentieth century. Elizabeth Cady Stanton and Susan B. Anthony wore the bloomer costume with enthusiasm, but also abandoned it eventually. Mrs. Stanton advised Miss Anthony, who did not want to relinquish the outfit, despite the jeering:

> We put the dress on for greater freedom, but what is physical freedom compared with mental bondage? . . . It is not wise, Susan, to use up so much energy and feeling that way. You can put them to better use. I speak from experience.

War and Freedom

When war came, American men and women were seriously divided in regard to its purpose. Many colonists still viewed themselves as transplanted Englishmen with close familial and cultural ties to the mother country. Many feared the words and deeds of the radicals who dumped English tea in the Boston harbor. American women, who have always played a key role in American wars, sent their sons and husbands off to battle hoping that the end would justify the means. Like women in every war, they tearfully watched their loved ones leave, not knowing whether they would ever see them again. Women nursed the wounded, folded bandages, and sent food to the soldiers. The Daughters of Liberty spun cloth and made shirts for the soldiers. Although they might have secretly questioned the validity of the war, they deferred to the judgments of the men around them.

Men, not women, voted for war in the Continental Congress;

83

Women at work during the Revolutionary War. (Bettmann)

women played no part in the deliberations that led to it. Their place continued to be in the home, and in the hastily established hospitals. Woman's modesty and "natural" diffidence, so went the argument, made it unthinkable for her to nurse men on the battlefield. As the weaker sex, women could not contend with the harsh realities of war.

This view ignored the fact that women managed their farms in their husbands' and sons' absence, took care of their husbands' business, and continued to handle all the domestic chores of the home. In the myriad physical tasks on the farm, women showed great capacity for endurance, great tolerance for physical and emotional pain. But their sphere remained limited, although neither the Revolution nor any subsequent war could have been fought and won without the participation of women. They helped feed, clothe, and care for the troops—services which enabled General Washington's badly trained army not only to survive but to succeed. Further, the women literally kept the home-fires burning; without the women, the men would have had no homes to which to return.

Abigail Adams reported to her husband John how a group of women treated a merchant who hoarded coffee during the war:

84

A number of females, some say a hundred, some say more, assembled with a cart and trunks, marched down to the warehouse, and demanded the keys, which he refused to deliver. Upon which one of them seized him by his neck and tossed him into the cart. Upon his finding no quarter, he delivered the keys when they tipped up the cart and discharged him; then opened the warehouse, hoisted out the coffee themselves, put it into the trunks and drove off.

The Natural Right to Own

One of the natural rights claimed by white settlers was private ownership of property. Land, like all other sources of wealth, became the possession of private individuals, who could use its resources for their personal gain. How different was this concept of ownership from the American Indian's idea of the land. As Osway Porter, a Chickasaw Indian, expressed it a century later:

> None of the full bloods ever wanted this land divided; I have been loving my own mother, and I love this country as I love my mother. I love it as I love my own father. I love its hills and mountains, and its valleys and trees and rivers, and everything that is in this country.

From the Indian's point of view, land could not be divided into parcels and distributed to different families. Private, individual ownership was inconceivable; for land belonged to everyone, as everyone belonged to each other. No wonder the Indian found the white man's pieces of legal paper strange and inexplicable.

White American Protestants, imbued with their belief in the individual over the communal, were just as puzzled by the notion that a tribe or community could all share in the riches of the land, working it and living on it. Convinced that their view was right and the Indian's wrong, farmers and exploiters ruthlessly claimed the open land for many generations, without interference or opposition.

James Fenimore Cooper (1789–1851), a popular nineteenth-century writer, well expressed the usual moral justification for the American view of private property:

85

> As property is the base of all civilization, its existence and security are indispensable to social improvement. Were it possible to have a community of property, it would soon be found that no one would toil, but that men would be disposed to be satisfied with barely enough for the supply of their physical wants, since none would exert themselves to obtain advantages solely for the use of others.

Cooper's argument that communal property-holding could result only in laziness, selfishness, and lack of progress was extremely popular in eighteenth- and nineteenth-century America. Individual possession of property ensured hard work, pride in accomplishment, and progressive accumulation of wealth. It was in the nature of men, contended Cooper and many who shared his philosophy, to rely on others as far as possible and to do as little as possible. In this sense, hard work was unnatural but would be practiced if the incentives were great enough. Human beings might not be born with a wish to work, but the promise of profit and private ownership could motivate them to strenuous action.

Boosters of the new industrialism heartily agreed with Cooper. In 1787, Tench Coxe, a vociferous advocate of industrialization, addressed the Society for the Encouragement of Manufactures and the Useful Arts. He told them:

> The lovers of mankind, supported by experienced physicians, and the opinions of enlightened politicians, have objected to manufacturers as unfavorable to the health of the people. Giving this humane and important consideration its full weight, it furnishes an equal argument against several other occupations, by which we obtain our comforts, and promote our agriculture. The painting business, for instance, reclaiming marshes, clearing swamps, the culture of rice and indigo, and some other employments, are even more fatal to those who are engaged in them. But this objection is urged principally against carding, spinning, and weaving, which *formerly* were entirely manual and sedentary occupations. Our plan, as we have already shown, is not to pursue those modes, unless in cases particularly circumstanced; . . . we are sensible, that our people must not be diverted from their farms. *Horses, and the potent elements of fire and water, aided by the faculties of the human mind, are to be in many instances our daily labourers.* After giving immediate relief to the industrious poor, these unhurtful means will be pursued, and will procure us private wealth and national prosperity.

86

Note the major purposes and advantages of industrialization according to Coxe: immediate relief for the industrious poor, private wealth, and national prosperity. Noble ends, surely. The clear implication is that all who care to work will work and all will prosper; no one will lose.

Another spokesman for industrialization at about the same time assured his audience that "agriculture, manufacturers and commerce, especially internal commerce, are in perfect harmony—they mutually aid and support each other—together they constitute national prosperity." This was the message, delivered again and again, from the defenders of industrialism. Machines would replace human labor and provide wealth for more people.

It was the natural right of individuals to profit from their labor as well as from their shrewd investments. It also seemed to be the natural right of every manufacturer to employ any and all workers at wages he determined. When do the natural rights of one group infringe upon the rights of another group? Were the rights of women textile workers and ten-year-old mine workers violated while industrialists pursued their right to make a profit? Who decided? Natural rights, indeed, were a weighty and ambitious issue. If the right to private property contradicts the Indian's right to collective ownership, whose right should prevail? Eighteenth-century white Americans avoided thinking about the serious implications of their lovely rhetoric.

Suggestions for Further Reading

Edith Abbott. *Women in Industry* (New York, 1910).

Katherine Anthony. *First Lady of the Revolution* (New York, 1958). A biography of Mercy Warren.

Mary S. Benson. *Women in Eighteenth Century America* (New York, 1935).

Elizabeth Commetti. "Women in the American Revolution," *New England Quarterly*, 20: 329–346 (September 1947).

Stanley Elkins. *Slavery: A Problem in American Institutional and Intellectual Life* (Chicago, 1959).

Familiar Letters of John Adams and His Wife Abigail Adams During the Revolution (New York, 1876).

Thomas Paine. "An Occasional Letter on the Female Sex" and "Reflections on Unhappy Marriages," *Pennsylvania Magazine*, August 1775.

Independence for Whom? 1775–1800

Report on the Condition of Woman and Child Wage-Earners in the United States. 19 vols. U.S. Senate Document 645, 61st Congress, 2d Session (Washington, D.C., 1910–1913). A valuable primary source.

CHAPTER FIVE

The Workers of America
1800 – 1860

. . . We have the agreeable contemplation of a people out of debt; land rising slowly in value, but in a secure and salutary degree; a ready though not extravagant market for all the surplus productions of our industry; innumerable flocks and herds browsing and gamboling on ten thousand hills and plains, covered with rich and verdant grasses; our cities expanded, and whole villages springing up, as it were, by enchantment; our exports and imports increased and increasing; our tonnage, foreign and coastwise, swelling and fully occupied; the rivers of our interior animated by the perpetual thunder and lightning of countless steamboats; . . .

This transformation of the condition of the country, from gloom and distress to brightness and prosperity, has been mainly the work of American legislation, fostering American industry, instead of allowing it to be controlled by foreign legislation, cherishing foreign industry.

> —Henry Clay, *In Defence of the American System,* speech delivered before the U.S. Senate, February 1832

I happened to arrive at the first factory just as the dinner hour was over, and the girls were returning to their work; indeed the stairs of the mill were thronged with them as I ascended. . . . The rooms in which they worked, were as well ordered as themselves. In the windows of some, there were green plants, . . . in all, there was as much fresh air, cleanliness, and comfort, as the nature of the occupation would possibly admit of.

> —Charles Dickens, description of a visit to the textile mill town of Lowell, Massachusetts, 1841

Democracies being, as nearly as possible, founded in natural justice, little violence is done to the sense of right by the institutions, and men have less occasion than usual, to resort to fallacies and false principles in cultivating the faculties. As a consequence, common sense is more encouraged, and the community is apt to entertain juster notions of all moral truths, than under systems that are necessarily sophisticated. Society is thus a gainer in the greatest element of happiness, or in the right perception of the different relations between men and things.

> —James Fenimore Cooper, *The American Democrat,* 1838

*T*he English and European settlers continued actively to change the landscape of the continent they now claimed as their own. By 1800, they had rid themselves of the British presence, pushed the Spanish farther south and west, and chased away or killed most of the Indians east of the Mississippi. Their primary task, on the eve of the new century, was to cultivate the rich land, build factories to produce new wealth for the country, and go on experimenting with the federal political system developed under the Constitution. Because influential leaders like Senator Henry Clay proclaimed that digging canals, building roads, and negotiating trade were "fostering American industry," most citizens agreed that the direction in which the country was going was a good one. And by circular reasoning, saying that it was good made it good.

But the cultivators of the land, the yeoman farmers, and the young workers in the new coal mines may have had their doubts. Farming continued to be a back-breaking, time-consuming enterprise; mining coal was even more arduous. As the century progressed, these two groups of workers—pressed by industrialization to produce more crops, more coal—found it harder and harder just to support their families. Farmers had to cope with soil that was often stubborn and unyielding. Ignorant of crop rotation or of ways to prevent soil erosion, many saw more work and fewer rewards in the supposedly promising future. Miners and factory workers shared that dreary vision as they contemplated years of dehumanizing labor in behalf of American industry. Fewer and fewer of them were emerging from the coal mines and the pig-iron factories to become skilled tradesmen,

91

merchants, or clerks. When they tried to organize themselves into unions, their efforts were fiercely resisted by mine and factory owners (in 1830 as in 1930). Though they displayed their frustration by drinking a lot and by frequently missing work, no major labor struggles took place. Industrialization became the way of the future, to the delight of the entrepreneurs and the resignation of the workers.

The Nation Industrializes

To European visitors, the growing cities, the mills and factories, and the fertile land of America all suggested the enormous success of this experiment in the New World. True, the English novelist Charles Dickens criticized the dirt of New York City and the boisterousness of Americans, but the nation's mechanical progress and its steady growth impressed him. The French observer Alexis de Tocqueville, who visited America in 1832, believed that democracy, with its principle of majority rule, might lead to a deadening conformity and to mediocrity—but he liked the openness of the people, their friendliness, and their good nature. Majority rule, as expressed by Jacksonian emphasis upon the common man, might have its bad effects, but the monarchies of Europe did not appeal to most Americans as a desirable alternative. The United States had no king, no aristocracy, no inflexible class system; it did have seemingly unlimited land, plenty of economic opportunity, and political freedom. To nearly all Americans, as well as to many visitors, these virtues far outweighed the dangers of undue conformity and of eliminating intellectual, political, and economic distinctions among the populace.

Michel Chevalier, another Frenchman, visited this country in 1834. Having observed the new towns springing up in the Pennsylvania anthracite region, he vividly described the villages hastily built around a newly discovered coal deposit:

> On the banks of the Schuykill, which has lately been canalled, and which, flowing from the coal-region, empties itself into the Delaware, near Philadelphia, may be seen the beginnings of a town, built during the time of the mining speculations, at the head of navigation. Port Carbon, for that is its name, consists of about thirty houses standing on the declivity of a valley, and disposed according to the

92

plan of the embryo city. Such was the haste in which the houses were built, that there was no time to remove the stumps of the trees that covered the spot; the standing trees were partially burnt and then felled with the axe, and their long charred trunks still cumber the ground. Some of them have been converted into piles for supporting the railroads that bring down the coal to the boats; the blackened stumps, four or five feet high, are still standing, and you make your way from one house to another by leaping over the prostrate trunks and winding round the standing stumps. In the midst of this strange scene, appears a large building with the words, *Office of Deposit and Discount*, SCHUYKILL BANK. The existence of a bank amidst the stumps of Port Carbon, surprised me as much as the universal neatness and elegance of the peaceful Philadelphia, or the vast fleet which is constantly receiving and discharging at the quays of New York, the products of all parts of the world.

The railroads, major beneficiaries of industrialization, connected seaports with the interior roads, and canals also brought the newer communities closer to the settled ones. Industrialization, moreover, produced new wealth and new enterprises for the citizens. By the 1840s, about 11 per cent of the population was living in urban areas, and the number was increasing. More and more farm boys were leaving their homes to find factory work in the thriving cities. They were joined by the new immigrants, arriving constantly, who remained in Boston, New York, and other ports.

Machine production took industry out of the home and into factories, where raw materials were transformed into finished products far more quickly and efficiently than in the homes. One woman working at spindles and looms in a factory could produce more cotton goods than ten women working on home spindles. The manufacturer could deliver his goods with greater speed, since the factories were usually located near some means of transportation—a river, a railroad, or a post road—by which the goods could be carried to many markets.

From the beginning of industrialization, women were a significant portion of the working population. In the manufacture of textiles, one of the first of the major industries, women workers often outnumbered men. In 1807, for example, 3,500 women and children worked in 87 cotton mills and outnumbered men by 7 to 1. Yet these women and children earned less than their male counterparts for comparable hours doing the same work. An eighteen-hour workday with a wage of $1.50 a week was not unusual, even at a time when people needed at least $10.00 a week to meet basic expenses.

At the age of eleven, Lucy Larcom (1824–1893) began working in the cotton mills of Lowell, Massachusetts. Her father had died and her mother had moved to Lowell with the children to run a boardinghouse for girls who worked in the mills. Lucy later wrote:

> I never cared much for machinery. The buzzing and hissing and whizzing of pulleys and rollers and spindles and flyers around me often grew tiresome.

But she believed that her tenure in the mill would be temporary, especially after she managed to spend three months in an elementary school. She found the learning exciting and hoped that she would not have to return to the mill.

> But alas! . . . The little money I could earn—one dollar a week, besides the price of my board—was needed in the family, and I must

Factory worker and writer
Lucy Larcom. (Culver)

return to the mill. It was a severe disappointment to me, though I did not say so at home.

It was several years before Lucy left the mill for good. When she did, she proved to be the exceptional woman whose example buoys the spirits of so many. She became a schoolteacher and, in the post–Civil War years, a successful writer of children's books.

At the same time that the myth of women as weak and fragile beings was gaining popularity among the middle class, women were demonstrating their strength and skill in shoe factories, cap-making shops, even in typesetting. They might have dreamed about living like the frail, delicate heroines of novels, but the reality of their life, and their nature, was wholly otherwise.

As machines became more and more important in the production of goods, human beings lost some of their uniqueness. Rows of men and women in a factory, performing repetitive, mechanical tasks, often seemed to resemble the very machines they were operating. Creative writers such as Herman Melville noted this. In one of his stories, he described how Lowell, Massachusetts, a textile town supposedly the model of industrial efficiency and virtue, turned its young women into dull machines, denying them any vitality. Human creativity, diversity, and imagination were not valuable traits in machine production. Each member of the labor force was taught a specific chore to perform and was expected to do it quickly and without deviation.

Unskilled workers, the cheapest human labor, were the most desirable factory employees, although skilled craftsmen remained essential in many operations. The growing numbers of Irish immigrants in the 1840s and 1850s competed for factory jobs with American workers, but no laborers were ever sure of steady work. When business was good—that is, when the suppliers had an abundance of buyers for their goods—all available workers were employed. When the market for a particular product diminished, often because the manufacturer optimistically overexpanded production, workers were summarily dismissed and unemployment ran high. There was no protection for them against these "bad times," no such thing as unemployment insurance. While private charities often aided the most helpless of the unemployed, workers usually had to fend for themselves, seeking whatever employment was available at whatever wage the employer chose to pay.

When business was bad, a manufacturer would not only fire large numbers of his workers but would cut the wages of those who were left. Coal miners and workers in the iron foundries of Pennsylvania, cap-makers in New York City, and textile workers in Lowell were the first victims of such industrial depression. In 1817, 1837, and 1857, financial panics resulted in economic disaster for many farmers and workers. When land prices went down, when demand for manufactured goods declined, and when banks subsequently called in their credits (and refused to grant further credit), the ordinary working citizen suffered. While most Americans became accustomed to alternate boom and bust periods, it was always the poorest people—those on the small farms and the unskilled workers in the factories—who suffered most. Senator Henry Clay's description of American prosperity in 1832, quoted at the beginning of this chapter, applied to "good times," not "bad times."

Added to the worker's perpetual uncertainty about what tomorrow would bring were dismal, often physically grueling, working conditions. Consider, for example, the following petition for a ten-hour workday submitted to the Massachusetts House of Representatives on March 12, 1845:

> The first petitioner who testified was Eliza R. Hemmingway. She had worked 2 years and 9 months in the Lowell Factories; 2 years in the Middlesex, and 9 months in the Hamilton Corporations. Her employment is weaving,—works by the piece. The Hamilton Mill manufactures cotton fabrics. The Middlesex, woollen fabrics. She is now at work in the Middlesex Mills, and attends one loom. Her wages average from $16 to $23 a month exclusive of board. She complained of the hours for labor being too many, and the time for meals too limited. In the summer season, the work is commenced at 5 o'clock, A.M., and continued till 7 o'clock, P.M., with half an hour for breakfast and three quarters of an hour for dinner. During eight months of the year, but half an hour is allowed for dinner. The air in the room she considered not to be wholesome. There were 293 small lamps and 61 large lamps lighted in the room in which she worked, when evening work is required. These lamps are also lighted sometimes in the morning.—About 130 females, 11 men, and 12 children (between the ages of 11 and 14,) work in the room with her. She thought the children enjoyed about as good health as children generally do. The children work but 9 months out of 12. The other 3 months they must attend school. Thinks that there is no

day when there are less than six of the females out of the mill from sickness. Has known as many as thirty. She, herself, is out quite often, on account of sickness. There was more sickness in the Summer than in Winter months; though in the Summer, lamps are not lighted. She thought there was a general desire among the females to work but ten hours, regardless of pay. Most of the girls are from the country, who work in the Lowell Mills. The average time which they remain there is about three years. She knew one girl who had worked there 14 years. Her health was poor when she left. Miss Hemmingway said her health was better where she now worked, than it was when she worked on the Hamilton Corporation.

She knew of one girl who last winter went into the mill at half past 4 o'clock, A.M. and worked till half past 7 o'clock P.M. She did so to make more money. She earned from $25 to $30 per month. There is always a large number of girls at the gate wishing to get in before the bell rings. On the Middlesex Corporation one fourth part of the females go into the mill before they are obliged to. They do this to make more wages. A large number come to Lowell to make money to aid their parents who are poor. She knew of many cases where married women came to Lowell and worked in the mills to assist their husbands to pay for their farms. The moral character of the operatives is good. There was only one American female in the room with her who could not write her name.

Rebecca Harding Davis, writing for *Atlantic Monthly* readers in April 1861, described the working conditions of iron-mill workers. First, their environment:

The idiosyncrasy of this town is smoke. It rolls sullenly in slow folds from the great chimneys of the iron-foundries, and settles down in black, slimy pools on the muddy streets.

Then their collective portrait—a bleak one:

Masses of men, with dull, besotted faces bent to the ground, sharpened here and there by pain or cunning; skin and muscle and flesh begrimed with smoke and ashes; stooping all night over boiling caldrons of metal, laired by day in dens of drunkenness and infamy; breathing from infancy to death an air saturated with fog and grease and soot, vileness for soul and body.

Because of inevitable economic ups and downs, the future did not look bright or hopeful for these ironworkers, most of whom were immigrants from Wales and Ireland. Many spent their whole working lives in the mills and never enjoyed a moment free of anxiety about losing their jobs.

The work performed in the iron mills was physically arduous. Mrs. Davis described the mills for rolling iron as "immense tent-like roofs, covering acres of ground open on every side."

> Fire in every horrible form: pits of flame waving in the wind; liquid metal-flames writhing in tortuous streams through the sand; wide caldrons filled with boiling fire, over which bent ghastly wretches stirring the strange brewing; and through all, crowds of half-clad men, looking like revengeful ghosts in the red light, hurried, throwing masses of glittering fire. It was like a street in Hell.

The same anxiety haunted the men in the coal mines, the women and children in the shoe factories, and the men and women in the textile mills—all of whom toiled long hours with little relief, only a minimal break for eating, and small wages. The human cost of transforming natural resources into salable products by machinery can never be adequately measured. Of course, the owners and executives profited happily, but to the workers in most industries, the American Dream of continuous progress, of individual accomplishment leading to success, and of high rewards for hard work was an unreal, unreachable goal.

It was indeed a paradox that, in the richest country in the world, dependent workers and marginal farmers lived side by side with wealthy businessmen and prosperous farmers. Poverty, as a social phenomenon, was a minor problem in the first half of the nineteenth century; there were few destitute people in comparison with the total population. Large numbers of farmers lived marginally, but they worked and managed to subsist. Yet in the growing cities of America, poverty was becoming visible. The immigrants, unfamiliar with the new environment, the unskilled farmboys, and the children of marginal farmers who went to the cities hoping for a better life—all formed the beginnings of a poor class. These groups, who passed their impoverishment on to their children, increased dramatically through the nineteenth century as industrialization and heavy immigration produced a large surplus population of vulnerable people.

The Myth of Rugged Individualism

Industrialization developed under the private enterprise system and its profits remained in private hands, even though the government encouraged industry through land grants to railroads and a favorable tariff policy. (Since American manufacturers could not compete with English-made products, a tax was imposed on foreign goods to make domestic products more attractive.) The theory was that individuals who worked hard and took risks deserved rewards resulting from their efforts. Thus property remained private, as did profit, and the old American idea of rugged individualism was adjusted to the new industrial reality. Both entrepreneurs and government officials justified aid to private industry as essential for national growth: investors would not put money into a high-risk enterprise—a railroad, for example—unless they were encouraged by government assistance.

In the pre–Civil War era, there were few very rich people in America. Fortunes were quickly made and lost in fur-trading and commerce. Manufacturing did not yield the fabulous profits in the 1840s that it would in the 1890s. On the eve of the Civil War, America was still a nation of farmers. Industrialization had really not yet arrived. When it did, the virtues lauded in an agricultural society, where each farmer worked for success on his own farm, were transferred to an industrial one. True, individual workers in a factory had little control over their lives; yet the same virtues, the same mythology governed everyone's thinking. The few examples of persons who, like Andrew Carnegie, achieved spectacular success through hard work convinced most people that individualism and industrialism were compatible. Just as individualism guided a nation of farmers, so it could guide a nation of industrial workers.

Not nearly so well known were certain career secrets of railroad executives who became successful, not through hard work, but through good connections with the government. Or those financiers who took advantage of inside information to make fortunes—and being born into a rich family did not hurt a future capitalist, either. On the other hand, an immigrant newly arrived from Ireland in the 1840s had no such opportunities, and could hardly begin on an equal footing with the member of an old New

England family. If the ambitious son of a Pennsylvania farmer wanted to become a lawyer, he would have to compete un-equally with the son of an educated Philadelphia attorney. Yet writers, politicians, and businessmen continued to preach indi-vidualism to the populace. Poor people were reminded that they caused their own poverty, by their own faults and weaknesses. Misfortune was the result of drunkenness, laziness, shiftlessness, preached the ministers; it had nothing to do with inequitable laws, favoritism, or nepotism.

Most people accepted the message of rugged individualism without question. They agreed that each husband, as the natural head of the family, had to support his wife and children, that if he failed to fulfill his responsibilities, the fault was his alone. And failure was a hopeless state. It was not self-respecting to accept charity unless you were utterly desperate. There were no gov-ernment agencies to care for the sick, the unemployed, or the destitute, and few citizens believed the government should be responsible for them.

Thus, government policy or lack of policy toward the needy reflected the popular views of the time. There were always jobs available to the industrious, so went the argument, and no up-standing citizen could be expected to pay taxes for the support of shiftless men. Another popular view was that each worker should negotiate on his own and enter into an individual agreement with his employer. Collective bargaining was considered sub-versive because it denied the worker a right to make his own contract.

As a result of this belief, labor unions were ruthlessly sup-pressed. Not only the legislatures but the Supreme Court sup-ported individualism by denying labor the right to organize in its own behalf. It was entirely legitimate for businessmen to com-bine and pool their resources for their mutual benefit, but not workers. Even the workers, captives of the rhetoric of individ-ualism and the promise of better times ahead, resisted unioniza-tion. They joined unions when times were bad and abandoned them when things got better. Women employees were especially reluctant to organize because they saw their jobs as temporary activities, to be carried on briefly before marriage and perhaps for a short time after. Most women workers were young, from 15 to 19 years old, and unmarried. Even those who worked after marriage seldom thought their jobs were as important as their household duties. Also, women workers shared the society's view that to be assertive or militant was manly behavior and hence unbecoming in a woman.

Female workers, therefore, though great numbers of them were employed in the textile industry, remained unorganized for many years. A few women's labor unions were formed in the early years of the nineteenth century but they did not last long. When male workers did succeed in organizing themselves, they rarely admitted female workers and made little, if any, effort to help women organize their own unions. The women had to do this on their own, and at their peril. In those days, being a male union organizer was a dangerous occupation; for a woman, it was nearly suicidal.

The philosophy of individualism, then, had many insidious implications. It convinced poor unemployed workers and subsistence farmers that they alone were responsible for their misfortunes. It discouraged workers from organizing for their own benefit. And, finally, it provided the industrialists with a rationale for opposing unions once they did get started.

The inherently evil effects of individualism were often disguised by the hypocrisy of its practitioners. Men who boasted of what they had accomplished on their own frequently owed their success to the help of others. Rare indeed was the person who attained prosperity and prominence without good luck, good timing, and good connections. Cooperation with others, rather than competition, was the key. Thus, oddly enough, the very people who preached individualism would actually practice collectivism. Surely, achievement by one's own effort is a worthy goal, but it is meaningful only when everyone starts from scratch, as it were—with all conditions except natural ability being equal. We have already seen that cultural values predetermine the case for most people, but the doctrine of individualism does not take this into account.

Women and the Professions

At the beginning of the century, men outnumbered women in the teaching profession, but as economic opportunities increased in industry, trade, and other professions, they took better-paying jobs and left teaching to the women. But women schoolteachers,

101

The Schoolmistress: her presence was greatly appreciated in the Mississippi Valley, 1840. (Culver)

like women in other fields, were paid far less than men. In the 1820s, for example, a woman teacher earned around twenty dollars a school session, while a man teacher earned one hundred dollars. By the 1840s, women teachers were paid about a third as much as were men, and the gap never narrowed throughout the century. By 1850, however, there were more women teachers than men. Unfortunately, teaching, never a high-status profession in the United States, sank even lower in prestige as it became dominated by women.

Despite this dismal state of affairs in the teaching profession, there were certain ambitious women who sought professional careers in two other fields, medicine and law. But when they tried to enter medical or law school, they found themselves frustrated. Men were admitted, often without question; women, never.

Education as the pathway to a profession was still a modest affair in the first half of the nineteenth century. Abraham Lincoln, we recall, read law in the office of a Springfield, Illinois, lawyer before going into practice for himself. The apprentice system was widely followed—but not invariably, as it was in the skilled trades. Some potential doctors and lawyers did go to school for their professional training. The length of that training, in both medical and legal education, varied from state to state and often from school to school. One year of formal medical study usually constituted the future doctor's professional training. Few states gave rigorous examinations or had standards for licensing practitioners; therefore school-educated physicians practiced alongside self-taught doctors.

The legal profession was also in an early stage of development. Some lawyers appeared before the bar after little formal training, while others had studied law in one of the great old European universities. The law was a busy profession, as Americans experienced new problems and wrote new laws based upon them. Real estate concerns, commercial transactions, and criminal matters all required attention in the growing nation, and the courts and jurists had to create their own standards of legality.

Some people believed that the legal and medical professions were becoming overcrowded. Both professions formed national organizations: the American Medical Association (1846) and the American Bar Association (1878). Both also limited the number of their members, thereby increasing the prestige and financial rewards of doctors and lawyers. Finally, both refused to allow women to enter their ranks. When, in 1870, Myra Bradwell appealed the Illinois law that barred her from practicing law, the court denied her appeal and gave this as its reason:

> The civil law, as well as nature herself, has always recognized a wide difference in the respective spheres and destinies of man and woman. Man is, or should be, woman's protector and defender. The natural and proper timidity and delicacy which belongs to the female sex evidently unfits it for many of the occupations of civil life.

Doctors also argued that a woman's delicate nature militated against her becoming a physician. The rigors of medical practice would be too much for her.

Yet some women insisted on becoming doctors and lawyers. Myra Bradwell capitulated to the extent of turning her legal knowledge to a related field. She founded the first weekly legal newspaper in the West, the *Chicago Legal News*, and served as both its editor and its business manager. She drafted the law, passed by the Illinois legislature, which established a married woman's right to her own earnings. She also worked for women's suffrage.

Myra Bradwell was an exceptional woman. The wife of a lawyer and mother of four children, she was able to engage in the legal profession, although on its periphery. She was fortunate in having the active support of her husband, if not the legal establishment. Most women, of course, were not so lucky.

Then there was Elizabeth Blackwell (1821–1910), who wanted to study medicine after having witnessed the agonies of a friend suffering from a "female" disease. At that time, women's modesty often prevented them from seeking medical aid when they were ill. When they did, the male doctors were frequently unfamiliar with their troubles. Elizabeth Blackwell, having decided to make medicine her career, studied privately for a few years and then tried to enter medical school. But she encountered only rebuffs.

Finally, a small medical school in Geneva, New York, admitted her more or less by a fluke. When the school's administration asked the student body to decide whether she should enter, the students, as a prank, voted her in. On January 3, 1849, after a year of study, she became the first woman to receive an M.D. degree in this country. After her graduation, Dr. Blackwell went to Europe to study further. She later wrote that her whole life was

> . . . devoted unreservedly to the service of my sex. The study and practice of medicine is, in my thought, but one means to a great end, for which my very soul yearns with intensest passionate emotion, . . . the true ennoblement of woman, the full harmonious development of her unknown nature, and the consequent redemption of the whole human race.

When she returned to New York, Dr. Blackwell began practicing medicine and opened a dispensary for women. In 1857, with the aid of her sister, Dr. Emily Blackwell, and Dr. Marie E. Zakrzewska, she started the New York Infirmary for Women and

Elizabeth Blackwell, first woman to receive the M. D. degree in the U.S. (N.Y. Infirmary for Women and Children)

Children. In 1868, the Infirmary opened a Women's Medical College as well, with Dr. Elizabeth Blackwell on its faculty. For most of the nineteenth century, women doctors got their formal medical education at this college, or the Philadelphia Women's Medical College, or else at one of the more radical medical schools that preached the water cure or eclectic medicine. In the field itself, the more avant-garde male physicians did support women's rights, but the staid American Medical Association and its university-affiliated medical schools eschewed all social reforms involving women.

In this period, when bleeding and purging were recommended to cure most illnesses and when the only effective medicines were quinine and morphia, many people needed medical attention. There were plenty of men who called themselves doctors, but their knowledge was limited, especially their knowledge of woman's physiology. Yet women who wanted to become doctors so as to help their sisters had little or no encouragement from male-administered medical schools. In order to raise the standards of the medical profession, these institutions were becoming more and more exclusive and restrictive. They worked zealously to limit the number of medical students admitted, and to close down the less respectable medical schools. Many earnest young men had to give up a fervent ambition to become doctors, but women who aspired to such a career had almost no hope at all.

Victim I: The Environment

During the first fifty years of the nineteenth century, there was no movement toward social sharing or any modification of the doctrine of individualism. Unlimited land was still available, the cities had plenty of jobs for newcomers, and the nation's progress was measured by the increase in population and the growth of cities and farms. In 1800, the U.S. Congress encouraged new arrivals to buy land by cutting the required acreage purchase in half, to 320 acres, and extending credit for four years. In 1804, Congress further reduced the minimum purchase to 160 acres and provided for installment payments. While it reversed itself in 1820 by eliminating installment purchasing, it permitted 80-acre tracts to be sold for as little as $1.25

per acre. During the 1820s, about 1,000,000 acres of government land were sold each year. Then from 1835 to 1837, after President Jackson removed government funds from the Bank of the United States, various state banks extended credit so generously that 40,000,000 acres were sold in that two-year period. This sale of public land at manageable prices and in modest units not only supplied revenue for the operation of the federal government but reinforced the belief that America was a nation of landowners. Anyone who had the stamina, the energy, and the determination, so argued the individualists, could become an independent farmer and be his own master.

But the farmers unwittingly abused their land. Few of them used fertilizers, and few rotated their crops; thus the soil was quickly depleted. Nor did the federal government show much concern for the preservation of natural resources. Not until the Civil War period was land set aside for public parks, and there was little effort to protect wildlife or to conserve any other features of the native prairies and forests. The prevailing view —prevailing up to the present day—was that the land and its riches were infinite, or at least always available. And the federal government, by selling millions of acres to individual citizens and by constantly encouraging settlement of its new territories, once more demonstrated its commitment to private ownership. Underlying this policy was the long-held belief that the land belonged to the white man and that the American Indian had to make way for him.

Victim II: The Indian

When American pioneers moved into the Indiana territory in the first decade of the 1800s, they encroached upon acknowledged Indian lands. Rather than moving away, paying for the land, or trying to negotiate amicably with the Indians (who were by this time wary and suspicious of white men), the settlers complained to the governor of the territory, William Henry Harrison, and demanded protection. In 1809, Harrison signed a treaty, known as the Treaty of Fort Wayne, in which the Indians agreed to the white settlement. But two years later two Shawnee Indians, Tecumseh and his brother, the Prophet, organized a confederation to resist further white encroachment. In the same year, Harrison, believing offense to be the best defense, attacked and destroyed the Prophet's village on Tippecanoe Creek. This deed later helped Harrison to secure the presidency of the United States.

Another Indian fighter, Andrew Jackson, asked Congress in 1829 to move all Indians into a specified Indian territory. The following year saw the passage of the Indian Removal Act, which forced the Indians to migrate to lands designated by the white men. Thus the U.S. government pushed the Indians away from their traditional territories: the Cherokees in Georgia had to move to Oklahoma, while Tecumseh's people were likewise forced farther west. Soon there would be no more open land for the Indians.

The steady, relentless expansion of white America was carried on in the name of progress and civilization. Yet neither the government nor the public took any recognition of the serious injustices perpetrated against the Indians. When the Supreme Court, under Chief Justice John Marshall, argued that the Indians were entitled to federal protection in the case of *Cherokee Nation v. Georgia* (1831), President Jackson ignored the ruling. The Court's decision read as follows:

> Indian tribes had always been considered as distinct, independent, political communities, retaining their original natural rights . . . and the settled doctrine of the law of nations is, that a weaker power does not surrender its independence—its right to self-government—by associating with a stronger, and taking its protection.

> The Cherokee Nation, then, is a distinct community, occupying its own territory, with boundaries accurately described in which the laws of Georgia can have no force, and which the citizens of Georgia have no right to enter, but with the assent of the Cherokees themselves, or in conformity with treaties, and with the acts of Congress.

President Andrew Jackson replied, "John Marshall has rendered his decision; now let them enforce it."

Without legislation and presidential leadership to enforce it, the Court opinion had little significance. Even when one branch of government tried to grant the Indians equal rights, the other branches disregarded the action. In 1834, when the forced re-

108

moval of the Cherokees occurred, 4,000 of the 14,000 Cherokees died on the westward trail. One eyewitness recorded that the trip, started in the mid-winter, resulted in incredible hardships on the Indians.

> Even aged females, apparently nearly ready to drop, were traveling with heavy burdens attached to their backs, sometimes on frozen ground and sometimes on muddy streets, with no covering for their feet.

Expansion was the dominant theme in the 1800s, and the whole vast continent was waiting to be settled. The new United States had ambitions to be a great nation, and one clear way of accomplishing this goal was by extending its borders. Seventeen new states were admitted to the Union between 1803 and 1859. The old Northwest Territory had been carved into states, as had the South. California became a state in 1850, Minnesota in 1858, Oregon in 1859. On the eve of the Civil War, there were thirty-three states in the Union—a dramatic increase since the thirteen colonies had boldly separated themselves from England some eighty years before. The land was to belong to the people and the people were to be white Christians, preferably Protestants of Anglo-Saxon ancestry. Jews and Catholics remained a minority. In 1840, there were about 15,000 Jews in America, primarily of Spanish and Portuguese origin. The period of Irish-Catholic migration began, in large numbers, in the late 1840s. The promised land of opportunity for all did not recognize large segments of humankind.

Victim III: The Southern Slave

Working in the South had special features. First of all, if you were black, you were a slave, unless you were one of the fortunate few who had been freed by kindly masters. Most masters, however, were interested only in getting as much manual labor as possible from the blacks whom they owned. True, white Southerners of means would frequently point out to their self-righteous neighbors north of the Mason-Dixon line that slave owners treated their "darkies" better than Northern mill owners treated their paid workers. But this was one of the many rationalizations by which Southerners tried to justify the existence of slavery.

Cotton planting, picking, and hauling occupied the majority of blacks in the deep South, in Alabama, Georgia, Louisiana, Mississippi, and South Carolina. There cotton was the major crop, and after the invention of the cotton gin in 1793, slave labor and cotton went hand in hand. The effects of this cruel partnership are suggested in the following vignette of Abby:

> Abby was a fifteen year old slave girl in Louisiana. Beginning in August, she picked cotton with the dozen other slaves on the plantation.
>
> She well remembered the first August—five years ago—when she started picking cotton. The overseer whipped her skinny shoulders so severely, as a warning and a reminder he said, that she ached for days afterwards.
>
> Abby rushed to the fields as the light was beginning to appear in the sky. She couldn't be late if she valued her life. The day was a long one; except for a 15 minute break to eat some cold bacon, she was expected to pick cotton until it was too dark to see.
>
> Upon leaving the field, after a back-breaking day, Abby had to help her mother grind some corn in their handmill for their late supper. First she stopped to feed the mules. "Oh for the thoughtless life of a mule," she mused.

Although rice, sugar, indigo, and timber were also planted and harvested, these were minor crops and far less profitable than cotton. By 1860 the Southern states were producing close to four million bales of cotton a year. By way of contrast, in 1784 eight bags of cotton had been sent to England.

While the Northern states had begun to industrialize and urbanize, the Southern states remained predominantly agricultural and rural. Most work in the South, therefore, was associated in one way or another with crops and cattle. Merchants, brokers, and a small professional group made up a sort of middle class, but most people remained on the land, their major source of wealth and status. The plantation system became the ideal way of life, the goal of every ambitious Southern farmer. Most Southerners, of course, farmed small acreages, worked the land themselves, and did not own slaves. But they were all faithful to the myth of the South as a region of rich plantations on which large numbers of blacks served their leisured masters and mistresses. And, as we have seen in an earlier chapter, to poor whites, slavery had an added psychological significance. Low as they were on the socioeconomic scale, they could always take comfort in the fact that there was a group of human beings on a still lower level.

Black slaves, besides working in the fields, often provided skilled labor on the plantations, as carpenters, blacksmiths, and tinsmiths. Black women became nurses and midwives to the white family, forming intimate ties with the master's wife and children. Indeed, one of the cruel ironies of the black slave culture was that a black woman was considered worthy enough to nurse a white child but unworthy of being treated as an equal in any other way. Free blacks, most notably in big cities such as New Orleans and Charleston, lived better than did the slaves, but the stigma of their black skin was inescapable.

While the Northern states were developing a democratic ideology for white males, the Southern states stuck to an aristocratic concept of education and society. Public education was not highly regarded in the South. Wealthy Southerners sent their children to private schools. An aristocrat's daughter was educated to be a proper hostess while her brother was trained for the ministry or law. But even a proper hostess could oversee the meat house and supervise the slaves. The sons and daughters of small white farmers did not need much schooling, it was reasoned, since they would spend their entire lives on their parents' farm. Black slaves, it was also assumed, should not be educated because any schooling might give them undesirable ideas. Only the white male elite required more than a rudimentary education; white males must be prepared for intelligent leadership. According to the census of 1850, the slave states had a white population of 6,184,477, of whom 581,861 were schoolchildren. But the state of New York alone, with a population of 3,097,394, had 675,221 schoolchildren—more than in all the Southern states combined.

Transportation, too, remained crude and backward in the South. State governments would not spend public money to improve roads between the seaports and the interior. Indeed, roads were poor everywhere. One traveler in Indiana as late as 1850 remarked that "the jolting of the wagon from the roughness of the road was almost intolerable." Thus, because the people were so isolated, so removed from other communities—far more than in the developing North and Middle West—the slave culture was preserved intact. In this society, where a small elite held power over all other segments of humanity, both whites and blacks suffered. The myth of ivory-towered Southern womanhood, of the genteel tradition, and of the graciousness of plantation life flourished at the same time as the Northern myth of individualism. Southern landowners (who made up a small proportion of all white Southerners) took pride in their love of the past, their families, and their hospitality. Abhorring the smelly, smoky cities of the North and enjoying their pastoral existence, they frequently ignored the black workers who made this good life possible. The success of the elite in inculcating their myth into the white majority enabled them to retain their power for many years.

Victim IV: The Frontierswoman

On the frontier, families lived in backwoods cabins which were, according to one traveler, "miserable holes, having one room only, and in that room, all cook, eat, sleep, breed, and die, male and female all together." Women not only performed all the domestic chores but helped with the planting and harvesting. They cooked over open fireplaces, milked the cows, fed the single men in the area, and often defended themselves and their children against hostile Indians when their husbands were off hunting or drinking. Many travelers to the Middle Western frontier in the first half of the nineteenth century commented on the hard-working women and the lazy men. Mrs. Eliza W. Farnham called the male population of Illinois in the early 1800s "unequivocally indolent. On a bright day they mount their horses and throng the little towns in the vicinity of their homes, drinking and trading horses till late in the evenings." Indeed, the picture painted by contemporary visitors is quite different from the romantic one of brave frontiersmen carving out a new existence in the wilderness.

The wives were lonely, though loyal and rarely complaining.

A frontierswoman's daily chores. (Culver)

They yearned for company and were extremely hospitable to passing travelers. One such traveler, Thomas Ashe, noted:

> On entering the house, which was a long one fitted up very well, the Kentuckyan never exchanged a word with his wife or his children . . . notwithstanding he had been absent several days. No tender enquiry, no affection or sentiment, but a contemptuous silence and a stern brutality which block up all the avenues to the heart.

The wife, Ashe continued, remained amiable and offered the visitor some toddy.

The religious camp meetings, the quilting parties, and the frolics held when a farm task had been completed were the women's only social activities. These, too, however, entailed extra work. The hostess had to serve refreshments and entertain her guests—and clean up after them.

Frontierswomen worked in the fields while their sisters in

113

settled New England and Middle Western communities tended their homes. There was always a critical shortage of labor in the newly settled areas and as a result women participated in all of the arduous physical tasks alongside their menfolk. Frontierswomen wore men's trousers years before Amelia Bloomer introduced the idea to New England women—because of practical necessity. One writer in Indiana during the 1800s observed:

> A strange figure emerged from the tall rank weeds into the road before us, and continued to move in front, apparently never having noticed our approach. The figure was undeniably human; and yet at bottom it seemed to be a man, for there were a man's tow-linen breeches; at top, a woman; for there was the semblance of a short gown, and indeed a female kerchief on the neck and a sun-bonnet on the head. . . . It originated in the necessities of a new country, where women must hunt cows hid in tall weeds and coarse grass on dewy or frosty mornings.

Women aged more noticeably on the frontier than did men. Because of constant childbearing and the immensely difficult job of maintaining a home, caring for the children, and working in the fields, a thirty-year-old woman was already old and worn out. One journalist commented: "Woman is expected to daily endure a strain that no man would tolerate for any length of time. Until what is modestly called housekeeping is recognized as a noble science that it really is, and is carefully studied, the slaughter of women by overwork will continue."

Because women were at a premium, however, they obtained certain advantages not granted their sisters in settled areas. In 1838, Kentucky, for example, granted widows or single women who owned taxable property the right to vote for their district school officials, who surely needed the support of this potentially dissatisfied constituency. Mississippi, in 1839, granted married women control over their own property, before any Eastern state did so. It was Wyoming territory and Colorado that granted women the vote after the Civil War. (For Wyoming territory to become a state, a certain number of voters were necessary.) In order to attract women to the new frontiers, Western territories granted wives the right to hold their land separately from their husbands. In the 1850s, single women in Oregon were given 320 acres if they would migrate there.

Victim IV: The Frontierswoman

Women remained in short supply throughout most of the nineteenth century in the West. Their lives were hard, and only loyal wives, daughters born in the new territories, runaway slave girls, Indian women, and adventurous white women risked leaving the security of a settled community for the unpredictability of the frontier.

The frontierswoman, whether the frontier was Illinois in 1805 or Wyoming in 1860, faced all kinds of hardships with courage and determination. She is the unsung heroic figure of the settlement of the West—she, not the series of Daniel Boones who have been memorialized in poetry and song.

Victim V: The Prostitute

Outside New England, prostitutes existed since the settlement of the country. As long as Puritanism exerted its power in New England, however, that region remained free of prostitutes. In frontier communities, Indian and black women were frequently forced into prostitution by the large numbers of bachelors who sought their services. In cities, such as New York and Charleston, prostitutes served married men as well as bachelors. And they were not entirely condemned by married women. Though prostitution was not a subject open to public discussion, many wives believed that the existence of prostitutes saved them from the constant sexual demands of their husbands, and thus provided one form of birth control.

As cities grew, so did the number of prostitutes. As new communities arose in the West, prostitutes followed the gold trail in search of a secure income. Some moral reformers in the nineteenth century inveighed against "white slavery" and blamed male excess and venality as causing prostitution. Others blamed industrialization, which exploited unskilled women workers and led many to become whores as a desperate alternative. One 1858 study of New York prostitutes showed that half of them had been servants or seamstresses (1,000) before turning to prostitution. It was much more lucrative for a woman to sell her body than to slave over a sewing machine twelve hours a day for a pittance.

On the other hand, prostitution was not always a matter of choice. Many innocent immigrant and farm girls, when they arrived in the big city, found themselves hustled off to a house of ill repute. Stories about this corrupt practice occasionally stirred outraged city officials to promise an investigation. But little ever came of their promises. The white slave traders and operators of houses of prostitution usually rewarded police officials sufficiently to assure their turning the other way.

One consequence of unsupervised prostitution was the rise in venereal disease. By the end of the nineteenth century, it was estimated that one in ten American men had syphilis. And they brought the disease home, thus infecting their wives and future generations as well.

Dr. Emily Blackwell wryly remarked:

> The higher sense of mankind says that the family is the essential unit of the state. Our practice says that the family plus prostitution is the essential unit.

Whether driven to prostitution by economic desperation or forced to prostitution by unscrupulous hustlers, prostitutes were a significant social group in America. They were victims of a sexual double standard that praised sexual prowess in men and condemned it in women, and they were the victims of an economic system that did not value human labor. The prudery and hypocrisy of American society, however, made prostitution a forbidden subject to discuss publicly. Everyone knew it existed, but everyone conspired to ignore that knowledge.

Human Work

Labor, too, was hedged with many restrictions. All occupations were not judged equally worthy for all human beings, but reflected a well-defined caste system. Slaves had their special kinds of work, as did poor white farmers. Skilled carpenters had their place in the vocational scheme and unskilled laborers theirs. Woman's work was a carefully specified series of chores associated with the home. Though women and blacks often demonstrated that they could leave their designated work-spheres and perform admirably in those reserved for white males, such a shift was permitted only when absolutely necessary. Skilled black workers might be tolerated and women doctors might be able to handle their professional responsibilities well, but neither blacks nor women were encouraged to believe that all categories of human work were open to them. Exceptions existed, but never became the rule.

Yet in the paradoxical manner in which many Americans' minds frequently operated, work remained highly respected. Whereas a variety of jobs were closed to large groups of people, everyone was told that work was a virtue. Still, if an ambitious black or a woman could not learn a professional skill, if immigrants' sons had no money to study medicine, and if many of the craft trades excluded foreigners—how was a person to engage in the work he really wanted to do? How could a curious youth explore new and different kinds of work? The standard-bearers of the American culture never faced these questions. Instead, they continually mouthed their faith in American industry and in the inevitability of human progress in this best of all possible worlds. Though clearly all work was not rewarded equally, the culture commentators loudly praised its value. Work was always praiseworthy, laziness always deplorable.

On the other hand, the sweat of a man's brow did not rate as highly in the American value system as the clever manipulations of a stock transaction. Work based on shrewd maneuvers received greater financial rewards than did physical labor. The farmer may have been noble, according to literary sources, but he did not reap the benefits gained by a successful merchant or manufacturer. In the words of Ralph Waldo Emerson, a man of letters—and of leisure: "The first farmer was the first man, and all historic nobility rests on possession and use of land." Truly, in an agricultural society where everyone works, even the large landowning farmer, there is a sense of equality among all persons. However, when a commercial and manufacturing economy develops and a whole group of people make profits without any physical labor, distinctions between various kinds of work emerge. An accountant is far removed from the products he itemizes in his ledgers. A capitalist who owns textile mills does not sweat in his own factories. And a shipbuilder can be far removed from his workers.

As the economy becomes more complex, more reliant on machines and experts, physical labor loses its dignity and its rewards. Those who profit by labor are often farthest away from it. The large shareholder in John D. Rockefeller's oil company

117

knows nothing about drilling oil, nor does he need to. The first Rockefeller himself, though beginning as a worker, gave up that role once he enjoyed financial success.

So it happened as America became industrialized. Shrewd investors made huge profits from industries they knew nothing about. Work and profits were separated, as were workers from the products of their labor. Indeed, work, if it happened to be physical activity, lost its value, even while it was being continuously advocated as essential to human success and satisfaction. If it happened to be mental activity, the rewards were higher, and the highest rewards went to those who no longer had to work at all. The goal of all work, then, was leisure.

This segmentation of work into different categories was just taking shape in 1860. The development of a completely industrial economy—of corporations, of shareholders, of absentee owners—was still in the future. But the foundation for that future was firmly established on the eve of the Civil War.

Suggestions for Further Reading

Mary Beard. *Woman as a Force in History* (New York, 1946).

Mary Beard. *America Through Women's Eyes* (New York, 1934).

Elizabeth Blackwell. *Pioneer Work in Opening the Medical Profession to Women* (London, 1895).

John R. Commons, *et al. History of Labor in the United States* (New York, 1935).

De Bow's Review. A nineteenth-century monthly periodical that published a great deal of agricultural and scientific information.

Elizabeth A. Dexter. *Career Women of America, 1776–1840* (Francestown, N.H., 1950).

E. Franklin Frazier. *The Negro in the United States* (New York, 1957).

Eugene D. Genovese. *The Political Economy of Slavery* (New York, 1965).

Ishbel Ross. *Child of Destiny: The Life of Elizabeth Blackwell* (New York, 1949).

Anne F. Scott. *The Southern Lady: From Pedestal to Politics, 1830–1930* (Chicago, 1971).

Anna Howard Shaw. *The Story of a Pioneer* (New York, 1915).

Kenneth M. Stampp. *The Peculiar Institution* (New York, 1956).

Alexis de Tocqueville. *Democracy in America* (New York, 1954).

CHAPTER SIX

Woman's Superior Moral Power,
1800–1860

Not her hand can build the city;
Not her voice should rule the State;
She must reign by love and pity—
Through her goodness make men great.

—*Godey's Lady's Book,* August 1879

We make our tables elegant with silver,
glass, and china: should our women be
less attractive than all around them?

—Sara Josepha Hale, *Manners; or Happy
Homes and Good Society,* 1868

*G*odey's *Lady's Book,* a well-known woman's magazine with 150,000 subscribers by 1860, preached the first of the two messages just above. The author of the second, Mrs. Sara Josepha Hale, was Godey's editor for forty years. During those four decades, she frequently reminded her readers that:

The station of woman as the companion of free, independent, civilized and Christian man is the most important she can sustain on earth—the most honorable, useful and happy.

To a good many women, this message meant that they should remain in the home, obedient to their husbands' every wish. To a few, it meant exerting a moral influence upon society; it meant engaging in reform activities.

119

Woman's Superior Moral Power 1800–1860

As good Christians, these women activists left their homes and became moral crusaders for temperance, penal reform, and the abolition of slavery. Frequently they were able to perform their missions without violating society's conventions. They participated in voluntary associations, in church-related groups, and in charitable activities. They did philanthropic work in their communities. Sometimes they became reformers, though not feminists—that is, they never agitated for specific woman's issues such as the vote, equal educational opportunity, or liberal divorce laws. Rather, in a lady-like manner, they spoke and propagandized for the rights of other deprived groups—using moral suasion to convince male authority figures to pass a desired piece of legislation or repeal an undesirable one. Some few women reformers, however, did espouse women's causes, and those few began, in a modest way, the women's rights movement.

These women reformers compared the plight of the American woman with that of the slaves. Both groups were denied their natural rights; both groups had to obey the authority of men. Many women reformers, therefore, became advocates of the emancipation of slaves as well as their own liberation. The first generation of suffragists, those emerging in the thirty-year period before the Civil War, usually espoused feminism as well as suffragism. Their belief that women should have the vote was part of their larger creed, which included women's rights as a whole. Later generations of suffragists would narrow their vision and concentrate on the woman's right to vote, to the exclusion of other feminist concerns. The reformers of the pre–Civil War generation, however—an exciting, diverse, and numerous group of expressive, active women—worked both for their own liberation and that of other downtrodden people.

Dorothea Dix, crusader for the mentally ill. (Brown Bros.)

Feminist Reformers

Dorothea Dix (1802–1887) was born in a Maine log cabin to poor, sickly parents. Her father was an itinerant preacher who never provided adequately for his family. Dorothea's early years were filled with hunger, fear, and sorrow. At the age of twelve, she ran away to her wealthy grandmother's house in Boston. But she rebelled against the strict discipline there, and two years later she moved in with an aunt. The two of them started a school, which proved successful.

For almost twenty years, Dorothea taught school and wrote children's stories and hymns, but she contracted tuberculosis and could not continue her teaching. She went to England to recuperate. While living there with Quaker friends, she witnessed efforts to improve sanitary conditions in hospitals and prisons. Upon returning to America, free now of financial worries as she had inherited her grandmother's fortune, she searched for useful work. In 1841, she found it: a minister asked her to take his place in a Sunday School class held in a prison in Cambridge, Massachusetts.

On the first day she appeared at the prison, Dorothea was appalled by the conditions. The rooms were dirty, unheated, and unventilated. Mentally ill patients were chained to chairs alongside criminals, since no distinction was made between the insane and the criminal. She could not sleep that night. And thus began one of the most spectacular one-woman campaigns in history. She started writing letters to the newspapers on the deplorable prison conditions. She lectured and traveled the length and breadth of Massachusetts collecting information on prisons.

Dorothea Dix drafted legislation to provide proper facilities for the insane as well as the criminal, and Massachusetts and then a dozen other states appropriated money to carry out her reforms. For over ten years she devoted herself to this cause and became associated with it in the public mind. No other person has ever done more to publicize the shameful neglect of prisons than did Dorothea Dix.

The Grimké sisters, Sarah (1792–1873) and Angelina (1805–1879), and Elizabeth Cady Stanton (1815–1902) were leaders in the abolition of slavery movement as well as the women's rights movement. All three learned much from their experience with abolitionism: how to address groups, convince the doubtful, and get petitions signed. They later applied this knowledge to their work in the women's rights movement. Another thing they discovered was that men reformers, notwithstanding their liberal convictions, were often strongly biased against women. They learned that abolitionist societies resisted the women who spoke for their cause just as traditional men's groups did. Separate women abolitionist societies and temperance groups were formed, as male abolitionists and temperance reformers would not admit women into their midst.

The Grimké sisters were colorful examples of certain people who, in every generation, rise above their cultural environment and indeed almost deny it. Daughters of a prominent slaveholder, both Sarah, the sixth child of the family, and Angelina, the ninth, rebelled against the life they were expected to lead. They abhorred slavery, vowed not to live in luxury while blacks remained enslaved, and preached abolition to their friends and neighbors in Charleston, South Carolina. After the sisters became converted to Quakerism—a liberal Protestant religion that upheld the equality of all mankind—they found that their words met with open hostility in their native town. In 1823, Sarah moved to Philadelphia, the city of Quakers and brotherly love. Six years later, Angelina followed her to the North.

Both sisters attended meetings of the Philadelphia Anti-Slavery Society and in 1835 became involved, in a dramatic and forceful way, with the abolitionist movement. When the prominent American abolitionist William Lloyd Garrison asked his fellow workers to welcome the British abolitionist George Thompson, Angelina Grimké wrote Garrison a letter supporting Thompson's work. Garrison was so impressed with the letter, and the fact that she was a slave-holder's daughter, that he printed it in his newspaper, the *Liberator*. Thereafter, the Grimké sisters spoke at various anti-slavery meetings in the North, and in the summer of 1837 undertook a speaking tour of New England. They were the first women in America to speak publicly before mixed audiences.

Both Angelina and Sarah believed in woman's equality because of their deep commitment to Quakerism and to the moral equality of all human beings. Sarah Grimké, in her *Letters on the Equality of the Sexes*, argued that "Whatsoever it is morally right for man to do, it is morally right for a woman to do." In fact, while working for the abolition of slavery, the Grimké sisters discovered

123

Sarah and Angelina Grimké:
Southerners who defied slavery.
(Brown Bros.)

another challenge—women's rights. Much to their dismay, they found that audiences resisted their message not only because of its radical content but because it was delivered by women. Furthermore, they learned that many male abolitionists still held the traditional view of woman's place in society. As Abby Kelley, another abolitionist spokeswoman, stated: "We have good cause to be grateful to the slave for the benefits we have received to *ourselves*, in working for *him*. In striving to strike his irons off, we found most surely, that *we* were manacled *ourselves:* not by *one* chain only, but by many."

Women organized their separate anti-slavery societies beginning in 1837—promoting the doctrine of "separate but equal," which was later applied to "free" black people. In 1840, when men and women abolitionists went to London to attend the World Anti-Slavery Convention, they were told that women delegates, such as Lucretia Mott, could not sit on the main floor of the convention hall alongside the men. In protest, American abolitionist leader Garrison sat in the balcony with the women. But to Elizabeth Cady Stanton, who was also present, and Mrs.

124

Mott, this event symbolized the need for them to carry on their abolitionist activities apart from the men. They did this, not in behalf of the slaves but in their own behalf.

Elizabeth Cady was born in 1815 in Johnstown, New York. Her mother was the daughter of Colonel James Livingston, a participant in the American Revolution, and her father was Judge Daniel Cady, a well-known lawyer who was elected to Congress the year Elizabeth was born. Her childhood, by her own account, was pleasant and cheerful. But when she was eleven, her only brother died and her father grieved mightily. "Oh, my daughter, I wish you were a boy!" he said to Elizabeth, and she responded: "I will try to be all my brother was."

Elizabeth resolved to study hard, to learn Greek, and to follow her father's legal interests. One of her great disillusionments, however, was the discovery that no one expected the same intellectual performance from a girl as from a boy. The seed of feminism was already stirring in Elizabeth Cady's heart.

She grew up to be precocious, curious, and critical of cultural forms that restricted women's behavior. She wondered why Judge Cady's law books denied married women equality with their husbands, and she wrestled with the problem continuously. When she married Henry B. Stanton, a noted abolitionist, in 1840, the minister had to remove the word "obey" from the marriage vows in order to get Elizabeth's approval. Their honeymoon voyage took them to England for the World Anti-Slavery Convention. It was eight years later (July 13, 1848) that Mrs. Stanton, the mother of a growing family (she eventually had seven children), called together several hundred women in Seneca Falls, New York, at her home, for the first women's rights meeting in the United States. It marked the beginning of the women's rights movement. Thus began a long and fruitful career as speaker, writer, and organizer in the cause of women's issues.

Of the resolutions they drew up following their statement of grievances, a woman's suffrage proposal passed by only a slim margin, while all the others passed unanimously. The resulting document, reproduced in its entirety in the Appendix, was modeled after the original Declaration of Independence, and was called the "Declaration of Sentiments and Resolutions." It began:

125

Woman's Superior Moral Power 1800–1860

We hold these truths to be self-evident; that all men and women are created equal; that they are endowed by their Creator with certain inalienable rights: that among these are life, liberty, and the pursuit of happiness . . .

Just as Thomas Jefferson's 1776 Declaration listed the colonies' grievances against the British Crown, so the Seneca Falls Declaration proceeded to list the abuses of women. The introduction stated:

> The history of mankind is a history of repeated injuries and usurpations on the part of man toward woman, having in direct object the establishment of an absolute tyranny over her. To prove this, let facts be submitted to a candid world.

There followed an extensive list of ways in which society prevented women from being educated, from earning a living on an equal basis with men, from maintaining a separate identity and existence, and from having political rights. In conclusion, the feminists who approved the Seneca Falls Declaration vowed to "circulate tracts, petition the State and national legislatures, and endeavor to enlist the pulpit and press on our behalf. We hope this Convention will be followed by a series of Conventions embracing every part of the country."

The original Declaration of Independence stands as the idealistic foundation of this country's history; it expresses the goal, more than the reality, of how Americans should view each other. The Seneca Falls Declaration of 1848 also stands as a dramatic articulation of an ideal: what women's rights ought to be in a democratic country.

Many male commentators either ignored the significance of the Seneca Falls meeting or mocked it. One newspaper writer described the women who attended it as "divorced wives, childless women, and some old maids." No worse fate could befall a woman than to be divorced, childless, or an old maid. Since the primary function of women was to produce children, those who did so were absorbed in the nurturing task. Presumably, then, only female misfits had the time and energy to go to Seneca Falls and complain about their status in America. The neatness of this logic acted as a powerful deterrent to women's open rebellion —and explained why more women worked in the abolitionist

Elizabeth Cady Stanton, leader of the first generation of women reformers. (Brown Bros.)

127

movement than the women's rights movement. Americans may be joiners, as Alexis de Tocqueville pointed out in the 1830s, but they join respectable church and community organizations, not reformist groups.

A Feminist Philosopher

Another lively, exceptional woman of this period was Margaret Fuller (1810–1850), who preached her own brand of feminism. She lived the life of a free woman, and assumed that if all women would do likewise, society would be reformed. Personally emancipated, she respected the work of the abolitionists, but spent her days writing about the condition of women in the United States, teaching, and conducting "conversations" with young women about their lives and their problems.

The brilliant daughter of New Englanders Timothy and Margaret Fuller, Margaret was educated largely by her father. As she later wrote: "[He] hoped to make me the heir of all he knew. I was often kept up till very late; and as he was a severe teacher, both from his habits of mind and his ambition for me, my feelings were kept on the stretch till the recitations were over."

Margaret Fuller fulfilled her father's wishes. She was the first woman reporter for Horace Greeley's New York *Tribune* as well as a writer and teacher. Raised in Cambridgeport, Massachusetts, she lived briefly in Providence, Rhode Island, and then in Boston and New York. She taught French and Latin at Bronson Alcott's school in Boston, where, in order to supplement her income, she started "conversation" classes for the educated women of the city. She conducted these classes for five years, during which time many famous women attended, among them feminist Lydia Maria Child and Nathaniel Hawthorne's future wife, Sophia Peabody. Margaret Fuller's article based on these conversations, called "The Great Lawsuit," was later expanded to become her famous book, *Woman in the Nineteenth Century* (1845).

To the young women who attended her classes, Margaret Fuller kept stressing the fact that each was an individual, a person with special interests and special needs that required fulfillment—a message considered highly unusual and radical for polite Boston society in the 1840s. She admitted that it was difficult to get women "to the point from which they shall naturally develop self-respect and learn self-help." She encouraged them to be whatever they chose to be: "Let them be sea captains if they will." She understood women's psychological dependency on men, as well as the use of male-devised standards for evaluating all accomplishments in our culture. "The intellect," she reminded her readers,

> no more than the sense of hearing is to be cultivated merely that Woman may be a more valuable companion to Man but because the Power who gave a power, by its mere existence signifies that it must be brought out toward perfection. . . . Let it not be said wherever there is energy of creative genius [that] she has a masculine mind.

While activists like Elizabeth Cady Stanton and the Grimké sisters acted on the assumption that women's brain power was the equal of men's, Margaret Fuller wrote about it. Her writings, combined with those of the Grimké sisters and Mrs. Stanton, constitute an impressive quantity of feminist literature. Margaret Fuller advised her women readers that:

> When the mind is once awakened to this consciousness, it will not be restrained by the habits of the past. . . . It is therefore that I would have Woman lay aside all thought, such as she habitually cherishes, of being taught and led by men. . . . I would have her free from compromise, from complaisance [and] from helplessness.

Transcendentalist,
feminist writer Margaret Fuller.
(N.Y. Public Library)

Some historians of ideas have included Margaret Fuller in their discussions of transcendentalism, but they have never explored the unique way in which she synthesized the transcendental philosophy with feminism. To her, human transcendence —based on the firm conviction that all human beings were precious—meant that women had to free their minds, bodies, and souls. "Man should prove his own freedom by making her free." And women should demonstrate their freedom by acting it out.

Feminists and Abolitionists

The anti-slavery movement and the women's rights movement were tied together in various ways. First, many women active in the abolitionist movement shared the feminist concerns of Mrs. Stanton and the Grimké sisters. Second, the leadership of the two movements often overlapped. Henry B. Stanton was a prominent abolitionist. Henry Blackwell, an abolitionist leader, had a wife committed to both causes (Lucy Stone), and a sister (Dr. Elizabeth Blackwell) and a sister-in-law (Antoinette Brown Blackwell) who were activists. In May 1838, Theodore Weld, another important abolitionist, married Angelina Grimké. Frequently, women led their husbands into reform activities. Wendell Phillips, for example, said that he became a staunch reformer because "my wife made an out-and-out abolitionist out of me; and she always preceded me in the adoption of the various causes which I have advocated." Anne Terry Greene Phillips convinced her husband of the legitimacy of women's rights, temperance, and abolition.

In logic, of course, though not in human nature, all abolitionists should have been women's rights advocates and vice versa. However, this was not always the case. While Garrison, Phillips, and, to a lesser degree, Weld sympathized with the feminist movement, they all believed that the cause of slavery deserved first priority. Only after the complete emancipation of all slaves should reformers turn their attention to women's rights. After the Civil War, this conflict over priorities resulted in the creation of a separate woman's movement. But in the period before 1860, women, however reluctantly, agreed with the male

130

abolitionists' assessment and worked faithfully for the freedom of the slaves.

Theodore Weld, for one, regretted the time and energy Sarah and Angelina Grimké devoted to the feminist cause. "I advocate ... that woman in EVERY *particular* shares equally with man rights and responsibilities," he wrote Sarah, but "notwithstanding this, I do most deeply regret that you have begun a series of articles in the papers on the rights of women."

After Angelina married Weld, she and her sister retreated to private life and stopped their vigorous writing and lecturing. Both were self-conscious about their retirement, and wrote friends that they were working for all women by showing that a woman reformer need not be ruined for domesticity. "Let us remember," wrote Sarah, "that our claim to stand on perfect equality with our brethren can only be substantiated by scrupulous attention to our domestic duties." The career/marriage dichotomy—the difficulty of combining home responsibilities with the demands of an active outside life—was not effectively resolved by the Grimké sisters. Though they rationalized their behavior, they did not help to solve the dilemma.

Elizabeth Cady Stanton, on the other hand, managed to become the leading feminist philosopher of this first generation of women's rights activists while at the same time raising a family of seven children. Her husband Henry supported her interest in the cause of women from the beginning. During the first two decades of their marriage, the 1840s and 1850s, she was too busy with her maternal chores to tour the country, but she still found time to write and to plan the strategy for the feminist movement. Her friend and staunch co-worker Susan B. Anthony once asked her for help in this way:

> Oh, dear, dear! There is so much to say and I am so without constructive power to put [it] in symmetrical order. So, for the love of me and for the saving of the reputation of womanhood, I beg you, with one baby on your knee and another at your feet, and four boys whistling, buzzing, hallooing "Ma, Ma," set yourself about the work.

And so she did. Mrs. Stanton wrote speeches for Miss Anthony to deliver. She drafted the 1848 Seneca Falls Declaration, and she spoke at the annual women's rights conventions held after 1848. Her rhetoric became known throughout New England and the Middle Atlantic states. Her phrasing was always dramatic and to the point. She told the New York legislature in 1860:

> There are certain natural rights as inalienable to civilization as are the rights of air and motion to the savage in the wilderness.
>
> The prejudice against color, of which we hear so much, is no stronger than that against sex. . . . The Negro's skin and the woman's sex are both *prima facie* evidence that they were intended to be in subjection to the white Saxon man.

Bringing the two reform movements together may have personally strengthened the women involved, but it convinced many others that both movements were radical, would lead to disruption and chaos, and were therefore totally undesirable. For their part, the moral crusaders, because they argued in simple, direct moral terms, did not fully appreciate the revolutionary nature of their demands. Supporters of freedom for the black people did not envision the immensely complicated changes in human behavior that would be required to make emancipation a meaningful accomplishment. While they recognized the need to educate the blacks, they could not anticipate the tremendous social, political, and economic consequences of emancipation. White Southerners, on the other hand, knew that their whole way of life would be in jeopardy if the moral reformers succeeded.

For the reformers in the woman's movement who based their argument on the natural rights theory, there could be no halfway measures, no restrictions on the implementation of those rights. To them, the natural rights of women were a moral imperative and therefore needed legal sanction. Once their message was effectively communicated to enough people, they believed, the simple power of moral justice would be sufficient to secure reform. Right would triumph because it *was* right. Their logic was direct and tight; yet most human actions are not guided by truth, but rather by tradition, custom, and accepted standards of behavior. Southerners in the 1840s justified a system they had lived with for over a century because they had developed a comfortable set of living patterns within that system and were unwilling

132

to change them. Moreover, to both sexes in the North and the South, the traditional notion of woman's place in the home and in society was deeply entrenched. Women had been around a lot longer than slaves and had always performed the same domestic functions. Assuring them their rights did not seem a compelling reason to alter age-long customs.

The reformers possessed an enormous amount of optimism about human beings, really believing that their innate goodness was stronger than their sinfulness. Frequently the abolitionists and feminists were members of the more liberal Protestant sects, such as the Quakers, that preached the essential goodness of humanity. Winning the public over to a righteous cause, they felt, was only a matter of education. If people learned about the extreme cruelty of slavery, if people knew about the laws that oppressed women, they would support all efforts to end these injustices.

Then, too, the moral crusaders had great patience and courage. Many worked for their reforms throughout their adult lives. Elizabeth Cady Stanton, for example, remained an active leader in the women's rights movement until the 1890s, when she was in her seventies. She and others blessed with long life lived to see their efforts result in only partial success. The Civil War legally ended slavery, but did not create the conditions that would provide true freedom for black Americans. Women gained some forms of equality in the law courts, but, at the century's end, they still could not vote. Yet the reformers in every generation are staunch, admirable people—first because they are aware of moral flaws in the accepted values of their peers, and second because they act on that awareness. Whenever their cause has potentially long-range and far-reaching effects, they fail, and for a single, simple reason: most human beings are unwilling to make radical changes in their way of life. When the desired changes are modest and nondisruptive, they stand a better chance for success.

The abolitionists and the feminists held annual conventions all through the 1850s, and kept their spirits high. Feminists were gratified by the passage of new state laws regarding married women's property rights. Mississippi in 1839 and other states (including New York) in the 1840s passed women's property acts, which gave married women the right to sign contracts, to

133

sue and be sued independent of their husbands, to manage and control the property they brought with them to their marriage, to work and keep their earnings. In 1850, however, women still could not sit on juries. In some states, husbands were still considered the owners of their children and of all household possessions; in case of divorce, which was rare, the husband kept the children and the property. Educational facilities discriminated against women at all levels. Professional schools would not accept women, and women who had studied law could not take the bar examinations in any state. The women's rights movement before the Civil War exposed and articulated the gross disadvantages under which women lived in America, but it did not effect significant changes in their status.

Demon Rum

Temperance was another cause supported by leading female and male activists of the period. They pointed out that drunkenness created all kinds of social ills. They reminded their audiences that a drunken, irresponsible husband could not support his wife and children and that his behavior had a bad effect on them. His wife often had to work, not only to feed the family but to pay the debts incurred by his heavy drinking. Drunken husbands caused poverty and vice, and upset the social stability of the community. Thus temperance, the movement to abolish drinking and encourage sobriety, gained momentum in the twenty years before the Civil War, especially in the crowded cities.

Actually, temperance was a middle-class answer to a strictly lower-class problem, since upper-class men who drank excessively were not viewed as a social burden or a danger to society. So it was middle-class women and men who formed temperance societies to educate the masses to abstinence. These societies, modeled along the same lines as abolitionist and feminist organizations, were formed in every state. "Abolish Demon Rum" was the watchword of the movement, in which many abolitionist and feminist crusaders were active. Susan B. Anthony, along with Lucy Stone, for example, gained a great deal of organizing and lecturing experience in the temperance movement, as well as in the women's rights movement.

Susan B. Anthony (1820–1906) was born in Massachusetts,

and even as a young girl displayed an independent spirit. She asked her teacher why he taught long division only to boys. His answer—"A girl needs to know how to read her Bible and count her egg money, nothing more"—did not satisfy Susan. She arranged to sit behind the schoolteacher and listen while he taught long division. Thus she demonstrated her strength of will, a trait she would apply to the temperance, the anti-slavery, and then the women's rights movements.

Susan had agreed with her father that liquor was an evil, so as a young schoolteacher in the 1840s, she campaigned for temperance. As she gained experience at speaking and organizing, she came into contact with other women leaders. Her meeting with Elizabeth Cady Stanton changed the course of her life—the two women became inseparable colleagues in the women's rights movement.

After the Civil War, Susan B. Anthony published *The Revolution*, the National Woman's Suffrage Association magazine, whose motto was: "The true republic—men, their rights and nothing more; women, their rights and nothing less." She became an acknowledged spokeswoman for suffrage and personally supervised many state suffrage campaigns. At the time of her death, she was one of the most famous and respected women in America.

Members of temperance societies did not always support other reforms. In 1853, Wendell Phillips of Boston, a delegate to a temperance convention in New York, tried in vain to get the convention to recognize women delegates. Lucy Stone and Susan B. Anthony, thanks to Phillips' efforts, were admitted to the meeting, but later a credentials committee decided that women delegates had no place there. Women could work in women's temperance societies, but they could not expect equal treatment at a male temperance convention. Wendell Phillips was hissed and jeered at so much for his support of women's rights that he concluded that "the men of New York do not understand the meaning of Civil Liberty and free discussion."

Imagine how much more difficult it was for women speakers advocating their own cause! Sarah and Angelina Grimké, Elizabeth Cady Stanton, and Lucy Stone, among others, endured many unpleasant and often terrifying moments during their years of public speaking. It is always disagreeable, in any age, to have one's words mocked. But for nineteenth-century women,

brought up to listen and defer to men, it could be a painful experience. They needed tremendous courage just to rise and speak. To continue speaking with patience and endurance, when their words were hissed at, must surely have been an awe-inspiring feat.

The Feminist's Dilemma

To the leaders of the nineteenth-century moral crusades, there was a natural logic in being an abolitionist, feminist, and temperance worker simultaneously, since each cause aimed toward the perfection of society. To many members of a single reform movement, however, the other causes were by no means of equal worth. Most temperance workers did not think woman's role needed changing; most abolitionists felt that their cause was supreme. It was the women leaders of all three movements who tried to preserve the connections between them and to advocate simultaneous reforms on all fronts. To Frances Willard, who led the Women's Christian Temperance Union in the post–Civil War period, temperance, women's rights, and socialism were all interrelated. To Elizabeth Cady Stanton, abolitionism and feminism were also tied together. Most male reformers did not appreciate these linkages.

The difficulty of devoting one's energy to more than one cause at a time undoubtedly contributed to the feminists' failure. But a greater obstacle to women's rights was the cultural commitment, shared by both the reformers and the conservatives, to traditional ideas. If even Theodore Weld had his doubts about the seriousness of women's rights, how could an ordinary husband, married to a tradition-minded wife and not to a feminist, be expected to change his mind about woman's role in society? Thus, only a few reformers remained committed to the three causes, taking comfort and encouragement from like-minded friends and never broadening their constituency substantially.

Susan B. Anthony (left) and Elizabeth Cady Stanton both devoted a lifetime to the woman's movement. (Culver)

To further complicate the already difficult task of comprehensive reform, there was a serious difference of opinion among the reformers as to what was meant by women's rights. To Wendell Phillips, the cause did not include the liberalizing of divorce laws. Indeed this issue, when proposed by Elizabeth Cady Stanton in 1860, lost her the support of many members of the women's rights movement. Reforming divorce laws hit at the very heart of the family, an institution which was considered sacred and beyond reproach. Moreover, the divergence of opinion on this single issue demonstrated that many reformers had not thought about the full meaning of feminist claims. To them, equality for women meant eliminating inequitable laws and allowing women free entry to institutions of higher learning; but to most women, and to men who were sympathetic to feminism, it did not mean changing the family framework. The debate in the 1850s and 1860s over the meaning of feminism is being restaged in the 1960s and 1970s—and equally divergent opinions are emerging.

The feminist reformers, like the abolitionists, did develop a coherent critique which listed all society's injustices toward women, but, with the exception of Mrs. Stanton and a few other bold leaders, they did not devise adequate solutions to the problem. To do this, a close examination of the family structure was certainly in order, which would include consideration of both marriage and divorce. In the nineteenth century, divorce was generally initiated by the man, on the rare occasions when it became necessary. He could divorce an adulterous wife, retaining possession of the children and all household items. The divorced wife was left without resources; she had no legal rights, no economic power, no social position without her husband. Even if a wife could initiate and obtain a divorce, how could she survive in a hostile community that unfailingly blamed the woman for the breakup of a marriage?

Elizabeth Cady Stanton had thought long and hard about all the areas of American life that required revising in order to make it more tolerable for women. Liberalizing divorce laws was only one of many changes she advocated. But to most people, including many reformers, divorce meant the ruin of society as they knew it; free love and promiscuity would replace morality. The family was society in miniature. If it was sick, society was sick. If it was healthy, all was right with the world. It took a person with a bold and daring imagination to conceive of a society built on human equality, and to visualize the steps needed to bring it about. Mrs. Stanton was such a person, but she found her reformer friends unwilling to entertain her radical ideas.

Even as we praise the moral crusaders of the pre–Civil War period for their efforts to publicize the evils of slavery, the enslavement of women, and the disastrous effects of liquor, we must also recognize their limitations. Their views of the future, for the most part, were narrow. Their imagination did not dare to explore the full possibilities of freedom for all. In their advocacy of human emancipation, they did not consider all the implications of their crusade. They were labeled "visionaries" by the populace—a word spoken in derision—precisely because their visions did not include concrete plans or practical details. Elizabeth Cady Stanton, however, was exceptional. She stood far above most male abolitionists in her perception of the links between abolitionism and feminism, as well as in her willingness to examine each and every social institution and change it if necessary.

Women Educators

Women, as we have seen, frequently got together to supply the needs denied them by male society. When men's schools and colleges refused to admit them, women started their own. But women educators generally accepted the male definition of education and of a "proper" curriculum for female students. Emma Willard's seminary in Troy, New York, founded in 1818, offered the classics (Greek and Latin) but not physical education. Most other "ladies' seminaries" agreed that the primary purpose of educating women was to prepare them to be good wives and mothers, along with a smattering of the liberal arts. Contrary to the message of Margaret Fuller, women were not educated to develop their intellectual interests and potentialities.

The men who advocated higher education for women always couched their support in acceptable cultural terms. The editor of the *Maysville* (Kentucky) *Eagle* told his readers in 1830:

> The cultivation of the female intellect cannot detract from the power, influence, and pleasure of man. It will bring no "rival in his

kingdom"—it will not render her conversation less agreeable—it will not render her judgment less sure and certain in the management of the domestic concerns of the family.

There was no way to break loose from these male standards. Men had to make sure that educated women would never compete with them—though they apparently thought that children would benefit from their mothers' ability to read Cicero in the original Latin! Both men and women believed that there were male areas and female areas of learning: mathematics and science for men, domestic and cultural arts for women. Spheres of knowledge, like spheres of life, were defined along sex lines.

Mount Holyoke, often regarded as the oldest woman's school in the nation, opened its doors in 1837. Mary Lyon, its founder and spunky leader, envisioned an institution where women would get a truly well-rounded education, not mere training for domesticity. Prior to 1837, she traveled around the countryside for three years in order to raise the money she needed, appearing at church meetings, sewing bees, and farmers' homes. The original financial endowment for the college was actually made up of small contributions from neighboring farmers. Once the college was established, at South Hadley, Massachusetts, Mary Lyon encouraged able and interested young women from all economic groups to study there, and she extended the traditional two-year seminary term to three years. Mount Holyoke under her direction was a worthy model for the superior women's colleges that developed after the Civil War.

But Mount Holyoke by itself could hardly change the general public's views on women's education. Most people continued to assume that young girls went to college to prepare for married

Mt. Holyoke Female Seminary, 1836. (Culver)

life, and that the only women who became professional educators were those who had unfortunately lost their chance for matrimony. Naturally, no married women would pursue a career, since marriage itself was a full-time occupation.

As late as 1940, this same point of view was expressed implicitly by historian William Sprague:

> The lady who was to perform a great role in the progress of western education, by making it possible for many young women of this class to teach in the new states, was Miss Catharine Esther Beecher (1800–1878).
>
> The early eighteen-twenties had found this oldest sister of Henry Ward Beecher and Mrs. Harriet Beecher Stowe engaged to the young and energetic Yale professor, Mr. Alexander Metcalf Fisher. But he perished in 1822, when the ship on which he was bound for Europe was lost at sea. Miss Beecher, therefore, prepared for a teaching career, and soon opened the Hartford Female Seminary.

Probably, given the cultural expectations of the day, Catharine Beecher *did* choose her career only after losing her chance for marriage. To all women, except the rare and unusual ones, marriage was the be-all and end-all of their lives. When Elizabeth Cady Stanton combined marriage with professional lecturing and crusading, she became one of a very small minority of married women who successfully juggled two full-time jobs. But teaching and "respectable" writing were among the few socially approved professions for single women.

Catharine Beecher opposed women's suffrage while Elizabeth Cady Stanton supported it. Mrs. Stanton recalled in her memoir one discussion with Miss Beecher on this subject:

> Catharine said she was opposed to woman suffrage, and if she thought there was the least danger of our getting it, she would write and talk against it vehemently. But, as the nation was safe against such a calamity, she was willing to let the talk go on, because the agitation helped her work. "It is rather paradoxical," I said to her, "that the pressing of a false principle can help a true one; but when you get the women all thoroughly educated, they will step off to the polls and vote in spite of you."

Women Writers

One field in which educated young women could express themselves was literature. Writing fiction for the moral uplift of
women readers was considered respectable work, and many
best-selling American novelists in the years between the Revolution and the Civil War were women. Their fiction seemed to
follow a certain general pattern. The beautiful heroine, yearning
and long-suffering, consumed by strong emotions and inner conflicts, paid dearly for any sexual indiscretion she committed.
Women loved these romantic novels, which provided them with
the vicarious excitement lacking in their own lives. While men
satisfied their fantasy needs by reading sea stories and frontier
tales, women read about the lost loves of a beautiful girl.

The first American best-seller was Susanna Rowson's
Charlotte Temple (Philadelphia, 1794), a novel that went
through two hundred editions and had innumerable imitators.
Charlotte Temple, a well-meaning but weak young woman, put
her trust in a scoundrel who seduced, impregnated, and abandoned her. She bore an illegitimate child and died repentant
shortly thereafter. Women loved reading about Charlotte's trials,
tribulations, and downfall. They empathized with her suffering
but agreed that immoral women had to be penalized for their
sinful behavior. None of them challenged the established mores
or questioned the morality of a society that punished the woman
but let the man go free. Few even wondered whether the whole
moral code did not need reexamination.

Though almost no one today knows the names of Fanny Fern,
Susan Warner, and Maria Susanna Cummins, these women
wrote more books, read by more people, than Herman Melville,
Nathaniel Hawthorne, and Henry David Thoreau. Fanny Fern's
romantic fiction sold hundreds of thousands of copies.

AMERICAN BEST-SELLERS BY
WOMEN NOVELISTS

1794–1860

1794: *Charlotte Temple: A Tale of Truth* by Susanna Haswell
Rowson
1794: *Mysteries of Udolpho* by Ann Radcliffe
1797: *The Coquette* by Hannah Foster

1803:   *Thaddeus of Warsaw* by Jane Porter
1810:   *The Scottish Chiefs* by Jane Porter
1815:   *Moral Pieces in Prose and Verse* by Lydia Huntley Sigourney
1828:   *Lucy Temple* by Susanna Haswell Rowson
1836:   *Awful Disclosures* by Maria Monk
1847:   *Home Influence: A Tale for Mothers and Daughters* by Grace Aguilar
1850:   *Greenwood Leaves* by Grace Greenwood
1850:   *The Wide, Wide World* by Elizabeth Wetherell (Susan Warner)
1851:   *The Sunny Side; or The Country Minister's Wife* by Elizabeth Stuart Phelps
1852:   *The Curse of Clifton* by Mrs E.D.E.N. Southworth
1852:   *Uncle Tom's Cabin* by Harriet Beecher Stowe
1853:   *Fern Leaves from Fanny's Portfolio* by Fanny Fern
1853:   *A Key to Uncle Tom's Cabin* by Harriet Beecher Stowe
1853:   *Heir of Redclyffe* by Charlotte Mary Yonge
1854:   *The Lamplighter* by Maria Susanna Cummins
1854:   *The Newsboy* by Elizabeth Oakes Smith
1855:   *Ruth Hall* by Fanny Fern
1856:   *John Halifax, Gentleman* by Dinah Maria Mulock
1859:   *Beulah* by Augusta Jane Evans
1859:   *The Hidden Hand* by Mrs. E.D.E.N. Southworth
1860:   *Malaeska, or The Indian Wife of the White Hunter* by Ann Sophia Stephens

In 1853, people bought 70,000 copies of *Fern Leaves from Fanny's Portfolio*. While Nathaniel Hawthorne lamented the paltry royalties he received for his book *Mosses from an Old Manse*, Susan Warner smiled happily over a $4,500 royalty check for six months' sales of *The Wide, Wide World*.

The fiction of the popular women writers was not of high literary quality, and this was why it did not endure. But it had a very important social function: it confirmed the moral values of the culture. While the women activist-reformers tried to change values, the women writers spoke for the majority and enforced the traditional social attitudes. Christian virtues were always upheld; sin was punished and virtue rewarded. Wayward behavior always led to evil consequences, and the Lord's approval or dis-

Frontispiece of novelist Fanny Fern's most popular offering. (Culver)

approval was personally experienced. Hawthorne may have written brilliantly about sin and retribution in *The Scarlet Letter*, but readers preferred a less weighty novel—Maria Cummins' *The Lamplighter*, a heart-rending story about an orphan girl that sold 40,000 copies in eight weeks. Mrs. E.D.E.N. Southworth, perhaps the most popular nineteenth-century woman writer, wrote a few romances a year and earned an annual income of $10,000. Her novel *The Hidden Hand, or, Capitola the Madcap* became an immediate best-seller.

Women writers, then, gained an economic independence and a power over their own lives that were unknown to most of their women readers. Frequently, they began to write out of economic necessity and, if they had a knack for this kind of fiction, found their efforts well rewarded. Some of them were middle-class wives who had time on their hands and took to writing as an outlet for their surplus energy.

Just as individualism was preached at every Fourth of July

144

celebration and by every politician at election time, so women writers assured their readers that there was an all-seeing God in heaven, that virtue was indeed rewarded—if not on earth, then in the next world—and that each individual was an important person whose behavior was noted. Their novels also confirmed the society's prejudices and long-held biases against deprived groups. In *Henrietta,* by one Harriet Scott, it is discovered that the heroine, who is about to be married, has Indian blood. The intended husband's mother, symbolizing the society at large, thinks to herself:

> Could anything be more horrible than for John to have children, her grandchildren, running about with a penchant for ornaments, for feathers, and for tomahawks!

The primitivism of this belief, popularly held in the nineteenth century, aptly illustrates the backwardness of so-called cultured people. Most white Americans thought that Indians passed on their ability to use a tomahawk to their children, in the same way that whites passed on the color of their eyes or hair. Bearing this notion in mind, we find it easy to understand why white Americans assumed that all black people inherited the ability to sing the blues and dance rhythmically, and that all Italian immigrants had the biologically engendered tendency to gesture with their hands. Whenever the majority wanted to degrade a particular minority, all they had to do was claim that some negative cultural trait was inherited and therefore unchangeable. It has been the task of reformers in each generation to convince the majority that group behavior is determined largely by environment, not heredity.

In this sense, the women writers supported both the prejudices and the ignorance of the dominant society. Further, their novels afforded a pleasant escape from unpleasant reality. Since their message was essentially conservative, it also provided readers with a neat, predictable universe. There were no surprise endings. The formula was known to all, and its success was based precisely on this fact. Readers did not want surprises, such as villains escaping or vice rewarded. In real life, those undesirable things occurred; in fiction, the world was more reasonable, just, and moral.

The most famous in her time and perhaps the most famous

American writer was Harriet Beecher Stowe (1811–1896). Her *Uncle Tom's Cabin,* published in 1852, did supply shocks and surprises, yet it became an immediate best-seller both in this country and abroad, selling 300,000 copies the first year. Written in serial episodes for a magazine, Mrs. Stowe's powerful, dramatic story made readers weep over the outrageous treatment accorded slaves. Though her personal knowledge of slavery was slight, her vivid imagination created a touching portrait of long-suffering slave Uncle Tom, of slaves George and Eliza who escaped, and of the villainous Simon Legree. Readers from far-off places wrote letters to Mrs. Stowe, and President Lincoln met her in 1861. Some people gave her credit, or blame, for starting the Civil War. In any case, her novel was a statement of moral indignation, one that attracted sympathetic responses from readers who had been ignorant of the ways of slavery. Mrs. Stowe continued to write novels, essays, and poems for many years, and all were enthusiastically received.

Woman's Darker Side

The subject of woman's sexuality was never openly discussed in the nineteenth century. After all, the moral custodian of the home was not expected to become concerned with such an evil matter as sex. For another interesting paradox in the American people's attitudes was already deeply established. It was acknowledged that woman's strongly sensual nature had tempted Adam (and all men since Adam) to sin but also, on the other hand, that woman's delicacy and morality prevented her from even thinking about sexual matters. (No one ever explained how both positions could be equally tenable.) The genteel woman of the nineteenth century—an ideal person whom middle- and upper-class women strove to emulate—knew little about her own reproductive system, less about the crucial matters of birth control and conception, and still less about the natural sexual feelings she experienced.

The culture deemed this the proper state of mind for women. Sexuality was man's domain, and serious unhealthy consequences were in store for the man who did not express his sexual feelings—within the matrimonial bonds, of course. Doctors con-

Harriet Beecher Stowe; her novel of slavery upset many readers. (Culver)

tributed to the general ignorance by accepting the view that woman's body was a mystery. Modesty, along with social inhibitions, prevented most women from ever being examined by a male doctor. No research on woman's physiology was done, so the mid-nineteenth-century woman had no way of learning about her body.

The birth control information available in that period was inadequate at best and thoroughly inaccurate at worst. The two most widely read books on birth control were Robert Dale Owen's *Moral Physiology* (1830) and Charles Knowlton's *Fruits of Philosophy* (1832). Owen recommended *coitus interruptus* as the most effective method of birth control, while Knowlton invented elaborate douching solutions of green tea, alum, zinc, or raspberry leaves for women to use after sexual intercourse. But Knowlton was "quite confident that a liberal use of pretty cold water would be a never-failing preventative." It goes without saying that neither man knew anything about effective birth control techniques, although Knowlton is to be credited with the suggestion that women had the right to control conception and should learn proper methods of doing so. On the men's side, let it be said that the vulcanization of rubber in 1843 led to a more durable condom. Men had used various sheaths from time immemorial but the rubber condom, thanks to Goodyear and Hancock, became a very popular birth control device.

Despite the myth of motherhood as the most desirable and holy state for womankind, many women tried desperately to prevent conception. The letters and diaries of mid-nineteenth-century wives reveal their anxiety over the risks of childbearing. There were many self-inflicted abortions. No wonder women dreaded sexual intercourse when the inevitable result seemed to be pregnancy. And no wonder they often resorted to abstinence—much to their husbands' dismay—as the safest and surest form of birth control.

The great majority of women, as we know, married; they endured (rarely enjoyed) sexual relations as their matrimonial duty. A few, however, did not marry because they were repelled by the prospect of a constant series of pregnancies. Such women might have been diagnosed by twentieth-century doctors and psychoanalysts as frigid, but any nineteenth-century woman would have informed them that she had been instructed, from childhood on, that sexual feelings were evil and must be re-pressed. Women were under obligation to satisfy their husbands sexual needs, but they were not expected to enjoy or participate equally in sexual relations.

A few liberated women in the first half of the nineteenth century spoke out for equal sexual rights. Among them was Frances Wright (1795–1852), a lively, attractive woman who was often condemmed as wild and irresponsible—what other kind of woman would entertain such eccentric and dangerous notions? Since her parents died while she was a child, she was raised in England by an aunt. She came to the United States the first time in the 1810s and wrote a popular book about her travels here. In 1828–1829, she lectured on women's rights and the need for women to be educated.

Her lectures convinced her critics that she was an atheist and free lover. She contributed to this impression by living in the utopian community at New Harmony, Indiana, for a while and then forming her own community in Nashoba, Tennessee. There she ran a plantation on which slaves were allowed to buy their freedom through their earnings. This action caused a great con-troversy and convinced still more people that she was a danger-ous radical. In fact, "Fanny Wrightists" became an insulting phrase used by critics of women's rights reformers.

Most women, of course, shared the culture's views about themselves. They feared change, did not dare to explore their bodies, and never rebelled against a male-dominated society that blamed them for introducing sin into the world. Wifehood and motherhood were, after all, sacred professions, sanctioned by parents, friends, preachers, and politicians alike. Who would dare challenge the system? As a result, the cloud of ignorance surrounding woman's physiological nature remained into the twentieth century. Generations of women felt either overt or covert disgust at the nasty business of sexual intercourse, and never understood the mysterious stirrings within themselves that they occasionally experienced. The birthrate declined sig-nificantly in nineteenth-century America. Whether by design and/or chance, families were smaller, and women's lives changed accordingly. But the definition of woman's role re-mained the same, as did the unbroken silence regarding woman's sexuality.

149

The Moral Anchor

In the home and in the lecture hall, women were generally acknowledged to be the moral anchors of society. As mother, woman inculcated in her children the accepted religious values and ethical principles of her day. As wife, she obeyed her husband and followed his lead. As activist-reformer, she reminded her audiences and readers of the immorality in their midst. And as giver of charity, she extended aid to the needy. In all these functions, women fulfilled society's expectations of them, but when they tried to use their moral energy to gain acceptance of themselves as equals, they were politely or rudely shunned. Those who dared to leave home and march for worthy causes were often admired for their character and courage, but not for their advocacy of equal rights for their sex.

The moralists of this period were listened to, but their words did not lead to action. Abolitionists aroused much interest in the problem of slavery, but they did not incite Northerners to wage war on Southerners; other factors caused the Civil War. The feminists did not change American attitudes toward women, nor did the graduates of women's colleges go out and revolutionize society. Women may have had superior moral power, but they were unable to use that power to gain equality for themselves —or for anyone else.

Suggestions for Further Reading

Ruth Finley. *The Lady of Godey's* (Philadelphia, 1931).

Eleanor Flexner. *Century of Struggle* (New York, 1973, paperback).

Willystine Goodsell. *Pioneers of Women's Education in the United States* (New York, 1931).

Sarah Grimké. *Letters on the Equality of the Sexes and the Condition of Women* (Boston, 1838).

James D. Hart. *The Popular Book: A History of America's Literary Taste* (New York, 1950).

Mae E. Harveson. *Catharine Beecher: A Pioneer Educator* (Philadelphia, 1932).

Elinor P. Hays. *Morning Star: A Biography of Lucy Stone* (New York, 1961).

Gerda Lerner. *The Grimké Sisters of South Carolina* (Boston, 1967).

Suggestions for Further Reading

The Letters of Theodore Weld, Angelina Grimké Weld and Sarah Grimké, 1822–1844 (New York, 1934).

Alma Lutz. *Created Equal: A Biography of Elizabeth Cady Stanton* (New York, 1940).

Alma Lutz. *Emma Willard* (Boston, 1929).

Perry Miller, editor. *Margaret Fuller: American Romantic* (New York, 1963).

Mabel Newcomer. *A Century of Higher Education for American Women* (New York, 1959).

Helen Papashvily. *All the Happy Endings* (New York, 1956).

Elizabeth Cady Stanton. *Eighty Years and More* (New York, 1971).

Barbara Welter. "The Cult of True Womanhood, 1820–1860," *American Quarterly*, XVIII (Summer 1966).

CHAPTER SEVEN

The More Things Change, the More Things Stay the Same
1861–1880

Just before the battle, Mother,
I am thinking most of you,
While upon the field we're watching
With the enemy in view,
Comrades brave are 'round me lying
Filled with thoughts of home and God,
For well they know that on the morrow
Some will sleep beneath the sod.
Farewell, Mother, you may never
Press me to your breast again;
But, oh, you'll not forget me, Mother,
If I'm numbered with the slain.

    —George F. Root, Civil War song

Gonna lay down my sword and shield,
Down by the riverside,
Down by the riverside,
Down by the riverside.
Gonna lay down my sword and shield,
Down by the riverside.

I ain't gonna study war no more,
I ain't gonna study war no more,
I ain't gonna study war no more.

    —Negro spiritual

Whan hit come ter de question er de female vote,
De ladies an' de culled folks is in de same boat.
Ef de Boss feelin' good, an' we eats out his han',
We kin shout fur freedom, an' foller de ban'.

The More Things Change . . . 1861–1880

We kin play at freedom, so long's we play.
But ef we gits thinkin', an' comes out an' say:
Case one's borned a female, an' one's borned black,
Is dat any reason fur sottin' [sitting] way back?
Is dat any reason fur sottin, da-put? [staying put]
You kin betcher bottom dollar dat de Boss's fut
Gwine ter sprout big claws, till dey comes clar thoo,
An' he climps hit heavy on bofe us two.
Case de tears er do mudder, nur de sign, er de cross,
Ain't shame all de debbil yit, outen de Boss!

—Rosalie Jonas, *Brother Baptis' on Woman Suffrage*

*T*he year 1861 provides an unhappy but essen-

Civil War

tial break in U.S. history. It was the year when war, civil war, overtook Americans. It signified the failure of negotiations and of human reasonableness. All wars are cruel, but civil war is crueler than any other. It forces families and friends to fight one another and citizens of the same country to kill one another. In America, an artificial geographical boundary separated the warring states: though southern Illinois had cultural and familial ties with the South, the state itself was part of the North. Branches of the same family found themselves fighting on opposite sides. Northerners who were sympathetic toward the Southerners' right to autonomy had conflicting loyalties. So did Southerners who secretly hated slavery and wanted to see it abolished.

When Fort Sumter, the federal military post, was attacked by Southerners on April 12, 1861, the Northern states had two rational choices open to them: they could accept the secession of the thirteen states which eventually organized as the Confederacy, or they could fight to require the readmission of these states to the Union. Abraham Lincoln, whose election to the presidency was a major reason for the South's actions, believed in the indivisibility of the United States of America. Thus he chose the second option, and the result was civil war. Never before had a war occurred between Americans. Indeed, most people could recall only one war in recent memory—the Mexican War of 1846–1848, in which the United States arrogantly seized territory from the Mexicans.

Americans, then, had no idea how devastating and horrible war could be. But they learned that bitter lesson in the four long years of the Civil War. The Southerners called it, and many still do, the War Between the States—a neutral designation that removed the onus of responsibility from the South but ignored the dramatic destruction of the body politic that a civil war can cause. The South had always maintained the priority of states' rights above national rights. The North took this opportunity to assert the principle of federalism, once and for all.

The human cost of the Civil War was enormous on both sides: more than 500,000 Americans died. By way of contrast, the total number of deaths in twentieth-century wars—World Wars I and II, the Korean War, and the Vietnam War—totaled 626,161. About 30,000 Confederate soldiers died in Northern prison camps. The tragedy of these tremendous human losses was so great that families of the dead kept reliving the war experience through the 1880s, the 1890s, and well into this century. Especially the Southerners. The white population of the South was smaller than that of the North, and the loss of 160,000 men was deeply felt. The North lost 364,000, but because of its larger population, and also its victory, was better able to support that loss.

The North won the war—that was the final bitter tragedy for the South. Southerners had lost their loved ones in vain. Their cause, its justness, had not been vindicated but repudiated. And in the Reconstruction period after the war, in which they were constantly reminded of their loss, the South created a number of myths—a myth of valor, of nobility, of selfless devotion to a lost cause—to assuage their hurt pride. They convinced themselves that they had been defeated only because of superior Northern manpower and industrial power, not because the North had justice on its side. The South never asked for forgiveness, never acknowledged that slavery, the institution it fought to defend, was an evil.

Because the war was unprecedented, no one knew how long it would last or even how it would proceed. The new President had to improvise and create agencies to handle wartime responsibilities. The Southern states hastily organized a new government in recognition of their status as a separate entity. It took months for each side to mobilize an army, gather war materials, and recruit military and civil leaders. The North had distinct advantages: its superior industrial capacity, its railroad system, and its large number of farmers who could provide needed food.

Free Northern blacks fought with the white Union troops, while Southern blacks were not allowed in the Confederate army. The first year was bleak for the Union because its soldiers were badly trained, but they improved with time and experience. The South had good military leaders but few of the other vital resources needed to win a war.

To most people, the real cause of the war was unclear. Northerners did not want to fight their Southern compatriots over black slaves. But white Southerners were uneasy about Lincoln's election because the previous forty years had seen a gradual erosion of Southern influence in the U.S. Congress. Political power, so crucial to favorable legislative policies, had slipped away from them. Long gone were the days of the Virginia dynasty, when Presidents Jefferson, Madison, and Monroe had reigned in Washington. Representation in Congress was heavily weighted in favor of the North. The new states of the Northwest now outnumbered the new Southern states, and the population of New England and the Middle West was vastly greater than that of the South.

It became harder and harder for Southerners to withstand the criticism of the abolitionists, the unfavorable tariff policies in Washington, and the widening chasm between a slave and a non-slave system. Boldly taking the lead, South Carolina seceded from the Union, followed by other Southern states. Jefferson Davis became president of the new Confederacy, a form of government that granted each state equal power. Though no one knew what the outcome of secession would be, many Southerners felt exhilarated by their decisive action. The South, they ardently believed, would prove its right to be an independent nation, with its own values, socioeconomic standards, and culture. After all, it was not inevitable that this great continent should support only one nation; on the continent of Europe many countries existed side by side. The Confederacy could coexist with the Union, two independent nations on the same land mass.

One Nation—Indivisible?

The power of ideas was readily demonstrated in Americans' belief that the United States was a holy entity, "one nation, indivis-

157

ible, with liberty and justice for all." The building of that nation, which began in 1776, took several generations; but by 1860 few doubted the existence, and the inviolable right to existence, of the United States of America. During the early administrations, nationalists had fought against advocates of a looser union —Hamilton's vision of a centralized commercial, manufacturing nation had won over Jefferson's dream of a decentralized nation of farmers. Other Southerners, in Jefferson's time and in later generations, doubted the efficacy of "one nation, indivisible." The elaborate political philosophy developed in the 1830s by John C. Calhoun expressed this problem directly.

> There is . . . but one mode in which this can be effected, and that is by taking the sense of each interest or portion of the community which may be unequally and injuriously affected by the action of the government separately, through its own majority or in some other way by which its voice may be fairly expressed. . . .

Calhoun argued that majority rule could harm the vital interests of one section (the South) and the only way to guard against that is to allow each region to have a voice in government matters.

Generally, however, the nationalists had their way. They imposed the same political structure upon all regions of the country, ignoring the significant cultural differences in the South. They demanded conformity to the Constitution and to all channels of federal government and law. Thus when South Carolina defied the Union, the nationalists, led by Abraham Lincoln, insisted on its preservation. In a sense, this absolute conviction of the rightness of the one-nation concept was carried into future wars, in which Americans fought for their country's form of government.

Whoever initiates a war—the President, the Congress, the military establishment—must always give the populace adequate reasons for doing so. In the case of the Civil War, these had to do with preserving the nation; in later wars, with bringing democratic nationalism to others. These reasons have always seemed sufficient. Rarely did a citizen of the North ask himself in 1861: "How will life in this nation be affected if the South secedes? Surely the present United States will be destroyed, but could not a new nation, carved out of the New England and

Middle Western states, be devised?" As for the other reason —bringing democracy to undemocratic nations—few Americans have wondered how any war could create the institutions and attitudes necessary to achieve new democracy in an old land. How could battles convert Spanish-held Cuba to democracy? How could war preserve and extend democracy in the countries of Europe or Asia? The power of our nationalism and our democracy is so great that Americans have accepted and never questioned the belief that their country is the most democratic one of all. Especially during the Civil War, there was no time for reflecting on the purpose and value of war, or for carefully examining the virtues of nationalism.

Another Myth: The Glory of War

Both sides entered the Civil War with romantic notions. Both believed that war itself had some positive virtues: it tested the contestants' manliness and brought out the masculine traits of valor and courage. Stephen Crane's *The Red Badge of Courage*, written after the war, effectively contrasted these false values with the real horrors of war. Yet prior to the Civil War and ever since, men continued to laud war as a maturing experience and an opportunity to show one's strength. Even at the end of the nineteenth century, Theodore Roosevelt rejoiced in the Spanish-American War because it gave him a chance to display his military and manly talents.

Men have always associated war with masculine characteristics. How impoverished the male imagination must be, we may well wonder, if it can find no other setting in which to demonstrate courage and valor. Are there no peaceful activities that can arouse these qualities? But for some reason, deeply rooted in what we call civilization, men have always felt that their physical nature, their size and strength, require testing, and war has provided the ultimate proof of prowess. Related to this is the idea that aggressive behavior, in the name of honor, family, and nation, is a virtuous form of action; fighting to preserve family traditions is noble and brave.

The whole romantic mystique of suffering for a cause fits into this mythology of manliness and warfare. Being wounded in battle was somehow considered an ennobling experience, dying

159

for one's country a glorious way of ending one's life. In the nineteenth century, individual sacrifice was the theme of many popular novels. A woman became a self-sacrificing heroine by languishing away because of unrequited love, while a man became a self-sacrificing hero by dying in battle. Some psychologists believe that people who habitually sacrifice themselves are haunted by unconscious guilt and self-hatred, and welcome suffering because it punishes them for some unknown crime. How else can one explain the willingness of endless generations of men to risk their lives for abstract concepts?

Many men in 1861, then, looked upon war as a super game, a sporting match, in which they could test their physical prowess, their manly ability to survive. This splendid game had its elaborate rituals and codes of gentlemanly conduct, its own rules and customs. How disillusioned and shattered were the true believers of this myth during the Civil War! The four-year slaughter was not glamorous or thrilling; its excitement was made up of panic and terror. Rifles mutilated bodies, and many one-armed and one-legged men lived on into the 1880s to remind Americans of war's tragic consequences.

The technology of war—the only aspect of it that has "progressed" throughout human history—improved continually over the four years. Gunpowder manufacturers and gun-makers worked constantly to create better and more effective ways to kill. Advanced artillery techniques, exploding shells, and more accurate rifles all were produced. While the cavalry still carried battle swords into the field, the foot soldiers faced their opponents with deadlier rifles. Indeed, one of the direst consequences of industrialization has been the stream of ever more horrible mass-produced weapons of destruction.

Women and the War

Due to the nature of this "new" war, all available human resources had to be fully used. Because of this pragmatic necessity, women were put to work at jobs never open to them in peacetime. During the course of each of our American wars, women have been told how valuable they are, how important their services are to the winning of the war. Their patriotism, courage, and loyalty are widely praised. The praise, however, is always short-lived. As soon as the hostilities end, so do the compliments and the jobs. Duties performed by women during wartime revert to males after the war, throwing women out of the job market. This pattern, established during the Civil War, has continued ever since. True, some women have managed to remain employed in peacetime (and their numbers have increased), but their jobs have usually been the lowest paid, with the least status.

Women contributed a great deal in the Civil War. Not only did they carry on their normal responsibilities, but they often had to assume their husbands' or brothers' tasks as well. In addition, women in every community folded bandages, preserved fruits for the soldiers, and sent medicines to the wounded. Through volunteer organizations, they performed many of the functions later assumed by the Red Cross. The U.S. Sanitary Commission was created, largely by the efforts of women, to supervise hospitals, provide supplies for the wounded, recruit nurses, and develop convalescent homes. In earlier wars, the government had made no provision for its wounded soldiers. Army infantrymen who were injured fighting Indians or Mexicans often died on the battlefield. During the Civil War, women pressured the politicians in Washington to set up hospitals and medical facilities for treating wounded soldiers.

But conditions in these hospitals were far from ideal, since medical science had not yet recognized the need for sanitation. A surgeon would wear the same white medical coat until it was entirely covered by caked blood, and would never wash his hands before performing surgery. No effort was made to sterilize an operating room or its equipment. As a result, many soldiers who had escaped death on the battlefield died of infection in the hospital.

Mary Logan, the wife of army officer John A. Logan of Illinois (later senator of the state), accompanied her husband to an army camp located on a river near Cairo, Illinois. She described it:

> Often it was deluged by overflows, whose waters stagnated in every depression and were soon covered by a green scum, almost cutting it off from the highlands by that dismal swamp. . . . Ague and other diseases from miasmatic influences frightened away many who came to make their homes and fortunes there.

Mary A. Livermore (seated, center) poses with other officers and nurses of the Sanitary Commission at Fredericksburg, 1864. (Culver)

Another Mary, Mary Livermore of Chicago, became the leader of the Northwest district of the U.S. Sanitary Commission. She displayed great talent as an organizer, and supervised the packing and distribution of vast quantities of food and medical supplies to the various hospitals located in the Northwest. Before the Civil War had ended, the Commission had organized 7,000 local societies and had spent $50,000,000. Mary Livermore enlisted the aid of countless women who made bandages and sewed clothing and wrote letters to the soldiers—like this one:

My Dear Friend,

You are not my husband or son; but you are the husband or son of some woman who undoubtedly loves you as I love mine. I have made these garments for you with a heart that aches for your sufferings, and with a longing to come to you to assist in taking care of you. . . .

162

One of the most flamboyant women leaders during the Civil War was still another Mary: Mary Ann Bickerdyke, known affectionately to many soldiers as Mother Bickerdyke. When the war began, she went to the smallpox hospital in Cairo, Illinois, to help improve conditions there. She started by washing and scrubbing everything in sight, thereby antagonizing the entire hospital staff. When a surgeon tried to throw her out, she counter-threatened to report his drunkenness to the proper authorities. Mrs. Bickerdyke won this battle as well as many others. Besides discovering the filthy conditions, she also found that staff members were pilfering food and supplies. One day when she saw the ward-master wearing clothes sent to the wounded by the Sanitary Commission, she grabbed him and made him disrobe! As the number of her assertive acts increased, so did the complaints from the largely incompetent staff, men who did not want a meddling female around. When General Sherman received one such complaint, he retorted, "Well, I can do nothing for you; she outranks me."

For the first time, women nurses staffed the army hospitals. The noted reformer Dorothea Dix, sixty years old, was appointed superintendent of women nurses for the U.S. Army. At the glorious salary of forty cents a day, women with strong backs, plain in

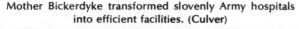

Mother Bickerdyke transformed slovenly Army hospitals
into efficient facilities. (Culver)

appearance, and over thirty years old were recruited into the nursing corps. Their dresses "must be brown or black, with no bows, no curls, or jewelry, and no hoop skirts." These plainly clad nurses witnessed many of the battles, as the hospitals were often set up close to the field of action.

Mary Livermore visited many hospitals on an inspection tour for the U.S. Sanitary Commission. Her description of one of them vividly captures the horrid conditions there:

> It was a miserable place. . . . The cots were placed inside the tents, on unplanked ground. The soil was so dropsical that wherever one trod, it sank under one's weight, and one immediately stood in a little puddle of water. . . . The hospital swarmed with large green flies, and their buzzing was like that of a beehive. . . . Many of them [the patients] did not lift their hands to brush away the flies that swarmed into eyes, ears, noses and mouths.

Mrs. Livermore was responsible for the cleaning and equipping of every hospital on the Mississippi River. She urged the acquisition of hospital boats, and many lives must have been saved as a result of her great work. Mother Bickerdyke, who also became famous for her hospital activities at Cairo, Huntsville, and Memphis, went to Fort Donelson, Shiloh, and Chickamauga, and accompanied General Sherman on his march to the sea.

In a war where battle casualties were very high, the work of the U.S. Sanitary Commission and the army corps of nurses cannot be underestimated. Ten thousand men were wounded at Antietam alone. But without the contributions of such women as Mary Livermore and Mother Bickerdyke, and such organizations as the Sanitary Commission, the death rate in the Civil War would have been even higher. Because of the women's efforts, the government assumed responsibility for the care of the wounded men. Indeed, whatever humaneness and human-ness was expressed during the war was due to women. Their accomplishments cannot be fully measured—or fully appreciated.

Histories of the Civil War give short shrift to woman's role in it; yet without her labors, the very inhumanity of the conflict would have been intensified beyond comprehension. Abraham Lincoln, though initially apprehensive about the value of the Sanitary Commission and the part played by women in the war, later made this full-hearted acknowledgment:

164

I am not accustomed to use the language of eulogy. I have never studied the art of paying compliments to women. But I must say that, if all that had been said by orators and poets since the creation of the world in praise of women was applied to the women of America, it would not do them justice for their conduct during the war. I will close by saying, God Bless the Women of America!

For many women, especially those who had been active in earlier reform movements, the war provided an opportunity to continue their good works. Many were restless, eager to do something constructive. Elizabeth Cady Stanton, for example, felt somewhat out of sorts at the start of the war because she could not find a place for herself in the new effort. Eventually, she organized the Woman's Loyalty League, which propagandized for the passage of the emancipation amendment, the Thirteenth. Through her efforts, plus those of Susan B. Anthony and their countless helpers, petitions bearing 400,000 names were presented to Congress in support of the amendment. Just as these women had accumulated thousands of signatures in favor of the abolition of slavery, so they repeated the process to insure the emancipation of the slaves.

Louisa May Alcott, destined for fame as the author of *Little Women*, wrote in her journal in 1862:

Thirty years old. Decided to go to Washington as nurse if I could find a place. Help needed, and I love nursing, and *must* let out my pent-up energy in some new way.... I want new experiences....

Women wanted to share with men the great experiences of life, even experiences of war, death, and destruction. Nursing was a respectable way for energetic girls to be useful in a time of crisis, and to escape the restrictive environment of their homes and their predictable lives. Young men went off to battle hoping for opportunities to prove their valor; young women became nurses, hospital volunteers, and workers in community organizations for much the same reason.

One woman who actually assumed a "manly" role during the war was Harriet Tubman (1823–1913), the runaway slave who before the war led three hundred slaves out of the South by the Underground Railroad. Now she became an unofficial spy and scout for the Union Army. In June 1863, she led a band of black soldiers up the Combahee River in South Carolina, burning plantations and freeing more than eight hundred slaves. Her behavior was bold, courageous, and quite untypical of women's usual wartime role. But then Harriet Tubman, the Moses of her people, had always behaved extraordinarily.

She was born a slave in Maryland. When she was fifteen, an overseer threw an iron weight at her, causing a deep wound in her skull and periodic fainting spells that remained with her throughout her life. Though she married a free black man, she remained a slave. When her master died in 1849 and it seemed that she would be sold to another person, she begged her husband to run away to the North with her. He refused, and she escaped by herself.

Harriet then resolved to help other slaves gain their freedom. She became a "conductor" on the Underground Railroad—the secret route from the South to the free North. Staying in the homes of friendly Quakers along the way, traveling by night, wading through swamps, and risking her life endlessly, Harriet Tubman made nineteen round trips in ten years. She was personally responsible for saving 300 slaves. The white South offered a reward of $40,000 for her capture. No one ever collected it.

Harriet Tubman lived into her eighties. The U.S. Congress granted her a $20.00 month pension when she was eighty, a belated tribute to a great woman.

Just as the male sex regarded fighting and tests of bravery as acceptable manly pursuits, most members of the female sex conformed with society's view of their role, that of mothers and nurses in war and in peace. Since it had always been assumed that all women knew instinctively how to be nurses, there were no nursing schools in America in 1860. Another decade would pass before nursing became a profession for which formal schooling was required. In the Civil War, women were permitted to become nurses simply because nursing was an extension of the mothering role for which they were uniquely fitted.

Women created life and preserved it—so went the common belief—while men destroyed it. Is it not strange that men espoused this sex distinction and built a whole cultural system on it? Were not some men uncomfortable at being designated as killers? Were not some women desperately unhappy at the thought of producing a new life that men would eventually destroy?

166

Harriet Tubman, the Moses of her people. (Brown Bros.)

The More Things Change . . . 1861–1880

Among the War's Casualties

Walt Whitman, the poet, was a male nurse during the Civil War. His essay, "The Real War Will Never Get in the Books," told the unwritten story of the wounded soldiers on both sides:

> Future years will never know the seething hell and the black infernal background of countless minor scenes and interiors, (not the official surface-courteousness of the Generals, not the few great battles) of the Secession war; and it is best they should not—the real war will never get in the books. . . . I have at night watch'd by the side of a sick man in the hospital, one who could not live many more hours. I have seen his eyes flash and burn as he raised himself and recurr'd to the cruelties of his surrender'd brother, and mutilations of the corpse afterward. . . .

The civilians—men, women, and children—suffered during the war as well. Food was in short supply in certain regions, and what food was available often cost a great deal of money. Few farmhands were left to perform hard physical tasks. Anna Howard Shaw, the future suffrage leader, recalled that there were no men "to grind our corn, to get in our crops, or to care for our livestock; and all around us we saw our struggle reflected in the lives of our neighbors." The remarkable fact is how well those at home succeeded in keeping their families intact. The women endured constant physical hardships, while the children pitched in and performed adult chores. Older people helped in every way they could. Neighbors helped neighbors in a true cooperative spirit. It is another irony of human nature that only during stressful, difficult times do people so completely help one another.

All this applies to women in both the North and the South. Southern women, black and white, also managed their farms and assumed male responsibilities. Because many of the battles were fought in the South, they saw more destruction and violence, saw their homes ravaged and their farms destroyed. In some cities food was expensive and bread unavailable; there were bread riots in Richmond and Mobile. And fires swept through the larger Southern cities: Richmond, Columbia, Atlanta, and Charleston.

168

The Confederate government had more difficulty than Washington in raising both troops and taxes to carry on the war. Here the overly developed sense of states' rights, so supremely characteristic of the Southern states, militated against broad-scale cooperation. Virginia's troops, for example, would vigorously object to crossing the state's borders in order to help their brothers in a neighboring state. Furthermore, the transportation system in the South was still painfully inadequate, so that fresh supplies might never reach the army which desperately needed them.

The Civil War exhausted everyone on both sides. Americans were stunned by its length and incredibly high human loss. Its effects would be felt for generations to come. Thoughtful young men like William James and Oliver Wendell Holmes, Jr., who were coming of age during the war, changed their career plans as a result of the experience. Both had literary aspirations, but both became convinced that they must pursue professions through which they could serve others in those troubled times—medicine and the law. Human improvement, to the extent of eliminating future wars, might well come about through the efforts of lawyers and physicians.

Older men who had survived the war worried about its effects. To most Northerners, fearful of the migration of the blacks into their midst, the abolition of slavery portended evils that might even be greater than the evil of slavery. White Southerners, for their part, had not been convinced by the war that slavery was wrong or that the North had a right to impose its view upon them. And indeed most Northerners did not regard the war as an ideological conflict; they had fought to preserve the Union, not to end slavery.

The Confederate flag continued to fly in New Orleans after the Civil War. Stories about the bravery of the "men in gray" were told far and wide, and the rightness of their cause became confirmed in the minds and imaginations of many Southerners. The North tried to impose terms in a settlement that allowed the victor to decide the rules of the game, but it could not change Southern attitudes. For a brief period after 1865, the North sent troops to occupy sections of the South, but their presence did not convince the Southerners that there was, or ever had been, anything wrong with their way of life.

169

The Future of Black Americans

On the eve of the Civil War, blacks made up 14 per cent of the Southern population—or 4,441,830—and 4,000,000 of these were slaves. The war itself was not fought to abolish slavery, though many people thought it did, thus providing a rationale for the carnage. In fact, the many abolitionists and feminists who were also pacifists believed that emancipation, the noblest of causes, was the only justification for the war. At the outset, Susan B. Anthony and Elizabeth Cady Stanton became impatient when Lincoln did not immediately proclaim the freedom of the slaves. He did so in September 1862, with the Emancipation Proclamation, which was to be effective the following January. Thereafter the slaves in the rebel states were to be free.

During the course of the war, escaped slaves and free blacks in the North took an active part in the long struggle. Nearly a quarter-million of them enlisted in the Union Army and Navy, and the same number worked as laborers in the Union forces. Some 38,000 of them lost their lives. Blacks who stayed in the South maintained the plantations, continued to work the land, and displayed loyalty to their masters. Undoubtedly they hoped and prayed for freedom, but meanwhile, under the watchful eyes of suspicious whites, they went on obeying their masters' com-

Black Union soldiers during the Civil War battle of Milliken's Bend. (Brown Bros.)

mands. Such were their long-standing patterns of behavior. Yet when emancipation freed all four million slaves, it brought vast, far-sweeping changes not only to their lives but to the lives of the white people with whom they had lived for so many decades.

Now the evil of race prejudice replaced the evil of slavery. In the cities of the North, the freed blacks were publicly and privately rejected by hostile whites. In Philadelphia, where dozens of black regiments had fought on the Union side, Negroes were forbidden to ride on railroad coaches. A wounded black soldier, in a hospital at the edge of the city, could never be visited by his family because they could not ride on the train. At this same time, three black men were jailed because they refused to get off a streetcar. Republican Philadelphia, however, was the only large Northern city that barred blacks from public transportation, and fortunately the taboo did not last long. The city's black population protested so loudly that a revised city ordinance was passed, enabling black people to use public vehicles.

In the South, the freed slaves often returned to their former plantations simply because they were unable to earn a living in any other way. Many became sharecroppers on the same land, earning a modest share of the crops they had always cultivated. Some moved to the new Southern towns and cities and found better opportunities there. One black man, Jordan Anderson, who had moved to a town in western Tennessee, learned that his former owner wanted him to return to the plantation. He replied in a letter:

> I want to know particularly what the good chance is you propose to give me. I am doing tolerably well here. I get twenty-five dollars a month, with victuals and clothing; have a comfortable home for Mandy,—the folks call her Mrs. Anderson,—and the children—Milly, Jane, and Grundy—go to school and are learning well.

Anderson told his former master that he would return to the farm under one condition:

> . . . and we have concluded to test your sincerity by asking you to send us our wages for the time we served you. This will make us forget and forgive old scores, and rely on your justice and friendship in the future. I served you faithfully for thirty-two years, and Mandy

171

twenty years. At twenty-five dollars a month for me, and two dollars a week for Mandy, our earnings would amount to eleven thousand six hundred and eighty dollars. . . .

You can be sure that Colonel Martin, the owner, never answered Anderson's letter.

Status Quo Antebellum

Reconstruction was the term given the immediate post–Civil War period during which the war-devastated South had to be rebuilt, the moral fiber of the people rehabilitated, and freedom for the blacks confirmed. The task, surely an ambitious and a mighty one, was never achieved. White Southerners, unrepentant, worked zealously to regain their political and economic power. They quickly learned the rules of the new game—the peace settlement imposed by Congress—and conformed to them superficially. But once they had pledged allegiance to the Constitution they had earlier defied, they blithely ignored it. For a while, in some states, the presence of Northern troops reminded them of their defeat and their new subservience. But the troops stayed only long enough to permit some Southerners to exaggerate the trials of "oppression": how they were shamed by corrupt Northern carpetbaggers, treacherous white Southern scalawags, and incompetent blacks. The myth was propagated so successfully, in fact, that white Northerners became convinced of its truth.

One reason why the task of Reconstruction was so difficult was that President Lincoln and Congress could not agree on how and when the respective Southern states should be readmitted to the Union, nor on whether they should be punished for their disloyalty. Lincoln and his successor, Andrew Johnson, followed a conciliatory policy, as a means of uniting the country once again. Radicals in Congress, however, violently opposed this view. In 1866 they forced congressional passage of the Fourteenth Amendment, which not only gave the vote to black Americans but also prohibited payment of debts or losses to any Southerner who had worked or fought for the Confederacy. The amendment was really a retaliatory move after the South had enacted the so-called Black Codes, which restricted the rights of blacks almost to the point of restoring slavery.

Eventually the political struggles of the Reconstruction period came to an end, but a far more demanding job remained to be accomplished. New black citizens had to be educated to take their place in a free society, and the society itself had to change its behavior and attitudes toward them. As we know a century later, this could not happen instantly or miraculously. The Freedmen's Bureau, created by Congress to educate ex-slaves, needed money, dedicated teachers, and a lot of time to attain its goal. Meanwhile all the state legislatures had to examine their laws and remove discriminatory references to blacks. All the courts had to redress the grievances of black people. All white Americans had to learn, slowly and painfully, how to treat the blacks as fellow human beings.

This last step has yet to be fully achieved, even though a hundred years have passed. Achieving it immediately would have required a miracle, and that never took place, despite the new laws and three new amendments to the Constitution. The federal government lacked the commitment to enforce its new laws precisely because its administrators shared the attitudes of white Southerners.

Altering human behavior is a most difficult feat, but in the post–Civil War period (and after) a few enlightened persons worked tirelessly to accomplish it: white and black women teachers who went from the North to the South to educate former slaves; Southern black men and women who lived and worked with their newly freed sisters and brothers; and white business-men who employed blacks at the same wages as whites. Sadly, their influence was as small as their numbers—though if each had had the moral strength of ten the result would have been the same. For most white people believed that the war, however bloody and prolonged, had changed nothing: blacks were inferior—no act of Congress could alter that fact. This was the wisdom that Western culture had inculcated into white Ameri-cans.

Reformers were convinced, then as now, that education was the key to the problem. If people could learn about the needs and natures of those who were less privileged, less fortunate, how could they help responding with warmth and sympathy? All human beings were educable; when education failed, it was be-cause of faulty communication and lack of sufficient understand-ing. Any white person who had a chance to mingle with educated blacks would immediately appreciate their worth, and hence the worth of all black people. Reformers with a religious bent would emphasize that God's children come in many colors but all are God's creations and all deserve equal consideration.

The reformers' pleas and the preachers' sermons fell on deaf ears. White Southerners refused to accept the blame for the war and rejected the Northern solution to the race problem. Nor did the freed blacks change suddenly into well-educated, skilled workers. Forced to adopt different life patterns, many of them faced the new world with bewilderment and dismay.

Thus ended the period known as Reconstruction. The rebuilding of the South was a shallow and makeshift job which reused the old foundations and the same worn-out materials. No new designs and no new materials were introduced to build a new social structure.

The Woman's Movement

To some veterans of the abolitionist movement, women's rights and black equality had always been tied together, since both causes had become part of the same crusade for human equality. Politicians who were committed to the emancipation of the slaves, however, did not see it this way. They did not extend their concern to the rights of women, nor did many abolitionists, black and white. Black freedom was going to be hard enough to ensure without simultaneously working for women's freedom. So these experienced politicians and abolitionists counseled patience to the women activists, telling them their day would come—eventually. Elizabeth Cady Stanton and Susan B. Anthony, mindful of the promises made to them in previous years, were infuriated by the message of patience. Feminists had worked diligently and selflessly for black freedom for thirty years. Now that the slaves were emancipated, why delay further the successful completion of their own mission?

Their pleas were disregarded. The male abolitionists, totally occupied with translating the ways of slavery into the ways of freedom, wondered how the women could be so narrow-minded, so shortsighted and self-interested. Frederick Douglass, the leading black abolitionist, sympathized with Mrs. Stanton's concern and frustration but told her that blacks had to be assured of their freedom before the reformers could turn their attention to the women of both races. In 1869, the woman's movement split over this critical issue, and Mrs. Stanton and Miss Anthony formed a separate organization—the National Woman's Suffrage Association (NWSA). Veteran feminists Lucy Stone and Julia Ward Howe, author of the "Battle Hymn of the Republic," formed a rival organization—the American Woman's Suffrage Association (AWSA). For twenty years, the woman's movement was divided between these two organizations; then, in 1890, they united to form the National American Woman's Suffrage Association (NAWSA).

Reformers everywhere—being aggressive, intelligent, and stubborn—often spend more time fighting among themselves than uniting against the common enemy. This fact of human behavior characterized the woman's movement as well as most subsequent reform movements in America. Socialists, communists, abolitionists, feminists, ultra-conservatives, and the New Left have all been plagued by factionalism and divisiveness within their ranks. The 1869 split in the woman's movement was the result of both personality and philosophical differences between its two leaders, Elizabeth Cady Stanton and Lucy Stone. Mrs. Stanton, a thoroughgoing feminist, insisted that the focus be only on women's issues, which included suffrage, the divorce question, help for working women, and censure of the church for its unfeminist perspective. Lucy Stone, on the other hand—married to abolitionist Henry Blackwell and a veteran of the anti-slavery struggle—wanted to focus on woman's suffrage after the emancipation of the slaves had been accomplished. She did not want to deal with such socially explosive issues as divorce; neither did she wish to antagonize the church or any other institution that might support her cause.

Both Elizabeth Stanton and Lucy Stone (she always retained her maiden name) had strong personalities, and each asserted her position. Obviously, their views could not be espoused by the same organization at the same time, thus the breakup of the previously unified woman's movement. This was the more unfortunate because the talent, membership, money, and public support of the movement were cut in half. Furthermore, it drastically narrowed the focus of feminism.

While Mrs. Stanton, with her broad vision, continually reminded her workers and followers that suffrage was only one of

Lucy Stone became a symbol of independent womanhood to future generations. (Brown Bros.)

many social issues related to women's emancipation, Lucy Stone gave suffrage top priority. The fact that both new organizations had the word "Suffrage" in their names helped her to identify this as woman's primary goal. The public jumped to the conclusion that once women got the vote, the fight for equal rights would be over. By no means, Mrs. Stanton reminded them. The feminist whole was far greater than any of its parts: feminism implied a revolutionary change in all human roles and all human values. But her message went unheeded, and the generation of women coming of age in the 1860s identified the vote as the be-all and end-all of their crusade.

The suffragists (their critics called them "suffragettes" and spoke the word mockingly) worked vigorously, enthusiastically, and often vociferously for their cause. When women got the vote, they claimed, miracles would happen. Politics would suddenly be purified and society itself elevated to lofty levels. Political leaders, in the interest of gaining feminine support, would pass laws beneficial to humanity. Implicit in the preachings of the suffragists was an assumption that has been carried over to the current women's liberation movement: that women as a sex are somehow finer than men—more concerned for others and less greedy, competitive, and aggressive. Their participation in the body politic would be an immeasurable boon to society.

This argument has been turned upside down by those who want to keep women in their traditional roles. Yes, say the critics, women are pure and fine, and thus are unable to live easily, if at all, in the hurly-burly world of politics and business. Better that they remain in the sheltered confines of the home, protected by loving males. In rebuttal, some feminists of the 1970s argue that women's biological nature may not differ much from men's, but most of them have been trained to cooperate, sacrifice, and forgo personal pleasures. Therefore they are better equipped to sustain the shocks of the post-technological age. Suffragists in the 1870s, on the other hand, often shared their society's view of women, hardly daring to consider the full implications of woman's equality with man. When Mrs. Stanton embraced the cause of free-love champion Victoria Woodhull, she was denounced not only by Lucy Stone's association, the AWSA, but by her own, the NWSA.

Victoria Claflin Woodhull (1838–1927) was a dynamic personality who attracted notice—by design. Born in Ohio, the seventh child in a family of ten, she distinguished herself by becoming a stockbroker in New York in 1870, by running for President of the United States in 1872, by lecturing on free love, and by generally making a public display of herself. Along with her sister, Tennessee Claflin, they began a newspaper, the *Woodhull and Claflin's Weekly,* and tried to make the staid suffrage organization a forum for their radical ideas. Within a few years, their fury subsided and they moved to London. But while in America, they succeeded in convincing an unsympathetic public that women suffragists were also eccentric advocates of free love. Mrs. Stanton's support of Victoria Woodhull cost her many supporters.

Elizabeth Stanton discovered that most self-proclaimed reformers, women and men, did not share her revolutionary fervor or her radical ideology. Most people, indeed, did not entertain even very moderate suggestions for change. In 1870, few considered suffrage for women a serious and real possibility, and fewer still were willing to explore the dimensions of feminism. Further, Mrs. Stanton learned that if she wanted her audiences to listen respectfully, she had to moderate her expressed views to fit their values, but in so doing, she had to dilute her message. No one would listen to her visions of the total transformation of the home and family. But though she may have modified her brilliant oratory, she continued her vigorous writing. Her *Woman's Bible* (1895 and 1898), examined biblical teachings from a feminist perspective—and shocked many a true believer. (See Appendix II.)

Mrs. Stanton tried to interest her own suffrage organization in considering the woman's relationship to the Judeo-Christian religions. She had little success. Most women did not want to debate the church and were shocked at the audacious Mrs. Stanton. In 1885, at the annual convention, she tried to get the meeting to adopt a resolution condemning Christianity for its attitudes toward women. Her subcommittee agreed to submit the following resolution, having toned it down and substituted Judaism for Christianity. But even in the muted form, the resolution was defeated:

Whereas, The dogmas incorporated in religious creeds derived from Judaism, teaching that woman was an after-thought in the creation, her sex a misfortune, marriage a condition of subordination, and

Satire on Victoria Woodhull, 1872. Overburdened wife rejects Victoria's advocacy of free love. (The Granger Collection)

maternity a curse, are contrary to the law of God (as revealed in nature) and to the precepts of Christ, and,

Whereas, These dogmas are an insidious poison, sapping the vitality of our civilization, blighting woman, and, through her, paralyzing humanity; therefore be it

Resolved, That we call on the Christian ministry, as leaders of thought, to teach and enforce the fundamental idea of creation, that man was made in the image of God, male and female, and given equal rights over the earth, but none over each other. And, furthermore, we ask their recognition of the scriptural declaration that, in the Christian religion, there is neither male nor female, bond nor free, but all are one in Christ Jesus.

A more "acceptable" woman's organization, with more respectable goals was the Women's Christian Temperance Union, formally established in 1874; it quickly became the largest women's organization of the period, with 200,000 members in all the states. Its second president, Frances Willard, energized the group and drew a good deal of public attention to it. A supreme organizer and a good speaker, she tied temperance to suffrage and many other woman's causes, urging WCTU members to work toward eliminating prostitution and improving education along with spreading the gospel of temperance. Frances Willard believed that if women had the vote, they could abolish the liquor trade; therefore, political power was a necessary precondition for nationwide temperance. On this issue, however, there was a division of opinion within the WCTU, and all local chapters did not follow Miss Willard's directives on woman's suffrage as zealously as she would have liked. In the South, for example, some WCTU chapters campaigned against convict-leasing (see Chapter Eight) and child labor.

The WCTU aptly illustrated the kind of woman's reform organization that the American society would tolerate—that is, one dedicated to the moral uplift of the male sex. The dominant cultural view had always been that women, the preservers of the home, had to help moderate male passions and male excesses. Although no one ever mentioned sexuality in women, men's sexuality was considered a natural male characteristic and was by no means taboo in gossip or serious discussions. Men, being men, would drink, smoke, and be unfaithful to their wives.

Women had the thankless but continuous job of trying to reform them, forgiving them when they strayed. In the name of promoting man's better nature, it was respectable for women to parade against Demon Rum and to send petitions to legislatures demanding that the sale of liquor be prohibited. They always behaved in lady-like, socially approved ways. Occasionally a WCTU zealot would smash barroom windows, but this was exceptional, not the rule. Yet Frances Willard's efforts to bring other feminist issues into the scope of the temperance movement failed—and for much the same reasons as did Mrs. Stanton's efforts within the suffrage movement. Most WCTU members concentrated on the single acceptable cause of temperance, with no further commitment to women's rights.

On the other hand, one of the few positive accomplishments that both temperance and suffrage workers could show for their years of endeavor was their own personal growth. Just as women abolitionsts benefited both the slaves and themselves while working in the movement, so temperance and suffrage workers developed their own inner resources while fighting their opponents. In the 1870s, many women achieved self-liberation, though they never saw their sex liberated. Then, too, Frances Willard, Elizabeth Cady Stanton, and Susan B. Anthony were only a few of many women who became models for the younger feminists of the day. Rheta Childe Dorr, a journalist in the 1910s, recalled hearing Susan B. Anthony speak in the 1880s, deciding then and there what she would do with her life. Countless women became active in their church groups, civic organizations, or WCTU chapters precisely because they had heard the voice of one of the great women leaders of the time. The pity, then as now, was that there were not enough such leaders to inspire many more young women to become active in social causes.

Women's Lives After the War

In the generation following the Civil War, there was a surplus of women because so many young men had been killed. True, immigration erased much of the surplus, especially after 1880. But still many women, either widowed or destined to be spinsters because their lovers had died in battle, found themselves jobs.

The More Things Change . . . 1861–1880

Women teachers increased tremendously in this period, although until 1850 men had dominated the teaching profession. Nursing, which had also been a male profession, likewise was woman-dominated; by 1890, there were nearly 40,000 women nurses. Yet prejudice and discrimination against working women still prevailed. Once women began to enter a male-designated field, it lost its professional status. Women teachers and nurses received less pay for the same work that men did, and administrative and other highly paid jobs remained in the hands of men.

The problems of Southern women, most of whom lived in agricultural communities, were often more severe than those of their Northern sisters. Nearly one-fourth of the million men who had served in the Confederate Army died on the battlefield or from disease; the state of Alabama had 80,000 widows. Quietly, without a great deal of flourish or publicity, the Southern women endured untold hardships, raised their families, and tilled the soil, often with the aid of their teenage children. Some widows were able to hire laborers, black or white, to help maintain the farms. Some town women opened schools, took in boarders, and sewed for a living. Though a small proportion of the upper middle class became interested in social reform, the majority found the daily chores totally time-consuming, demanding, and exhausting.

(All women worked, but those who worked outside of the home were particularly vulnerable to exploitation.)One working-woman writer, in an article in *Harper's Magazine* (1869), summarized the working woman's dilemma as well as the solution to it:

> But, although I admire the time-worn simile of the oak-tree and the clinging vine quite as much as those masculine advocates of the charming helplessness theory, yet I can not help asking, "How about those vines that have no oak-tree to cling to, or who have found the oak in which they have trusted turn out a mere reed, which, if they have no self-sustaining power, only serves to drag them to the earth, to be trampled by every cruel or careless passer-by?"

Working women had no alternative, she continued; they had to work—or to starve. "Is it just, then; is it fair, is it humane even, to exclude them from *any* occupation where they could make a fair living on the shallow pretense that such an occupation is not feminine?" A working woman wanted only one thing: ". . . the right to work, and a fair day's wages for a fair day's work." The author further stated that women required practical education and full rights to equal employment. "In conclusion," she noted,

> I would say to the working woman, if you wish to succeed be in earnest. This, after all has been said, is the lever with which you may and must move the world. Put your heart into your work. Make a business of it. Don't always look and do as something to be taken up for a few months, or at most, years, and then to be laid aside, never to be resumed. Whatever work you·elect, whether hand-work or brain-work, take it up as if for life.

Women and Unions

The 1870 census showed that more than 300,000 women were working in factories and other plants, especially in the cigar-making, textile, and laundry industries. Their wages were low, their working conditions often unspeakable. Before that census was taken, in 1869, the New York City Women's Typographical Union No. 1 was organized, as was the Daughters of Crispin, a union of women shoemakers. Other unions were formed in New York and in the factory towns of Massachusetts—most of them, unfortunately, short-lived. Factory owners would retaliate ruthlessly against striking workers, and most new unions did not have the resources to sustain a long strike.

In general, women workers were reluctant to join unions, partly because of their inbred diffidence and partly because they hoped that marriage would soon remove them from their factory jobs. But certain fiery women speakers and organizers, such as Mother Jones, became legends in their time.

Mother Jones (1830–1930) was born in Cork, Ireland. She and her family came to America in 1835, and her father became a laborer on the railroads. Mother Jones attended elementary school and planned on becoming a teacher. She taught briefly at a convent in Monroe, Michigan, and then moved to Chicago to establish a dressmaking business. She preferred sewing, in her words, "to bossing little children."

Mother Jones married an ironworker in 1861 and had four

Mother Jones leads strikers, 1913. (Brown Bros.)

children. Tragedy struck her family in 1867 when a yellow fever epidemic swept through Memphis, where they lived. Her husband and four babies all died. Mother Jones then returned to Chicago and the dressmaking business.

After the Chicago fire of 1871, she became interested in the plight of workers. She joined the Knights of Labor, the major union of the time, and devoted the rest of her long life to organizing workers in all industries.

Women Go to College

As the Civil War came to a close, women were on the march, despite many frustrations and defeats. An early, tremendously significant victory was the opportunity for higher education offered to middle- and upper-class girls. Vassar College, established in Poughkeepsie, New York, in 1865, became the first academically superior women's college. Matthew Vassar, the wealthy brewer who endowed it, explained his purpose in creating a college for women in a speech to the trustees:

> It occurred to me that woman, having received from her Creator the same intellectual constitution as man, has the same right as man to intellectual culture and development.
>
> I considered that the *mothers* of a country mold the character of its citizens, determine its institutions, and shape its destiny.
>
> Next to the influence of the mother is that of the *female teacher,* who is employed to train young children at a period when impressions are most vivid and lasting.
>
> It also seemed to me that if woman were properly educated, some new avenues to useful and honorable employment, in entire harmony with the gentleness and modesty of her sex, might be opened to her.

Mr. Vassar's remarks reflected the nineteenth-century view of women's education. The purpose of educating women was, first, to make them good mothers and wives; second, to prepare them to be effective teachers of the next generation; and, finally, to permit them to be gainfully employed in work that was "in entire harmony with the gentleness and modesty" of their sex. But the school went beyond his expectations in its academic excellence.

The 353 young women who came to Vassar College in 1865 ranged in age from fourteen to twenty-four. Their fathers were merchants, lawyers, manufacturers, and (in smaller numbers) ministers, farmers, and doctors. Indeed, it was usually the girl's father who decided that she would attend college—though in later generations the mothers would play the influential role. When the first Vassar class arrived on the campus, they found that it consisted of one main building, modeled after the Tuileries in Paris; thirty teachers, twenty-two women and eight men; and a religious aura that would permeate their lives. A look at the daily schedule for 1865 reveals a great deal:

6 a.m.   Rise; attend morning prayers
7 a.m.   Breakfast
7:30–9 a.m.   Put room in order; Silent Time (a period of prayer and religious meditation)
9 a.m.–12:40 p.m.   Study period

185

1 p.m.   Dinner
2–2:40 p.m.   Recreation time
2:45–5:45 p.m.   Study period
5:45–6 p.m.   Change dress
6–6:30 p.m.   Supper and evening prayers
6:30–8 p.m.   Silent Time
8–9 p.m.   Study time
9–10 p.m.   Free
10 p.m.   Lights out

Included in the curriculum were mental and moral philosophy, Greek and Latin, English, mathematics, astronomy, physics and chemistry, physiology, hygiene, German, French, and art and music. The students were expected to commit to memory a good deal of the subject matter presented to them, and to repeat it in an essay on the final examination.

Athletics were encouraged, and the girls were told to bring outdoor clothing suitable for sports. They played tennis in the 1870s and 1880s, basketball in the 1890s. They also competed in track and field events, priding themselves on their parallel concerns for intellectual and physical development.

That first generation of college women, whether educated at Vassar or, a few years later, at Smith (1875), Wellesley (1875), or Bryn Mawr (1885), believed they were special people destined to do special things. Over 60 per cent of all graduates before 1912, for example, had jobs at some time in their lives. And the women who entered the state universities that became coeducational in the last three decades of the century also felt like pioneers opening new pathways for women. As a result, an impressive number of the first generation of women graduates went on to take postgraduate professional training in education, law, medicine, and that new profession, social work.

The *Vassar Alumnae Register* has recorded the achievements of a few of those early graduates:

'77: Susan Miller Dorsey, first woman to be superintendent of a metropolitan school system.

'78: Harriet Stanton Blatch, warrior for women's legal rights.

'80 Julia C. Lathrop, first director of the Federal Children's Bureau.

186

These are simply a few examples of the many women college and university graduates whose lives were committed to a career. This is not to say that they avoided marriage, though a high percentage of them did. Rather, it is to say that they defined their lives in other than the traditional way; being a wife and mother did not constitute the sum total of their self-image and their aspirations. But in the 1870s, as in the 1970s, it was often difficult to combine a career and marriage.

One Vassar alumna, class of 1897, recalled some years later:

> In my day at Vassar, the women professors seemed definitely and outspokenly to discourage the students from marrying, and encouraged them instead to study for a PhD and have a "career." For example, I remember hearing Professor Abby Leach say of an outstanding alumna who had just married, "It's a pity she has thrown away her life and buried herself that way. She might have had a distinguished career."

Over 50 per cent of Vassar graduates from the classes of 1867 to 1900 married. In the first two decades of the twentieth century, the proportion rose to over 60 per cent and from 1907 to 1931 to over 70 per cent. These figures, though based on incomplete returns, show a general trend. Most women chose marriage, then as now. But it was the minority of college-educated women, beginning in the 1870s, who organized the woman's clubs, the settlement houses, and the nursing schools. And it was from those small but impressive ranks that the suffragists, the feminists, and the social workers emerged.

Black Leaders

In the post–Civil War period of ferment and progress, black men and women arose to speak for their people's needs. As in the white abolitionist movement, the older black leaders, free blacks and ex-slaves, shared their influence and experience with younger black leaders. Frederick Douglass made room for Booker T. Washington, who, like Douglass, had been born in slavery. Black women—among them Ida Wells, Mary Church Terrell, and Fannie Barrier Williams—led a variety of causes. Ida Wells became a leading spokeswoman against Southern

187

lynching. Mary Terrell helped organize, and became the first president of, the National Association of Colored Women, and Fannie Williams founded the first nursing school for black women at Provident Hospital in Chicago. Like the white reformers, they engaged in a variety of educational, legislative, and reform activities.

The number of educated black men and women was pitifully small, because of blatant discrimination against blacks in colleges, universities, and professional schools. Being a black *woman* was a double disability. Recall how difficult it was for Elizabeth Blackwell, a white woman, to gain admission to a medical school; then imagine the ordeal of Caroline V. Still, one of the first black woman doctors, who finally interned at the New England Hospital for Women and Children. In 1872, the first black woman lawyer, Charlotte B. Ray, was graduated from Howard University Law School. That university had been established after the Civil War to educate black students, but it had only a

Howard University, established during Reconstruction for black Americans. (Brown Bros.)

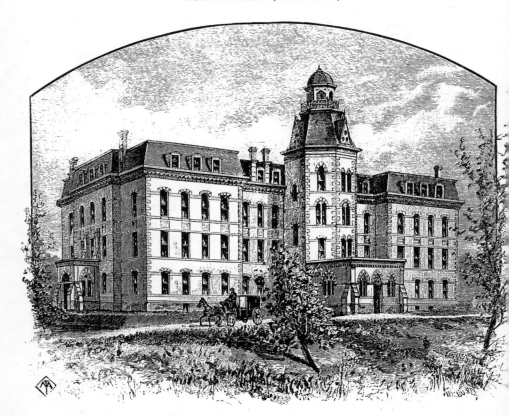

few counterparts. The resources of black schools and colleges have always been limited, and the number of well-to-do blacks who could afford to educate their children has been distressingly small.

Many black women became teachers in the segregated Southern black schools. Often woefully underprepared for their task—as were most white women teachers (many of whom had only six years of elementary-school education)—they found the job frustrating at best and hopeless at worst.

Outstanding among them was Charlotte Forten (1837–1914), a member of an upper-class black family in Philadelphia. Her father, a successful sailmaker and inventor, amassed a fortune. Charlotte was educated by private tutors and then went to a normal school in Salem, Massachusetts. She taught school for a few years, but poor health forced her to retire. She then spent her time attending lectures, anti-slavery meetings, and social affairs.

The outbreak of the Civil War stirred her to action. After the Union soldiers had captured the Port Royal islands, off the coast of South Carolina, volunteers were called for, to teach the emancipated slaves. Charlotte went to Port Royal and taught there from August 1862 to May 1864. She instilled a sense of pride in her black students and told them of the heroes and heroines of their people. She described the activities of Harriet Tubman and reminded her students that freedom was now their legacy.

The agricultural demands of the South made it difficult to keep children in school for any length of time, since both black and white boys were needed in the fields. Further, the white Southern legislators allocated to black schools only one-tenth the amount of money they gave to white schools. Considering that public education for white children was badly underfinanced in the South, it is easy to understand why black schoolchildren were hardly educated at all.

Nevertheless black parents were greatly concerned about their children's schooling. William Pickens, an organizer for the National Association for the Advancement of Colored People in the 1910s, paid tribute to his mother in his autobiography. That hard-working woman, he recalled, always stressed the importance of education and was chiefly responsible for his own advanced learning.

During Reconstruction, most black Americans still lived in the South, and most black leaders worked to improve life in their own communities. One of these leaders, Booker T. Washington, gained a national reputation in the 1890s for his efforts to provide vocational and agricultural education for his people. Whereas the blacks in the North tried to get the government to eliminate discrimination against their race, Southern black leaders generally counseled self-improvement and self-help.

In the violent and hostile atmosphere of the South, black leaders who criticized the white establishment could be either castrated or lynched. For example, in 1875, in Clinton, Mississippi, Charles Caldwell was the black leader of the local militia. White men resented Caldwell's position and one day started a riot which resulted in his death, as well as the massacre of more than forty blacks during a four-day slaughter.

Mrs. Caldwell, the widow, testified before a congressional committee:

> I know there was two dead men there, but I did not think it was my husband at the time.
>
> I stood right there, and as I stood there they said to me, if you don't go away they would make it very damned hot for me; and I did not say anything, and walked off, and walked right over the dead man.

Only by running faster than the posse could such leaders escape the cruel reprisals planned for them. So, as time went on, younger blacks with ambitions to be leaders and articulators of their people's problems did not stay in the South. If they did, they would quickly learn how to moderate their wishes and state their grievances in "acceptable language." Just as the white Grimké sisters could not preach abolition in the South in the 1830s, neither could black leaders advocate black equality there in the 1870s.

For, as we have seen, the white South had not changed. Its people demonstrated their long-held belief in the inferiority of blacks by using both violent and nonviolent methods to keep them in their place. In the North, things were better, despite many forms of discrimination. But white Southerners, once they regained political power, used threats to get blacks to vote their way, or else rewrote the laws to disqualify them from voting at all. In addition to appropriating almost no funds for black education, the whites kept black farmers landless and in

190

debt and discriminated against all blacks in many other ways. The result was unofficial slavery. Yet few blacks left their Southern homeland at this time, though the trend shifted dramatically in later years.

A Promise Fulfilled: The Forgotten American Indian

"They made us many promises, more than I can remember, but they never kept but one; they promised to take our land, and they took it." So commented one Indian in Dee Brown's *Bury My Heart at Wounded Knee*, a graphic account of the white man's deceitful and violent treatment of American Indians. No treaty was honored by white Americans; no word was sacred to them. In exchange for Western lands, they promised the Indians weapons to kill buffalo and food to feed their hungry children —and violated all their promises.

The drive westward continued through the 1860s and 1870s. After the interruption of the Civil War, white pioneers moved across prairies, great rivers, and mountains in their covered wagons. Wherever they decided to settle, they established the governmental and cultural structures they had known back home in New York or Ohio or Illinois, and staked out the land for whites only. (The U.S. government did sign treaties with Indian tribes in the Great Plains—only to break them when it was convenient to do so.) Indian Commissioner Francis C. Walker commented in 1871: "When dealing with savage men, as with savage beasts, no question of national honor can arise. Whether to fight, to run away, or to employ a ruse, is solely a question of expediency." The idea of thus parceling land, putting wire fences around it, and privatizing it was beyond the Indians' imagination. As Chief Crazy Horse once said, "One does not sell the earth on which the people walk." Land belonged to no single individual but to all living things. From a late twentieth-century point of view, it appears that the American Indian understood the natural environment far better than did the American white man—how to live with the land, not to exploit it. Private property was the white man's way; communal property, the way of the Indian.

Few white Americans at that time bothered to learn about the diverse cultures of the Indians. Some scouts and military men learned tribal languages, but they never regarded the Indians as equals who were worthy of respect and from whom they could learn something about the universe.

The reservation system, devised during this period, became the white man's answer to the Indian problem. Because so many buffalo had been killed, along with the Indians, a vital source of food for Western tribes was disappearing. Legislators and the militia had the idea of setting off reservations for Indians *and* buffalo. This notion assumed that the groups to be contained on reservations were not adult human beings entitled to their natural rights, responsibilities, and freedoms. It assumed that those in power could control the behavior of these people without fear of disobedience. It assumed, finally, that American Indians were pawns to be placed wherever the white man chose. Such cruel arrogance on the part of human beings toward other human beings seems incredible. But it was no crueler than slavery, and no more arrogant than denying half the population of the country, the female half, equal rights.

Unfortunately for both the Indians and the white men, there were few people around like George Catlin, the American painter. Catlin traveled widely in the West, grew familiar with the language and customs of various Indian tribes, and came to appreciate the beauty and dignity of their culture. In 1868, in a report to the Smithsonian Institution, he wrote his "Indian Creed":

> I love a people who have always made me welcome to the best they had.
>
> I love a people who are honest without laws, who have no jails and no poorhouses.
>
> I love a people who keep the commandments without ever having read them or heard them preached from the pulpit.
>
> I love a people who never swear, who never take the name of God in vain.
>
> I love a people who love their neighbors as they love themselves.
>
> I love a people who worship God without a Bible, for I believe that God loves them also.
>
> I love a people who have never raised a hand against me, or stolen my property, where there was no law to punish for either.
>
> I love a people whose religion is all the same, and who are free from religious animosities.

A Promise Fulfilled: The Forgotten American Indian

I love the people who have never fought a battle with white men, except on their own ground.

I love and don't fear mankind where God has made and left them, for there they are children.

I love a people who live and keep what is their own without locks and keys.

I love all people who do the best they can. And oh, how I love a people who don't live for the love of money!

Catlin praised the American Indians' deeply humane culture. His appreciation, however, remained almost unique. Critics of the white man's policy toward the Indian were usually either ignored or silenced.

In this period began the tales of Indian fighters (regarded as heroes, not criminals) and the whole mythic tradition of the cowboy and the West. The lone cowboy battling Indians and cattle thieves became the stuff of which romantic novels—and later movies—were made. Generations of Easterners developed a sentimental, idealized picture of the winning of the West from these wholly fictitious tales. Like the South, the West created its

A George Catlin painting of the Sioux Indians. (American Museum of Natural History)

own myths, and the only Indians who appeared in them were those doomed to death. The cattle ranchers were the Western correlative of the Eastern businessmen. Absent from the cast of heroes and villains were the farmers. The small wheat-farmer in Nebraska—who had as hard a time making a living as the cotton-farmer in Mississippi or the corn-farmer in Iowa—was neither glamorous nor adventurous. Hence the cowboy became the central figure.

The depth and strength of the cowboy image in popular American mythology owed something to his fictional predecessors. These were the explorers and pioneers who fascinated readers of James Fenimore Cooper—solitary men confronting the perils of an unknown wilderness. They were never portrayed as intruders into another people's land and culture, but as intrepid souls braving natural dangers and overcoming them through cunning and skill. It was man against nature in many pre-cowboy westerns, not white man against American Indian. As cattle ranches developed in the West (with cowboys) and cities and towns multiplied in the East, Western tales grew even more appealing to city dwellers. Most of them had never seen lofty mountains and foothills and wide-open plains, but they could read about them in dime novels. In the next century they could see them in motion pictures, too, where Tom Mix and later John Wayne portrayed the sturdy, hard-riding cowboys.

The mythology of the West helped white Americans to accept their own cruel behavior toward the Indians, rewriting history in such a way as to justify their actions. In stories of white men conquering the West, and cowboys riding the range, there were no evil or treacherous deeds, only deeds of courage and valor. White America would not face up to its treatment of the native population until the 1960s, when the remnants of the great Indian tribes of the past rose up in indignation and demanded their rights. The myth of the West was largely a male dream—an adventure of danger, risk, excitement, and high stakes. Neither women nor Indians counted.

The Forgotten Land

"Man has too long forgotten that the earth was given to him for usufruct alone, not for consumption, still less for profligate waste." So wrote George Perkins Marsh in 1864. In his classic study, *Man and Nature,* Marsh pointed out that man is the only living creature that ravages nature not for sustenance alone but "with reckless destructiveness." Other creatures destroy only to survive, but man arrogantly misuses nature for selfish and extravagant purposes. He outlined the disastrous consequences:

> In short, without man, lower animal and spontaneous vegetable life would have been constant in type, distribution, and proportion, and the physical geography of the earth would have remained undisturbed for indefinite periods.

Most people were totally ignorant of Marsh's book as well as the ideas he was propounding. To the majority of Americans, felling the forests and converting iron ore to steel meant progress. Replacing buffalo-grass sod with cattle ranches, turning timber into houses, and leaving a gaping hole in a mountainside were all viewed as acts of advancement. Man was conquering nature, imposing his will upon it. Industrialization, of course, accelerated the rape of the environment, as factories consumed large quantities of coal and iron ore to produce steel for railroads, machinery, ships, and bridges.

Smoky landscapes soon became a familiar sight in industrial areas. Pittsburgh, the center of steel production, became known as Smoky City. There as elsewhere soot and dirt abounded. Water supplies were polluted by industrial wastes dumped into lakes and rivers, often resulting in epidemics of typhoid, dysentery, and related diseases. People never considered the long-range effects of their actions. Because manufacturing was defined as a social (and individual) good, its by-products must also be good. Or at least the end surely justified the means.

When factories produced more goods, buyers had more things to buy. Acquiring more and more things—the products emerging from the smoking factories—became the great American goal. Meanwhile, neither the federal, the state, nor the local governments imposed any restrictive laws on manufacturers who polluted both air and water. Lumber companies made no effort at reforestation or at cutting trees selectively. Forest fires were frequent, but the damage was ignored. While the Chicago fire of 1871 has remained a vivid historical milestone, few now recall that in the very same summer a great fire in Wisconsin burned more than 1,250,000 acres of timber and took 1,500 lives.

Not only were the air and water being polluted, but the wildlife of the nation was being indiscriminately destroyed. Hunters seeking a few salable neck and tail feathers killed egrets, herons, and spoonbills—and women proudly wore those feathers on their hats. The bison were destroyed as railroads and cattle moved relentlessly across the Western plains. Surely the natural devastation in all areas—air, water, land, animal life—was not as extensive as the damage wrought by the combustion engine in the twentieth century, but decades of total disregard for the environment portended future catastrophe. White men, confident of their superiority, believed not only that the continent was theirs for the taking, but that its natural riches were infinite.

The government made minimal efforts to salvage the environment. In 1864, during Lincoln's administration, Congress granted Yosemite Valley to the state of California for "public use, resort, and recreation." This was the beginning of the national park system. Yellowstone, Sequoia, and Mount Rainier national parks came into existence in the same period, and Yosemite was later returned to the federal government. A national forest system developed a few years later. Yet other efforts to preserve natural resources were hampered by the struggle between private and public interests. Private developers wanted to convert natural waterfalls into electrical plants. Real estate dealers believed that spectacular scenic tracts should be used for profitable land development. And lumber interests fought all moves to place forests in the public domain.

The conservation movement as we know it was not organized until the turn of the century—by engineers, naturalists, geologists, and artists who loved the beauty of their natural surroundings and fought to preserve it. Its forerunner in the 1870s was a group of professional men who had studied geology and engineering in universities and wanted to apply their new knowledge to the environment. Most of them were conservationists rather than preservationists; that is, they wanted the land and its resources to be used scientifically and managed intelligently. The preservationists wanted the natural environment to be kept as it was, with no conversion to human use. Once again members of a reform movement differed among themselves as to their ultimate goals and the best method of accomplishing their purposes.

The majority of Americans in 1880 still lived on the land, though the population of the cities was growing dramatically. Most still cherished the American Dream and believed that, de-

196

spite the depression years of 1873–1875 and 1893–1895, things were and would be all right. No serious challenge to the accepted mythologies arose. No charismatic leader emerged to protest America's treatment of Indians, women, or blacks. No establishment politician campaigned on the platform of revolutionizing American society. Women reformers, and men, kept on making speeches and enlisting new supporters; they too believed that success was just around the corner. The fact that they were free to present their views convinced them of the essential openness of the American mind. Little did they realize that they were allowed to preach only because they posed no threat to the status quo.

Suggestions for Further Reading

John B. Andrews and W. D. P. Bliss. *History of Women in Trade Unions.* Volume X of *Report on Condition of Woman and Child Wage-Earners in the United States.* U.S. Senate Document 645 (Washington, D.C., 1910–1913).

Nina Brown Baker. *Cyclone in Calico: The Story of Mary Ann Bickerdyke* (Boston, 1952).

Ray Billington, editor. *The Journal of Charlotte Forten* (New York, 1961).

Alice Blackwell. *Lucy Stone* (Boston, 1930).

Dee Brown. *Bury My Heart at Wounded Knee* (New York, 1971).

Earl Conrad. *Harriet Tubman* (Washington, 1943).

Stephen Crane. *The Red Badge of Courage* (New York, 1894).

Vine Deloria, Jr. *Custer Died for Our Sins: An Indian Manifesto* (New York, 1969).

Alfreda M. Duster, editor. *Crusade for Justice: The Autobiography of Ida B. Wells* (Chicago, 1970).

Arthur H. Fauset. *Sojourner Truth: God's Faithful Pilgrim* (Chapel Hill, N.C., 1938).

John Hope Franklin. *From Slavery to Freedom.* Rev. ed. (New York, 1967).

Ida Husted Harper. *The Life and Work of Susan B. Anthony* (Indianapolis, 1899).

Mary Livermore. *My Own Story of the War* (Hartford, Conn., 1889).

Mary Elizabeth Massey. *Bonnet Brigades: American Women and the Civil War* (New York, 1966).

John Wesley Powell. *Report on the Lands of the Arid Region of the West.* Edited by Wallace Stegner (Cambridge, Mass., 1962).

Benjamin Quarles. *The Negro in the Civil War* (Boston, 1953).

The More Things Change . . . 1861–1880

Anne F. Scott. *The Southern Lady* (Chicago, 1971).

Elizabeth Cady Stanton, Susan B. Anthony, Matilda Joslyn Gage, and Ida Husted Harper, editors. *The History of Woman's Suffrage.* 6 vols. (New York, 1969). An invaluable source.

Mary Church Terrell. *A Colored Woman in a White World* (Washington, D.C., 1940).

Frances Willard. *Glimpses of Fifty Years* (Chicago, 1892).

CHAPTER EIGHT

Old and New Problems
1880–1900

Of course 'twas an excellent story to tell
Of a fair, frail, passionate woman who fell.
It may have been false, it may have been true.
That was nothing to me—it was less to you.
But with bottle between us, and clouds of smoke
From your last cigar, 'twas more of a joke
Than a matter of sin or a matter of shame
That a woman had fallen, and nothing to blame,
So far as you or I could discover,
But her beauty, her blood and an ardent lover.
But when you were gone and the lights were low
And the breeze came in with the moon's pale glow,
The far, faint voice of a woman, I heard,
'Twas but a wail, and it spoke no word.
It rose from the depths of some infinite gloom
And its tremulous anguish filled the room.
Yet the woman was dead and could not deny,
But women forever will whine and cry.
So now I must listen the whole night through
To the torment with which I had nothing to do—
But women forever will whine and cry
And men forever must listen—and sigh— . . .

—Kate Chopin, *The Haunted Chamber*

I am tired of fighting. Our chiefs are killed. Looking Glass is dead. Toohulhusote is dead. The old men are all dead. It is the young men who say yes and no. He who led the young men is dead. It is cold and we have no blankets. The little children have no blankets, no food. No one knows where they are—perhaps they are freezing to death. I want to have time to look at my children and see how many of them I can find. Maybe I shall find them among the dead. Hear me, my chiefs, I am tired. My heart is sad and sick. From where the sun now stands I shall fight no more forever.

—Chief Joseph, Surrender speech

I have struck a city,—a real city,—and they call it Chicago. The other places do not count. San Francisco was a pleasure-resort as well as a city, and Salt Lake was a

199

phenomenon. This place is the first American city I have encountered. It holds rather more than a million people with bodies, and stands on the same sort of soil as Calcutta. Having seen it, I urgently desire never to see it again. It is inhabited by savages. Its water is the water of the Huglei, and its air is dirt. Also it says that it is the "boss" town of America.

—Rudyard Kipling, *From Sea to Sea*, 1899

*T*hese quotations aptly suggest both old and new problems facing Americans in the 1880s: the centuries-old man-woman problem; the destruction of the American Indian, also an old problem; and the growth and, in a sense, the death-producing quality of the city, a new problem.

Old Problem: Women

In 1890, as we mentioned, the woman's suffrage organizations merged into one, the National American Woman's Suffrage Association. Elizabeth Cady Stanton, now an old woman, was the first president of the combined organization. The suffragists concentrated on winning state support, spending enormous amounts of energy and money to persuade male voters to add a woman's suffrage law to the constitution of their respective states. This state-by-state strategy proved to be extremely time-consuming, with unimpressive results. New York, Pennsylvania, and every other major state east of the Mississippi failed to grant women the vote. In the West, on the other hand, four states did provide for woman's suffrage: Wyoming (Territory) in 1869, Colorado in 1893, and Utah and Idaho in 1896. These few successes only highlighted the many failures, and suffragists were deeply discouraged, although they did not abandon the state-by-state strategy until after 1910.

As for other issues in the women's rights movements, again the difficulty was inconsistency in state legislation. By the 1880s, the law had been adjusted in a number of states to permit married women to retain their earnings and to own property in their own right. Each state law, however, varied from the others, and there was no federal legislation that applied to all the states. Even as late as the 1920s, Texas did not allow married women to sign contractual agreements. (This created an awkward situation when a woman was elected governor but could not legally sign a bill!) Women could not sit on juries in any state. Most women could not vote, and few could initiate divorce proceedings against their husbands. Some feminists advocated a federal divorce law that would give all women this right, but no such law was forthcoming.

Divorce, always a controversial issue, was becoming more prevalent by the turn of the century. From 1880-1900, the number of divorces doubled. To the traditionalists, this portended the destruction of the family and the end of civilized society. To liberals and feminists, it affirmed the human right of unhappily married couples to end an intolerable relationship. The arguments and public debates over divorce continued well into the twentieth century, with doomsayers predicting the breakdown of the family and with divorce advocates arguing that liberal divorce laws were essential for true liberation.

While the number of colleges and universities increased dramatically during this period, higher education for women was largely confined to the women's colleges. Brave indeed was the girl who ventured into a coeducational public university. Still, more and more women were graduating from college (in 1900 5,237 women and 22,173 men graduated from colleges), and, after 1880, women were becoming leaders in many areas: suffrage, temperance, nursing, education, settlement houses, and the peace movements of the early twentieth century. More and more of them were entering the legal and medical professions. By 1900, they established a proportionate representation of their sex that would be preserved throughout the new century: about 3 per cent of the nation's lawyers and 6 per cent of its doctors were women. In the twentieth century, as earlier, both law and medicine remained high-level professions that jealously guarded their elite status. Each generation of bright, courageous women had to fight to gain admission into the privileged fold.

The culture's dictates on proper behavior and appropriate work for women did not change. Women continued to be segregated in "womanly" work areas in the factories, offices, and schools of America. And they could not receive training as engineers, forest rangers, or skilled carpenters.

In 1890, a woman lived, on the average, about thirty years after her last child entered school and about twelve years after that last child married. By contrast, in 1950 a woman could expect to live forty years after her last child entered school and about twenty-five years after that child married. These statistics suggest not only that by 1950, women's childbearing period ended earlier than did their grandmothers', but also that women were living longer, thanks to better sanitation, health services, and medical knowledge. Therefore, women in 1950 faced a far longer period in which to do constructive work, after their childbearing tasks ceased. Yet their basic life patterns remained unchanged throughout those sixty years. Working women of the mid-twentieth century were still victims of the same cultural limitations and salary discrimination that had existed in 1890, 1860, and 1800.

Old Problem: Black Americans

In the closing years of the nineteenth century, most black Americans lived in the South. Great numbers of them stayed on the land, sharing their crops with onetime white masters and enduring the hardships imposed on poor farmers by weather, deteriorating soil, and unprincipled people. The Ku Klux Klan and similar groups had their ways of perpetuating the blacks' servility. Another practice by which whites kept blacks "in their places" was convict-leasing: Southern industrialists found that it was much cheaper to lease convict labor from the state than to pay free workers a decent wage. The states encouraged this system because it reduced the cost of maintaining prisons and caring for the inmates. It was no accident that the conviction rate in the South was far higher for blacks than for whites, since Georgia coal-mine owners and Alabama steel manufacturers preferred to lease black convicts rather than hire either black or white workers. Mrs. Matilda Smith, a member of a penal reform committee, noted one chain gang:

> Ten black men and three white men were chained at their ankles, one to the other. They were all sweating heavily, and their bare chests glistened in the sun.
>
> They were taking a five-minute break before returning to their work of laying railroad tracks for the new Georgia line. A ladle and pail of

203

water was passed among them. Each man scooped up all the water he could drink before passing it to the next man.

The guard stood by, watching, his gun lying across his shoulder.

Mrs. Smith and her reform committee members moved on silently after witnessing this scene.

The old song "I Owe My Soul to the Company Store" was the musical version of a frequent complaint by black and white workers in both North and South. This store sold the necessities of life on credit and was owned by the steel factory or the coal company. Whether a worker lived in Pullman City, near Chicago, or in Birmingham, Alabama, he found that the boss kept the ledger and decided how much each worker owed, how much he had paid, and for how long he was in debt to "the company store."

Southern poverty knew no color boundaries. Farmers and laborers, black and white alike, lived in dirt-floored shacks and leantos that could blow away in a heavy wind. The term "poor white trash"—coined by upper-class whites, particularly in the

Black chain gang at the turn of the century. (Brown Bros.)

South—described a whole class of people who did live among trash and had little if any opportunity to change their material conditions. Novelist Erskine Caldwell's depiction of poor Georgia farmers in the twentieth century applies just as well to a large number of marginal farmers in the late nineteenth century.

Blacks who lived in the cities of the North and South also had a constant struggle to earn a meager livelihood. Chicago segregated its black residents and restricted their employment to jobs in laundries or as domestic servants. Desperate jobless blacks often became strikebreakers, thus creating tensions between black and white workers. Within their own communities, of course, black businessmen provided insurance and other services to their people, but the relationship of blacks to whites was always circumscribed and clearly defined.

In Southern cities, by contrast, there was no residential segregation. Blacks and whites lived close to each other, even though the schools and all public facilities were segregated. The various Jim Crow laws—that is, laws designed to separate the two races—were set up after Reconstruction as a means of keeping blacks in subservience. So while the North discriminated against blacks by limiting their residential and employment opportunities, the South wrote laws that built an elaborate system of separate schools, separate washrooms, and separate restaurants. Blacks could not buy tickets on the main floor of a Charleston theater, nor could they sit in the front section of a Birmingham streetcar.

The U.S. Supreme Court upheld this system of racial segregation in its *Plessy v. Ferguson* decision of 1896, when the justices argued that "separate but equal" facilities were not discriminatory. (The counter argument that separate is always unequal went unheeded in the 1890s.) The suit was brought in order to test the legality of segregated railroad-car facilities, and the Court's decision was simply that if railroads provided decent cars for blacks to ride in, they were fulfilling their constitutional obligations. The psychological effect of segregating people according to color was not considered. Just as Indians on reservations were doomed to a separate and inherently unequal life, so did the Supreme Court doom black Americans in condoning racial segregation. For there was ample evidence to show that "separate" provisions for blacks were never even intended to be "equal." Separate educational facilities, for example, were not equally funded, since Southern black schools received one-tenth of the money allocated to white schools. The picture was indeed bleak for the supposedly free black Americans. No white union admitted them, no white school allowed them to enroll, and few whites helped them to gain a measure of autonomy.

One great need, in their quest for autonomy, was education. Herein lay the tremendous contribution of Booker T. Washington. He himself was educated at Hampton Institute, a school created during Reconstruction and headed by its white founder, Samuel C. Armstrong. Washington later built his own black school in Tuskegee, Alabama, modeled after Hampton. His Tuskegee Institute trained black youths in scientific farming and vocational trades. It preached self-reliance as it imparted knowledge, and encouraged its graduates to live according to white people's religion, to practice thrift, and to work hard. Yet the American Dream never included blacks. Many hard-working black farmers waited vainly to reap the rewards of their industry.

Another noted black educator was Lucy Laney (1854–1933), who was born a slave in Macon, Georgia. Through the aid of her former master's sister, she went to elementary and high school, and graduated from Atlanta University in 1886. Lucy resolved to help other black people gain an education. She founded the Haines Normal Institute in Atlanta the same year she graduated from college. Beginning with seventy-five students, she worked to expand the school and to obtain sufficient funding for it. With the help of the Presbyterian Board of Missions for Freedom, the school increased in size and, by the time of Lucy Laney's death, had nearly 1,000 students.

Black women's clubs were organized locally to perform charitable and educational services. Similar in purpose and nature to white women's clubs, the National Association of Colored Women was formed in 1896 and, led by Mary Church Terrell (1863–1954), it had more than 100,000 members in 26 states within four years. While one local chapter would be organizing a hospital for blacks, another would be developing a kindergarten program for the black children of its community.

One of the first black women to graduate from Oberlin College, Mary Church Terrell was an articulate and prominent spokeswoman for black Americans' rights. An extraordinary person, she spent her long life working for the freedom of black people. She was a good speaker and writer for a variety of causes. In addition to heading the NACW, Mrs. Terrell campaigned against lynching, became a charter member of the NAACP, and worked for the suffrage movement as well. She represented black women at many national and international meetings.

Mrs. Terrell ranked with Jane Addams and the other women leaders in the early 1900s who devoted their lives to worthy causes. Near the end of her life, she continued the struggle by marching in Washington, D.C., to protest segregation practices in the nation's capital.

As the black population moved northward into the cities, Mrs. Terrell and her fellow members of the NACW created new chapters in the urban North and tried to involve black women in good works for their communities. Their efforts dramatized the reality of racial segregation that forced black women to create their own community organizations. A small but significant minority of educated blacks was emerging in the last two decades of the century. Many were trained professionals —ministers, lawyers, teachers, university professors, and high school principals. In 1897, the American Negro Academy, a scholarly forum, was founded in Washington, D.C.. By 1900, a significant, though small, black middle class was forming. Its members organized for their common good and pursued private goals as well—just like their white counterparts.

Mary Church Terrell,
prominent speaker and
writer for racial equality, c. 1900.
(Culver)

Old Problem: The Environment

Another old but increasingly urgent problem that faced Americans at this time was the effect of industrialization and unwise agricultural practices upon the environment. Here, an awareness of certain immediate dangers did lead to some intelligent steps, particularly in the big cities. Chicago, faced with widespread epidemics caused by polluted water, reversed the flow of its major river. This remarkable engineering feat saved a continuously fresh water-supply for its citizens. During the 1890s, the U.S. Congress passed a number of rivers and harbors acts that prohibited dumping waste materials into rivers. The simple purpose of these measures was to eliminate obstructions that could damage ships. How could any legislator foresee that in the 1960s and 1970s ecological experts would use these laws, particularly the Water Refuse Act of 1899, as legislative weapons against water polluters!

On another front, city planners began to consider ways of beautifying the urban environment. New York City's Central Park preserved a vast tract of greenery and scenery as early as the 1860's, and other cities followed New York's lead. A Kansas City report in 1893 revealed the growing enthusiasm for counteracting the effects of industrial ugliness:

> There has been in our city thus far no public concession to esthetic considerations. We are but just beginning to realize that by beautifying our city, making our city beautiful to the eye, and a delightful place of residence, abounding in provisions that add to the enjoyment of life, we not only will do our duty to our citizens, but we shall create among our people warm attachments to the city, and promote civic pride, thereby supplementing and emphasizing our business advantages and increasing their power to draw business and population.

Inevitably, in all attempts to spend money for parks, landscaping, and tree planting, the planners reminded penny-pinching legislators that pleasant cities attracted new business opportunities. Indeed, this was the only effective appeal. Profit-minded officials would hardly respond to the idea that a smoke-filled atmosphere, dirty streets, and crowded, grimy buildings choked the human spirit. It was useless to assure them that open spaces within an urban environment gave citizens

208

room to think creatively, use their imaginations, and relax from their labors. After all, the business of a city was business, and landscape architects and park planners succeeded only when they could convince the power-holders that their plans would not cost a lot and would encourage prosperity.

The federal government continued to preach its message of noninterference in the economy—all the while providing subsidies to railroads in the form of land grants, direct loans, and army freight contracts. The government also aided steamship lines and stagecoach firms, though it scrupulously avoided giving any help to individual workers and farmers. On the other hand, the Western ranchers were not interfered with when, in the 1880s, their cattle grazed on government land. Mining companies, railroads, and lumber companies took timber from government landholdings illegally but without molestation. Thus, the government encouraged big business and big agriculture, and rationalized its favoritism by claiming that bigness meant prosperity for the nation—that big farms, big cattle ranches, and big factories ultimately benefited the whole population.

Old Problem: The American Indian

The destruction of the American Indian—as a vital culture, as a society living in harmony with the land and nature—was accomplished in the final decades of the century. In 1890, the battle at Wounded Knee Creek, where the Sioux were slaughtered by the Army, ended any major Indian resistance. Ended, too, were the hypocrisy and double-dealing that accompanied so many formal treaties and informal promises between the U.S. and the various Indian tribes. As an anonymous Indian observed, the only promise the white man ever kept was that he would take the Indians' land.

A nation of multiple tribes, of millions of Indians, was thus reduced to fewer than a million people. They were now restricted to reservations, where self-rule and self-determination were replaced by white men's laws. The American Indian was not a U.S. citizen, so said the federal government. He could not vote or participate in government affairs. Except in the eyes of a few compassionate, conscience-ridden reformers—whose voices were never loud enough to be heard—the American Indian no longer existed.

The New Reality

Andrew Carnegie, a young Scottish immigrant, confirmed the myth that America held endless opportunities for hard-working youth. Beginning as a bobbin boy in a Pittsburgh cotton factory at $1.20 a week, Carnegie went on to become one of the richest men in the world. From the cotton factory to a telegraph office, to a clerkship in the Pennsylvania Railroad, Carnegie eventually parlayed his earnings and his stock profits into a huge sum. With this he set up the first corporation in America, the United States Steel Company.

Andrew Carnegie, always proud of his achievements, was a forceful spokesman for rugged individualism, expressing his deep conviction that America was indeed the land of opportunity. He also wrote frequently on the virtues of the poor:

I cannot tell you how proud I was when I received my first week's own earnings. . . . I have had to deal with great sums—many millions of dollars have since passed through my hands; but putting all these together, and considering money making as a means of pleasure giving, or . . . of genuine satisfaction, I tell you that $1.20 outweighs all. It was the direct reward of honest manual labor. . . .

You know how people are all moaning about poverty as a great evil; and it seems to be accepted that if people only had money, and were rich, that they would be happy and more useful, and get more out of life. There never was a graver mistake. As a rule there is more happiness, more genuine satisfaction and a truer life, and more obtained from life in the humble cottages of the poor than in the palaces of the rich. . . .

I always pity the sons and daughters of rich men who are attended by servants, and have governesses at a later age; but am glad to remember that they do not know what they have missed. They think they have fathers and mothers, and very kind fathers and mothers too, and they enjoy the sweetness of these blessings to the fullest, but this they cannot do: for the poor boy who has in his father his constant companion, tutor, and model, and in his mother—holy name—his nurse, teacher, guardian angel, saint, all in one, has a richer, more precious fortune in life than any rich man's

210

son can possibly know, and compared with which all other fortunes count for little.

It is because I know how sweet, and happy and pure the home of honest poverty is, how free from care, from quarrels, how loving and how united its members, that I sympathize with the rich man's boy, and congratulate the poor man's boy, and it is for these reasons that from the ranks of the poor the great and the good have always sprung and always must spring.

Surely the poor of Chicago, Pittsburgh, New York, Birmingham, or Tuscaloosa in the 1890s did not always share Carnegie's sentiments.

But the middle and upper classes agreed with him as they continued to mouth the platitudes of individualism in an increasingly collectivist society. Fewer and fewer sons of the poor could hope to approach the amazing success of Andrew Carnegie, but his example encouraged them to keep on trying.

On the other hand, the realities of life for the new industrial poor were depicted by some imaginative writers and artists of the time. Stephen Crane's *Maggie, a Girl of the Streets* (1894) vividly portrays the grim daily routine of many people.

The girl, Maggie, blossomed in a mud puddle. She grew to be a most rare and wonderful production of a tenement district, a pretty girl.

None of the dirt of Rum Alley seemed to be in her veins. The philosophers, upstairs, downstairs, and on the same floor, puzzled over it.

When a child, playing and fighting with gamins in the street, dirt disguised her. Attired in tatters and grime, she went unseen.

There came a time, however, when the young men of the vicinity said, "Dat Johnson goil is a puty good looker." About this period her brother remarked to her: "Mag, I'll tell yeh dis! See? Yeh've edder got t' go on d' toif er go t' work!" Whereupon she went to work, having the feminine aversion to the alternative.

By a chance, she got a position in an establishment where they made collars and cuffs. She received a stool and a machine in a room where sat twenty girls of various shades of yellow discontent. She perched on the stool and treadled at her machine all day, turning out collars with a name which might have been noted for its irrelevancy to anything connected with collars. At night she returned home to her mother.

211

Old and New Problems 1880–1900

Not wanting a life of prostitution, ("d' toif" as her brother called it), Maggie chose to work in a collar factory, but the daily deadening routine eventually led her to the streets and to her doom. Crane's novel, like those of Theodore Dreiser, Frank Norris, and other naturalist writers of the period, was darkly pessimistic. The poor people they wrote about were pale, lifeless, puppet-like—machines in a machine-run world not of their making. Their choices were few, and their future, it appeared, would be a mere repetition of the present.

Men and women workers expressed their discontent with their jobs in a variety of ways. They slowed down the production lines, were frequently absent, and came to the job drunk. Some engaged in union activities; others worked when they had to and loafed at other times. Women workers were much more vulnerable to exploitation than men. Not only did they receive less pay for the same jobs, but they were often seduced by their male supervisors and threatened with dismissal if they told what had happened. At the end of a long workday they went home to long hours of housework. All in all, the writers whose fiction portrayed the harshness of American working-class life exaggerated little, if at all.

Farmers, also discontented with their lot, organized their own unions, the Farmers Alliances in the 1880s, and in 1890 formed their own political party, the Populist party. Recognizing the importance of women in agriculture, the Populists included woman's suffrage among the planks in their national party platform.

Mary Ellen Lease (1850–1933), one of the most dynamic organizers and leaders of the farmers, had lived in Kansas since 1873. A lawyer as well as the mother of four children, Mrs. Lease was thirty-five years old when the Populist party was formed. She had already gained an impressive reputation from her strong, forthright speeches at Farmers Alliance meetings. "Raise less corn and more hell," she told farmers as she attacked the "greedy, governing class" that exploited them. General James B. Weaver, the Populist candidate for President in 1892, called her "our Queen Mary," and when Kansas elected a Populist government, Mrs. Lease became a member of the State Board of Charities. Unfortunately she found, much to her dismay, that even Populists, once they held office, were as susceptible to compromise and cooperation with the powers-that-be as were traditional politicians.

But during the brief period when the Populist party promised to become a viable political force on behalf of farmers, Mrs. Lease and many other women played an important part in its activities. "Wimmin is everywhere," said the humorist Josh Billings, referring to the many Farmers Alliance doings in the early 1890s. Women cooked the Alliance's picnic dinners, sang in the glee clubs, and marched in the processions. They formed an essential part of the farmers' reform movement, as well as every other reform movement of significance.

Another aspect of the new reality was the continuing influx of European immigrants to these shores. Millions came from Eastern and Southern Europe—Russia, Poland, Italy, Greece —and changed the texture of life in American cities and towns. In earlier years, most immigrants were English, Scottish, Irish, German, and Scandinavian. Except for the Irish, they all shared the Protestant religion as well as a commitment to the agricultural way of life. Many Germans settled in Pennsylvania, slowly learned English, and gradually accepted the legal and social system of America. The Scandinavian farmers of Wisconsin and Michigan lived on land which resembled that of the "old country," and unobtrusively maintained their traditions while training their children in the new country's ways.

The immigrants of the 1880s and 1890s, however, spoke Yiddish, Russian, Italian, and Greek, and followed various non-Protestant religions such as Judaism and Catholicism —Roman, Greek Orthodox, and Russian Orthodox. The Jews who fled from the pogroms of tsarist Russia often remained in the port of entry, New York City or Boston, to become workers in the garment industry or merchants. The Italians also preferred to live in the big port cities. Many Poles gathered in Chicago, where they set up ethnic communities and preserved their ties with the old country. All these newer immigrants seemed dedicated to their own culture, which was significantly different from that of the American WASM. They had brought it with them and wanted to keep it alive in the new soil of the Promised Land. And the fact that they looked different, sounded different, and worshipped differently was reason enough, in intolerant America, to persecute them.

"I didn't know that was your mother," the settlement house worker said to the young girl.

"Well, she, she . . .," stammered the girl in response, obviously flustered and upset by the exchange.

"Why, what's the matter?"

"I, I didn't want anyone to know she's my mother."

"Why not?"

"Well, she talks with an accent and dresses in those old fashioned clothes—I wish I had a mother who looked American!"

"But your mother is a skilled seamstress and knitter. You should be proud of her ability—and besides—no one should be ashamed of their mother, whatever she does or however she looks or sounds."

"I guess not," the young girl replied unconvincingly.

The new immigrants reacted realistically and prudently to intolerance. Their reasoning was simple: the sooner they became Americanized, the sooner they would be tolerated. The longer they remained different, the longer they would be discriminated against and denied entry into schools and jobs and better neighborhoods. In one sense, they were more fortunate than the Indians and blacks because their skin-color did not give them away. Changing their names, learning proper English, and dressing like Americans could win them acceptance by the majority—whereas a black- or brown-skinned person could not escape discrimination so easily. But the immigrant women had another problem: they soon found that the New World was not new at all in its view of woman's place and woman's role. Since the age-old traditions still applied, their lives did not materially improve.

By 1900, the United States had a very heterogeneous population. Could so many people, of so many national origins, live together in harmony? Would the dominant WASM culture impose its will on the new citizens? Only the future would tell.

Because the new arrivals needed many kinds of help, private citizens (mostly women) in large cities established "settlement houses" in immigrant neighborhoods. Famous to this day are Jane Addams' Hull House on Harrison and Halsted streets in

Chicago and Lillian Wald's Henry Street Settlement on the Lower East Side of New York.

Jane Addams (1860–1935) was born and raised in Cedarville, Illinois, where her father was a prominent businessman and politician. She attended Rockford Seminary, a woman's college, an experience that marked her as a member of a privileged minority —college-educated women. During the 1880s, she traveled to Europe on two separate occasions. She observed the London settlement houses, visited Tolstoy in Russia, then returned to the United States still uncertain of her future and anxious about the lack of direction in her life.

In 1889, her friend Ellen Gates Starr suggested that the two of them set up a settlement house in Chicago. Thus began Hull House (Hull was the name of its original owner), located in an immigrant neighborhood. Jane Addams became the driving force behind what was to become an enduring institution. She lectured, wrote, and was known all over for her social welfare projects on behalf of immigrants. She campaigned for reform-minded politicians and supported legislation to improve working conditions for all industrial workers.

Lillian Wald (1867–1940) was a middle-class Jewish woman born in Cincinnati. Breaking expected cultural patterns, she became a nurse and established a settlement house in New York City in 1893. Called the Henry St. Settlement House, it became famous as a sanctuary for immigrants interested in learning about health care as well as American history. In 1902, Lillian Wald organized the world's first public school nursing system. She lectured and wrote against the evils of child labor and became a peace advocate at the outbreak of World War I. Her career paralleled Jane Addams' in many ways, and in their time the two women were equally well known and respected.

Groups of women, usually single women and often college educated, lived in the settlement houses, taught English and citizenship, and made friends with the newcomers. In addition, a broad range of services was developed within these communities. Lillian Wald dispensed prenatal and maternal information to immigrant women. Settlement house workers often cooperated with public officials in providing local services to the community, as when Jane Addams was appointed garbage inspector for her neighborhood in order to ensure proper garbage collection. The workers also enlisted the aid of city officials in

215

Henry St. Settlement House nurses, 1905. (Bettmann)

improving housing and working conditions. Often, too, they supported local trade unions and marched with union workers.

True, the settlement house staffs did try to impose their brand of Americanism on the new immigrants. They stressed such middle-class values as cleanliness, neatness, and discipline, and emphasized the need to adjust to these values. But let it be said to the credit of Jane Addams, Lillian Wald, and their co-workers that they always respected the variety of ethnic groups in their neighborhoods, and encouraged each family to preserve its religious, cultural, and social traditions. Jane Addams made a point of telling youngsters to be proud of their parents and never to be ashamed of their foreign accents.

This was a period in which the government denied any responsibility for the welfare of its individual citizens. In fact, President Grover Cleveland told Americans that it was their responsibility to support the government, not the government's to support them. So the settlement houses of Chicago, Boston, New York, and other Northern cities assumed a major social burden. As a result, the women and men who staffed the settlement houses later became the backbone of the twentieth-century professional social welfare establishment. Many of them went on to careers in the U.S. Labor Department and various state agencies.

In the cities of the South, such as Atlanta, the Methodist Church set up home mission societies to aid the urban poor and also dependent women. The Southern women who led and participated in these missionary enterprises organized training programs for black girls, advocated the banning of child labor, and worked for penal reform. Many joined the Women's Christian Temperance Union and supported a wide range of other social causes. Among them was Belle Kearney (1863–1939), who was born of slave-holder parents in Mississippi. She later wrote: "There was born in me a sense of the injustice that had always been heaped upon my sex, and this consciousness created and sustained in me a constant and ever increasing rebellion." First in the temperance movement and then as a suffragist, Belle Kearney organized WCTU chapters and, later, suffrage associations throughout Mississippi. She believed that Southern women, though more diffident than their Northern sisters, could also rise up in moral outrage when they saw injustice around them.

217

Like their Northern sisters, Southern women were deeply concerned about the human problems created by the growth of cities and of industry. Mill workers, black and white, skilled and unskilled, needed help, and both black and white women strove to supply it. Thus, women reformers, in the North and the South, entered the vacuum of social concern, a vacuum not filled by anyone else.

New Ideas

To intellectuals, no less than to scientists, Charles Darwin's theory of evolution challenged traditional systems of thought in many areas. Although that theory integrated the ideas of earlier philosophers and scientists, Darwin was credited with—and often blamed for—its formulation. On the positive side, this new concept that life evolved from the simplest forms, like the one-celled amoeba, to the most complex, *Homo sapiens,* did suppy a comprehensive explanation for the complexity of living things. More than that, the eternal struggle of all creatures for existence, with only the fittest destined to survive, provided the script for a drama in which all life, animal and human, grew and changed continously.

On the other hand, the idea that human beings had evolved from simpler forms of creation offended not only the religious fundamentalists but many secular persons who felt that human beings were different and special. Then, too, the environmentalists, who had always discounted heredity as a factor in survival, were disturbed by the principle of natural selection —that some members of each species have an inherited capacity to survive while others cannot adapt to the changing environment. Eventually, and very gradually, all these groups learned to live with Darwinism and, indeed, to adapt Darwin's theory to their previously held ideas. Theologians even argued that the biblical story of the Creation was still true. God could have created the earth and its inhabitants in seven days if each day symbolized a billion years of evolution. Hence the Genesis story retained its authority.

Flexible intellectuals made Darwin's ideas relevant to the world of the 1880s and 1890s. Only a few swallowed Darwin whole and preached the doctrine of a dog-eat-dog world in which the strong and able survived and the weak and stupid failed—a very unpleasant philosophy. A group of "reform Darwinists," following the lead of sociologist Lester Frank Ward, claimed that man could direct his own evolution, that people were capable of altering the environment so that all human beings could survive. These reformers envisioned a society which would manage its environment for the benefit of all. Then the physically weak and the poor would not have to die in a harsh, unsupervised Darwinian jungle. After all, they proposed, if human beings had invented clothing and shelter to protect themselves from the weather, why couldn't they devise institutions to prevent starvation, disease, and oppression of the poor? Although Darwin's ideas were valid only in the natural world, not the social milieu created by men, the reformers thought they could be adapted, through human ingenuity, to serve mankind.

Other optimistically inclined reformers found in the theory of evolution the handle they had been looking for. To them, Darwin's theory fitted in with the accepted American belief in progress, since society in urban-industrial America had moved from a simple to a very complex stage during the nineteenth century. Many American intellectuals saw themselves as part of a superior Western culture and saw all other cultures as marked off on a descending scale of human organization. Any culture, argued American anthropologist Lewis H. Morgan, that was illiterate (today we would say preliterate) and without a technology was of a lower, simpler order. This system of classification has endured a very long time. A century later, Americans still believe that a society that has no written language is primitive; only societies that have machinery and a literature are "civilized."

The Darwinian frame of reference could be applied to any human group. For example, some nineteenth-century experts on child-raising viewed children as simple, primitive creatures. Just as the people of New Guinea were unsophisticated by Western standards, and thus lower on the evolutionary scale, so were little children. They had to be tamed, educated, and socialized in order to become acceptable citizens. In the same way, women, blacks, and Indians were considered to be lower than white men on that scale. Darwin, who certainly had no intention of doing so, unwittingly gave intellectual respectability to an old, discriminatory scheme of thinking.

219

Old and New Problems 1880–1900

Fortunately, not everyone agreed with the theologians, scientists, and reformers who made such elaborate efforts to assimilate the theory of evolution into their own systems of thought. One of the most original thinkers of the century was Elizabeth Cady Stanton, whom we have met in earlier chapters. Her *Woman's Bible,* published in 1895, looked critically at the Old Testament from the feminist perspective. She boldly challenged the accepted theology at the same time that other critics were reexamining the Bible in the new light of Darwinism. A careful reading of Genesis made Mrs. Stanton wonder why there were two versions of how God created woman. In the first chapter of Genesis, woman is created as the equal of man ("male and female created He them"). In the second chapter, she emerges from Adam's rib. Mrs. Stanton's explanation was this:

> It is evident that some wily writer, seeing the perfect equality of man and woman in the first chapter, felt it important for the dignity and dominion of man to effect woman's subordination in some way. To do this a spirit of evil must be introduced, which at once proved itself stronger than the spirit of good, and man's supremacy was based on the downfall of all that had just been pronounced very good. This spirit of evil evidently existed before the supposed fall of man, hence woman was not the origin of sin as so often asserted.

By 1895, some people had accepted the Darwinian view of creation; few, however, were prepared to adopt the feminist one.

Then there was Charlotte Perkins Gilman (1860–1935), a leading feminist theoretician of the generation after 1880, who used the evolutionary model as the basis for her study *Women and Economics.*

An interesting and gifted woman, she transcended her upbringing to become a prolific writer and contributor to the women's rights movement. A New Englander, Charlotte recalled her childhood as bleak and loveless. Her father deserted the family, and her mother worked hard to support the children, but they moved frequently—nineteen times in eighteen years.

As an adolescent, Charlotte showed talent in art and design and later earned money painting "commercial cards." She also wrote poetry. At twenty-four, she married artist Charles Stetson and the following year gave birth to a girl. After that, melancholia overtook Charlotte, leaving her listless and despondent. Various rest cures only offered temporary relief.

220

Eventually she and Charles separated and were divorced. When he married her best friend, their daughter Katharine went to live with her father, causing an uproar in the community. Meanwhile, Charlotte began writing and lecturing. Her *Women and Economics,* published in 1898, made her a popular, influential writer and speaker on behalf of women—their rights and their potentialities.

Charlotte Gilman argued that the urban-industrial world was a fine example of evolutionary change but that women's role had not kept pace with that change. Although American progress had resulted in quantities of machine-made products, women remained in the home, tied to age-old domestic functions. The task ahead, said Mrs. Gilman, was to apply the advanced technology of industrialization to the home and thus free women from household drudgery. The specialization of labor and the use of individual expertise could be applied in the home with great success. Since all women were not equally good cooks or housekeepers, why not collectivize the cooking and cleaning functions? She envisioned a technologically equipped home in which expert cooks prepared food for many families and expert nurses cared for preschool children. Then career-minded and professionally trained mothers could do the kind of work that brought them the highest satisfaction. "The more absolutely woman is segregated to sex-functions only, cut off from all economic use and made wholly dependent on the sex-relation as means of livelihood, the more pathological does her motherhood become."

In short, Mrs. Gilman believed that progress in the machine age had to be accompanied by greater opportunities for human development—most notably female development. Society could not hope to achieve its full human potential without permitting women to realize and express their special talents. Little did she know that the technological changes she advocated would ultimately be made in American homes—but without any accompanying changes in women's lives.

Economist Thorstein Veblen, one of the most astute commentators on American society at the time, saw dangers in the widespread acceptance of industrialization. He did not look upon industrialization as a sign of a highly evolved culture, but rather as a less than desirable condition. One of its negative consequences, he believed, was the accumulation of great wealth by the very few who owned the means of production. The rich displayed their wealth in a variety of ways, such as bedecking their women with jewelry, furs, and showy clothes—"conspicuous consumption," he called it. They built large mansions on Fifth Avenue in New York City and Astor Street in Chicago, importing marble floors from Italy and filling sixty rooms with unique pieces of English and French furniture.

In all societies, Veblen noted, the richer and more successful find ways to display their station in life. In an industrial society, which had the potential for producing truly fabulous fortunes, women were used as ornaments, as figures to show off their husbands' wealth. Actually, rich women had no other useful function—if this passive role could be called useful. In an agricultural and commercial society, even rich women performed household and nurturing tasks. But in an urban, industrialized society, they were no more than mere figurines, upon whom their husbands showered luxuries. Veblen further observed that since human beings are imitators, mimicking the behavior of others, poor and middle-class people looked upon the rich as desirable models. Therefore society as a whole directed itself toward conspicuous consumption. The rich were the taste-makers, and all others strove to follow their lead.

This value system and this mode of human behavior portended horrible consequences. Veblen foresaw a nation of competitive, grasping people, each trying to outdo the other by acquiring more and more wealth, each trying to impress more and more people with his own success. The prospect was most distressing—the struggle for existence would become translated into a struggle for material possessions. Since capitalism does not permit all persons to profit equally, there would always be losers in this game; yet everyone would continue to play it. The value system, Veblen concluded, needed serious revising. Not only was its waste of human and material resources wholly irresponsible, but what kind of society would make idleness its highest virtue? The "idle rich" were the envied ideal in its scale of social worth. The American industrial culture, rather than bringing human beings together to engage in production for constructive use and to share resources, encouraged competition, the accumulation of unnecessary luxuries, and the spending of endless hours in frivolity.

Veblen's writings depicted a society gone wrong; its supposed evolutionary changes had not led to a better life for human beings but to selfishness, competition, and acquisitiveness. Still, to most people, evolution and progress were by now synonymous. Progress meant industrial expansion, not human improvement—though Charlotte Perkins Gilman and Thorstein Veblen agreed that no nation, no culture could "progress" without elevating the status of its women.

The progress of American society was measured by its new cities, its gross national product, its growing population, and its export figures. This was human-directed evolution, a telling example of American self-confidence. It provided the rationale for whatever measures the power brokers chose to enact. New buildings and new smokestacks became signs of progress. So did man's shaping of the physical environment to his own will, and so did filling up the continent with white people. Once again, Americans displayed their ability to accommodate new ideas to older ways of thinking, and to manipulate the human and natural environment to their own ends.

Women Writers Speak Out

In the last years of the century, as in all previous years, the critics of the dominant philosophy wrote, painted, and spoke their disapproval. While the Stephen Cranes and the Theodore Dreisers were picturing the bleak reality of industrial America in their fiction, a new group of women writers questioned, often in covert and subtle ways, the role of woman in America. They were a minority compared with the popular women writers who continued to grind out romantic novels, but they did break away from the successful formulas to describe the lives of anguished, frustrated women.

Among them was Kate O'Flaherty Chopin (1851–1904), who, while writing about Creole life and Southern women in New Orleans, expressed feminist yearnings that gained few sympathetic followers in her lifetime.

She herself was not a Southerner, but was born in St. Louis of an Irish immigrant father and a French mother. In 1870, she married a French Creole banker, Oscar Chopin. They moved to New Orleans and then to a sugar plantation in central Louisiana, where Kate had six children. In 1883, Oscar died of swamp fever, and Kate moved back to St. Louis where she began writing stories about the Creoles. They were indulgently viewed as local-color dialect pieces. Then came *The Awakening* (1899), a novella which caused a sensation.

The Awakening tells of Edna Pontellier, an upper-class New Orleans woman who finds her existence unbearable. Her love for a young man whom she meets at a summer resort makes her "realize her position in the universe as a human being, and . . . recognize her relations as an individual to the world within and about her." She later tells a friend that she would give her life for her children, but "I would not give myself." When asked to explain this remark, she says she cannot. Eventually she moves out of her husband's house and resolves "never again to belong to another than herself." The subversive, explosive material in this story might well have sparked the feminist movement, but it did not. When, at the end, Edna Pontellier walks into the ocean and drowns, most readers probably thought that this was the only possible conclusion to an idiosyncratic, troubled life. Few would believe that Edna's cry for help might also have been locked in the breasts of countless women of her time.

In this new fiction, the feminist plea was usually disguised. Mary E. Wilkins Freeman, a rather popular and able writer, always wrote about New England women who lived Spartan lives in village farming communities. In one story, "A New England Nun" (1891), Louisa waits fifteen years for her betrothed to return from Australia, where he has gone to make his fortune. When he comes back, she learns that he loves another woman. She releases him from his obligation to her because she does not want to change the comfortable routine that she developed during his absence. The author concludes: "If Louisa Ellis sold her birthright she did not know it, the taste of the pottage was so delicious, and had been her sole satisfaction for so long. Serenity and placid narrowness had become to her as the birthright itself."

Rarely indeed did American fiction (as well as American society) project the message that women might be content to remain unmarried. But "serenity and placid narrowness," a quaint phrase, suggests a life of happiness, not of sustained frustration. Another theme, which would become much more explicit in the twentieth century, also appeared in "A New England Nun": that a woman could, and would, consciously

Mary Wilkins Freeman, creator of fictional heroines.
(Brown Bros.)

choose spinsterhood and risk the unpleasantness which that
status conferred, rather than live with a man she did not love.
Mid-twentieth-century psychoanalysts might hint at a lesbian
overtone here, or some type of neurosis. Another explanation,
however, might arise from a realistic assessment of marriage,
with its family obligations, postponement of personal pleasures,
and constant demands for self-sacrifice. An extremely brave
woman who arrived at this assessment might very well prefer
personal freedom to the multiple responsibilities inherent in a
heterosexual, married relationship. Selfish, yes; unnatural, no.

Margaret Deland was also a popular author of the time. In her
Old Chester Tales (1898), she, like Miss Freeman, wrote about
New England women. The heroine of "The Promises of

225

Dorothea" lives with two maiden aunts, one of whom has been bedridden for more than thirty years—ever since she was jilted at the altar. The other aunt, a domineering woman, is determined that Dorothea will live the same confined life that she and her sister do. But Dorothea breaks loose and marries an older man who has returned to Chester for a visit. The theme of liberation—in this case from restricting, life-destroying spinsters—pervades Margaret Deland's stories. While "A New England Nun" portrays spinsterhood as a desirable, self-determined life, "The Promises of Dorothea" suggests that spinsterhood may be a denial of life, a living death.

Although these stories, along with many others, pictured women in varying states and circumstances, female readers preferred dramatic or melodramatic tales of women's tribulations. The self-sacrificing heroine had a tremendous appeal, reflecting the accepted idea that woman's role, be she married or single, was to sacrifice, to forgo self-gratification in ensuring the pleasure of others. In fiction, as well as in fact, there were few Edna Pontelliers who cried out for their right to be individuals, different from anyone else. Most women repressed their feelings of discontent, or exhibited them only in covert ways. Most

Popular novelist
Margaret Deland.
(N.Y. Public Library)

suffered and endured in stoical fashion. But the women's fiction of the late nineteenth century both described and prophesied the feelings many women would express in years to come.

Suggestions for Further Reading

Jane Addams. *Twenty Years at Hull House* (New York, 1910).

Robert Bremner. *From the Depths: The Discovery of Poverty in the United States* (New York, 1956).

Dee Brown. *Bury My Heart at Wounded Knee* (New York, 1971).

Kate Chopin. *The Awakening and Other Stories* (New York, 1971).

Allen F. Davis. *An American Heroine: The Life and Legend of Jane Addams* (New York, 1973).

Allen F. Davis. *Spearheads for Reform: The Social Settlements and the Progressive Movement, 1890–1914* (New York, 1967).

Vine Deloria, Jr. *Custer Died for Our Sins* (New York, 1969).

R. L. Duffus. *Lillian Wald, Neighbor and Crusader* (New York, 1938).

Charlotte Perkins Gilman. *The Living of Charlotte Perkins Gilman* (New York, 1935).

Charlotte Perkins Gilman. *Women and Economics* (Boston, 1898).

Arthur Mann. *Yankee Reformers in the Urban Age* (Cambridge, Mass., 1954).

August Meier and Elliott M. Rudwick. *From Plantation to Ghetto* (New York, 1966).

Lillian Wald. *The House on Henry Street* (New York, 1915).

C. Vann Woodward. *The Strange Career of Jim Crow* (New York, 1966).

CHAPTER NINE

Women Remaking the World

1900–1914

As a colored woman I cannot visit the tomb of the Father of this country, which owes its very existence to the love of freedom in the human heart and which stands for equal opportunity to all, without being forced to sit in the Jim Crow section of an electric car which starts from the very heart of the city—midway between the Capitol and the White House.

> —Mary Church Terrell, *What It Means to Be Colored in the Capital of the United States*, 1907

Dante is dead. He has been dead for several centuries, and I think it is time that we dropped the study of the Inferno and turned our attention to our own.

> —Elizabeth Platt Decker, President, General Federation of Women's Clubs, 1904

You know at twenty I signed on to serve my country for the duration of the war on poverty and injustice and oppression, and I take it . . . that it will last out my life and yours and our children's lives.

> —Florence Kelley, Social reformer, 1910

Whether a product of the working-class or the middle-class, she was always curious, rebellious, and high-spirited. If she discovered sweatshop conditions from first-hand experience, she became outraged, joined a union, and began organizing other women.

If she became a reformer after learning about a particular social problem from a newspaper account, a friend's remarks, or a professor's outrage, she too became actively interested in *doing* something about it.

She was confident of her own powers as a person; she rejected the cultural definition of a woman and her parents' generational goals for women.

229

Women Remaking the World 1900–1914

She was better educated than her mother, convinced that she could control her own destiny, willing to experiment with life-styles. She sometimes tried marriage, often did not. If she had children, she tried to raise them while pursuing a social cause or a career. She struggled all her life with the problem of being involved in the world while maintaining a home. She never gave up fighting for the causes in which she believed.

—*Portrait of a Feminist, 1910 Style*

*A*merican women entered the twentieth century with the same obligations and responsibilities that had always occupied them. They continued to manage the home and the family. They remained the providers and preservers of a warm, stable home atmosphere. In addition, they helped to humanize society through their volunteer activities, and they worked in factories and offices. Those of the growing middle class frequently joined women's organizations and worked for the betterment of the poor and the orphaned. The college educated entered the "helping professions"—social welfare, nursing, and teaching. The concept of woman as helper harks back to the Hebraic interpretation of the word "Eve," and as social problems increased in industrial, urban America, Eve's descendants found their help urgently needed.

New Women Leaders Emerge

Each generation contributes new leaders as well as new issues to its particular causes. In the early twentieth century, a number of exciting and able women assumed leadership in a variety of reform efforts. Alice Paul (1885–), a Quaker from Philadelphia, had learned from experiences in England in the 1900s that the cause of woman's suffrage could succeed only when militant tactics were employed. Hence she infused new strategies into the rather staid National American Woman's Suffrage Association (NAWSA), and drew widespread attention to the suffrage movement.

231

Women Remaking the World 1900–1914

Carrie Chapman Catt (1859–1947), a former school superintendent from Mason City, Iowa, worked with Elizabeth Cady Stanton and Susan B. Anthony in state suffrage campaigns during the 1890s. She herself was credited with organizing the victorious campaign for suffrage in Colorado in 1893. She served as president of the NAWSA from 1900 to 1904, when she resigned to head up the International Woman Suffrage Alliance. In 1920, after the ratification of the Nineteenth Amendment, Mrs. Catt organized the League of Women Voters to help educate women in political matters.

Elizabeth Gurley Flynn (1890–1964), who at the age of fifteen in 1905 spoke eloquently on the street corners of New York City, told her audiences that workers deserved and demanded better wages and better working conditions. "Gurley," as the workers called her, became a leading organizer for the Industrial Workers of the World (the "Wobblies"), a radical union formed to

Suffrage leader
Carrie Chapman
Catt. (Bettmann)

Elizabeth Gurley Flynn addressing strikers in Patterson,
N.J., 1913. (Brown Bros.)

organize unskilled coal miners, copper miners, and textile workers.

Crystal Eastman (1881–1928), a New York City lawyer with a master's degree in social work, was a leading spirit in the woman's peace movement after 1914, as well as a leading spokeswoman for feminism. Emma Goldman's stirring speeches advocating anarchism were widely publicized in the press. Crowds gathered wherever she spoke, as they did to hear Gurley, Alice Paul, Crystal Eastman, and other charismatic new thinkers and activists. And the first fourteen years of this century were exciting ones for all who were infected by the belief in human progress. Reformers delighted in the opportunity to work for worthwhile causes. Life had a guiding purpose for Jane Addams and Lillian Wald. Life presented great challenges to union advocates such as Sidney Hillman, Rose Schneiderman, and Mary Anderson. The future appeared full of hope to Norman Thomas, a budding young Socialist, and to Eugene Debs, a well-known Socialist leader. Achieving the perfect society seemed quite possible, though these social reformers knew that a great deal of hard work would be needed to accomplish that mighty goal.

Women with jobs also united during these years to demand better working conditions. In 1909, a general strike called by shirtwaist workers took thousands of employees, mainly women, away from their factory jobs. The Women's Trade Union League, organized in 1903 by middle- and working-class women, publicized the plight of strikers, enlisted the financial aid of wealthy women, and helped draft favorable workers' contracts. Working girls who spoke out at labor meetings in New York City and Philadelphia gained a sense of power over their own lives that they had never known before. In the trade union movement, Agnes Nestor and Mary Anderson of Chicago found comradeship and a heightened commitment to meaningful work. Women and men built a whole life style upon their devotion to unionism.

Middle-class women such as Margaret Dreier Robins and Florence Kelley also discovered a new purpose in life by crusading for working women. Florence Kelley worked as executive secretary for the Consumers League, a propaganda organization aimed at gaining protective labor legislation for women and children. She and her supporters saw that these workers, more than men, were particularly vulnerable creatures of industrialism and needed special laws to protect them. So the Consumers League worked long and hard to get the states and the federal government to pass maximum-hours and minimum-wage laws for women, together with child labor laws that prohibited young children from working in factories. The League's successes were few and their disappointments many, but its members remained committed to their cause for decades. Later, when some feminists suggested an equal rights amendment which would erase all protective laws from the books, Florence Kelley was enraged and went into action against it. She found herself fighting other women crusaders as well as the apathetic populace, which cared nothing about women's working conditions or women's rights.

CASE STUDY OF A WORKING WOMAN

Interview No. 2.—An early marriage did not give Anna T. the leisure and economic security she expected. Instead her burdens

Florence Kelley,
social reformer.
(N.Y. Public Library)

235

increased, and now she is glad if she has food and clothing for her family. In 1912, shortly after her father died in Hungary, Anna at the age of 16 came alone to the United States. With neither friends nor relatives to help her find work she followed women on their way to work and on her own initiative found a job in a cigar factory, where she began as a bunch maker and earned $2.50 the first week. Within a year she married a laborer, but he was often ill, his job was too heavy, and he lost much time, so they could not count on a full week's pay. In the 10 years of her married life she had given birth to six children, four of whom were living at the time of the interview. But childbirth never interfered long with her status as a wage earner; she worked within a week or so of confinement and always returned when the babies were very little. Sometimes her baby was brought to the factory for her to nurse during working hours.

Since 1912 Anna has worked 9 hours, 10 hours, day after day, and now one week's pay barely covers the monthly rental of $15. She lives in a dingy house with no gas and no sewer connection, but she is thankful that, having lived in communities where bunch makers are in demand, she has always been able to find work.

—Caroline Manning, *The Immigrant Woman and Her Job,* 1970 reprint, p. 14.

Most of the social reformers of the period believed, with the majority of Americans, not only that political democracy was the best human institution ever created, but that capitalism could be purged of its injustices to permit the full development of human potentialities. All that was needed was a greater public awareness of social ills; then the people themselves would gladly correct them. This faith in the good will of an enlightened public **has always** characterized reformers. There was no deep pessimism or sense of futility, for reformers felt the world could be changed and their labors would be rewarded.

The women activists, on the other hand, were not so optimistic. Surely they must have wondered at times whether their day of victory would ever come. Veterans of the woman's suffrage campaign could only have shuddered at the tenacity with which male Americans kept on denying them the right to vote.

One of America's best known women: Jane Addams.
(Brown Bros.)

Lillian Wald, nurse, settlement house leader, and peace advocate. (Brown Bros.)

Recalling the hope and excitement of the 1870s and 1880s, they might well have been discouraged. But the truly amazing feature of the movement was the suffragists' unswerving devotion to their cause.

Jane Addams and Lillian Wald had begun their careers with settlement work in the 1880s and by the 1920s had broadened the scope of their activities to include crusading for suffrage and pacifism. Crystal Eastman organized the Wisconsin state suffrage campaign in 1913, then went on to join Alice Paul in the formation of the Congressional Union, a more militant suffrage group. Still later, Crystal Eastman became the executive secretary of a pacifist organization called the American Union Against Militarism and also the chairwoman of the Woman's Peace Party in New York City. Elizabeth Gurley Flynn saw the inside of many jails in her travels across the country organizing workers for the Wobblies. After 1914, she too spoke against war and temporarily interrupted her union work for peace work.

World War I disrupted many lives, as we shall see in the next chapter. But before 1914, almost everybody was convinced that the world could be improved through peaceful means. There was no serious malaise among the intellectuals or the population at large. The intellectuals who gathered in New York City's Greenwich Village enjoyed a community of like-minded people. Even when their ideas were unacceptable to the general public, they found sympathetic listeners in the Village. Human knowledge seemed to be expanding at such a speedy and exciting rate that Village intellectuals felt they were on the brink of great social discoveries and breakthroughs. Many years later, Elizabeth Gurley Flynn recalled the euphoria of this period:

> I felt then, as I do now, it's a rich, fertile, beautiful country, capable of satisfying all the needs of its people. It could be a paradise on earth if it belonged to the people, not to a small owning class. I expressed all this in my speeches for Socialism.

In her speeches, Gurley declared again and again that America had the ability to change itself. And as Alice Paul worked for a national suffrage amendment, she was convinced that she and her co-workers could eventually persuade legislators to pass it. The task would be long and hard, the labor back-breaking, but it could and would be accomplished. The

239

suffrage leaders, the labor leaders, the writers who advocated reform, and the public speakers all shared this conviction.

Feminist-philosopher Charlotte Perkins Gilman continued to write about every dimension of woman's life in America. One subject that aroused her critical attention was women's fashions, against which she directed her strongest barbs. True to her evolutionary socialist perspective, Mrs. Gilman argued that social conformity, as exemplified by the fact that women dressed according to male standards, characterized a lower form of social development. As human beings evolved, they became more individualistic and socialistic, in the best sense of those terms. They abandoned the herd instinct and the desire to look, think, and act like every other member of their group. Hence the need to conform displayed, sad to say, the American woman's immature development as a human being.

There were, however, Mrs. Gilman suggested, other reasons for women's slavish devotion to fashion.

Charlotte Perkins Gilman, feminist philosopher.
(Brown Bros.)

Here we have three lines of approach: one the economic dependence of women upon men, which, as we have shown, causes her to
vary in costume in order to win and hold his variable taste; another
the tendency to "conspicuous expenditure," shown by Veblen,
which causes both men and women to exhibit clothes, rather than
wear them—the more the better; and third, a result of our artificial
classification of society, in which social position is indicated by
dress, with the consequence that the natural tendency to conform
and to imitate is reinforced by the desire to resemble someone
higher up, a species of "protective mimicry."

Mrs. Gilman's critique, written in 1915 for her magazine *The
Forerunner,* remains a perceptive and accurate description of
women's devotion to fashion in the latter part of the twentieth
century. "The girl growing into youth and womanhood, finds
nothing to check the doll-and-baby influences, or the imitative
instinct." Although her extensive discussion of this subject was
dispassionate on the whole, Mrs. Gilman could not resist
expressing her exasperation with her sisters:

Only in dress, and almost wholly in the dress of women, is it
possible to dictate to half the adult population as if they were a lot of
hypnotized dummies.
"Fix your eyes on Me!" say the Leading Couturiers. The eyes
are fixed—glued—in silent adoration.
"Think exclusively about clothes in relation to the orders I
give!"
They think exclusively.
"Now then, attention! Act promptly please! Up with the waist-
line!"
It goes up.
"Down with the waistline!"
It goes down.
"Away with the waistline!"
It goes away.

There is no better gauge of woman's continued dependency
upon male standards than fashions in dress. Charlotte Perkins
Gilman, like economist Thorstein Veblen, appreciated that fact.
The new technology could produce more dresses in a variety of
colors and styles, but it did not free women from dressing
according to the dictates of male designers, male manufacturers,

and their husbands' views of proper womanly attire. Only women could do this for themselves.

Another aspect of woman's life that provoked the ire of this fearless feminist was the alimony granted to divorced wives—a further sign of their dependence on men. Mrs. Gilman's words on this subject are only now, in the 1970s, being echoed by social critics. Here is what she wrote about it in *The Forerunner* for March 1912:

> Alimony is the meanest money that is taken—by women. It is bad enough to marry for money; it is bad enough to maintain an immoral marriage for money; but to give up this mercenary commerce and then take money when no longer delivering the goods—! There is only one meanness to be mentioned in the same breath; taking "damages" for "breach of promise."
>
> Some hold it a man's duty to "support" his wife, on the ground that her position as his wife prevents her from earning her living. When she is no longer his wife then it doesn't hold. . . .
>
> Some argue that the husband should provide support for his children; "his" children, note. They are also "hers" surely. But even if he should have the whole burden of their maintenance —that is not "Alimony." Divorcees without children, young women, quite competent to earn their livings, eagerly claim alimony, take it and live on it; never giving a thought to the nature of their position.
>
> But a woman's health is often ruined—she is in no condition to earn her living—is urged.
>
> Very well. If a woman is really injured by her marriage, she should sue under the employer liability act. She should claim damages—not alimony.

"New" Women

At this time the term "new woman" arose to describe a new type of young working girl. She was probably a secretary, or stenographer, or clerk in a large or medium-sized city. She lived away from home in one of the growing number of apartment buildings and enjoyed far greater freedom than her mother had. Her presence on the urban scene was due, of course, to the fact that more and more girls were completing high school, going on to college, and getting jobs.

On the surface, women's rights seemed to be making

progress—but only on the surface. On the eve of World War I, women still could not vote. Most employed women worked at low-paying jobs, and most wives followed essentially the same life pattern as did their mothers. Few women looked on themselves as individual beings who could carry on a rewarding existence without a husband and a family.

The professional organizations still barred women, regardless of their qualifications. With only a few exceptions, such as Dr. Sarah Stevenson of Chicago, the American Medical Association refused membership to women doctors in the belief that men were better suited to practice medicine. Women lawyers still found it difficult to try cases in court or to receive impartial treatment in law school. "Woman's work" was no more broadly defined than it ever was, though isolated examples of women in diverse male occupations could be found. Statisticians, always eager to disprove an accepted thesis, displayed figures showing that women were represented in more than three hundred of the nation's major job categories. The fact that women carpenters, plumbers, and bricklayers even existed seemed to prove, to those who wanted to believe it, that women now had equal job opportunities with men. In reality, the presence of a few women in a variety of jobs proved nothing about the general working conditions in these jobs, and certainly did not signify true progress. Male carpenters did not encourage or aid women who wanted to enter their field; the bricklayers union did not admit women.

As always, most women married and had children. Large families, with six or seven children, were still the norm. By and large, even highly educated women accepted their traditional roles as wives, mothers, and preservers of the culture. Consider these excerpts from a report on Vassar College graduates:

Class of 1897, married: "I liked domestic life before I went to college—and have liked it ever since. As one of a large family I had been used to cook, sew, clean, iron, mend, etc., and I have been doing these things all my life, with enjoyment, in bringing up a family of five children."

Class of 1908, single, with a job: "My own experience and my observations convince me that the college graduate adapts herself to domestic life more intelligently than any other woman. Having

243

learned how to go at and master any job—intellectual or executive or manual—as any student who took part in Vassar's extracurricular activities certainly did, a girl can master household management as well as office routine, salesmanship, or teaching."

Class of 1911, married: "I do not blame college for my lack of domestic training, but rather my earlier home life. I think girls should be taught household essentials by the time they are in their early teens. Luckily I have a patient and tolerant husband."

Class of 1912, married, with a job: "My home is my hobby, and I have never looked upon my way of life as including a 'double job.' I enjoy home-making, just as I enjoy professional work."

Class of 1912, married: "Vassar showed me how to overcome the difficulties of domestic life. Housekeeping was a bugbear to me, but I read up on it and planned schedules that work out satisfactorily enough."

—Agnes Rogers, *Vassar Women: An Informal History*, 1940

The National American Woman's Suffrage Association plugged hopefully along despite serious opposition to its cause. The Women's Christian Temperance Union also persevered and propagandized for the abolition of liquor. Both movements had to wait until 1920, after the war, to experience the sweet taste of success. Indeed, the fact that suffragists had to work for fifty years before woman's suffrage became the law of the land indicates how difficult it has been, and is, to bring about any kind of significant change in American society. Of course, both the advocates and the opponents of suffrage assigned entirely too much importance to its ultimate effect on the country. The advocates promised the uplifting and purifying of politics, and the opponents predicted the immediate downfall of the family. Neither group was right, but because both foresaw dramatic social changes as a result of suffrage, the reformers had to fight an unduly long battle to achieve it.

The Socialist Party of America was the first political party to recognize women's rights and, in theory, equal rights for black Americans. But the party did little to express its support of either cause. (*Political note:* Black Americans who voted—that is, those who lived in the North—generally voted Republican out of gratitude to Lincoln for his Emancipation Proclamation. The

Democrats began cultivating the black vote during this period, but did not have any major success until the Franklin D. Roosevelt era.) The Socialist party saw women as an exploited class, just like workers. If the working class could be granted its rights, they reasoned, then women would win theirs. Many feminists agreed. Just as the nineteenth-century women abolitionists identified the cause of women's rights with the cause of freedom for blacks, so the early twentieth-century feminists identified the woman's movement with Socialist goals. Unfortunately, many of them discovered (as did their predecessors in an earlier generation and their successors in a later one) that the attitudes of male reformer-radicals were often quite traditional when the issue was women's rights. Lena Morrow Lewis, a Socialist party organizer, was exiled to Alaska when rumors spread that she was guilty of a sexual indiscretion. But the male involved with her did not suffer the same fate.

Many of the feminists who identified with the Socialist party and voted for its candidates retained their independence in every other way. Elizabeth Gurley Flynn considered herself one of the Wobblies and a free spirit. Emma Goldman labeled herself an anarchist, free of all organizational restraints and all restricting definitions. Henrietta Rodman, a schoolteacher who spoke and wrote about feminism, was a socialist. In fact, socialism became the fashionable philosophy for all good critics of American society. Walter Lippmann, a college graduate in 1912, considered himself a socialist, though he soon gave up that designation. Reformers who criticized the evils of industrial capitalism saw socialism as a desirable alternative, but although they spoke of it in glowing generalizations, they could bring forth few concrete illustrations to show how a socialist state would operate. Not until the Russian Revolution of 1917 did radicals have a real-life demonstration of effective socialism at work—or so they thought.

Black Spokespeople

We poor colored women wage-earners in the South are fighting a terrible battle. . . . On the one hand, we are assailed by white men, and, on the other hand, we are assailed by black men, who should be our natural protectors; and, whether in the cook kitchen, at the

245

washtub, over the sewing machine, behind the baby carriage, or at the ironing board, we are but little more than pack horses, beasts of burden, slaves!

. . . I believe nearly all white men take, and expect to take, undue liberties with their colored female servants.

—*More Slavery at the South,* by a Negro nurse, *The Independent,* January 25, 1912

Black leaders similarly remained committed to the American Dream and to its realization for all black Americans. During the opening years of this century, two key black organizations worked for the true emancipation of their people: the Urban League and the National Association for the Advancement of Colored People. Whereas the Urban League concentrated on helping Southern blacks adjust to life in all the major cities of the North, the NAACP used the courts to test civil rights laws for black Americans.

Both blacks and whites supported the two organizations. W. E. B. Du Bois, the first black man to receive a Ph.D. from Harvard, became the editor of the NAACP's magazine *Crisis.* Under his leadership, this magazine, from its inception in 1912 until 1934, was one of the most eloquent voices for black freedom in America.

By 1900, a significant minority of educated blacks had emerged to assume leadership in their own communities. These leaders, primarily educated in the North and often mulattoes born into free Northern families, had all the characteristics of reformers and intellectuals in general. They wrote well, spoke well, held university appointments, and propagandized for their cause. Kelly Miller, a sociologist at Howard University, contributed frequent articles to *Crisis* and personally promoted many efforts in behalf of blacks. Alain Locke edited a collection of black writing in the 1920s that demonstrated the distinguished literary talents of a number of black authors.

Booker T. Washington was still the most visible and well-known black leader in the country. Perhaps because the thought or prospect of a sizable group of capable black leaders made white Americans uncomfortable, they preferred to recognize one black man as the spokesman for his people. Despite an increase in black migration to the North during the opening years of the century, the majority of black Americans continued to live in the South. There the black ministers in hundreds of communities maintained a strong influence over their people. While black university professors and Harlem intellectuals were a minority compared with the black clergy, the three groups, taken together, represented a far richer and more diverse group of leaders than white Americans realized. After Booker T. Washington talked with President Theodore Roosevelt in the early 1900s, Washington became the most popular Negro in the nation, but he did not speak for all black people any more than one white person can truly speak for all whites.

One of the cruel disillusionments many black Americans experienced at the time was their reception in the North. The *Chicago Defender,* a well-known black newspaper, told Southern blacks who migrated to the North that they had come to a land of opportunity, free of lynching, Jim Crow laws, and racism. Unfortunately, this optimistic assertion was far from accurate. The North did discriminate heavily against blacks, though usually in subtle ways. In business and industry, blacks were the last hired and the first fired. They were shunted into the worst housing any city had to offer, and their children were segregated in inferior schools. The cold winters of Chicago and New York were a further ordeal for the black Mississippians who came North without overcoats. And another kind of chill afflicted many of the newcomers, the chill of loneliness. The close personal relationships of the rural Southern community, they found, did not exist in the North; strangers lived all around them. Finally, black families had a hard time making ends meet. At least when you lived on the land, thought many Southern blacks, you always had something to eat. Life was much more precarious in the North.

New York's Harlem, which became a haven for emigrating blacks during this period and on into the twenties, offered them little sense of kinship or comradeship based upon color. Its population included black foreigners from the Caribbean islands—strange, unfamiliar people who seemed as unfriendly as the whites. The hostile atmosphere of the big city infected these members of the same race, and they often fought among themselves. Just as all women in America never could work together for their common benefit, so all black people did not perceive that their interests were the same. The individualistic

247

creed of America, combined with its class distinctions, has always separated groups that might otherwise have acted in concert to achieve common goals.

White Northerners showed their hostility toward the newly arrived blacks by throwing stones at those who moved into white communities, arresting blacks on trumped-up charges, mistreating laborers on the job, and starting race riots. Between 1900 and 1914, there was at least one race riot a year in the United States, with an equal number in the North and in the South. Between 1910 and 1914, 347 lynchings were recorded, and 100 in 1915. Now white Northerners knew what white Southerners had been telling them for years—that the North would no longer be smugly tolerant when faced with a race problem of its own. Northern liberalism could not endure the test of experience; it gave way to the same racist attitudes that white Southerners had always had.

Black leaders in the North continued to work within their communities for the uplift of their people, but most black reformers believed (as did white reformers) that despite Northern discrimination, conditions in the South were worse for blacks. Thus, the leaders focused much of their energy on enlisting Northerners' aid in their fight against lynching, convict-leasing, and Jim Crow laws. Black reformers knew better than to preach any such changes in the South. In fact, if they valued their lives, they stayed in the North.

In 1925, Walter White, a longtime executive of the NAACP, published a novel called *Fire in the Flint*, which vividly described Southern examples of violence, discrimination, and lynching. It became a best-seller in the North but had no sale at all in the South. Southern white booksellers would never even stock a book that was written by a black man and criticized life in the South. In the pages of *Crisis*, NAACP reporters wrote about the evils of convict-leasing, segregated schools, and black sharecropping, but although the NAACP managed to establish some local groups in the South, discretion and diplomacy had to be used to avoid conflicts with the sensitive Southern white power structure. Pre–Civil War Southern politicians would never entertain negative comments about their social system, and white politicians of the twentieth century carried on the same tradition. So all efforts to inform Northerners about conditions in the South did little to change the lives of Southern blacks.

248

Within black society, light-skinned Negroes frequently attained positions of leadership. Mulattoes, with white benefactors in their past, were often better educated than their blacker brothers. Then, too, some blacks tended to have more respect for light-skinned Negroes than for those with darker skins. They adopted the white American view that white is right—meaning that the lighter a black man was, the closer he was to acceptance by the desirable white society. In Philadelphia, the black upper crust had an exclusive organization called the Blue Vein Society which had one entrance requirement: a visible blue vein in a black person's forehead. Sad to say, white Americans had succeeded in inculcating their own warped values into many black Americans. Yet the phenomenon is understandable. Blacks adopted white standards because whites represented power and prestige. The powerless identified with the powerful, a natural human pattern.

The idea of blackness as evil and ignorance, and of whiteness as virtue and knowledge, seems to be as old as Western civilization. In a white society, those who dominate impose their will on all others. Slavery in America confirmed the inferiority of dark-skinned peoples, and the white-is-right notion persisted after the slaves were freed. Both white people and blacks were captives of the same ideology, and both tried to live by it. Blacks, therefore, suffered mentally and emotionally because of their color. Some blamed themselves for their sorry fate and, if their skin color was light enough, tried to pass into white society.

Black intellectuals as early as the 1910s lamented this slavish imitation of the white man, and urged blacks to be proud of their race. It was during the 1920s that Langston Hughes, one of America's great poets, proclaimed "Black is beautiful." To encourage racial pride, black teachers in the South told their pupils about Harriet Tubman, the black slave woman who worked for the Underground Railroad; about Frederick Douglass, an escaped slave who spoke and worked for freedom; and other black heroes. But it was a difficult task. Surely they all wanted to believe this, but it was hard for them to translate the belief into reality. And in a materialistic society, in which the white power brokers dangled alluring tangible rewards before everyone's eyes, how could anyone resist working toward those rewards within the framework of the system?

Still, in this period there were no major revolts by blacks or unskilled white laborers. Sharecroppers did not rise in rebellion. Women did not walk out of their homes en masse. From oppressed and discriminated-against groups came leaders who articulated their causes with moving eloquence but with no great success. From the woman's movement came suffragists, feminists, and Socialists who merged their causes with the working-class movement. Blacks created their own organizations to cope with the multiple and diverse problems facing their people. But the U.S. Congress did not pass either the woman's suffrage amendment or an anti-lynching law. The provisions of the Fourteenth and Fifteenth amendments regarding the rights of all citizens continued to be ignored, and U.S. presidents generally avoided these explosive issues.

Winners and Losers

Those who fought to conserve and preserve the natural environment continued their uphill battle against power companies that wanted to surround Niagara Falls with a commercial jungle, and lumber companies that tried to take over thousands of acres of government land. Every proposal for a new national park faced towering opposition—and a desperate struggle. The editors of *The Outlook* magazine reminded their readers in 1901:

> At this stage, when the tide of commercial energy is at the flood, those who care for the mind and the soul of America should watch with a vigilant eye the encroachments of trade on beauty, and should organize themselves together to protect that natural wealth which God has given the people of the United States; which belongs not only to them, but to their posterity and to the world, and which they have no right to alienate.

Such warnings from many sources did not impress the industrialists. True, the collective expertise of increasing numbers of engineers, geologists, and land surveyors did provide some enlightened information on the use and waste of natural resources. But it was often disregarded, especially when agencies like the Army Corps of Engineers willingly gave private industry the right to pollute the waterways and to dam rivers for its own profit.

250

Precious metals were eagerly torn out of the ground, bringing devastation and ruin to land and people alike. Elizabeth Gurley Flynn recalled what Butte, Montana, looked like at the turn of the century.

> A practice then prevailed to burn the sulphur out of the copper in great piles near the mines, before it was sent to the smelters. The poisoned fumes pervaded the city and killed all vegetation. Not a blade of grass, a flower, a tree, could be seen in this terrible city. A sprawly, ugly place, with dusty shacks for the miners, it had an ever-expanding cemetery out on the flat lands. The city of the dead, mostly young miners, was almost as large as the living population, even in this very young city.

Both human and natural life died rapidly as nature's riches were gobbled up by profiteers.

The first President of the twentieth century, Theodore Roosevelt, spoke out for conservation with a forcefulness hitherto unknown in the White House. A great lover of the outdoors, Roosevelt organized the Inland Waterways Commission, held conferences on conservation, established national bird sanctuaries, extended the acreage of the national forests, and generally publicized the need to conserve natural resources. Since the buffalo had all but been destroyed as a viable species, in 1905 President Roosevelt signed an act of Congress creating the first American game preserve, which contained fifteen buffaloes.

A great many pieces of conservation legislation were passed by Congress in the first decade of the century, but sufficient funds were never appropriated to do any job effectively. Further, few conservationists had a broad view of their field. Irrigation experts, soil experts, wildlife preservationists all saw only their own specific problems, never integrating them into the ecological system as a whole. The result was a series of piecemeal efforts to deal with, if not actually conserve, our natural resources, along with a feeling on the part of uninformed Americans that conservation was not a serious social problem.

Meanwhile the middle class of America—white-collar workers, blue-collar workers, some farmers, and professional persons—was enjoying the fruits of industrialization. Now peo-

251

ple could travel across the country on one of five transcontinental railroads, and they could communicate by telephone and telegraph with remote parts of the globe. But the lower class did not benefit from the new industrialization. In the cities, the unskilled workers (often recent immigrants) lived in crowded slums. In the country, tenant farmers and sharecroppers, both black and white, were huddled in thin-walled shacks on their own land. Wherever these people lived and worked, their meager earnings barely paid for necessities. Many of them, out of frustration and hopelessness, spent their money on liquor and immediate pleasures.

Before the First World War, factory-produced home appliances, automobiles, and other goods were not cheap. In fact, only the middle and upper classes could afford the consumer products coming off the newly created assembly lines. In the early 1900s, the automobile was still an unusual phenomenon, a luxury. An American car in 1908 cost $2,500, and its high cost made skeptics doubtful whether the automobile would ever be a major form of transportation. The roads were poor, and there was no such thing as a highway system. Furthermore, the accident rate was already high. Frederick Dwight wrote in *The Independent,* a popular magazine of the day, that in Massachusetts in 1907, 62 people had been killed and 640 seriously injured in automobile accidents. He concluded his discussion of the automobile by saying:

> I think the time when motor vehicles are desirable assets to society at large is yet to come, and that at present a certain excess must be charged to them in the debit column. They have engendered a reckless personal extravagance that must bring remorse and suffering to many some day. They have produced a new contempt for authority and an unusually lawless and irresponsible class. Finally, with little or no compensating advantage to the communities thru which they hurry, they have caused the taxpayers heavy expense for roads, have almost driven the more leisurely from them, and have then proceeded to destroy the highways themselves. All of these things are doubtless curable and will be remedied in time. At present, however, they exist.

A number of interesting points come to light in this passage. For one, even in the first decade of our century, at least some people had apprehensions about motor vehicles. Frederick

Dwight foresaw a vastly accelerated pace of living as the leisurely carriages gave way to the frantic new high-speed (some thirty miles an hour) monsters. Dwight's conclusion, however, truly typified the disposition of most social critics: "All of these things are doubtless curable and will be remedied in time." This naive assumption, based on faith in reason, technology, and progress, led white American males to believe they could discover solutions to all existing problems, even war. There would never be war again, many "civilized" Americans proclaimed in 1900, while complimenting themselves on their new inventions and their material prosperity.

When the twentieth century began, Europeans had not had a major war for almost a hundred years. Americans, separated from the European continent by the Atlantic Ocean, were sure that if war did break out in Europe they could, and would, stay out of it. They had enough to do in their own country. Already the United States was rapidly overtaking England and Germany in the industrial race, and the American continent still contained more than 500 million acres of uncultivated Western lands. True, California and Oregon were settled and were thriving states of the Union, but between the West Coast and the East were vast unsettled tracts. Millions of immigrants were attracted to these shores during the first fourteen years of the century, all infected by the same optimism and faith in the future, all convinced that America was the Promised Land whose streets were paved with gold.

The new system of values, by which money and material possessions were translated to mean personal happiness, became confirmed in the twentieth century. In the earlier agricultural society, people had placed far more value on other human beings, family background, religious ties, and educational achievement. Now, in an urban industrial society, city people were thrown together without knowing anything about their neighbors. And where the sense of a stable community life was lacking, the only way of judging and evaluating a person's worth or status was by outward, material signs—the clothes one wore, the house and furnishings one possessed, the carriage one drove. All these, taken together, provided an accurate barometer to gauge a person's economic and social position. And as Veblen had pointed out a decade earlier, the richest people in the community showed off their wealth through ostentatious display.

Of course, the economic yardstick for judging human worth was not invented in the twentieth century. Even in Puritan New England, a rich man had greater power and influence in a community than a poor man. Indeed, in those days, religious-minded people associated material success with spiritual rewards: the Lord favored the endeavors of those who worshipped him. Thus, an equation between the material and the spiritual developed, and though the religious element of the equation was soon forgotten, the material determination of a person's worth remained.

The costly process of becoming an industrialized, urbanized society was paid for by the poor and the underprivileged in this country. But because Americans evaluated everything in material, rather than human, terms, there was no serious effort to redress people's grievances or to humanize capitalism. The successful and the unsuccessful shared the same philosophy of individualism, the same belief in progress. Socialists who suggested distributing profits equally among workers were viewed by the majority as dangerous subversives who wanted to destroy the American way of life. Workers did not rush in huge numbers to join the Socialist ranks. Although the Socialist party enjoyed its greatest success in the early twentieth century, it was never able to impress the legitimacy of its philosophy on the majority of Americans.

New Visions

The artists and writers of this period, as in other eras, looked at the world with a perception far different from that of the majority. In 1913, the famed New York Armory Show of modern French painting revealed some completely new and disturbing concepts of reality. Marcel Duchamps' "Nude Descending a Staircase" caused a sensation. This abstract painting, in which neither a nude nor a staircase could be discerned, startled art lovers with its unique representation of continuous movement. The Impressionist painters, as they strove to break up light itself into the colors of the spectrum, seemed to fragment reality, to destroy traditional images. Picasso painted the human form in novel and shocking ways. T. S. Eliot's poetry, in similar fashion, departed from the nice sentiments and predictable forms of earlier poets.

Social scientists—influenced by that discoverer of the unconscious mind, Sigmund Freud—claimed that each individual's deeply hidden nature was a subject worth exploring and that each culture, too, could provide valuable insights into mankind's way of interpreting reality. Commentators on foreign policy, surveying the Western world in the early 1900s, decided that the United States and Russia would be the most powerful nations of the twentieth century. Meanwhile, the followers of Karl Marx were convinced that the capitalist nations had entered their final stage before destruction—the imperialistic stage—and that their end was imminent. Feminists, for their part, maintained that the twentieth century was to be the "woman's century."

In a sense, all these diverse groups were committed to the evolutionary theory. They all believed that Western industrial society had evolved to its present stage after passing through earlier forms of development. When it came to their predictions for the future, however, their views differed dramatically. The industrialists saw technology taking over all human activities; the communists saw revolutionary socialism emerging as the best and final form of human society; and the feminists saw women at last fulfilling their human potentialities in the twentieth century.

The industrialists' prophecy seemed to be coming true. Machines were taking over more and more human functions. Mass production and the assembly line became a perfected manufacturing process, best exemplified a few years later by Henry Ford and his Ford Motor Company plant. However, the promise of progress, of more material goods for more people, was fulfilled for only a few—certainly not those who toiled in the sweatshops of the textile and cigar-making factories, or in the sunless depths of coal and copper mines. Children still worked in cotton fields as well as in textile mills. Farmers, black and white, picked cotton for pennies, harvested sugar and rice and grain, and raised foodstuffs for consumers. After several decades, workers still benefited little from industrialization; their wages were low, their future precarious. They had no job security, no unemployment compensation, and no pension plans. And those who protested against these conditions found their places taken by other workers the next morning.

To the spokesmen for the new technology, then, the future held exciting visions of machines replacing human labor, of a rising standard of living, and of all people benefiting and no one

255

suffering. Surely this vision attracted many followers—more and more, in fact, as the century advanced, although the reality seemed to point in another direction entirely. There were disturbing signs that technology could destroy huge numbers of human beings in wartime, that technology seriously threatened the natural environment, and that technology did not deliver its benefits equally to all human beings. But the opening years of the twentieth century, at least until 1914, convinced the hopeful that the future would be better than the present and that the American people had found the way to solve all problems peaceably.

Babes in America

In the spring of 1903 I went to Kensington, Pennsylvania, where seventy-five thousand textile workers were on strike. Of this number at least ten thousand were little children. The workers were striking for more pay and shorter hours. Every day little children came into Union Headquarters, some with their hands off, some with the thumb missing, some with their fingers off at the knuckle. They were stooped little things, round shouldered and skinny. Many of them were not over ten years of age, although the state law prohibited their working before they were twelve years of age.

—The Autobiography of Mother Jones

In 1900, 25 per cent of all boys ten to fifteen years old and 10 per cent of all girls the same age worked for wages. Eleven-year-old boys went into the mines, and eleven-year-old girls bent over sewing machines for ten or twelve hours a day. Thus, substantial quantities of goods were produced by ill-paid child labor. Reformers tried to get child labor laws passed, but had little success.

Most children still received only a minimal education, although the high school movement had spread significantly among the middle class. Of course, the longer children went to school, the longer they remained out of the work force. But those who were born of poor parents had to leave school early to help support their families, and farm children had to interrupt their studies every year at harvest time. Only the children of the upper class and the growing middle class could benefit from a high school and college education, and college was still a luxury of the few.

The fact that these more fortunate youngsters were able to complete their high school education gave rise to a highly significant social development—a prolonged period of financial and emotional dependence on their parents. In the 1770s and the 1870s, twelve-year-olds had been breadwinners, but in the 1900s, upper- and middle-class youth stayed in school at least until the age of seventeen. Most important, the whole process of growing into adulthood, of accepting adult responsibilities, was delayed. Indeed, parents encouraged their adolescents to remain childlike and dependent. One clear sign that a family was well off was the fact that its teenage children could keep on going to school instead of going to work.

Child-raising manuals, already a staple for the reading public in the nineteenth century, became a best-selling commodity in the twentieth. Parents wanted answers to a host of new problems. Mothers not only wanted to know how to deal with colicky babies, an old problem, but now they sought advice on adolescent development, on dating practices, and on discipline for restless teenagers with time on their hands. The longer the period of childhood, the bigger the problems. City youngsters spent more hours away from home and often rejected their parents' standards of behavior in favor of their peers'. Thus, a paradox arose in the parent-child relationship: the less time children spent in the home, the more rebellious they became; and the longer they were dependent on their parents, the more strongly they resented parental advice and authority. This trend, which began early in the century, has become a major social problem in its final decades.

The noted psychologist G. Stanley Hall recognized parents' anxiety in his book on adolescence:

> . . . Never has youth been exposed to such dangers of both perversion and arrest as in our own land and day. Increasing urban life with its temptations, prematurities, sedentary occupations, and passive stimuli just when an active, objective life is most needed, early emancipation and a lessening sense for both duty and discipline, the haste to know and do all befitting man's estate before its time, the mad rush for sudden wealth and the reckless fashions

set by its gilded youth—all these lack some of the regulatives they still have in older lands with more conservative traditions.

—G. Stanley Hall, Preface to *Adolescence,* 1904

Charlotte Perkins Gilman, for her part, rose to youth's defense.

We do not begin to appreciate the usefulness of youth. Youth has been admired, idealized, envied, well-nigh worshipped; but it has never been appreciated. . . .

Our next mistake in treatment was in the unnatural selfishness with which human parents have regarded their duty to children as an investment, and expected it to be paid back with interest.

The frank and practical poor expect their children to begin to work for them long before they are grown up; and rich and poor alike expect an amount of care and service, a prolonged submission, which young people quite naturally object to render. Then they are blamed for "ingratitude."

As has been before observed in these pages, parental duty is a law of nature. Filial duty is an invention of the patriarchs. Nowhere else in the whole animal kingdom is there found this sordid parentage.

It has not been good for youth. It has checked the wide free growth of new power, new hope, new ambition, and chained the child to family care at an age when such care should not exist.

We have not understood, as yet, what young people are for, because we have not understood human life in general. We supposed, in our ancient undeveloped minds, that there was no more to human life than to that of other animals; that we had merely to keep ourselves alive and to reproduce our kind; with, to be sure, a keen post-mortem interest in our individual souls, but none whatever in our general humanity.

Since we found that the period of immaturity with us was longer, and required much labor and care on the part of parents, we took this as a sort of personal grievance, and short-sightedly fell back on the children, expecting them to make good for our exertions.

So the child has been exploited by the parent—more especially the girl child—, and there was no legitimate escape until the young person could establish a new family relation and begin to repeat the same game. . . .

Young people are the advance guard of civilization. To them belongs the splendid duty of leadership. They are the torch-bearers, the pioneers, the planters of new banners. All the care and service

258

necessary for a free and full development, bringing out the utmost powers of the individual, should be guaranteed to youth by Society—not from any parental instinct of blind affection and perverted self-interest, but from a recognition of Society's need of youth.

The parent does not own the child.

The parent has no right to take toll from childhood; to demand back again all or part of what has been given.

Parentage is not only an animal function; it is a social obligation. Society has its parentage to fulfill, a care extending to all children alike, guaranteeing to them those conditions requisite for their right growth.

The community, so far, has seen but dimly its obligation to youth, and youth is equally uncertain about its obligation to the community.

This calls for new ethics. We seize the contumacious child and hammer in ancient commandments of honor and service to parents. What do we teach the child of honor and service to the state?

We pet and indulge the child, providing it all the pleasure and amusement we can pay for, and expect a commensurate return in care and duty. But we do not recognize in the child a Citizen—a member of Society—and teach to him and to her as the basis of all morality, duty to the Society to which they belong.

So we find young men huge children, selfish, boisterous, crude, quarrelsome; and young women ridiculously dressed, behaving as if life were a place of amusement.

These young people are neglected. They are Social orphans. They have not been taught their own real place in life, with the rights and duties, labors and honors, appertaining.

It is the duty of youth to bring its fresh new powers to bear on Social progress. Each generation of young people should be to the world like a vast reserve force to a tired army. They should lift the world forward. That is what they are for.

> —Charlotte Perkins Gilman, "What Young People Are For,"
> *The Forerunner,* III (January 1912).

Changing Roles

As urban industrial society grew more complex, human tasks became fragmented and specialized. The old-time handyman who knew how to fix everything became an increasing rarity

—partly because factory workers had no chance to acquire a variety of skills on jobs that dealt with only one small part of a manufacturing process. For them, such specialization brought only monotony, doing the same thing day after day with no conception of the overall scheme to which they were contributing.

Monotony likewise marked the lives of city women, who, after sending their children off to school each morning, faced hours of idleness and boredom. Housekeeping was simplified by iceboxes, sewing machines, and canned foods, and domestic help was plentiful and cheap. At last middle-class women were freed from traditional domestic chores, but how would they fill the empty hours? That was the question, and a good many women found at least partial answers. They occupied themselves with good works, community activities, and social dilly-dallying.

Role changes affected almost every segment of society, in city and country alike. The life of a middle-class woman born in New York City and coming of age in 1900 was very different from her mother's. She had more education, worked in an office before marriage, and probably lived in a small apartment afterward —experiences her mother had never known. The life of an Iowa farm boy was not so different from his father's, although both he and his father had to learn to use the new farm machinery; but farm boys too were better educated than their parents and often grew bored and restless. Eager to taste the excitement of urban centers, large numbers of country lads left the farm to seek their fortunes in the city. And the immigrant, of course, encountered manifold changes. For him and his family all the unfamiliar features of the new country (including language) made each day's experiences strange and difficult.

All Americans, then, of all ages, colors, and backgrounds, found their lives altered by the productive power of machines —some for the better, some for the worse. Indeed, as the social changes accelerated, whatever remained of traditional living patterns often appeared almost ludicrous. How could women be told that their place was in the home when machines were removing many of their functions within the home? How could they be told that they were delicate and frail at the same time that women workers were forced to toil twelve hours a day in unventilated factories? How could workers be reminded of the importance of their individual jobs when these were being taken over by machines? How could farmers be praised as the backbone of the nation when each year their sons and daughters left the farm for the city? How could politicians talk about equality of opportunity in America while blacks, American Indians, and women continued to be denied their rights? How could children be expected to obey their parents unhesitatingly when their increased education made them doubt traditional values? None of these questions were answered before 1914. In fact, most of them are still unanswered as the twentieth century draws toward a close.

Suggestions for Further Reading

Mary Anderson. *Woman at Work* (Minneapolis, 1951).

Mary Dreier. *Margaret Dreier Robins* (New York, 1955).

W. E. B. DuBois. *Dusk of Dawn* (New York, 1940).

W. E. B. DuBois. *The Souls of Black Folk* (Chicago, 1903).

Harold U. Faulkner. *The Quest for Social Justice: 1898–1914* (New York, 1931).

Eleanor Flexner. *Century of Struggle.* Rev. ed. (New York, 1973).

Charlotte Perkins Gilman. *The Home: Its Work and Influence* (New York, 1903).

Josephine Goldmark. *Impatient Crusader: Florence Kelley's Life Story* (Urbana, Ill., 1953).

Aileen S. Kraditor. *The Ideas of the Woman Suffrage Movement, 1890–1920* (New York, 1965).

James R. McGovern. "The American Woman's Pre–World War I Freedom in Manners and Morals," *Journal of American History*, LV (September 1968).

Maud Nathan. *The Story of an Epoch-Making Movement* (New York, 1926).

June Sochen. *The Black Man and the American Dream, 1900–1930* (Chicago, 1972).

June Sochen. *Movers and Shakers: American Women Thinkers and Activists, 1900–1970* (New York, 1973).

June Sochen. *The New Woman: Feminism in Greenwich Village, 1910–1920* (New York, 1972).

CHAPTER TEN

The Hope Dashed
1914–1920

Rents were very high for colored people in Cleveland, and the Negro district was extremely crowded, because of the great migration. It was difficult to find a place to live. . . . An eight-room house with one bath would be cut up into apartments and five or six families crowded into it, each two-room kitchenette apartment renting for what the whole house had rented for before.

—Langston Hughes, *The Big Sea*

I believe a great many suffragists, who are not pacifists, felt decidedly aggrieved that their services had been so lightly pledged to a government which has denied to them for forty years a fundamental democratic right.

—Crystal Eastman, Letter to a friend, 1917

"I Didn't Raise My Boy To Be a Soldier"

—World War I song

World War I, the Great War, not only destroyed many lives, but tore people apart in other ways as well. Black Americans, moving to Northern cities for the first time in great numbers, faced new kinds of exploitation. As writer Richard Wright (1908–1960) later recalled:

In the South, life was different; men spoke to you, cursed you, yelled at you, or killed you. The world moved by signs we knew. But here in the North cold forces hit you and push you. It is a world of things.

Feminist-pacifists who saw men voting for war felt their frustrations erupt from within. What kind of society were they living in? Old men pledged the lives of young men, while powerless mothers watched their sons go off to foreign shores.

Many men still had the same romantic notions of war in 1914 as they had had in 1861. War was still the test of masculinity, bringing out the male virtues of courage and valor. But though people's ideas about war were old-fashioned, the weaponry of war had become highly sophisticated. Mass technology had made possible such means of destruction as asphyxiating gas, higher caliber rifles, and more accurately directed shells. The joy of martial struggle—originally a confrontation between a few chosen antagonists—was lost in wholesale massacres. Quick, gentlemanly wars were a thing of the past; wars were now prolonged, agonizingly devastating affairs.

In 1914, both the Germans and the English predicted a short summer war—a six-week war, boasted the Germans. But trench warfare made the battles longer and the outcome more dubious. Each side dug in along a line of defense and shot across No Man's Land at the similarly entrenched enemy. The novel *All Quiet on the Western Front,* written by a German, Erich Maria Remarque (1897–1970), brilliantly describes the sheer monotony and brutalizing effects of war in the twentieth century.

Women and Peace

Until 1917, the United States looked upon the European war with detachment, believing that the power struggle of European nations was of no immediate concern to Americans. President Woodrow Wilson confirmed this popular view by instructing the public to be neutral in thought and action. Peace groups were formed to insure the implementation of the President's message. The Woman's Peace Party, organized in 1915, propagandized for peace and a speedy end to the European war. Above all, the party worked to keep American expenditures for militarism at a minimum and to discourage legislators from preparing for war.

Jane Addams, founder of the Hull House settlement in Chicago, was elected national president of the Woman's Peace Party, thus lending her name and reputation to an organization which proclaimed in the preamble to its first set of resolutions:

> As women, we are especially the custodians of the life of the ages. . . . As women, we feel a peculiar moral passion of revolt against both the cruelty and waste of war.

Even these few words reveal a great deal about how both sexes viewed women. It was assumed that women, as the custodians of life and preservers of culture, naturally abhorred war. Since, as mothers, they created life, they would be repelled by its wanton destruction and waste of human resources. Members of the Woman's Peace Party, therefore, legitimized the party's existence by asserting their traditional maternal role. The "naturalness" of women's love of peace did not, in fact, prevent men from going off to war.

Women did not form large-scale peace societies during the Civil War or the short-lived Spanish-American War. But in this century, beginning with World War I, the peace groups they founded have endured to this day. Generally, they used the traditional mothers-of-men argument, and believed it themselves. Their pacifism was sparked less by humanistic concern than by one central, oft-repeated theme: that war brought sorrow and tragedy to mothers and prevented them from fulfilling their role. These women pacifists sang the popular 1915 song "I Didn't Raise My Boy To Be a Soldier" as they paraded on Fifth Avenue in New York, trying to convince everyone of the rightness of their cause. Obviously, all women were not pacifists. Indeed, once the United States entered the war, in April 1917, most of the women pacifists suspended their propaganda activity and patriotically supported the war effort. But from 1914 to 1917, they spoke for peace.

Women marching for peace, 1915. (Culver)

The Hope Dashed 1914–1920

Prominent among them was Crystal Eastman (1881–1928), whom we have met in earlier pages. Dark-haired and bright-eyed, she personified the new woman. She came from upper New York State, where her parents were Congregational ministers. Her mother, Annis Ford Eastman, had set a fine example for her daughter. In the 1870s she had written a high school graduation speech on women's rights, she had become a minister, and she had raised her daughter and her sons to be independent, self-reliant people.

Crystal came to New York City in 1903 to do graduate work in sociology. After receiving a master's degree from Columbia University, she went on to law school. She worked in the settlement houses of New York, observed working conditions for immigrants, and lived in Greenwich Village, where a community of intellectuals and radicals gathered. Throughout the 1910s, she worked for women's suffrage, feminism, workmen's compensation laws, and the peace movement. She defined the woman's movement more broadly than did the suffragists and found few supporters for her comprehensive brand of feminism.

In 1920, she moved to England with her husband, Walter Fuller, and her child. She returned to this country in 1928 and died here at the young age of forty-seven.

Between 1914 and 1917, Crystal Eastman made the New York City branch of the Woman's Peace Party one of the most militant pacifist groups then in existence. To her the European war was imperialist, a war this country should not support for any reason because mass killings are never justified. She spoke against the "preparedness" bills in the U.S. Congress and the New York State bills that would provide military training in high schools. If you prepare for war, she argued, you will engage in war. Miss Eastman was sensitive to the fact that the Woman's Peace Party did not admit men into its membership. How could a humanistic organization have such a policy? She thought long and hard about it:

> For a feminist—one who believes in breaking down sex barriers so that women and men can work and play and build the world together—it is not an easy question to answer. Yet the answer when I finally worked it out in my own mind, convinced me that we should be proud and glad, even as feminists, to work for the Woman's Peace Party.

266

Since women did not have the vote in 1916, she reasoned, the peace party could develop solidarity of purpose among women; when they gained suffrage, they would know how to use it for their own purposes.

As a pacifist, she argued that her primary function was to "establish new values, to create an overpowering sense of the sacredness of life, so that war will be unthinkable." But Crystal Eastman's arguments did not sway the public or the legislators. Her pacifist brother Max Eastman (1883–1972) talked with President Wilson less than a month before Wilson asked for a declaration of war, but he and other pacifists were not persuasive enough to prevent that declaration.

After war was declared, Miss Eastman tried to redefine the role of a peace group during wartime. What could the Woman's Peace Party do? As a lawyer, she was greatly interested in preserving the civil liberties of all citizens in this period of hostilities. Historically, the minority critics of an administration's wartime policies have been deprived of their rights lest their opposition endanger the national welfare. But she believed that people who spoke out against war still deserved the legal protection guaranteed by the Constitution's Bill of Rights. If citizens could not express dissident opinions in wartime, then what was the meaning of free speech in a free society? A major result of Crystal Eastman's concern was the formation of the American Civil Liberties Union, which still exists in the 1970s.

Jane Addams was greatly disturbed by Crystal Eastman's radical interpretation of pacifism. She herself believed in a low profile for pacifists during the war, though she continued as president of the Woman's Peace Party. Miss Eastman wondered what patriotism really meant in a country that did not even grant women the right to vote. Yet both these women leaders stood high above the majority of Americans, who agreed unquestioningly that loyalty to the government had to supersede other concerns until the war was over. Members of the National American Woman's Suffrage Association, for example, pledged their support to the President and volunteered to serve the war effort in all possible ways.

Many suffragists, as Crystal Eastman wrote to a friend in the letter quoted at the opening of this chapter, were upset by the

NAWSA's expressed commitment. How could suffragists support a government that did not include them in its electorate? But theirs were minority voices. Their pleas—that women could not hope to realize their potential in a war-filled world and that women should never support a war for which they had not voted—were drowned out by the patriotic chorus. As in all previous generations, women and men alike accepted the power-holders' interpretation of reality and conducted themselves accordingly. The few who shared Crystal Eastman's feminist-pacifist perspective found themselves in trouble with the government. A number of issues of *Four Lights,* published by the Woman's Peace Party, were confiscated by the Post Office as dangerous material. (An example of such "dangerous material" was the following passage from an article by Mary Alden Hopkins, "Woman's Way in War," in the issue of June 2, 1917: "It takes a minute to destroy a boy into whose making have gone 18 years of thoughtful care.") Max Eastman's magazine, *The Masses,* was forced to suspend publication, and Socialist speakers such as Elizabeth Gurley Flynn and Rose Pastor Stokes found themselves under indictment for suggesting that the war's purpose was less than noble. Indeed, a significant number of radicals were jailed for their opposition to the war.

Free speech seemed to be a luxury no longer available, or so thought the anti-war socialists and pacifists. Crystal Eastman wondered how a war deemed not to be an American concern in March 1917 could become an immediate, burning issue one month later. The borders of this country did not seem to be endangered, and though the British were having difficulty defeating the Germans, American pacifists argued that our sympathy for the British did not justify our joining them in active combat. A hastily passed Sedition Act in 1917 became the legislative justification for putting socialist Kate Richards O'Hare (1877–1948) in jail as well as anarchist Emma Goldman (1869–1939). Numerous Wobblies, anti-war socialists, and pacifists found themselves behind bars because they spoke and wrote against American involvement in the European war. Their indomitable spirit is vividly expressed in the following letter, written in 1919 by Kate Richards O'Hare to her family from the women's prison at Jefferson City, Missouri:

> So far I seem to feel no sense of shock whatever. I entered quite as calmly as I have registered at hundreds of hotels and the clang of the

cell door did not disturb me more than the slamming of my room door by a careless bell boy. I have either much more poise, courage and strength of character than I dreamed of possessing or I am psychologically stunned. . . .

The work in the factory does not trouble me in the least. I understand that I have broken all records for beginners in making jumpers. I feel a little stiff and sore, but it is nothing serious. I feel sure that I will be able to make the "task" by next week, which is 55 jumpers each day. . . .

I want the comrades with whom I have worked for years with all my strength, to feel that they must not be bitter if I am taken away for a little while to be with the bitterly wronged victims of our social stupidity. . . .

Tell the comrades to go on with my work and all will be well.

Love and kisses to my darlings and greetings to the friends and comrades.

The analogy between anti-war sentiment in World War I and in the Vietnam War of the 1960s is striking, but by no means a chance development. Even the Civil War had its opposition movement, though never as articulate and widespread as the peace movement during World War I. But from the Civil War on, the tragic loss of life and the devastation of the land in modern war remained bitter haunting memories for decades to come. The conclusion of World War I did not fulfill either side's need for satisfaction. The victors did not feel victorious; indeed, Britain and France lost almost an entire generation of their young men on the battlefield. On the other hand, Germany, labeled the loser, went through a period of chaos and, though suffering from inflation, managed to recover and in the mid-twenties was in better economic shape than the victors. The memory of the defeat, however, would live on in the minds of Adolf Hitler and his followers, and the 1929 depression gave the fascists a chance to rekindle their resentment.

By the 1960s, the accumulated memories of wars that never solved any human problems made the younger generation of Americans doubt the validity of the Vietnam War. Surely the college youth of 1964 could not remember World War II, and probably knew very little about the war of 1917. But they did know that the world in which they lived needed a great deal of reforming and that this could not be done in time of war. The pacifists of the World War I generation, on the other hand, were older than the college-age activists of the 1960s, and were motivated by their ideological commitment to socialism and pacifism. They knew, from their study of history and their observation of world affairs, that both Britain and Germany were guilty of imperialism, and they did not want the United States to fight on the side of an imperial power.

Women and the War

As in previous wars, the majority of women served their country in every possible capacity. Farmers' wives maintained their farms with whatever help was available. Working-class women whose husbands had gone off to fight replaced them in their jobs. And upper-class women worked as volunteers to help the war effort. Many women took over jobs previously designated as "male," and performed them competently and efficiently. Unprecedented numbers worked in munitions factories, steel mills, and chemical plants. As had happened in the past and would happen in the future, they were commended for their patriotism but were replaced when the war was over.

The U.S. Department of Labor formed a special department to oversee women working in ordinance factories. After the war, this agency became the Women's Bureau of the Labor Department, whose function was to collect data on women workers. From 1920 on the Bureau, led by Mary Anderson (1879–1964), a former trade union organizer, worked—not always unsuccessfully—for federal labor laws to protect women workers.

Both at home and overseas, the Red Cross took over and enlarged the services performed by the U.S. Sanitary Commission during the Civil War. Many wounded soldiers benefited from the medical supplies sent by the Red Cross. Nurses joined the newly created U.S. Army Corps of Nurses and served in military hospitals in France. Indeed, women cooperated with the government and voluntary organizations to aid the war effort in multiple ways. Of course, both sexes believed that women were not equipped for actual fighting, but both agreed that woman's natural nurturing role could be important in war, as in peace. Hence it was acceptable and highly desirable for women to reassure wounded patients, read to them, write letters for them, and send them gifts.

270

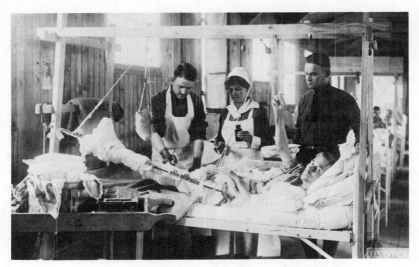

Red Cross nurses assist doctors in a hospital, 1918.
(American Red Cross)

The casualty rate mounted as the war went on. Since U.S. participation was relatively brief, Americans did not suffer the huge losses that the Europeans experienced. While 112,000 Americans died during the war, nearly nine million Europeans lost their lives in battle, and an equal number of civilians also perished. Human history had never before seen such a bloodbath. The dollar cost to the United States equaled the total cost of running the country from 1791 to the outbreak of the war!

War in the twentieth century was indeed a new and terrible experience. Gone were the romantic notions of a valiant struggle between brave men; that myth died on the battlefields of Europe. During the 1920s, when world disarmament was frequently discussed, people fervently vowed that there must never be a repetition of 1914–1918.

Suffrage and Temperance

Alice Paul, the militant suffragist leader of the Congressional Union, broke with NAWSA during the war. She and her group, the National Woman's Party, demonstrated in front of the White

271

House, were arrested, and refused to stop their activities once the U.S. entered the war in 1917. She insisted on pointing out that while American troops were fighting in France to save the world for democracy, the women of America had no democracy at all. Sentenced to prison, they were force-fed and subjected to inhumane treatment; upon their release, they toured the country to publicize their cause.

Throughout the war, Alice Paul and the NWP membership continued unrelentingly to remind President Wilson that American women could not vote. After the war and the passage of the Nineteenth Amendment, Miss Paul and her organization turned their energies to agitating for an equal rights amendment. She has been involved in this activity ever since. During the 1920s, she obtained three law degrees and worked, through the League of Nations and other international organizations, for the legal rights of women all over the world.

Historians disagree about Alice Paul's role in the passage of the suffrage amendment. Some see her as an obstructionist whose antagonistic behavior almost lost the vote for women; others view her militancy as necessary to win that vote. Surely, many legislators were appalled at women who demonstrated, at women who picketed, and at women who stubbornly refused to eat in jail—all this was behavior unbecoming to a lady. Not only did Alice Paul shatter the stereotyped image of a lady reformer—one who was always polite and hoped that the legislators would read her petitions—but she created a great deal of publicity for the suffrage cause. She never let Americans forget that getting the vote for women was a piece of essential unfinished business.

In 1919, the necessary votes were mustered in Congress to pass the woman's suffrage amendment. After a difficult campaign to have the amendment ratified by two-thirds of the states, the Nineteenth Amendment became the law of the land in 1920. The struggle had been long, almost too long. Now that women had the vote, would the body politic be changed for the better, as the advocates had prophesied? Would the traditional family be destroyed, as the critics feared? The twenties would become a time of testing for the new amendment.

The year 1920 saw another so-called victory on the legislative front: the passage of the Eighteenth Amendment—the temperance amendment, or Prohibition, or the Volstead Act, as it was

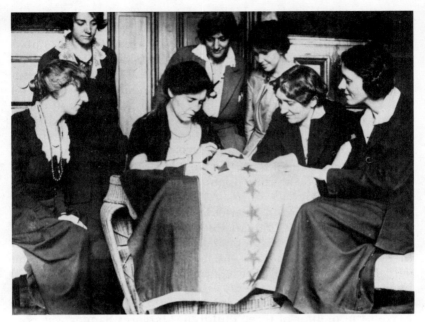

Alice Paul (seated 2nd from left) stitches the 36th star on a banner in 1920 signifying the ratification of the suffrage amendment. (Wide World)

variously termed. Temperance workers were usually conservative reformers; that is, they fought for the preservation of traditional values and parted company with more radical groups, like the feminists who advocated disseminating birth control information. While all feminists were suffragists, most temperance reformers were not feminists, and only a few were suffragists. They stood firmly for the integrity of the home and for a high moral tone in society. They abstained from liquor and zealously argued that drinking ruined families and victimized wives and children. Many feminists, on the other hand, did not believe that the government had the right to legislate morality. Although they wanted to see drunkenness eliminated, they feared governmental intrusion in citizens' private lives.

Whereas the suffrage amendment was enforced from the time women began voting in elections in 1920, the temperance amendment never had sufficient government support to be successfully implemented. Stopping all production and consumption of alcohol would have been difficult and probably impossible. The federal government's Justice Department did not have enough agents to supervise all areas of the country. Moreover, law-enforcement agencies, especially local police forces, tended to disregard violators of the Eighteenth Amendment. Indeed, many policemen received financial bribes to keep quiet. The result was the creation of a huge crime syndicate, organized to satisfy America's unquenchable thirst for liquor. People were willing, however reluctantly, to have women vote, but not to give up their gin and whiskey. The "roaring twenties" roared underground in speakeasies and other illegal drinking spots, with the law-abiding populace blithely ignoring a law they did not want.

A more specific and clear-cut victory for woman was largely the work of one remarkable woman, Margaret Sanger (1879–1966), who in 1916 opened the first birth control clinic in the United States. Before she had succeeded in making the subject (and issue) of birth control respectable, her clinic had been closed down repeatedly, she had been indicted, and her writings impounded by the government. Trained as a nurse and herself the mother of three children, Margaret Sanger was convinced that the only way women could exercise any freedom or independence was through knowledge of birth control. She devoted a long life to that cause.

Democracy for Whom?

Black Americans wondered uneasily what the war meant to them. As patriotic citizens, they had believed in President Wilson's reasons for entering the war and had dutifully served their country in battle. But the irony of black men serving a country that did not serve them—like that of women working for a war they had not voted for—upset the sensitive, and exasperated the critics of American policy. Within the black intellectual community, the President's words sounded hollow and untrue. How could black Americans fight to make the world safe for democracy when blacks themselves were not safe in Mississippi? Why should black men lose their lives for abstract principles that had never been applied to them? But blacks, like

Birth control advocate Margaret Sanger, 1915. (Bettmann)

women, hoped that things would be different after the war and that the promise of human equality would finally be fulfilled.

More than 360,000 black men served in the armed forces of this country. In the Army, where most of them served, they were segregated from white troops and frequently led by white officers. The newly created Air Corps shunned blacks, and the Navy assigned them only menial duties. One of the few reforms eventually gained for black soldiers was the initiation of a black officers' training camp.

W. E. B. Du Bois (1868–1963), among the nation's outstanding intellectuals of any color, campaigned in the pages of *Crisis*, the NAACP magazine, for the rights of black Americans. Du Bois had reluctantly supported President Wilson in 1912, and found his faith seriously shaken by Wilson's blatant discrimination against blacks. In his most blistering editorial in *Crisis*, DuBois told all his readers, especially the black soldiers returning in 1919:

> This is the country to which we Soldiers of Democracy return. This is the fatherland for which we fought! But it is our fatherland. It was right for us to fight. The faults of our country are our faults. Under similar circumstances, we would fight again. But by the God of Heaven, we are cowards and jackasses if, now that the war is over, we do not marshal every ounce of our brain and brawn to fight a sterner, longer, more unbending battle against the forces of hell in our own land.
>
> We return.
>
> We return from fighting.
>
> We return fighting.
>
> Make way for Democracy! We saved it in France, and by the Great Jehovah, we will save it in the United States of America, or know the reason why.

Du Bois' militant tone was not reckless or irresponsible. Its intensity had gradually developed after many years of patient devotion to reason and moderation. However, 1919 was not the year for black Americans to be patient. Returning black soldiers were greeted by their communities with the same discrimination as before the war. White employers continued to hire blacks last and fire them first.

The summer of 1919 witnessed so many race riots that some people grimly called it the "red summer." Seventy blacks died at the hands of racist mobs. Race riots broke out in the Southern states of Alabama, Mississippi, Florida, and Georgia, but the worst one occurred in Chicago. On July 27, a black boy was swimming in Lake Michigan when, according to witnesses, he inadvertently swam over to the "white" section of the water. Whites on the shore began throwing stones at him. The result was the boy's death and a riot that eventually took thirty-eight lives and injured over five hundred people. Fires broke out in various parts of the city, and many residents fled their homes. White racists never expected blacks to defend themselves or to retaliate. But they did, and the human losses were great.

The extent of the riot was so shocking that a commission was created to investigate the causes. The Chicago Commission Report of 1919 still stands as a rational, comprehensive explanation of why the riot occurred. The report also contains reasonable recommendations on how to prevent future violence, but the Commission was unable to state how race prejudice could be eliminated. How could white people be changed so they would not hate black people and behave badly toward them? All observers agreed that the black Chicagoans' grievances were legitimate. All conceded that housing and jobs and education for blacks were inferior to those of whites. All agreed that racial tension was bad for the city and for everyone. But getting rid of prejudice is not like curing a simple illness.

In the four years 1915–1919, the black population of Chicago had more than doubled—from 50,000 to over 125,000. The black residential district, already bulging, became hopelessly overcrowded, and black residents looked for homes elsewhere. Tensions arose within the neighboring white communities. White residents bombed the homes of recently moved-in blacks—a nasty practice that would be repeated endless times in the large Northern cities. Indeed, the center of racial violence now shifted from the South to the North, and though lynchings continued in the South, Northerners were shocked to find the race problem uncomfortably located within their midst. Still, white Northerners did not have to learn racism anew; it was part of their heritage. As discussed in the early chapters of this book, they shared with white Southerners a deep disdain for anyone who was not white.

Labor unions ignored the race problem and concentrated on advancing the interests of white workers—a difficult uphill struggle throughout the twenties, since employers manipulated both races to their own advantage. Black workers continued to be powerless, unable to organize in their own behalf. In Chicago and New York, black politicians were able to acquire a modest influence, but their constituency was still too small to enable them to extract major benefits from white power-holders. The situation was bleak. More than one and a half million black Southerners had migrated to the North in the hope that life would be better there. But reality did not fulfill that hope.

The two large black organizations, the NAACP and the Urban League, worked to alleviate the intolerable conditions for blacks in the North. But neither organization had enough money or staff to make a serious dent in the problem. To help sixty thousand recent arrivals adjust quickly to a new community was an impossible task. Black sociologists tried to maintain accurate records on newcomers from the South, but they had no way to keep track of them all. The Urban League could establish day-care facilities for black working mothers in smaller communities like those in Brooklyn, but had little success in sprawling Harlem. Educated blacks who did social work in this period understood the black Southerners' problem, but could not solve it without the assistance of whites, in the form of money, trained personnel, and above all, respectful treatment.

During the war, many blacks had jobs in the booming war industries, just as women did. Then after the war, both blacks and women suffered the same fate. Not only were they fired to make room for returning white soldiers, but the munitions factories closed down and the country experienced a recession. This was not unexpected, since a period of economic adjustment always occurs after a war, until workers previously employed in war-related plants are transferred to peacetime enterprises. In this process, however, the least skilled workers and the discriminated-against minority groups always suffer most.

Black women found jobs rather easily, because they were needed as cleaners, cooks, and nursemaids in the laundries, hotels, and homes of Northerners. As a result, they often had to support their families while their husbands vainly looked for work. This situation, in which doors were open to black women and closed to black men, would soon create immense psychic problems within the black family—another important by-product of white discrimination.

After the woman's suffrage amendment was passed in 1920,

278

some reformers wondered whether it would benefit black women as well as white women—especially in the South where black men had been virtually disfranchised by the white power-holders. Over two million newly enfranchised black women lived in the South. When suffragists suggested to Alice Paul that the voting rights of black women would be a continuing vital issue, she replied that the year 1920 was not the time to discuss that question. Rather, she said, the suffragists should enjoy their new political power and make plans for other battles in the future. Yet as the reformers had foreseen, when black women went to the polls in Alabama or Georgia, they found that white election officials had a bag of tricks ready to prevent them from voting. If a black woman could read a complicated text put before her, the white official would find some other obscure reason why she was ineligible to vote. And any woman who persisted was threatened with violence if she did not obediently slink away.

Suffrage meant little to black people in the South, and did not mean as much as it should have to people in the North. Although black men and women voted in Philadelphia, Chicago, and New York, all their representatives in Washington were white men, and the Congress paid no heed to the needs of black Americans. Not until 1928 did Oscar Du Priest of Chicago become the first black legislator in Congress since Reconstruction. Southern Democrats controlled most of the major committees of Congress and avoided, like the plague, any mention of civil rights.

Most black Southerners remained sharecroppers and tenant farmers while their brothers and sisters in the North struggled to sustain themselves in the unfamiliar city culture. As Richard Wright recalled, life in the North had new rules. For one thing, although public transportation was not segregated, blacks were expected to know where to sit. There were no signs in store windows saying "No Negroes Allowed," but most white merchants did not welcome black customers. Thus, discrimination in the North was covert, not overt. If blacks moved into changing neighborhoods, they sent their children to schools along with white children, both native and foreign born. Gangs would quickly form along racial and religious lines, and long-lasting hostilities would develop between them.

In the North, blacks and whites might go to school together, or sit near one another on streetcars, or work next to each other

279

on assembly lines, but there was no understanding between the races—just as there had never been in the South. The status quo was preserved, at the cost of any major steps toward human progress. So World War I did not save the world for democracy, and the United States, after participating in that war, did not even establish democracy on its own soil.

The Environment

The words of reformers usually fall on deaf ears until practical necessity dictates the same course of action they have advocated. Consider the federal government's attitude toward improving the country's inland waterways. The U.S. Congress had always been very stingy in appropriating funds for this purpose, ignoring the warnings of engineers. The few senators interested in preserving the nation's resources, notably Senator Newlands of Nevada and Senator Norris of Nebraska, ordinarily failed to get their legislative proposals passed. During the war, however, farmers found the railroads congested and began shipping their wheat via the St. Lawrence River. But they discovered, much to their dismay, that the waterway was too full of obstacles and bottlenecks to be useful as an important means of transportation. The urgent need for wide distribution of food then prompted Congress to appropriate funds for improving the St. Lawrence waterway.

In another matter, a series of natural disasters brought less effective government action. Periodically, about every five years the Mississippi River overflowed and flooded its valley, doing great damage to crops and homes. The Army Corps of Engineers, the government agency responsible for building levees along the river, continually insisted that it had the problem under control. Then, in 1912 and 1913, the floods were so devastating that Congress proposed a substantial appropriation to deal with the problem. Still, the Army Engineers insisted that the only workable solution was higher and higher levees. The Flood Control Act of 1917 provided an unprecedented amount of money for this purpose, but the floods continued. Conservationists believed that the Army Engineers took too narrow a view of the problem. Any effective flood control program, they

280

maintained, had to include reforesting adjacent lands, creating storage reservoirs, and instituting soil conservation methods in the area.

It is intriguing to learn that reformers interested in the natural environment faced some of the same difficulties as did the feminists, pacifists, and socialists with their proposed reforms. Each group that offered a comprehensive, many-sided solution to its particular problem faced stubborn opposition from the conservative majority or from other reformers who interpreted the problem more narrowly. All soil conservationists, for example, did not agree that their work had to be coordinated with flood control efforts, just as suffragists were not concerned with birth control, or temperance workers with any other women's issues.

The federal government continued to sell valuable natural resources, for a fraction of their worth, to private industry—for example, public land surrounding waterfalls. The hydroelectric power developed from these waterfalls, while benefitting many in the area, became privately owned. Lumber companies kept on cutting down trees indiscriminately, and the smokestacks of American steel mills puffed on furiously. Indeed, America's industrial capacity was widely credited as being the key factor in winning World War I. Industrialization and technology, which produced the goods needed in war and peace and provided jobs for the populace, were always regarded as progress.

A Foreign Revolution

The Bolshevik Revolution of 1917 had a tremendous effect on American intellectuals. At last there was to be a socialist nation in the world, with a government based on equal rights for all. Now American reformers would be able to see at first hand whether human beings could treat one another with equal respect and consideration. Early visitors were enthusiastic, though guardedly so. Lenin, the Bolshevik leader, faced strong opposition for a few years and spent most of his time in Moscow, marshaling support for his policies. John Reed, a friend of Crystal Eastman, reported the excitement and drama of the revolution in his book *Ten Days That Shook the World,* and firmly predicted its success. The Bolsheviks promised to grant equal rights to women and to eliminate all social and class distinctions.

Feminist-pacifist Crystal Eastman visited Communist Hungary in the early twenties and observed great hopefulness among the people. Anarchist-feminist Emma Goldman, who was deported from the United States at the same time, ended up in Soviet Russia and heartily disagreed with the sympathetic American intellectuals. She saw Lenin's promises go unfulfilled as his revolutionary ardor dissipated into a new tyranny. Lenin, she said, had replaced the tsar's brand of authoritarianism with his own. But most American radicals did not listen to Emma Goldman. Rather, they chose to believe the optimists who saw Russian Communist rule as the wave of the future, heralding a revolutionary period in which equal human rights would be established once and for all. This faith buoyed the spirits, however temporarily, of many U.S. liberals, who hoped for a Lenin of their own to revolutionize American society.

Feminists, like the Socialists, continued their long search —lifelong, in some cases—for models of truly humane societies. The quest seemed more urgent since the war's end in 1918. These thoughtful people shuddered at the human ability to destroy life, with the aid of lethal machines of war. Somehow the model for a good society must be found and set in operation before technological man destroyed all life permanently. But as always, the minority of Americans who criticized the dominant culture gained little popular support. It was the rare person who agreed with Crystal Eastman that 1920 was the beginning, not the end, of an era. She proposed a vigorous new feminist campaign dedicated to:

Removing all legal discriminations against women

Encouraging child-raising practices that would free children from sex stereotyping

Making birth control information freely available to all women

Providing motherhood endowments for women who chose to be mothers

The majority of women, however, were delighted with the war's end, the granting of suffrage, and the return to normalcy. Crystal Eastman's call for concerted action fell on deaf ears. Few agreed with her hope that

... with the feminist ideal of education accepted in home and school, and with all special barriers removed in every field of human activity, there is no reason why woman should not become almost a human thing.

The nation heaved a sigh of relief that the war was over and proceeded to rebuild its society in the image of the past.

Suggestions for Further Reading

Jane Addams. *Peace and Bread in Time of War* (New York, 1922).
Harriet Stanton Blatch. *The Mobilization of Woman-Power* (New York, 1918).
Merle Curti. *Peace or War: The American Struggle* (New York, 1936).
Rheta Childe Dorr. *A Woman of Fifty* (New York, 1924).
Elizabeth Gurley Flynn. *I Speak My Own Piece* (New York, 1955).
Charlotte Perkins Gilman, *The Living of Charlotte Perkins Gilman* (New York, 1935).
Emma Goldman. *Living My Life.* 2 vols. (New York, 1931).
Alan P. Grimes. *The Puritan Ethic and Woman Suffrage* (New York, 1967).
Alice Henry. *The Trade Union Woman* (New York, 1915).
Inez Haynes Irwin. *The Story of the Woman's Party* (New York, 1921).
Florence Kelley. *Modern Industry in Relation to the Family, Health, Education, Morality* (New York, 1914).
Henry F. May. *The End of American Innocence* (New York, 1959).
William L. O'Neill. *Everyone Was Brave: The Rise and Fall of Feminism in America* (Chicago, 1969).
Doris Stevens. *Jailed for Freedom* (New York, 1920).
Lillian Wald. *Windows on Henry Street* (Boston, 1934).

CHAPTER ELEVEN

Buy, Buy, Buy
1920–1929

We find the Negro woman, figuratively, struck in the face daily by contempt from the world about her. Within her soul, she knows little of peace and happiness. Through it all, she is courageously standing erect, developing within herself the moral strength to rise above and conquer false attitudes. She is maintaining her natural beauty and charm and improving her mind and opportunity. She is measuring up to the needs and demands of her family, community and race, and radiating from Harlem a hope that is cherished by her sisters in less propitious circumstances throughout the land. The wind of the race's destiny stirs more briskly because of her striving.

—Elsie Johnson McDougald, *The Double Task: The Struggle of Negro Women for Sex and Race Emancipation,* 1925

Charleston, Charleston, da da de-de da da . . .

—Popular song of the twenties

*I*n the twenties, as in earlier decades, many admirable women, black and white, worked hard, earnestly, and often without fanfare to gain their natural rights. On the other hand, there was also a new kind of woman, whom the public came to accept as the current image of all (young) American women. This gay, mindless, pleasure-seeking creature, dancing to the music of jazz bands until the small hours of the morning, was immortalized in popular fiction and films. But neither the serious-minded, dedicated worker for women's rights nor the "flaming youth" flapper was anything like the majority of American women. Most of them worked hard during the day, cared for their children, cleaned house, and cooked meals. On summer nights, they would rest from their chores in a rocking chair on the porch

The flapper image: superficial difference.
(Missouri Historical Society)

or, in slum areas, on the front stoop of their tenement home. Very few shared the life of the social activist or the flapper.

One ex-feminist, who had settled down with a man and a child, wrote to the *New Republic* in 1926:

> At present I am merely background—pleasant, important, perhaps necessary background, I admit—for two other individuals. I have no separate, integral life of my own. I long for engrossing, satisfying work. Instead, my days are devoted to a round of petty, tiresome details, with the benefit and effort of these two individuals as an end. I, who was once such a pronounced, assertive ego, am now become supine, self-effacing.

Few women who assumed domestic responsibilities publicly admitted to this despair, but surely many of them shared the writer's sentiments.

Still, the image of the carefree short-skirted young girl

286

enjoying life each moment of each day had a great deal of allure—for young women as well as young men. All of us, from time to time, have delicious fantasies about being irresponsible, under no obligation to anyone, and wholly devoted to the pursuit of pleasure. The assumption in an increasingly middle-class society was that young people would indulge their personal whims before they settled down to marriage, a job, and adult responsibilities. Thus, for the children of middle- and upper-class parents who could afford to give them a college education, the period of youth became longer than it had ever been—a period of freely enjoyed pleasures financed by indulgent parents.

The image of the flapper was unconsciously linked with the older cultural image of women as frivolous pleasure-seekers, as temptresses of men. The novels of F. Scott Fitzgerald and the silent movies about the young, such as *Our Dancing Daughters* (1928), portrayed upper-middle- and upper-class youth spending their time entirely on personal gratifications. They had no thought of social problems, no preoccupation with work or a profession, and no concern for domestic responsibilities. Mary Heaton Vorse, a labor reporter and a member of the Greenwich Village feminist community before World War I, observed a group of flappers aboard a ship returning from Europe in the late 1920s. She reported that she was appalled by their self-centeredness, their utter lack of interest in anyone but themselves. And Charlotte Perkins Gilman complained about the flappers' easy morality and their trumpeting of Freudian justifications for their behavior. She called Freud's writings "solemn philosophical sex mania."

1928
"Our Dancing Daughters"
MGM Production
starring
Joan Crawford as Diana Medford, the flapper
who toasts herself in the movie:

"To myself! I have to live with
myself until I die! So I hope I
like myself!"

Most flappers married and assumed, eventually, the same life style as their mothers. Though they claimed to know about sex and birth control, they still believed that four children was the ideal family size, that they were in fact different from their mothers, and that they married for love, not convenience. In actuality, they were not a new social type; their views and behavior were closer to their parents' than they would comfortably admit. Marriage and a family remained women's primary role. Of course, thanks to the mass-produced consumer goods that rolled out of the factories, young unmarried and married women dressed differently from their mothers, wore make-up and regularly attended that new social institution, the beauty parlor—but the differences were all on the surface, not substantive.

A Nation of Consumers

The decade of the 1920s resembled contemporary America in one respect at least: the widespread preoccupation with purchasing more and more consumer goods. Advertising in the United States acquired the status of a major industry, precisely because the new industrialists had to hire experts to publicize their merchandise and make it attractive to buyers—i.e. women. So advertising plus the new prosperity enabled housewives to spend more and more money on new apparel, furnishings, appliances, canned goods, and entertainment. Since factory-made clothes could be sold more cheaply, it was possible for the secretary, the garment worker, and the middle-class housewife to wear the latest fashions, and only the discerning shopper could distinguish the difference between expensive "originals" and their mass-produced imitations.

Charge accounts, installment buying, easy credit payments, and loans from finance companies led city dwellers into a ceaseless round of getting and spending. A buyer no longer had to delay his purchase of living-room furniture or a washing machine until he had enough money to pay for it. On an easy-to-buy, no-money-down credit system, he was encouraged to buy it, enjoy it, and pay for it monthly. Further, advertisers informed buyers that fashions changed, and newly bought products must be replaced frequently just to "keep in style."

288

Clothing manufacturers, cosmetics producers, and appliance dealers stayed in business by convincing the buying public that goods could be discarded while still usable and that being stylish was more important than being prudent.

In the Twenties

A fashionable 1914 ankle-length skirt became a knee-high skirt in 1920

No more petticoats and corsets

The cosmetics industry grew from a $17 million business to a $141 million business in 1925

Women smoked in public and read advertisements that told them to "Reach for a Lucky instead of a sweet"

Interestingly enough, America's new materialism, which affected (and infected) every class of society, gave rise to a false interpretation of democracy—though this did not become apparent for a good many years. Because all people could afford to dress alike (who could tell a Chanel original from a factory imitation?), wear their hair in similar styles, and (in later decades) drive cars, it was easy to believe that all Americans were at last being treated equally. No one stopped to consider that a secretary spent far more of her monthly budget on clothes than did an upper-class lady of leisure, or that all classes had become slaves to perishable manufactured products. The gap between classes, in fact, widened rather than narrowed during the surge of industrialism: the rich continued to get richer while the poor remained poor.

Workers' jobs were still precarious, many farmers still lived marginally on unsympathetic land, women continued to be locked into socially determined roles, and black Americans received the same discriminatory treatment they had always received. If one took a good look at society as a whole, one might well conclude that very few groups of people really benefited from consumer industrialism. But superficial appearances —clothes, hairdos, furniture—convinced many that all the new, easily available products were yet another example of American

289

progress. Since most people wished for progress, their "wishing made it so." Moreover, just having money to spend and spending it can give anyone a feeling of importance—a sense of power. In the 1920's, women were considered, and considered themselves, the chief beneficiaries of this power.

Women as buyers, therefore, were a significant social phenomenon of this period. Newspaper and magazine advertisements, billboards, and radio commercials all begged the little lady to try the latest brand of soap, smoke cigarettes, and buy the latest kitchen equipment. Women bought their husbands' and their children's clothes as well as their own, bought groceries, linens, and household utensils. These responsibilities, highlighted by the blandishments of advertisers, convinced them that they indeed had power. Rarely did a woman consider that her husband could (and often did) veto her latest purchase. His no could override her loudest yes. Rarely did it occur to her that she was never paid for her household work, her child care, and her cooking. Yet women were the only unpaid workers in a money economy. No one rewarded them in the only way such a society rewards workers—by paying them for their labors.

When a husband consented to let his wife buy a frivolous new dress, it was out of the goodness of his heart—or in response to her cajoling or her skilled manipulation. She actually had to demean herself in order to get money to spend, while her husband kept reminding her how long and hard he had worked to earn it. Though she too worked to earn whatever money she received from him, neither she nor her husband interpreted her weekly allowance as a salary.

Thus, the woman's purchasing power was not real but delegated—a privilege that a husband or father could take away any time he chose. Although the role of purchaser-consumer gave her the idea that she was free and independent, in reality she was now doubly enslaved: to the husband-breadwinner and to the new industrialism.

But this enslavement was inconceivable to women with cash in their handbags and shopping lists in their hands. In a society that glorifies money and material goods, the power to buy can stir heady emotions. Shopping was a serious pursuit for middle- and upper-class women in the 1920s; it served to fill up their time and gave them a sense of importance. A woman felt good trying on dresses in a shop and finally—momentous decision—choosing the one that seemed most flattering. Shopping was a magic cure for despondency or boredom, especially in the new department stores with their bewildering array of styles and colors. And all the while, advertisers screamed their message to buy, consume, and buy some more.

Mass entertainment, in various forms, was available to amuse all classes of city dwellers and enrich its promoters. Movie houses, nickelodeons, and dancehalls attracted middle- and working-class people who wanted to forget their daily problems. Speakeasies appealed to the more affluent and daring, who liked to drink highballs in nightclub surroundings. Indeed, during the 1920s, entertainment became a major industry. One debatable result was that it turned people into sedentary observers—for instance, in movie houses—rather than active participants in recreation of their own devising. True, the dancehalls did a big business in the twenties, and many people still sang around the family piano; but a trend toward passive amusements, which was to grow alarmingly in coming decades, began at this time. Amusements were a purchasable commodity, like soap, and the public consumed new movies as they consumed new products.

At the turn of the century, an enterprising black business-woman, Madame C. J. Walker, made a fortune manufacturing hair-straightener lotions and skin preparations for black people. By the 1920s, cosmetics for white women had become a major industry as well. In earlier years, women who wore make-up were considered disreputable, but this attitude changed completely with the coming of the flapper. No woman, black or white, was fully dressed unless she wore make-up. In addition to Madame Walker, two white women became millionaires in the new cosmetics industry: Helena Rubinstein (1871?–1965) and Elizabeth Arden (1884–1966).

Elizabeth Arden, born Florence Nightingale Graham, decided early that her home town, Woodbridge, Canada, was too small for her. A restless and ambitious young woman, she left Woodbridge for Toronto at the age of eighteen and worked in a variety of jobs—from bookkeeper to receptionist. In 1908, she went to New York and got a job as secretary in a beauty shop on Fifth Avenue. Florence became intrigued with the facial treatments given at the shop, and in 1910 went into the beauty business, which was just beginning to boom, with a woman partner.

The partnership, however, was short lived. Undaunted, Florence took the name Elizabeth Arden and borrowed $6,000

from a cousin in order to open her own salon on Fifth Avenue.
Within a year, she had paid off her debt and made a profit. Within
five years, she moved to larger quarters, was manufacturing some
of her own products, and started a branch salon in Washington,
D.C.

In the 1920s, Elizabeth Arden salons became the most
fashionable beauty salons for wealthy women—except for
Helena Rubinstein's. Within another decade, Elizabeth Arden's
empire consisted of nineteen salons all over the world and a list
of more than a hundred beauty products bearing her name. By
1938, it was estimated that American women spent $300,000,000
on beauty items, of which Elizabeth Arden received a goodly
share.

All these highly successful businesswomen behaved much
like the industrial giants of a previous era. They began modestly,
became ruthless competitors, worked hard to promote their
products, and succeeded in making cosmetics a respectable and
essential part of every woman's life. Indeed, the cosmetics and
movie industries, the new big businesses of the twenties, aptly
demonstrated the current emphasis on buying and spending in a
consumer-oriented society.

A number of new industries developed from ingenious
conversions of wartime to peacetime production. One manufacturer, who had made cotton products during the war, switched to
making sanitary napkins for women—and Kotex was created. His
enormous profits were largely due to the fact that his product,
along with all sorts of other products made exclusively for
women, was advertised in women's magazines and the woman's
pages of newspapers. The *Ladies' Home Journal*, one indicator of
changes in women's styles, reminded its readers that lip rouge
was an absolute necessity. A decade earlier, the subject of
make-up and facial beauty had been taboo. Interestingly enough,
the Internal Revenue Service reported that beauticians were a
new occupational group in the 1920s.

Feminists and Other Women

But what had happened to the prewar feminists? What had
happened to the suffragists, the temperance workers? Those
feminists who had also been pacifists and socialists were
seriously demoralized by the war. Henrietta Rodman returned to

high school teaching after 1918, until illness prevented her working and led to her untimely death. After 1920, feminist-pacifist Crystal Eastman went to England with her family to write and to observe the woman's movement there. She returned in 1927 but died the following year at the age of forty-five. In this period, too, Freda Kirchwey, an outstanding writer as well as wife and mother, became an editor of *The Nation,* a magazine for intellectuals, and actively promoted women's issues in its pages.

The suffrage organization, NAWSA, of course dissolved, though flushed with victory after passage of the suffrage amendment. One-tenth of its membership went into the newly formed League of Women Voters. The Woman's Peace Party became part of the Women's International League for Peace and Freedom, which still exists in the 1970s. Alice Paul's National Woman's Party (NWP) campaigned throughout the decade for an equal rights amendment for women. The General Federation of Business and Professional Women spoke for the special interests of career women, and a nation-wide network of women's clubs carried on many social, cultural, and philanthropic activities. The Women's Trade Union League fought a never-ending battle to keep itself a viable organization. The Women's Christian Temperance Union, though pleased with the passage of the Eighteenth Amendment, continued to propagandize for temperance. And the International Ladies Garment Workers Union succeeded in organizing nearly half of all women working in the clothing trades—a success enjoyed by few other unions.

Women's religious, ethnic, and racial organizations, such as the National Council of Jewish Women, performed community services for their particular groups. During the twenties, the Women's Joint Congressional Committee, a watchdog and pressure group in Washington, was formed. Made up of representatives from many women's organizations, the WJCC presented their collective views on such issues as federal aid to education, maternal and infant health bills, and minimum wage-and-hour laws.

Most of the women's organizations opposed the NWP's equal rights amendment, which gave rise to strong tensions within the woman's movement. Proposed by Alice Paul in 1923, it read:

Men and women shall have equal rights throughout the United States and every place subject to its jurisdiction.

293

Seemingly, no one interested in women's rights would object to this statement. However, the women's labor unions, plus all civic and religious groups that supported them, vigorously opposed the amendment because it would wipe out the protective labor laws for women which they had worked long and hard to obtain. Ideally, all women wanted to be treated as men's equals. But in light of the present industrial reality, women unionists argued, women would be mistreated and abused once the protective labor laws were removed.

Mary Anderson, a long-time union organizer and then administrator of the Women's Bureau of the Department of Labor, recalled in her memoirs the bitter struggle between the advocates of the equal rights amendment and the trade union women who opposed it. She argued against the amendment because

> ... it might upset or nullify all the legal protection for women workers that had been built up through the years, which really put them on a more nearly equal footing with men workers.

In the future, the opponents conceded, when factories would provide humane conditions for both sexes, equal rights would be appropriate. Advocates of the amendment, on the other hand, insisted that it would improve working conditions for men and women alike.

Throughout the twenties, bitter disagreement on this issue raged between the National Woman's Party and most other women's organizations. Each side spent a great deal of time and energy propagandizing for its point of view. Whenever a congressional committee considered the equal rights amendment, both sides sent representatives to argue their cause. Observers of the woman's movement as a whole often lamented that the women activists used up more of their time fighting among themselves than uniting against the common enemy. And indeed, little progress was made toward getting the public to think seriously about woman's role. Most people interpreted the new consumer products designed especially for her as signs of progress, and lightly dismissed the deeper aspects of the problem.

At the same time, two basic structures of American society, marriage and family life, were changing. The divorce rate was rising steadily, though the rate of remarriage was also high. Middle-class parents practiced birth control and consciously

294

tried to limit the size of their families. Margaret Sanger's work, begun in the 1910s, had gained a measure of respectability by the twenties, and birth control clinics were now available to middle-class women and, on a limited scale, to working-class women as well. Many states, however, still had laws prohibiting the sale of birth control information and devices—reflecting the deeply held commitment to women's role as mothers. But more and more urban areas failed to enforce the laws; birth control devices, notably the diaphragm, became widely used along with such male devices as the time-honored condom.

Despite a decline in family size and the mounting divorce rate, the concept of the "nuclear" family as the essential unit of American society persisted. In 1926, feminist Rose Pastor Stokes (1879–1933) wrote an article for *Collier's* magazine entitled "There Are Few Bad Divorces." The editors of the magazine warned their readers that if they were offended by unorthodox ideas, they should not read the article! In it, Mrs. Stokes argued that marriage was a failure in capitalistic America.

> Dominant in my struggle for the new society is the hope that once the complete factual basis is laid—once economic security becomes the heritage of every member of society—permanence in the love relation will become widely possible.

Marriage, however, was still sacred, and the woman's role in the family remained her central purpose in life. Whether a woman had seven children or only three, she was still expected to stay at home, be with them, and work for them. Her household tasks might have been lightened by vacuum cleaners and other appliances, but still her major responsibilities lay in the home. If she had a job, this continued to be regarded as an unimportant part of her life. In the 1920s, as in the 1790s, marriage was the only approved state for women. Divorcees always remarried as quickly as possible, not only to acquire financial security for themselves and their children but to gain respectability.

Writers as Cultural Commentators

The elite and the popular arts blossomed richly and variously in the decade of the 1920s. Gifted writers, men and women, produced an amazing number of truly great works. Ernest

295

Hemingway, F. Scott Fitzgerald, and William Faulkner; Ellen Glasgow, Edith Wharton, and Willa Cather; black male writers Langston Hughes and Wallace Thurman, and black female writers Jessie Redmon Fauset and Nella Larsen—all created powerful prose and poetry. (And this list is selective, not inclusive.) Drama, painting, sculpture, dance, music, and film also flourished in a true renaissance of the arts.

Yet it was in this period, too, that some American intellectuals found themselves stifled by the narrow traditional views of their countrymen. They went to live in Europe, usually Paris, where the atmosphere seemed more conducive to free creative expression, and were known as expatriates. Other intellectuals remained at home, while frequently complaining of the Philistinism of their countrymen. They read H. L. Mencken's barbed attacks on American ideas and customs while continuing to follow them.

Women writers, always an important group in America, did not disappoint their readers during the 1920s. Edith Wharton's (1862–1947) distinguished novels of New York society (i.e., *The Age of Innocence*, 1921) and her classic *Ethan Frome* (1912) had a strong popular appeal. Willa Cather's (1873–1947) short stories and novels about the Middle West (*O Pioneers!*, 1913; *One of Ours*, 1923; *The Professor's House*, 1925) have had an enduring fame. And Ellen Glasgow (1873–1945) wrote of Southern women who came vividly alive for readers everywhere, particularly in her *Barren Ground* (1925). While each of these writers used regional backgrounds as settings for their stories, their themes were universal. With superb insight and craftsmanship, they portrayed human dilemmas that reached the hearts of both sexes.

Other women writers wrote for women and about women, following the example of a long line of popular female novelists. Fannie Hurst (1889–1968), Gertrude Atherton (1857–1948), and Edna Ferber (1887–1968) may have had a limited literary skill, but in their time were best-selling authors whose work often departed surprisingly from traditional romantic themes. Some of Gertrude Atherton's heroines, for example, were women who rejected marriage and conventional living in favor of a career. Similarly, Edna Ferber created heroines who had careers and declared, "I'm spoiled for sewing bees and church sociables and afternoon bridges."

The heroines of Willa Cather's and Ellen Glasgow's novels

296

Popular novelist
Edna Ferber. (Bettmann)

usually played traditional roles but attained strength, self-awareness, and courage within an environment not of their making. All were brave, interesting women, often restless but always authentic, and always grappling with real-life problems. What a boon these books were for the woman reader! She could share the joys and troubles of heroines whose lives were like her own, or identify in fantasy with those who defied social conventions and lived according to their own predilections.

Fannie Hurst was one of the most successful popular novelists of the period. Her tear-jerking dramas about vulnerable, often victimized women were serialized in magazines and made into movies as well. Her *Star Dust: The Story of an American Girl* (1921), though not a best-seller, is interesting because it reveals a sensitivity to feminist issues that did not appear in her later writing. Perhaps one reason for the relative unpopularity of *Star Dust* was its unconventional heroine. Lilly Becker is a dissatisfied young woman who marries reluctantly (a most untypical way to behave) and finds married life worse than she had expected it to be. "I just can't rake up enthusiasm over French knots. Something in me begins to suffocate and I can't get out from under. I hate it." She leaves her husband, who refuses to give her a divorce, and goes to New York to begin a

297

career. She has few talents, however, though many aspirations. Then, shortly after she arrives, she discovers she is pregnant—a condition that has always defined and confined women.

After giving birth to a baby girl, Zoe, Lilly takes a job as a secretary. Now all her hopes and dreams are focused on her daughter. "I don't know which way the vision is pointing," she muses, but. . .

> I'm going to clear the way for you, Zoe. No Chinese shoes for your little feet or your little brain. Free-to-choose—to be! That's the way I'll rear my daughter! Queer I never think of him, her father. . .

These sentiments are rarely met in the popular novels of any period. For a woman novelist to suggest that marriage is restrictive and repressive and that women are enslaved defies the traditional American view. But *Star Dust*, which does not end satisfactorily from the feminist point of view (Zoe marries the man Lilly has secretly loved), did explore, though tentatively, a subject untreated in most fiction of the period. And in the end, Fannie Hurst capitulated to public sentiment by having Lilly sacrifice her personal happiness for Zoe's. Women were supposed to suffer in silence and sacrifice themselves for their loved ones. Thus, at the last minute, the novelist fulfilled her readers' expectations.

In the Pulitzer Prize-winning drama of 1920, *Miss Lulu Bett*, Wisconsin writer Zona Gale (1874–1938) also daringly departed from popular tradition. When the play opens, Lulu Bett is unmarried, "a maiden woman," living in the home of her younger sister and brother-in-law. She is "the family beast of burden," the unwanted extra woman, the spinster—whom Americans always regarded as society's embarrassment. Lulu Bett does the household chores uncomplainingly, grateful for a roof over her head. But she has no identity, no socially accepted function—until she marries. Then she becomes, in the eyes of everyone, a human being. The marriage does not turn out well and she returns to the town, but before the play ends she is to marry again, and thus reenter the zone of acceptability.

Zona Gale raised some intriguing points in this play, only to conclude it in a typically conventional way. The very fact that marriage was once more represented as a woman's only means to happiness shows how powerful and limiting the American myth

Fannie Hurst (2nd from right) visits the Hollywood set
where her novel "Back Street" is being made. (Culver)

The stars of the play
"Miss Lulu Bett" 1920. (Culver)

was. Only within marriage does Lulu Bett gain identity and a sense of purpose. On the other hand, by making her heroine an unmarried woman, Zona Gale did point up the unjust and irrational dimensions of that American myth.

Miss Gale herself was sympathetic to the woman's movement, had written for feminist publications, and understood the positions of such New York City feminists as Crystal Eastman and Henrietta Rodman. But neither she nor Fannie Hurst dared to portray a woman who led a rich, purposeful life independent of a husband and marriage. Both authors were themselves independent, but both upheld traditional values in their writings. They did suggest some of the cruelties single women faced, but were not able to reject the established assumptions.

Most of the fiction and drama of the period, however, did not even go that far. Imaginative, able writers—not always the popular ones—have often been the prophets of cultural change, but in the 1920s few perceived the injustices wrought upon women by male society. Fitzgerald's *The Great Gatsby* (1925)

300

dramatically portrayed the depravity of the materialistic American Dream, and Faulkner's novels captured the corruption that slavery had wrought upon all Southerners. But none of their work described the yearnings of unfulfilled women. In the writings of Willa Cather and Ellen Glasgow and other fine women novelists, only rarely did the strong women characters articulate feminist desires.

During the supposedly emancipated twenties, then, male novelists seemed to revel in creating female characters who depicted the traditional idea of women as simultaneously seducers and mothers of men. Daisy Buchanan, Fitzgerald's heroine in *The Great Gatsby*, is the prototype of the blonde, empty-headed beauty supposedly desired by every American male.

Meanwhile, black women novelists Jessie Redmon Fauset (1884–1961) and Nella Larsen (dates unavailable) were writing abut the dilemmas of black people, particularly women. In Jessie Fauset's novel *There Is Confusion* (1924), well-to-do, talented Joanna Marshall encounters race prejudice when she tries to become a professional dancer. At one point in the novel, Joanna's brother-in-law establishes the author's views on race relations in America:

> But every colored man feels it sooner or later. It gets in the way of his dreams, of his education, of his marriage, of the rearing of his children. The time comes when he thinks, "I might just as well fall back; there's no use pushing on. A colored man just can't make any headway in this awful country." Of course, it's a fallacy. And if a fellow sticks it out he finally gets past it, but not before it has worked considerable confusion in his life.

The heroine of an early story, titled "Emmy" (1912), finds that her mulatto boyfriend is torn by a conflict all too familiar to black youth: his love for a black girl versus his desire to succeed in the white world. Ultimately, both love and success come to the hero and heroine. Indeed, this author's stories—though dealing with discrimination against blacks—usually end happily, with the evil of racism forgotten. Nella Larsen's novel *Quicksand* (1928) sensitively describes the uncertain identity of a mulatto woman who feels uncomfortable in both the white and the black worlds. At the end, she marries a black minister and resigns herself to a life of poverty and many children.

These two black women writers spoke out firmly for the goodness and worth of the black culture. Their heroines and heroes learn to live proudly with their personal problems in the black world. Yet both these novelists avoided the issue of racism by omitting any white characters who could have inflicted suffering on the blacks. Nella Larsen, the more talented of the two, did touch upon the identity problem of the mulatto, which meant deciding whether to "pass" into white society. The problem was invariably solved by the mulatto's acceptance of his/her black identity and rejection of the white world and its values.

Black writers in the twenties still struggled with a fundamental question: Whom were they writing for, and why? Were they writing for white people, to impress them with the superior qualities of blacks? Or were they writing for both races, honestly portraying the weaknesses and strengths of blacks? They debated this problem among themselves but did not emerge with a single answer. Meanwhile, very creditable fiction was produced by black Americans in Harlem, Philadelphia, and Chicago; and black magazines, such as *Crisis* and the Urban League's *Opportunity*, encouraged black poets and prose writers and conducted regular poetry and short story contests. The mass hero of black America in the twenties was Marcus Garvey, a Jamaican who briefly enthralled large audiences with his message of black pride.

From black universities—notably Atlanta, Fisk, and Howard—came graduates who joined the growing black middle class. Black college graduates, however, were few in comparison with the total black population; among the few black professionals, black women outnumbered black men. Partly because of discriminatory admission policies, the number of black students in white colleges was pathetically low. Still, a black intelligentsia existed, made up of highly imaginative, creative people. But many gifted black writers were lost to America simply because commercial publishers believed that a book by a black would not sell. Both Nella Larsen and Ellen Glasgow wrote about the problems of women, but Miss Glasgow's books reached (and therefore influenced) far more readers than those of Nella Larsen, a black.

Finally, one of the most popular and enduring books of the twenties was not a piece of fiction but a how-to manual—*Etiquette: The Blue Book of Social Usage* (1922) by Emily Post (1873–1960). It was bought and avidly read by middle- and upper-class white women who wanted to know how to set a proper table, answer a wedding invitation, or introduce guests at a dinner party. Books telling people how to accomplish some specified thing have always had a good reception in pragmatic America. Americans want to know how to win friends and influence people, how to prepare an invitation list, and how to do their own electrical work. So Emily Post, along with the writers of light fiction, found her place on the bookshelves of the twenties.

Popular Fare

An immensely significant new medium, an entirely unique form of entertainment, probably affected the values and ideas of more Americans than any medium had ever done before: the movies. An important product of the new technology, the silent film-story replaced the brief "moving pictures" of the 1900s, and movie houses replaced the old nickelodeons. The people who acted in these films were as well known to Americans as their own families. They came to symbolize certain American attitudes and traits, like the diametrically opposite views of women pictured by two immensely popular stars, Mary Pickford (1893–) and Mae West (1892–). Mary Pickford, "America's Sweetheart," was passive, demure, and charming. She had a shy, winsome smile, looked eternally innocent, and was a blonde Virgin Mary. Mae West, on the other hand, epitomized the eternal sexual temptress, Mary Magdalen. Her famous line, "Come up and see me sometime," drew smiles from millions of men. The two images combined—virgin and temptress, purity and corruption—represented America's concept of woman, a concept accepted by both sexes and reinforced by Hollywood's films.

Actually, "America's Sweetheart" reached the height of her popularity a few years before Mae West came on the scene (and screen). While Mae West was still getting her basic training in burlesque, a parade of movie sirens preceded her as sex symbols. Known as vampires, or "vamps," these darkly mysterious temptresses wore long, slinky gowns, had black hair and heavy-lidded eyes, and exuded an aura of smoldering passion. They

Mary Pickford (left) America's sweetheart of the early
cinema and Mae West, America's sexual temptress.
(Brown Bros., Culver)

had exotic names like Theda Bara and Nita Naldi. Their sexual
charms lured the innocent males, though sweet young heroines
usually won the battle at the film's end.

Both Mary Pickford and Mae West were successful
businesswomen who exploited, for their own considerable profit, the film images they created. Mae West, who wrote and
directed many of her movies, showed a side of the Eve image
rarely seen in the popular American media. By enjoying sex and
choosing her sexual playmates—and frankly advertising this
fact—she gave woman's sexuality a public expression it had
never had before. In books, plays, and films, the temptress is
often portrayed as a good-hearted prostitute who is willing to be
reformed if the right man comes along. There is never any
intimation that she enjoys her work and has chosen it willingly
and freely. Mae West departed from this stereotype and brought
her own fresh interpretation to the role. She leered at men,
flirted with them outrageously, and blatantly enjoyed the whole
process. She did not appear wearied or resigned to her fate;
rather, she reveled in it. In Mae West, the siren was transformed
into a breathing person.

304

When sound films came into being at the end of the twenties, Mae West continued to produce her standard films, though Mary Pickford retired on her untaxed millions. But in the thirties, during the golden age of Hollywood, multiple images of women emerged to compete with her. After 1934, when the Will H. Hays Office (the film industry's self-regulatory agency) established its code of decency, Mae West's explicit sexual references were taboo. But by then "going to the movies" had become a major recreation for Americans and Hollywood had added some interesting variations to its depictions of women.

The popular songs of the twenties reflected the idea of the woman-temptress in such slang expressions as "golddigger," "jazz baby," and "vamp." Women singers confirmed the seductive image of themselves by belting out lyrics like"I'm all that evil music is. . . . I'm a wicked vampire." Cole Porter's "Let's Misbehave" (1928), along with innumerable other songs, contributed to the same image. By the end of the decade, the torch song had become popular, with its message of loss and despair. The torch singer, abandoned by the man she loved, reverted to another typical image of woman—as long-suffering, dependent on men, and always available. Fanny Brice's rendition of "My Man" (1921) reinforced the cultural view of woman as eternally self-sacrificing: "Whatever my man is, I am his forevermore."

That women were human beings with diverse natures and multiple possibilities for fulfilling their needs was still an unknown concept. Women were defined by their sexuality. The attractive woman received first prize—a handsome, popular man—and other women dogged her trail waiting for the rejects. Women's lives continued to be tied to men's. Popular songs, along with movies and novels, reflected these long-held cultural views.

Environmental Experts Speak Out

Just as every decade has its literary commentators, its artists, and its musicians, so every decade produces its scientific and professional critics of established policy. In the field of the environment, engineers, geologists, and land resource experts sometimes disagreed with the government's approach to the use of natural resources. Despite the continuing encroachments of industry, the federal government remained the largest landlord in the West, the owner of valuable rivers, and the regulator of mineral rights. But the government, run by conservative Republicans throughout the twenties, believed in private enterprise and the right of individual entrepreneurs to exploit public resources. Presidents Harding, Coolidge, and Hoover feared that public ownership smacked of socialism and willingly granted private power companies the right to use natural resources freely. When the government created a regulatory agency, such as the Federal Power Commission, private industry exerted great influence over its activities.

The Teapot Dome scandal during the Harding administration is only one of many examples of the government's giving public property to private interests for their profit. The Federal Power Commission always decided in favor of the big power companies. Ranchers continued to let their cattle range on public lands because of lax federal regulation. The Army Corps of Engineers allowed private industrialists to dump their wastes in America's rivers—if they applied for a permit to do so. Although the belief that "the land belongs to you and me" was immortalized in song, in reality the public land became the private domain of commercialists. Sometimes public officials were paid nicely for their special favors; sometimes they simply gave land away without personal compensation. In either case, the public and the country's natural resources suffered. Conservationists who, like Gifford Pinchot, objected to government policy never gained the public support that Ralph Nader won in the 1970s. Pinchot was not able to prevent private enterprise from profiteering on public resources.

From time to time, natural crises did force government officials to take note of their folly, though only temporarily. In 1927, the nation had the most destructive flood in its history. The Ohio and Mississippi rivers overflowed, and before the winter snows had melted in the spring, more than 700,000 people had been left homeless and 250 were dead. The property damage totaled $364 million.

The levees built by the Army Corps of Engineers proved inadequate to contain the floodwaters, and Gifford Pinchot called the Army's tenacious unwillingness to consider other methods of flood control the "most colossal blunder in engineering history." Conservationists committed to a multi-purpose

306

view of river development and flood control joined Pinchot in his attacks on the government's futile stopgap solutions to the serious problem. Though additional funds were then appropriated to study other solutions, not until the 1930s did the government take a truly comprehensive view of the flood problem.

During the 1920s, Senator George W. Norris of Nebraska failed a number of times to get presidential support for the large-scale development of the Tennessee River Valley at Muscle Shoals, Alabama. Other conservationists who advocated the development of the Colorado River–Boulder Canyon Project and the Columbia Basin project also failed. But by the end of the decade, professionals within the appropriate government agencies were largely in favor of a multiple-purpose plan for water development. Unfortunately, they still had to wait for a sympathetic President and a willing Congress before the plan could be put into effect—a situation that did not exist until the New Deal era.

Most Americans and most politicians operated under a dual concept—first, that natural resources should be developed by private industry for private profit, and, second, that these same resources were infinite and inexhaustible. The result was the exploitation of the environment without permitting the public to share equally in the benefits derived. Profit-minded private industrialists kept the price of electricity high throughout the 1920s; consequently, the farms and poorer urban areas were without electricity for many years. Surely hydroelectric power was a natural resource to which all Americans had an equal right. Yet only the rich benefited from electricity—those who sold it at high prices and those who could afford to pay for it.

Coal, oil, pure water, and trees, among other resources, are not easily replaceable; indeed some, such as oil, are finite and irreplaceable. Nevertheless, to this day Americans, tied to their notion of inevitable progress, insist that technology will invent new resources after the old ones have been exhausted. If American inventiveness could develop plastic substances to replace rubber, they say, the same inventiveness would find replacements for coal and oil. George Perkins Marsh in the 1860s, Stuart Chase in the 1920s, and Rachel Carson in the early 1960s forecast the terrible consequences of despoiling the natural environment, but their words went largely unregarded.

307

The ecological view that human beings are only one class of living things in a vast natural system is beyond the comprehension of most people. To the frontiersman, a bison did not have the same right to live that a human being, preferably a white American male, had. Just as it was Christian to kill heathen Indians and to enslave black people, it was proper to kill birds for their beautiful feathers. A certain amount of natural destruction is, of course, essential for the needs of each living group as well as for the delicate balance of the system. Animals kill each other in order to survive, and human beings too must live, though it is questionable whether their slaughter of animals is always tied to the need for food. Conservationists on this continent have always objected to the wanton, irresponsible killing of wildlife no less than to the thoughtless destruction of other natural resources.

In 1925, American author Stuart Chase wrote a book, *The Tragedy of Waste,* praised by intellectuals and conservationists for its well-developed arguments and its commitment to ecology. But no major conservation program was set up to implement Chase's views. His words remain relevant to this day:

> It is not difficult to draw a very gloomy picture of the despoliation of a continent. The rape has been colossal and unparalleled in history. More difficult is the attempt to appraise the real economics involved, for, on analysis, the simple dramatic sequence breaks down into many baffling and confusing parts. If an Industrial General Staff had been written into the American Constitution, with power to control natural resources in the public interest, enormous waste might have been averted, but the drive of the pioneers westward would have been altogether a different and, one fears, a tamer, phenomenon. It is doubtful if the arts of invention would have progressed as rapidly. The prospector, the speculator, the plunger, and the stark individualist have been woven into the whole fabric of the American scene.

Chase went on to excuse, in a sense, the waste that had occurred. Wouldn't each of us do the same thing? he questioned. "But somewhere this mad dance of destruction must abate." Then he proceeded to describe the available natural resources and ways of restricting their use so as to conserve them wisely.

But, as we have seen, the Presidents during this decade vetoed all legislation aimed at developing comprehensive water or regional development plans. Any such plans, they stated, were outside the domain of the government. In other words, they shared the same attitudes and values, the same cultural blindness, as did American leaders in the seventeenth century. They accepted scientific discoveries only when these did not conflict with traditional beliefs—*and* when they did not cost a great deal of public money. As a result, everyone suffered, including the traditionalists. Most scientists, contrary to popular belief, are not eager innovators. Like preachers, doctors, teachers, and farmers, they are limited by the views and values of their culture. Only a few bold ones transcend the cultural boundaries.

Changing Times?

Women were now voting in the United States, but much to the embarrassment of ex-suffragists, their votes had no perceptible effect. The Presidents they helped to elect were, if anything, less distinguished than in former decades. The U.S. Congress tried to deal with important social issues, but with little success. And the level of local politics remained low.

The League of Women Voters tried to educate women to vote intelligently, even though no similar organization existed to educate men voters. Apparently the League, captive of its culture's view of women, agreed that women needed special training to vote, while men, knowing all about political issues, needed none. The assumption seemed to be that women had never read newspapers, followed political campaigns, or listened to political speeches before 1920.

It is true, however, that the suffragists had not told women that they could use their new political power to vote as a bloc on women's issues. Feminists like Crystal Eastman had long articulated the need for such action, but it had never been stressed by the suffragists themselves. Rather, they emphasized the right of each woman to vote for candidates of the political party of her choice (meaning her husband's or her father's choice), never suggesting what she should do if neither party spoke to specific women's issues. Indeed, most suffragists did not believe there were specific women's issues. The League of Women Voters would not put the subject of birth control on its national agenda for discussion and did not support a national divorce law.

309

The woman's movement was splintered into many branches in the twenties—the Woman's Party busied itself with the equal rights amendment, the Women's Trade Union League tried to keep its organization alive during a period when union membership dropped, and other women's groups lobbied for the 8-hour day for women and the end to child labor. They all worked in worthwhile vineyards but they all experienced frustration and failure. Thus, the 1920's marked the end of an important period in the woman's movement. Feminism had little popular appeal, and women and men remained unenlightened about its true human significance. The supposedly emancipated flapper represented most people's notion of woman's progress toward self-fulfillment. And women themselves felt that their new role as buyers of consumer goods offered them a respectable way to express their desire for power and autonomy.

The American Indians had been successfully obliterated from the public mind. The Southern blacks remained invisible, while those newly arrived in Harlem learned quickly that the North was no more sympathetic to blacks then the South had been. The decade ended with a great depression, another jarring reminder that economic progress was not inevitable. But most people continued to look for better times, never questioning the fundamental rightness of the family-centered, capitalistic, consumer-oriented world they had created.

Suggestions for Further Reading

Mary Anderson. *Woman at Work* (Minneapolis, 1951).

Harriot Stanton Blatch and Alma Lutz. *Challenging Years* (New York, 1940).

Clarke A. Chambers. *Seedtime of Reform: American Social Service and Social Action 1918–1933* (Minneapolis, 1963).

J. Stanley Lemons. *The Woman Citizen: Social Feminism in the 1920s* (Urbana, Ill., 1973).

William E. Leuchtenburg. *The Perils of Prosperity, 1914–1932* (Chicago, 1958).

Mercedes M. Randall. *Improper Bostonian: Emily Greene Balch* (New York, 1964).

Rose Schneiderman. *All for One* (New York, 1967).

Martha Wolfenstein and Nathan Leites. *Movies: A Psychological Study* (Glencoe, Ill., 1950).

CHAPTER TWELVE

Human Miseries and Joys
1929–1945

If it is up to the women, as the chief bursars and disbursers of the family income, to help restore national prosperity by spending wisely, how much more is it up to the women to fix the standards not only of living but of life!

—Anne O'Hare McCormick, *The New Frontier*, July 1932

Great Spirit, Great Spirit, my Grandfather, all over the earth the faces of living things are all alike. With tenderness have these come up out of the ground. Look upon these faces of children without number and with children in their arms, that they may face the winds and walk the good road to the day of quiet.

This is my prayer; hear me! The voice I have sent is weak, yet with earnestness I have sent it. Hear me!

—Black Elk, A Prayer, 1930

When women go wrong, men go right after them.
—Mae West, in *She Done Him Wrong*, 1933

*T*he depression that started in the fall of 1929 lasted for a decade, and no one in the United States was unaffected by it. Journalist Anne O'Hare McCormick (1881–1954) told her women readers in the *Ladies' Home Journal* what their role should be in alleviating the horrible economic conditions, giving them the impression that if they spent money prudently and maintained a high moral tone, prosperity would return. American Indian Black Elk prayed for help to the Great Spirit, to whom he had always directed his supplications. Economists advised the President, the Congress, and the nation

311

on what measures to take as the unemployment rate rose and remained high throughout the decade. When Franklin D. Roosevelt became President in 1933, he promised the American people a "New Deal." Now that the reckless twenties had ended in disaster, the New Deal proposed vigorous intervention in the lives of the people—in contrast to the laissez-faire policy of former President Hoover.

F.D.R. captivated the people with his winning smile, his sonorous voice, his fireside chats, and his personal warmth. The nation, or so it thought, now had a President who cared about its citizens and explained things to them. Using radio and the press with great effectiveness, Roosevelt communicated with his constituents in novel and unprecedented ways. Each deprived group gained hope anew and began to believe, after three ineffectual Hoover years, that the nation was on the road to recovery. Young people, old people, black and white people, all had great faith in the new President, and the flow of emergency legislation from the White House to Capitol Hill during the first three months of the administration confirmed that faith. New agencies were created to aid the farmers, give jobs to the unemployed, and provide direct funds for the destitute.

Work and Workers

Symphony orchestras were federally financed during the thirties, as were writers and artists in federally sponsored projects. Young men built highways and worked on conservation programs in the national forests. Farmers received financial aid, and public works jobs gave employment to unskilled workers, engineers, and businessmen. Yet despite these impressive attempts to provide for each special-interest group in the country, the New Deal measures failed to satisfy everyone, most especially women and blacks.

In both cases, traditional cultural attitudes were responsible for the dramatic oversight. Americans still believed that women worked outside the home only in order to earn pin money or to kill time. Middle-class people still assumed that men should be the sole support of their wives and children. The fact that women were either the sole supporters of, or essential contributors to, many families, black and white, never seemed to occur to them.

Obviously, the many working-class women whose earnings provided necessities for their families knew the falsity of this popular view. But it was not working-class women who wrote the New Deal laws or passed out the jobs in agencies. When Anne O'Hare McCormick told her middle-class readers to spend wisely, she showed a total ignorance of the economic reality faced by millions of working women: too little money even for bare necessities.

Unemployed Northern blacks fared better than their Southern counterparts, because they received more federal aid, but they were worse off than unemployed whites. In the South, where racist white politicians administered the New Deal programs and gave out the relief checks, discrimination between blacks and whites was blatant and complete. Although blacks in the North did get their relief checks, they were deprived of job opportunities, particularly the defense-factory jobs that became available toward the end of the decade. Black leaders A. Philip Randolph of the Brotherhood of Sleeping Car Porters and Walter White of the NAACP tried continuously to persuade President Roosevelt to act in behalf of Negroes. But F.D.R.'s reliance on the political support of Southern Democrats made him less than enthusiastic about taking any action that might antagonize them.

Historians praise or damn Franklin Roosevelt, depending upon their ideology (he was either too liberal or not liberal enough), but they have not given sufficient attention to his administration's attitudes toward women and minority groups. The Economy Act of 1932 stipulated that if both a husband and a wife worked for the government, it was the wife who had to be dismissed when a cutback in personnel was called for. Just as eighteenth-century wives lost their separate identity once they married, so twentieth-century wives were told that they did not have the same right to work as did their husbands. In 1935, out of 1.6 million workers engaged in government projects, only 142,000 were women.

Although labor unions gained recognition during the Roosevelt years, union women continued to be paid less for doing the same work as union men. The American Federation of Labor preached equal pay but allowed employers to write contracts that included salary differentials between men and women.

Rose Schneiderman (1882–), a union organizer and president of the Women's Trade Union League throughout the

313

twenties, became the first and only woman member of the National Recovery Administration's Labor Advisory Board. This remarkable woman was the child of Polish immigrants who came to America in 1890. Her father, who was a tailor, went to work in the garment industry. When she was thirteen, Rose got a job for $2.25 a week as a clerk in a department store. However, she soon discovered that she could earn more money as a machine operator in a cap factory. Five years later, she and another woman organized the first local of the United Cloth Hat and Cap Makers Union. She remained a dues-paying member for over forty years.

Active in the Women's Trade Union League, she became a vice-president in 1906 and president twelve years later. She participated in every major textile strike and organized women workers in the shirtwaist, corset, and cap factories. She was a spokeswoman for suffrage as well. She ran for the U.S. Senate on the Labor Party ticket in New York in 1920. Defeated but undaunted, she declared that women would learn to use their powers as voters.

> I am just as disappointed in woman's suffrage as I am in men's suffrage. . . . Women have done very little in four years of voting, but men have done tragically little in a hundred and fifty years. Why suddenly demand that women do the outstanding thing which we've given up expecting from men?

When she was appointed to the NRA's Labor Advisory Board, union women took heart at this sign of progress, but their hopes were dashed when Miss Schneiderman was unable to gain any meaningful improvements for working women. There were seventy-one NRA codes in 1935 that provided lower pay for women doing the same job as men.

The millions of non-union women, of course, suffered even greater neglect. Since no one spoke for their interests, those who were able to keep their jobs, or obtain jobs, during the depression considered themselves lucky. They would work for whatever they could get. Men workers were grossly underpaid, it is true, but women suffered from the special salary discrimination always reserved for their sex. In the Southern textile mills, for example, women worked longer hours than men for less pay.

314

Union leader Rose Schneiderman. (Wide World)

Indeed, the lowest-paid man earned more than the highest-paid woman. Black women, damned by their double disability, worked for pennies in the cotton fields and in the laundries.

Women Journalists of the Thirties

Martha Gellhorn (1908–   ), a journalist and novelist, recorded some of the bleak realities of the period in her book *The Trouble I've Seen* (1936). Her direct, honest report on four families who were victims of the depression completely destroyed the old illusion that only lazy people went on relief. Anne O'Hare McCormick, traveling around the country, wrote about the nobility of American women who worked the land in Idaho, scrimped and saved from their meager incomes, and made do with their limited resources. Full of faith in the economic richness of the country as well as in the political vitality of the system, she encouraged her women readers to participate in local politics and help improve community life. Many other journalists, women and men, reported on life in the United States during the depression. Although they graphically described the grim conditions they saw, they still shared the American belief in progress, and most of their writings ended on a hopeful note. The future would be, had to be, better than the present.

Mrs. McCormick achieved eminence as the second woman to be awarded the Pulitzer Prize in journalism (1937). From 1935 until the late forties, she was a respected foreign commentator on the editorial page of the *New York Times*. Indeed, many women journalists were observers of foreign affairs as well as domestic events. Dorothy Thompson (1893–1961), Freda Kirchwey (1893–   ), and Martha Gellhorn all traveled widely in Europe throughout the thirties and reported on conditions abroad.

Of the 15,000 women in journalism in 1930, these four —Martha Gellhorn, Freda Kirchwey, Anne O'Hare McCormick, and Dorothy Thompson—were among the most successful. Mrs. McCormick, in her regular *New York Times* articles, described the everyday life of the Germans, French, Danes, Austrians, and Czechs, comparing the cultural values of each people and relating these to their respective ways of life. She warned her readers of the dangers of fascism and was convinced that the representative system of government, as exemplified by the United States, was the best in the world. In many articles, she urged women to enter politics because they had "the power and the capacity to save America by making democracy work."

This oft-stated theme reflected Mrs. McCormick's faith in the power of the ballot and of local participation in politics. It also revealed her limited view of women's potentialities and capabilities. She never advocated a woman for President or indeed for elective office. To her, the League of Women Voters provided a suitable structure for women's political participation. When the United States entered World War II, she frequently complained about the absence of women in national decision-making positions. Yet she did not realize that one reason for the lack of women leaders lay in the prevailing attitude toward women's political participation. They could work to get men elected to office or engage in nonpartisan propaganda activities, but they could never run for office themselves. Thus, they had no way of gaining active experience in the elective sphere, where candidates run for office, hold office, and continue to rise to higher level political jobs. Although Mrs. McCormick considered herself an advocate of women's rights, her notion of how they were to be achieved fit comfortably into the traditional view of woman's role: to work for the benefit of others rather than for herself.

Dorothy Thompson wrote for the *New York Herald Tribune,* then the *New York Post* and the *Ladies' Home Journal.* Her columns, revealing her intimate knowledge of foreign affairs, discussed the growing menace of Hitler and Mussolini. Some people called her the "First Lady of journalism" while others considered her a first-rate pest. She gained a reputation as a foreign correspondent in the 1920s, covering events in Berlin, Vienna, London, and other capitals of Europe until Hitler ordered her out of Germany in 1934. By 1939, *Time* magazine considered her the second most influential woman in America (Eleanor Roosevelt was the first).

Dorothy Thompson's columns ranged from discussions of Soviet Russia and the rise of Nazism to the role of women in America. Strong, aggressive, and known for her bold opinions, she told her *Ladies' Home Journal* readers in 1939 that women should concentrate on being good mothers rather than good secretaries, short-story writers, lawyers, or motion picture stars.

317

Journalist Dorothy Thompson. (Brown Bros.)

"It's a better thing to produce a fine man than it is to produce a second-rate novel, and fine men begin by being fine children."

Years later, in the early 1950s, Dorothy Thompson changed her mind. After she read the writings of feminist-philosopher Simone de Beauvoir, she became committed to the feminist point of view. But in the late thirties, she believed that the most significant and rewarding role for a woman was that of mother. Moreover, her advice to women accurately reflected current reality. Men *did* make all the major decisions in the world, and if women wanted those decisions to be just, they had to influence their sons accordingly. But a true feminist would advocate educating both boys and girls in humanistic values, so that, as adults, the sexes would share power equally.

Like Anne O'Hare McCormick and Dorothy Thompson, Freda Kirchwey , editor and publisher of *The Nation,* wrote on foreign affairs. Indeed, as a commentator and interpreter of world events, she was the most brilliant of the outstanding women journalists. Neither Mrs. McCormick nor Miss Thompson expressed views of international relations as perceptive and prophetic as Freda Kirchwey's. For that matter, few male commentators on that subject possessed her penetrating insight. During the thirties, she struggled with her own pacifist background as well as with isolationist Oswald Garrison Villard (her respected colleague who, after selling her *The Nation,* continued to write a column on international affairs). She was greatly concerned about the Nazi threat to Western Europe. France and Great Britain were unwilling to act boldly against Hitler, and the United States seemed equally reluctant. The strong isolationist sentiment in this country restrained Roosevelt from committing American resources to war or military defense. But Freda Kirchwey forthrightly recommended a policy of collective security in which the United States would unite with its European allies to preserve the peace. She criticized the Munich pact of 1938 by which the British and French gave Hitler control of the Sudetenland and Czechoslovakia.

When Hitler invaded Poland in September 1939, she observed the worst of her prophecies coming true.

> The consequences of war are so devastating that no nation has a right to plunge in unless all other means of resistance have failed. It is the tragedy of Europe that peaceful means of resistance were

never applied; instead, surrender was tried as a weapon. That is
why Europe is at war.

Throughout the thirties, Miss Kirchwey walked a delicate
tightrope, keenly aware that empires, be they German or British,
were exploitive and that preserving freedom often meant fighting for it. This seeming paradox constantly bothered her, but she
resigned herself to the fact that warfare may be necessary under
certain conditions. After the war, she counseled the creation of a
world order that could minimize the danger of war, an order that
would guarantee the right of each people to rule themselves.

As a feminist, Freda Kirchwey was deeply concerned about
the treatment women received in undemocratic America. She
supported F.D.R.'s appointment of Frances Perkins as Secretary
of Labor—the first woman to hold a Cabinet position—and of
many other women to government posts. When Florence Allen
became the first woman appointed to the Federal Circuit Court
of Appeals, Miss Kirchwey pointed out in an editorial that both
Secretary Perkins and Judge Allen

> . . . are only exceptions to the general rule that women are still
> discriminated against in the professions and in public life. It is still
> fair to say that the woman doctor has to wait longer, the woman

320

lawyer to work harder, the woman politician to be more outstanding than the man who would achieve a correspondingly high place. The fight for women's rights was not won when women got the vote; we still need good heads and stout spirits of both sexes to make equality in the professions an accomplished fact.

In 1940, speaking to a group of women at Hunter College on "The Role of the College Woman in a Shaken World," Miss Kirchwey told her audience that she had been raised in the early 1900s to believe in woman's equality and in its eventual accomplishment. But two world wars had shown her that democratic rights, once obtained, are still not guaranteed.

> The women of my generation represent an age of innocence, a period which no longer seems normal, realistic, solid but, on the contrary, somewhat fantastic. Democracy, we know now, must be continually created and continually defended; never for one moment can it be taken for granted. . . . And so the role of the educated woman today is almost painfully clear. However she goes about doing it, she has only one job. She must—as a mere act of self-preservation—fight for the social and political system which bred and protects her; for with its death, she dies, too.

Thus Freda Kirchwey, with voice and pen, ably synthesized the feminist-humanist perspective. She recognized that a peaceful and open world was essential to the fulfillment of human rights in any country. Sad to say, however, too few readers benefited from her astute commentaries, for *The Nation* was continuously plagued by financial worries throughout the troubled thirties.

Martha Gellhorn was another admirable woman journalist in a period when women journalists were still a rare breed and men jealously guarded their exclusive rights to the field. She was the only accredited woman war correspondent who reported, at first hand, the Russian bombing of Helsinki. In fact, she reported many of the major events in Europe from 1937 on. She had been in Madrid during the Spanish Civil War, and she was in Czechoslovakia when the Nazis occupied that country. Americans who read her accounts of all these memorable experiences in *Collier's* magazine saw through her eyes the excitement and the tragedy of war in Europe. Martha Gellhorn's reports focused on the people of war-torn countries, their personal sufferings.

War correspondent
Martha Gellhorn
leaving for San Francisco
with husband
Ernest Hemingway.
(Culver)

Her detailed descriptions of individuals and their lives, as well as her interviews with men in power, became her journalistic trademark.

Consider, for example, this passage from her report on the bombing of Helsinki:

> A boy of nine stood outside his home in Helsinki and watched the Russian bombers. He was blond and plump and he stood with his hands on his hips and with his feet apart and looked at the sky with a stubborn, serious face. He held himself stiffly so as not to shrink from the noise. When the air was quiet again he said, "Little by little, I am getting really angry."

This woman war correspondent broke through still another barrier—she entered a war zone and lived there in great physical danger. Men and war had always been associated together. For a woman journalist to invade this wholly masculine sphere represented a bold, if not shocking, departure from tradition. Martha Gellhorn's daring intrusion has remained exceptional; the number of women war correspondents has continued to be small.

Fiction as a Source of Feminist Thought

Popular women novelists such as Fannie Hurst, Edna Ferber, and Pearl Buck (1892–1973) fascinated their readers with stories of the sufferings of individual women, but they never preached or adopted a strident tone. Many of the heroines emerged as courageous, independent women, but their strength came from the impelling inner force that only extraordinary women possess—never from social forces in the outside world. Above all, the novels were interesting and engaging. Women readers enjoyed learning about life in China from Pearl Buck, about life in America's recent past from Edna Ferber, and about life in contemporary New York City from Fannie Hurst.

These popular women novelists never used their books as a forum for feminism. Yet in their personal lives and in interviews, they frequently supported women's rights. Fannie Hurst, for the first five years of her marriage to Jacques Danielson, maintained her own apartment and her separate professional and social life. She believed strongly in woman's need for independence, a point she stressed in her speeches before women's groups. In 1941, Pearl Buck wrote a book, *Of Men and Women,* that forcefully articulated the feminist cause. By and large, however, these women writers consciously omitted from their fiction any trace of their philosophical commitment to feminism. When they wanted to express themselves on women's rights, they did so in person or in a work of nonfiction. This prudence, though surely a shame, was understandable. If a woman author wanted her books to sell, she dared not flout the reigning cultural rules that governed the content of "women's fiction."

Nevertheless, one woman writer of the thirties, Tess Slesinger (1905–1945), had the courage to develop the feminist theme in her fiction. Interestingly enough, she was a forgotten literary figure until very recently, although in her day she achieved modest fame. Her short stories, which appeared in *The New Yorker,* among other periodicals, were well received by critics. In 1934, at the age of twenty-nine, Tess Slesinger published her first novel, *The Unpossessed,* and in the following year a collection of short stories, *Time: The Present.* She moved to Hollywood in 1935 with her husband, Frank Davis, and subsequently wrote film scripts. Unfortunately, she died of cancer

323

when she was only thirty-nine. Although her literary output was small, it reveals a powerful talent.

In *The Unpossessed*, Tess Slesinger created two feminist heroines. Using the internal-monologue form, she told the story of Margaret and Elizabeth, both torn between the life roles open to educated middle-class women in the twentieth century. They find no simple new model to follow. Neither the traditional pattern of wifehood and motherhood nor a career in the world of work seems to promise self-fulfillment. Margaret fancies herself a "new woman" because she lived with the man she loved before marrying him. She works in an office and spends a great deal of time pondering her purpose in life.

> It struck her how from her earliest days it had been dinned into her that a woman's life was completed by her husband; and now . . . how utterly false that might be.

When she considers committing adultery with an attractive friend, she wonders:

> And if it *were* infidelity? if it *were* disloyalty? Mustn't she be Margaret first, before a friend and wife? And if her life, unlike her mother's, were *not* completed by her husband?

Margaret never answers these questions either to her own satisfaction or the reader's. As the narrator states at one point: ". . . she sought a thread and a meaning, and expected them both from him. But that was impossible; it was sentimental; moreover, it had failed." Margaret is too well educated to enjoy keeping house and to be challenged by her job. She can find no life pattern that appeals to her, no experiences that have a lasting value for her.

Elizabeth is similarly restless and anchorless. She is a free spirit, a woman who loves men and leaves them. But she too is powerless to shape her own destiny.

> Why, I am an emancipated lady, Elizabeth, I play the game like a man. Elizabeth—you donkey, you sentimentalist, you cry-baby, you sissy—what in hell do you want, every damn thing that's going? The answer is Yes, Yes, Yes! But choice involves sacrifice, is largely a matter of elimination. . . .

324

She is never able to make a permanent choice, and the cards seem stacked against her.

> She reflected how little, at best, she had to do with her own destiny. She lived in a frame of men's reactions, building herself over from one man to the next; her character seemed compounded on what various men had told her she was.

Tess Slesinger discovered, possibly through agonizing personal experience, how helpless women were to determine the course of their lives. Surely she must have had many friends who also sought personal solutions to the problem of woman's identity, but few women writers, in the 1930's or earlier, spoke out on the same theme. Her perceptive and exceedingly sensitive treatment of the educated woman's dilemma sounds amazingly current. The revelation that a supposedly free woman can be living within a "frame of men's reactions" reinforced whatever frustration she might have felt—as it would for any creative woman. Tess Slesinger joined the slim ranks of feminist writers in each generation who reached an important point of personal awareness and communicated that awareness in their fiction.

Another important American woman writer who came of age in the 1930s was Mary McCarthy (1912–   ). After graduating from Vassar, she began writing drama criticism and various essays for New York magazines, then turned to short stories and novels. Her collection of stories titled *The Company She Keeps* (1942) centers on the identity problem of a bright, sensitive young woman not unlike the writer of the stories. Margaret Sargent searches for a sense of self. As a child, she tries to fit in with groups of her peers, but finds that such conformity goes against her innermost feelings. As a young adult, she comes to understand that her extreme introspection, her ability to stand back and observe herself as well as others, keeps her from expressing her own personality. She tells one man she meets that her favorite poetic line comes from Chaucer: "I am myn owene woman, wel at ese."

The Company She Keeps dramatically portrays a most unusual woman at the same time that it presents a social problem faced by all women. Socially determined roles are expected to provide women (and men) with identities, but if a person does not fit comfortably into any socially approved role, what identity does that person have? That is the question Mary McCarthy asked. In her best-known book, *The Group,* she captured the life struggles of a whole generation of women college graduates, those who graduated from Vassar with her in the class of 1933. The composite portrait is not a cheering one. The girls who married soon after graduation have become trapped in domesticity, maternity, and boredom. Those who chose careers have become frigid or lesbians. The business world does not welcome women, the professions ignore them, and the home and family do not excite them.

Mary McCarthy's fiction ranged over a wide assortment of people; among others, her satiric pen dealt with academics and New York City intellectuals of both sexes. Although the unique problem of women's identity in America concerned her, it was not her sole preoccupation. However, all her writings, taken together, comprise an impressive body of sensitive, thoughtful prose on the condition of being human—and a woman—in the twentieth century. Mary McCarthy's writing, along with the less well-known work of Tess Slesinger, foreshadowed a concern that would attain widespread public expression in the next generation.

Eleanor Roosevelt: A Heroine for All Times

Women may have been economically and psychically depressed in the 1930s, but they did have their heroines who gave them courage to persevere. Eleanor Roosevelt (1884–1962), the most important First Lady in U.S. history, heartened millions of women. She acquired a lasting fame wholly apart from her husband's and became a phenomenon in her own time. This feat was extraordinary, and would be under any circumstances, but the fact that F.D.R. was a dynamic, masterful President only heightened her achievements. Organizations from all over the world wrote to her at the White House, inviting her to speak to them. Magazines solicited her writings, and reporters informed their readers of her every move.

In 1933, when F.D.R. became President, his wife was already an experienced and accomplished public figure. She had campaigned for her husband throughout New York State in the

Eleanor Roosevelt: A Heroine for All Times

late twenties, had worked for the women's division of the Democratic party, and had gained valuable experience in lecturing and politicking. While her husband was President, she assumed the role of First Lady with grace, charm, and ease, immediately placing her inimitable stamp on the role. During Roosevelt's first fifteen months in office, she traveled more than fifty thousand miles. Everywhere she went she expressed great interest in human beings and human welfare. And she went everywhere. A 1933 *New Yorker* cartoon captured this aspect of her activity. Two coal miners are working with their picks. One looks up and says, "For gosh sakes, here comes Mrs. Roosevelt." She became a one-woman crusade for the rights of the young, of blacks, and of women. She defended her husband's New Deal programs but always remained open to the challenges of his critics.

Eleanor Roosevelt had grown into a remarkable human being through much personal travail. She had known suffering and tragedy, but instead of becoming bitter and withdrawn, she

Eleanor Roosevelt visits Ohio miners, 1936. (Brown Bros.)

chose to look outward, try to understand other human beings, and take constructive action in their behalf. At the same time, she never sacrificed her own values. "I am sorry," she told one of her adoring women interviewers, "if I hurt anyone's feelings, but one must do in this life the thing that seems right to oneself." Anti-Roosevelt congressmen complained that she swayed women to F.D.R.'s side, but women and men alike listened to this charming woman tell them why the National Youth Administration was important, or why more money had to be allocated for human services. In a letter to a friend in 1941, she wrote:

> Somewhere along the line of development we discover what we really are and then we make our real decision for which we are responsible. Make that decision primarily for yourself because you can never really live anyone's life, not even your child's. The influence you exert is through your own life and what you become yourself.

These profound words, though expressed in private, were demonstrated in Eleanor Roosevelt's public life throughout the thirties and forties.

One of the many women reporters who followed Eleanor Roosevelt around in the 1930s characterized her in this way:

> She is only a Right-Wing feminist. She utters New Deal preachments in pure Brahmin accents. She hasn't entirely escaped Old New York, tho she looks forward to a kindlier social order. And she has no intention of relaxing her efforts to bring it about.

Eleanor Roosevelt always spoke in favor of women's marrying and raising children. She regarded the home and the family as valuable social institutions worth preserving. But she also spoke in favor of women's participation in politics, business, and education. In answer to questions from her *Ladies' Home Journal* readers, she advised that a woman could have a full-time career only if she could manage two careers. If she had the energy, the time, and a supportive husband, then she could maintain a productive life outside the home—difficult conditions, indeed, for the average wife and mother.

"Right-wing feminist," then, is a good description of Eleanor

328

Roosevelt's philosophy. She never attacked the basic institutions of the society but told American women that they could combine a career and marriage if they were, in effect, superior. Wealthy women should do philanthropic and social work, she recommended, because it was not morally right for anyone to remain idle. As for women with jobs, they must be protected by labor legislation to ensure humane working conditions. She was an articulate supporter of the Women's Trade Union League and a personal friend of Rose Schneiderman, its president. Mrs. Roosevelt campaigned for her good friend Caroline O'Day, who ran successfully for Congress in 1934.

Ever the realist, Eleanor Roosevelt knew that neither men nor women always behaved according to humane standards. And she stated on numerous occasions that neither men nor women voted intelligently but she hoped both sexes could be educated to do so. "Women have used this suffrage," she wrote, "as far as I can tell, approximately as much as men have."

Above and beyond all the causes she advocated, Eleanor Roosevelt conveyed the image of a self-fulfilling woman. She lived her life according to her own principles and counseled her listeners to do the same. She reminded her woman readers that the only way to change unjust conditions was to work for that change. Most significantly, she told them that women simply did not have the power or influence to make their lives worthwhile. "I have heard people say that the United States is a matriarchy —that the women rule. That is true only in nonessentials." The feminist message emerged clearly in those words, although most American women did not discern their full import. They admired the First Lady but did not appreciate the significance of her message. Indeed, Eleanor Roosevelt herself may not have realized all its implications.

For if women were to implement the First Lady's philosophy, certain important alterations in sacred institutions would be required. How could career women—or, rather, *why should* career women have to assume two full-time jobs? Why shouldn't women hold elective offices? Why shouldn't both men and women workers be treated with dignity and receive equal wages and opportunities? Americans never seriously entertained these questions. Neither did Eleanor Roosevelt. She faithfully accepted the rightness of American institutions as well as the basic educability of both sexes. She believed that knowledgeable men and women could create the good society. In other words, she hoped for peaceful change within the established system.

Americans, however much they admired Eleanor Roosevelt, displayed their basic traditionalism in answering a 1940 *Fortune* magazine poll that asked: "What do you think Eleanor Roosevelt should do if she does not return to the White House next year?" Only 7.3 per cent of the women and 5.8 per cent of the men believed that she should be elected or appointed to some high government office. Mrs. Roosevelt herself said she did not think the American people would accept a woman President. Men and women still shared the idea that power should be held by men, not women. Political, economic, military, and diplomatic decisions were in the male's sphere of influence, not the female's. No wonder only a few people said they would support Eleanor Roosevelt for elective office in 1940.

Thanks to F.D.R.'s unprecedented third and fourth terms, Eleanor Roosevelt remained in the White House until 1945. Thereafter, as the respected widow of the President as well as the acknowledged spokesperson for human rights, she continued to serve the country and the world through her work with the newly formed United Nations. Before she died, she had become a legend, and had provided American women with an exciting example of an independent, fully realized human being.

Women Movie Stars

American women in the 1930s found many other cultural heroines in the movies. By now the movies were the most popular form of entertainment, as well as one of the largest industries in the nation. The drab years of the depression were Hollywood's golden era, with big studios like MGM, Warner Brothers, and Paramount turning out hundreds of films for eager movie-goers. Schoolgirls who spent Saturday afternoons at the ornate movie houses knew and loved the films of Joan Crawford, Bette Davis, and Katharine Hepburn. Men and women watched Greta Garbo and Clark Gable with the same absorption. Movie magazines informed the eager public about the personal lives of the stars, and fan clubs perpetuated their popularity.

330

PROFILES OF THREE MOVIE STARS

Katharine Hepburn (1909–)
Upper-class background.

Born in Hartford, Connecticut; her father was a urologist-surgeon, her mother a social activist.

Bryn Mawr College graduate. Played in theaters, summer stock in New York area. Went to Hollywood in 1932. Within a year, won an Academy Award for her performance in *Morning Glory* (1933). Married a Philadelphia lawyer in 1928, was divorced in 1935.

No children.

Record three-time Academy Award winner.

Bette Davis (1908–)
Middle-class background.

Born in Lowell, Massachusetts, to a patent attorney and a frustrated actress.

High school education. Parents were divorced when she was eight. Attended John Murray Anderson's acting and dancing school in New York.

Acted in theaters, summer stock. Went to Hollywood in 1930. Married her high school sweetheart in 1932.

Three children, four marriages. Divorced three times, widowed once.

Twice winner of the Academy Award.

Joan Crawford (1908–)
Working-class background.

Born in San Antonio, Texas. Parents divorced when she was three months old. Mother remarried but divorced her second husband.

Meager education.

Became a dancer and actress at an early age.

At sixteen, went to Hollywood to enter movies.

Married her first husband, Douglas Fairbanks, Jr., in 1929.

Four children, four marriages, divorced three times, widowed once.

One Academy Award.

Among the many types of movies of the period were the "women's films," so called because they starred women and were directed to women audiences. They included stories of career women, domestic comedies, and teary melodramas.

Katharine Hepburn, feminist on and off screen.
(N.Y. Public Library)

Katharine Hepburn built a reputation playing the roles of a woman lawyer, athlete, and aviatrix. Rosalind Russell starred as a businesswoman in countless films. Joan Crawford became a female Horatio Alger in *Mildred Pierce* (1945) and often portrayed dissatisified, restless women. Although each of these leading ladies was frequently defeated by society before the end of the movie, the image of an adventurous, striving soul remained in the audience's mind. Many a young girl grew up admiring Katharine Hepburn's portrayal of an aviatrix in *Christopher Strong* (1933), of a women's rights crusader in *A Woman Rebels* (1936), and of an international columnist in *Woman of the Year* (1942), along with other similar roles played by Bette Davis, Joan Crawford, and Rosalind Russell.

Then, too, career-woman films provided endless fantasies for married women who longed for a larger life. So they flocked to a Bette Davis or a Katharine Hepburn movie in order to experience vicariously the thrill of trying a case in court and of traveling all over the country. When the film ended, so did the dream. In fact, the dream ended in the final moments of the film when

332

Katharine Hepburn fell into the arms of Spencer Tracy (or another equivalent hero) and conceded that love and marriage were all she ever wanted anyway. The old cultural imperative prevailed. According to Hollywood, career women were usually masculine and aggressive until they fell in love with the "right" man, who then softened them, feminized them, and tamed them. They lost all worldly ambitions and submisively returned to their rightful place—the home.

In *Take a Letter Darling* (1942), Rosalind Russell gave up a career in advertising in order to spend her days with Fred MacMurray. And in the comic conclusion of *Woman of the Year*, Katharine Hepburn tearfully demonstrated her incompetence in the kitchen. But during these films the women in the audience would identify with a forceful, decisive woman who had a separate identity and purpose in life and whose financial and psychic independence they could admire. Some chose to ignore their favorite star's capitulation at the end of the film. Others were comforted by the surrender, which showed that the mighty can fall, too. Even Katharine Hepburn would succumb at the

Actress Bette Davis changes a tire in "The Bride Came C.O.D." (1941). (Culver)

Movie star Joan Crawford, a heroine to many. (N.Y. Public Library)

end; even Bette Davis and Joan Crawford could not break away from the traditional life pattern. Love and marriage, according to the utterly conservative Hollywood taste-setters, had to go together. Moreover, one *could* not have love without marriage and *should* not have marriage without love.

The stereotyped image of a career woman as mannish and therefore undesirable confirmed the society's view that every normal woman would marry and stay home. A woman must be mannish to venture forth into man's world—and mannishness would never do. Male characteristics were appropriate for men

334

in the marketplace and the professional office, but never for women. Thus, career women in the movies fulfilled a double function: they satisfied woman's fantasy needs for other life experiences at the same time that they enforced the culture's view of woman as wife and mother. Anyone who, in the 1970s, views the films of the 1930s may, however, emerge with a very different interpretation. Nowadays those career women appear quite natural, sympathetic, and authentic; their strivings seem legitimate and entirely understandable. But movie critics in the thirties, who never failed to note Joan Crawford's high-fashion gowns and often commented favorably on the acting talent of Katharine Hepburn or Bette Davis, never discussed the social significance of the women these stars depicted.

Domestic comedies, especially those starring Carole Lombard, satisfied women's need for varied experiences in a different way. Carole Lombard would be a beautiful rich girl or a girl "on the make" who devoted her days and nights to pursuing men. She was often a dizzy blonde who seemed clearheaded only when bent on capturing a man. In *My Man Godfrey* (1936), for example, Carole Lombard was an aristocratic young woman who fell in love with the butler and spent her days trying to attract his attention. In *Love Before Breakfast* (1936), the theme varied somewhat: she resisted the advances of the man she loved while still covertly pursuing him. The hero, played by Preston Foster, was domineering and she would not be dominated, though in the end, of course, she was. The further implication in many of these movies was that women enjoy the romantic chase but always want to be caught. And Hollywood obliged by making countless variations of the same theme.

The teary film melodramas gave women the emotional catharsis they also greatly needed. They watched Bette Davis die in *Dark Victory* (1938). They wept for her in *The Old Maid* (1939). They saw her play a self-sacrificing heroine who gave up her lover in *Now Voyager* (1941). Since women have always sacrificed for others in real life, in this sense the movies portrayed reality. A woman's life was made up of relations with others, and those relationships frequently required sacrifices. Women movie fans, therefore, adored crying in the theater as their favorite movie star also sacrificed herself for the one she loved. All women were comforted to see their fate shared by other women who were beautiful, rich, and famous.

335

The women movie stars of the thirties became the popular heroines of their generation. Somehow, seeing a Bette Davis or a Joan Crawford movie seemed to enrich a woman's daily life. Thus, the movies provided women audiences with an important fantasy satisfaction. During the depression, reality was especially unpleasant for millions of American women, but their spirits were buoyed and their experiences broadened by watching their favorite stars. Even if they could not travel all over the globe, they could watch Katharine Hepburn do so. Even if they could not behave commandingly, they could admire Bette Davis in a domineering role. The life of any human being includes his/her dream life, and the movies of the thirties gave women many dreams.

Women Reformers

At the same time, large numbers of women continued to devote their energies to organizations promoting women's causes. The National Woman's Party propagandized for the equal rights amendment without much success. The League of Women Voters educated women on legislative issues. Advocates of birth control worked for the removal of a federal ban on the shipping of contraceptive information and material. Margaret Sanger, the determined organizer of the first birth control clinic in this country in 1916, was still fighting for birth control reform in the 1930s. From 1924 to 1934, she and her cohorts had tried to get the U.S. House of Representatives to allow the medical profession to distribute birth control information, each time meeting with failure.

One of Mrs. Sanger's able colleagues was Mrs. Thomas Norval Hepburn, mother of actress Katharine Hepburn and long a crusader for women's rights. Mrs. Hepburn told the House Judiciary Committee members, at a hearing in 1934, that the Catholic Church's objections to birth control, as well as the legislators' skepticism, were ill founded. "Race suicide talk is just as ridiculous as was that of those who said, when we women wanted the vote, that it would destroy the home."

Added Mrs. Sanger: "The forgotten woman can have her child's teeth and adenoids cared for at clinics. She can send her children to get free luncheons. She can do nothing for her own most pressing problem." But the committee remained unimpressed.

Others who spoke for birth control reminded the legislators that many people privately used contraceptives, despite the federal ban. One outraged congressman declared, ". . . there has never been a contraceptive in my home. I have six children." Mrs. Hepburn replied, "I also have six children."

Yet despite the intensity of emotions and the sincerity of the reformers, the legislators did not vote to end the ban on contraceptive information and devices until 1937. They still held the long-established majority opinion and refused to consider women's rights in the birth control issue. The integrity of the family and the superiority of men were, as usual, the rationale for their position. The New Deal congressmen preferred the old deal.

Natural Calamities

Americans experienced natural as well as man-made catastrophes in the 1930s. The Ohio River Valley flood of 1936 and another in 1937 caused half a million people to abandon their homes in eight states—Ohio, Pennsylvania, West Virginia, Indiana, Illinois, Tennessee, Missouri, and Arkansas. Pittsburgh declared a state of emergency. The dire warnings of the advocates of regional multi-purpose flood control programs had come true, and President Roosevelt sent a message to Congress proposing the creation of seven regional boards to deal with the flood problem.

> Experience has taught us [he wrote] that the prudent husbandry of our national estate requires farsighted management. Floods, droughts, and dust storms are in a very real sense manifestations of nature's refusal to tolerate continued abuse of her bounties.

His recommendation resulted in the commitment of additional funds not only to conservation but to the continuation of the Tennessee Valley Authority, one of the few regional programs already under way.

Roosevelt had followed the lead of his cousin Theodore Roosevelt in supporting conservation measures and accepting

337

the multi-purpose concept of many experts. F.D.R. was very much aware of the abuse of the national forests, soil, and waterways. In the same message to Congress, he noted that

> ... provision should be made for the effective administration of hydroelectric projects which have been or may be undertaken as a part of a multiple-purpose watershed development. The water-power resources of the Nation must be protected from private monopoly and used for the benefit of the people.

Unfortunately, too many of the hydroelectric resources had already been preempted by private power companies. Further, to many people, the theme of public ownership of utilities smacked of socialism. To anti-Roosevelt observers, the TVA and all other regional planning projects spelled the end of private enterprise and were to be fiercely resisted. Only in times of natural disaster did Americans seriously consider the importance of long-range planning to protect natural resources.

The dust storms of the mid-thirties also affected thousands of lives. The dry soil left by the severe drought was picked up by winds and blown in huge clouds across the flat land. Much of the tragic devastation was due to mismanagement of farmlands. If the farmers had planted more trees, rotated their crops, built reservoirs to conserve the rainfall, the rich topsoil would not have blown away. But without knowledge of these conservation measures and without instruction in terrace planting, farmers were helpless. They went on planting their crops in straight lines rather than along the natural contours of the land. As a result of this mismanagement, soil erosion had become a mammoth problem by the 1930s. Hugh H. Bennett, director of the Soil Conservation Service, wrote and lectured on the evils of soil erosion, and his experts in the Service provided information and funds to encourage farmers to use their land wisely.

The lack of rainfall in the Great Plains heightened an already bad situation. In Oklahoma, where there were few natural streams and few man-made reservoirs, the farmers waited patiently for the rains to come. When they did not, the crops died and with them the farmers' livelihood. Hundreds of families every month left their farms and moved on, usually to more fertile parts of the West.

Mrs. Caroline A. Henderson and her husband had farmed in

Oklahoma for twenty-eight years before they had to face the drought of the mid-thirties. She wrote to a friend in Maryland describing the conditions under which she and her family lived during the worst of this period.

> Wearing our shade hats, with handkerchiefs tied over our faces and vaseline in our nostrils, we have been trying to rescue our home from the accumulations of wind-blown dust which penetrates wherever air can go. It is an almost hopeless task, for there is rarely a day when at some time the dust clouds do not roll over. "Visibility" approaches zero and everything is covered again with a silt-like deposit which may vary in depth from a film to actual ripples on the kitchen floor.

But the Hendersons stuck it out. They did not want to abandon their home of so many years. They kept on working —and praying for rain.

The life of an Oklahoma farmer was a hard and solitary one. Mrs. Henderson related how the family took a sixty-mile trip on the new federal highway on a Saturday, the farmers' marketing day, and saw only one car on the road. She could look across their 640-acre farm and not see a human face. Her letters, published in the *Atlantic Monthly* in 1936, pictured the life of many farmers over many centuries. Each year, the farmer's future was determined by the weather, the railroads, world prices, and consumer demand. Although he could improve his farming techniques, a farmer could not control the other powerful forces that decided his future. But Mrs. Henderson epitomized American stubbornness; she hung on and continued to believe in better days to come. She praised the New Deal agencies for their constructive help—and also the direct relief agencies, while proudly noting that most people in her county were working and did not have to depend on direct government relief.

The farmer's wife, if Mrs. Henderson was a good example, kept a cheerful demeanor and by so doing held her family together. She worked alongside her husband in the fields and cared for the home as well. Boys and girls alike participated in the regular farm chores. The Hendersons' daughter Eleanor drove the tractor during the summer, before returning to work in the fall.

The floods of the Ohio Valley and the dust storms of the Great

Plains hurt thousands of people, but the Hendersons, and scores of others like them, continued to believe in the human ability to survive natural disaster. The isolated farmers may have had radios, but they had no Bijou Theater to provide them with pleasant film fantasies. Indeed, they probably would not have had the dime necessary for admission. Sixty million Americans went to the movies every week during the thirties, but the Hendersons and their counterparts were not among that number. They survived the depression by relying largely on their own resources.

A Woman Novelist Looks at Women

On the eve of the second time in the century that the United States entered a world war, novelist Pearl Buck wrote a book, *Of Men and Women* (1941), that she believed dealt with a serious American problem. The examples of Nazi Germany and militaristic Japan portended evil for the status of women, observed Miss Buck. The Nazis subjected their women to inhuman tasks. If America did not alter its attitudes toward women, she feared the same fate would befall her sex in the U.S.

> If all women could be born with inferior minds and men with superior ones, the scheme for the home could doubtless be perfectly satisfactory. But unless that can be done, it is not satisfactory.

Miss Buck was positively frightened by American women's submissiveness and passive obedience to their male masters. Both sexes, she wrote, had to redefine their views of women's education and women's lives. Otherwise, one-half of the American population would become subservient slaves and follow the model of fascist countries.

The analogy between Nazi Germany and the United States in regard to sex roles did not appeal to most Americans. Pearl Buck's comparison seemed shocking and ill considered. How could anyone compare democratic America with Nazi Germany? The thought was positively unpatriotic. After Pearl Harbor, the United States fought both Japan and Germany to save political democracy and capitalism, and, by implication, to save the nuclear family, the home, and the patriarchal order. All Western civilization was jeopardized by the maniac Hitler, and anyone who saw similarities between the Nazis and the Americans on any level was mad or addlebrained.

Pearl Buck was neither, and she did not push the analogy too far in her book. Rather, she used the point to start a discussion of women's roles in the United States and to analyze the basis for Americans' utter traditionalism. Having spent a good deal of time in China, she was profoundly shocked, on returning to this country in the late 1930s, to discover the rigid sex-role definitions that were still applied to women in America.

The American home, she pointed out, no longer resembled the frontier home of the past century. It had been transformed by modern industrial living. While its physical structure remained, the tasks of the home had either been removed or simplified. The schools educated the children, the washing machine speeded the laundry tasks, and the factories made the clothes. Since the home took so little time to maintain, the modern woman was left with time on her hands and loneliness in her

Novelist and feminist writer Pearl Buck plays chess with her three adopted daughters. (Wide World)

heart. In the twentieth century, men and women alike still defined women in terms of their wife-and-mother role. So they dutifully remained in the home and lived a life that became increasingly functionless. Pearl Buck blamed women for their fate, and argued that they had to rouse themselves from their lethargy. They must raise their children, of both sexes, to become fully rounded human beings with life purposes other than the traditional ones.

Pearl Buck criticized women for their lack of involvement in world affairs. By staying at home, in a safe but insignificant capacity, the American woman contributed to the blundering of humanity. How can women claim righteousness and virtue, she asked, when they continue to tolerate war?

> Yet to continue to bear children only to have them slaughtered is folly. But to take as a solemn task the prevention of war would be an achievement unmatched. In the process women would become inevitably concerned in human welfare, to the betterment of all society as well as of themselves. It is the only hope I see of the end of war.

Women contributed to their own impotence by accepting it. They were as guilty as their husbands of perpetuating the status quo.

> Where is this moral superiority that will do nothing but knit while heads roll off in revolutions and war crashes upon our great cities so that ruins are all that we shall have left if the world goes on as it now is?

Women pacifists during World War I had organized a woman's peace party with the hope that women would join out of natural interest. Unfortunately, that hope did not materialize. Pearl Buck echoed the same message:

> Women fulfill themselves in having the babies, and men fulfill themselves in destroying them. There ought to be some other more profitable form of pleasurable sacrifice for the human race than this sacrifice of the innocents.

342

Women and War

How could this cycle be broken? Didn't women have any power over their own lives as well as the lives of their children? Was there no way for women to organize for peace instead of standing by and watching warlike acts proceed? Pearl Buck raised all these important questions during the war year of 1941. But another Pearl forestalled any public desire to answer them —Pearl Harbor. The Japanese attack on that U.S. naval base guaranteed the legitimacy of World War II. If women secretly wondered why men continually blundered into war, they kept their anxieties to themselves. Like their husbands, great numbers of them voted for President Roosevelt in 1940 and again in 1944, but they did not do so in blind obedience. American women felt as committed to their country as did their fathers, brothers, and husbands. When it came to love of country, women did not view themselves as a separate sex with certain qualities that set them apart from men. Although they were, in the popular phrase, "the mothers of men," they were also the wives and daughters of men whose ideology they shared. So Pearl Buck's *Of Men and Women* came at the wrong time to revolutionize American thinking about man-woman relations.

Women, after all, were accustomed to their age-old role of givers, sharers, and sacrificers. As Margaret Barnard Pickel, an adviser to women graduate students at Columbia University, told *New York Times* readers in a 1944 article, "A Warning to the Career Woman":

> A successful woman once said that women had to be three times as clever as men and work five times as hard to get the same promotion and salary. "Once you accept that," she added, "you can go forward without bitterness." Whatever the situation is after the war, I think women should go forward without bitterness, without the resentment that makes the load heavier and the prospect bleaker.

Career women, mothers, unskilled women workers, volunteer women workers, and all other women should never expect too much and then they wouldn't be disappointed.

Returning soldiers after World War II, as after all other wars, took away from women the higher-paid jobs and the professional

343

posts they had held for three or four years. Women engineers and chemists made room for the men, their predecessors, as did skilled women workers in the automobile plants and steel mills of America. Rosie the Riveter was a good wartime propaganda image, but that image disintegrated the minute the boys came home. When labor was desperately needed to keep the defense plants working, women were eagerly recruited, but when the war was over, they were dismissed or voluntarily left their lucrative jobs and went back home.

In New York State, women constituted 33 per cent of the work force during the war, and after the war, 25 per cent. So not all women returned to the home. In fact, after the war there were more women in the labor force than at any previous time in American history. But the same inequities prevailed: not only did women draw less pay than men for doing the same jobs, but they had to take jobs in traditional female-designated areas. Most women who worked (and for the first time more married women worked than single women) were typists, secretaries, and clerks. Two-thirds of all professional women were teachers or nurses. The rigid categories of work, defined along sex lines, remained unbroken, even if they had been changed temporarily during the war. Both employers and employees considered wartime work patterns as emergency variations that would be discontinued after the war. Even the unions would not permit women to continue working in automobile or steel plants once male workers had returned to their jobs.

A number of women writers of the period (before, during, and after the war) advised women workers to organize on their own behalf. Mary Heaton Vorse, a labor journalist who had been reporting on unions since the 1910s, suggested that working mothers ask the government to provide child-care centers and to set flexible schedules for them. Dorothy Thompson told her *Ladies' Home Journal* readers that both factories and schools would have to adjust their routines to accommodate working women. She envisioned schools that would provide hot lunches and after-school programs for the children of mothers doing war work. Many women's organizations recommended that factories install nursery facilities to lighten the double load of working mothers. But industry made no serious effort to change its procedures, even though women constituted a third of the labor force in 1944. Indeed, the women themselves did not act on these suggestions.

Mothers with full-time jobs, not a new phenomenon in the working class, now became acceptable in the middle class too. But communities rarely had adequate day-nursery facilities to care for preschool children. Some federal child-care centers were created in war-industry areas under the Lanham Act, as were some private centers, but the demand far exceeded the supply. In 1945, less than 10 per cent of the children of working mothers were cared for in government facilities. So each day the mothers of preschool youngsters had to leave them with willing (or unwilling) relatives, or else some other makeshift arrangement had to be invented.

Dorothy Thompson, for one, grew increasingly impatient with American women for their inability to organize themselves in order to meet their own needs. Why didn't women agitate for day-care centers? Why didn't women propagandize for a revision in the tax laws to make baby-sitting fees a deductible expense? But this zealous journalist never received satisfactory answers to her questions. American women, according to a Gallup poll in 1943, generally agreed with American men that young children should not be put in day-care centers unless this was absolutely necessary. Fifty-six per cent of the women interviewed said they would not take jobs in war plants if it meant leaving their children in a free day nursery.

In privatized, family-centered America, Dorothy Thompson's ideas—shared by Fannie Hurst and other forward-looking women—appeared subversive at worst and impractical at best. But American mothers had to be charged with inconsistency and/or hypocrisy. Increasing numbers of them would leave their preschool children at home with untrained baby-sitters, hardly a desirable alternative to entrusting them with professional nursery staffs. Leaving one child in the care of one untrained adult, they rationalized, was better than putting one child in a group of many other children cared for by one trained adult. Charlotte Perkins Gilman's idea of expert care in all areas of home care and child raising lay dormant. A significant debate on the subject never occurred.

In the spring of 1941, Eleanor Roosevelt recommended that young women be drafted into a one-year program of compulsory service to their country. This suggestion was received with boos and yells of protest. Draft women into the Army? Unthinkable! But the public misunderstood Mrs. Roosevelt. She never suggested military training for women, but simply that, during an emergency, young women along with young men should be summoned to serve the nation. They could work in hospitals, canteens, and offices. They could help during air-raid watches and perform a multitude of essential wartime tasks. Yet the cultural imperatives against women's participating actively in any military context blocked the idea. Despite this taboo, however, more than 250,000 women enlisted in the armed forces during World War II, and many women officers continued their distinguished military careers after the war was over.

The popular song "Don't Sit Under the Apple Tree" told the women who stayed home that fighting men expected loyalty from their wives and sweethearts, but a great many women had little time for sitting under apple trees. As they had done in previous wars, they worked long and hard—in the home, in offices and factories, on farms—and served their country in numerous volunteer organizations. Nothing had changed from war to war. Women uncomplainingly devoted themselves to keeping the family intact, sacrificing their personal needs for the war effort and the welfare of society. With dignity and courage, they accepted food rationing and air-raid drills, endured loneliness and fear. They wrote regularly to their husbands abroad and prayed for their speedy return.

Women as a Social Problem

Frequently, writers who dealt with the "woman question" did not fully perceive the import of their own words. In 1946, for example, *Life* magazine's editors noted that the American woman was still not a full political partner in this country, although women made up the numerical majority of voting citizens. They did not vote as a bloc, did not get elected to political offices in proportion to their numbers, and did not exert a leading influence on political life. But the editors did not know what to make of these facts, and could suggest no concrete reforms, simply because they did not understand the larger, more complex matrix from which the facts emerged. Women had contributed to the building of the nation but always within socially approved spheres. Furthermore, because outstanding accomplishments were defined by men, women's work never received recognition.

It was in 1944 that career guidance counselor Margaret Barnard Pickel advised women graduate students at Columbia that they should be content to be the "helpers and servers" of society. Considering herself realistic and levelheaded, she never suggested alternative life roles and values. After the war, she told the students—

> Women will have scope on a larger scale for their home-making talent. It seems likely that there will be a building program calling for women skilled in interior decoration, in the buying of furniture and fabrics, in landscape gardening. Women trained in institutional management and in dietetics will be in demand.

Thus, even women educators reinforced the cultural imperatives regarding the proper spheres of their sex.

As an anthropologist, Margaret Mead (1901–) understood the significance of child-raising practices but did not devote sufficient attention to that problem in a 1946 *Fortune* magazine article, "What Women Want." Rather, she recommended neighborhood nurseries for mothers who wished to work, and encouraged husbands to share household tasks. Surely these were practical suggestions for the immediate present, but she did not advocate any changes in the way children were brought up to think of their roles and their future life patterns.

The social commentators of the forties who looked at women's problems—anthropologists, sociologists, journalists—consciously detached themselves from their social environment. Pearl Buck compared the U.S. with China, Margaret Mead compared Americans with South Sea islanders, and Dorothy Thompson compared them with Europeans. Another contributor to the growing literature on women's roles was Mirra Komarovsky (1906–), a sociologist at Barnard College. In an article in the *American Journal of Sociology* (1946), Professor Komarovsky noted the serious discrepancy between the two dominant roles women were expected to play in the American culture—the "feminine" and the "modern." The feminine, of course, was the traditional wife-and-mother sex role that could be played only by women. The modern role could be played by either sex; it entailed professional work, knowledge of and interest in the larger society, and participation in the workings of that society.

347

Women, especially college-educated women (whom Professor Komarovsky had used as a sample for her research), developed strong conflicts over these roles. While in college, they could easily perform the modern role; but after marriage they reverted to the feminine one, losing all connections with the modern. Once the college-educated woman had her first child, she no longer read even the newspapers and was totally uninformed on world affairs. Why should she, when, after marriage, no one asked her opinion about anything important? How, then, could married, educated women achieve and maintain both roles throughout their lives? A very important question, but one which Professor Komarovsky did not answer satisfactorily. The problem would persist, she concluded, "until the adult sex roles of women are redefined in greater harmony with the socioeconomic and ideological character of modern society." How and when would there be such a redefinition? Who would initiate it? How long would it take? Being an academic analyst of society, and not a feminist reformer, Professor Komarovsky cannot be faulted for failing to provide answers to these questions. Yet restless, uncomfortable women readers in 1946 might have wondered when the miracle would happen.

Black and White

White American attitudes toward blacks did not change during World War II either. Of 107,000 workers employed by the aircraft industries in 1940, only 240 were blacks. Said an executive of North American Aviation, "Regardless of training we will not employ Negroes in the North American plant. It is against Company policy." Another executive, of Standard Steel, said, "We have not had a Negro worker in twenty-five years, and do not plan to start now." White women workers in defense plants were far more acceptable (on a temporary basis, that is) than able-bodied black men. Seventy-five thousand experienced black carpenters, painters, plasterers, cement workers, bricklayers, and electricians could not gain employment in the early forties. Of 56 war-contract factories in St. Louis, each employed an average of three black workers.

The war may have created an emergency demand for labor, but white Americans resisted changing their long-held views about blacks. Governor Frank M. Dixon of Alabama rejected a government contract to use the cotton mills in the Alabama State Prison for war production because of a nondiscrimination clause. Rather than hire black workers, he refused the contract. The Red Cross would not accept Negro blood even though the process of storing blood plasma had been invented by a black physician, Dr. Charles Drew of Howard University Medical School. Black organization leaders were increasingly alarmed by this wartime racial discrimination. What would the Roosevelt administration do to end it?

A. Philip Randolph, the head of the Brotherhood of Sleeping Car Porters and the first black union leader to gain stature within the American Federation of Labor, suggested to the leadership of the NAACP and the Urban League that a mass march be planned in Washington to protest the government's lack of action in behalf of black Americans. He pointed out that prejudice prevailed in employment, in the armed services, and in every other area of life. Black soldiers remained in segregated units, and tensions between black and white GI's persisted. Having gained the support of many black leaders and organizations, Randolph set about the mighty task of publicizing the proposed march. He spoke and wrote words of encouragement to black citizens all over the country in order to recruit marchers who would be ready to express their frustrations in front of the White House.

When President Roosevelt learned about the planned march, he conferred with Randolph and other black leaders. In order to avoid a huge demonstration in Washington (Randolph promised 100,000 marchers), F.D.R. agreed to issue an executive order outlawing discrimination in federal-contract defense plants. The Fair Employment Practices Commission (FEPC) was established to supervise the enforcement of this order. And although prejudiced attitudes and behavior did not change instantly—or even gradually, in some cases—the employment picture for black workers improved after 1941. Roosevelt's action, however modest a beginning, demonstrated an awareness of racial discrimination, which the federal government had virtually ignored for decades.

All during the years between the two world wars, the NAACP had worked steadily through the courts to gain civil rights for black Americans. In the spring of 1941, the Supreme Court ruled that railroads operating in interstate commerce could not refuse Pullman accommodations to blacks. Another modest beginning—one that led to the slow reversal of former Court decisions which had legitimatized the segregation of, and discrimination against, black Americans. In 1944, the Courts outlawed the white primary in Texas, paving the way for similar action in other Southern states, but it would be twenty years before large numbers of black voters fully realized their political power in the South. The power of the federal government to enforce black suffrage rights was not established until the 1960s.

Racial tensions remained high in all sections of the country, particularly wherever black citizens entered spheres designated as white. If black workers competed with white workers over jobs or if black residents moved into previously all-white communities, violence was sure to occur. On June 20, 1943, in Detroit, a race riot took place that resulted in the death of twenty-five blacks and nine whites. Scores of people were injured, and property damage ran to more than two million dollars.

It all started when black people tried to move into a government housing project with the government's approval. The white tenants in the Sojourner Truth housing project, named after the courageous black woman who escaped slavery and became a well-known abolitionist speaker, protested the government's action. The government reversed itself in response to the white opposition, but the blacks moved in anyway. With some help from Ku Klux Klan members, the whites started attacking the black tenants. The full-scale riot that ensued lasted thirty hours.

The Detroit race riot of 1943 was only one ugly example, among many, of the eruption of racial hatred and violence that has characterized white-black relationships in this country. Franklin Roosevelt's executive order and the Supreme Court's decisions were not sufficient to alter basic beliefs and attitudes. They simply marked the beginning of efforts to reverse deeply held convictions. It would be another generation before a concerted attempt on the part of the judicial and legislative branches of government was undertaken to redress racial grievances.

Suggestions for Further Reading

Andrew Bergman. *We're in the Money: Depression America and Its Films* (New York, 1971).

350

Suggestions for Further Reading

Caroline Bird. *The Invisible Scar* (New York, 1966).

Horace Cayton and George S. Mitchell. *Black Workers and the New Unions* (Chapel Hill, N.C., 1939).

William H. Chafe. *The American Woman: Her Changing Social, Economic, and Political Roles, 1920–1970* (New York, 1972).

Betty Friedan. *The Feminine Mystique* (New York, 1963).

Molly Haskell. *From Reverence to Rape: The Treatment of Women in the Movies* (New York, 1974).

Joseph Lash. *Eleanor and Franklin* (New York, 1971).

Rose Schneiderman. *All for One* (New York, 1967).

June Sochen. *Movers and Shakers: American Women Thinkers and Activists, 1900–1970* (New York, 1973).

John Steinbeck. *The Grapes of Wrath* (New York, 1939).

Suggestions for Further Reading

CHAPTER THIRTEEN

New and Old Anxieties
1945–1960

It's still the same old story,
A fight for love and glory . . .

　　—From the song *As Time Goes By*

[Women] don't assert their *own* experiences, affirm their *own* instincts, believe in their *own* wisdom, or struggle for their *own* values. And therefore, they don't release for society the unique power which is in them.

　　—Dorothy Thompson, 1951

1948: Twenty people died in Donora, Pennsylvania, because of a severe episode of air pollution.

1952: Four thousand people died in one week in London because of air pollution.

War and Peace

*W*ars, being the cataclysmic events that they are, always produce jarring aftermaths. The survivors cannot forget the bloody reality that dominated their lives for so long; families of the victims have to begin again, painfully but stoically. Eighteen-year-old boys who went into the Army in 1942 came out looking like thirty-year-olds in 1945. The war robbed the young of their youth. It made young girls assume responsibilities for which they were unprepared and forced young men to act out the aggressive masculine traits they had learned to subdue. And these same traits had to be repressed and forgotten once peace returned.

In 1945, twenty-two-year-old veterans went back to school, sitting uncomfortably beside naive eighteen-year-olds. The economy, like an old, unreliable automobile, spurted and stopped unpredictably. Returning GIs demanded their old jobs

353

—jobs eagerly sought by young men entering the labor force and previously held by women.

Young girls hoped to stop working, marry their sweethearts, and begin a life of tranquil domesticity. But middle-aged married women who had worked in defense plants hoped to keep their jobs, despite the priority given the returning veterans. Now that the war was over, everyone believed that prosperity and good times were at hand, that there would be enough jobs for all who wanted them.

Price controls, rationing, and government regulations were removed, often in haste and without proper planning, because President Truman knew the people wanted a return to normalcy. Even more important to Americans than economic stability and security was the restoration of their daily patterns of living. Wives wanted to cook dinner for their husbands, listen to the radio with their sons beside them, and gossip about trivial things with their girl friends. They wanted to forget about writing letters overseas and about worrying every night lest their husbands, fathers, and brothers would not return safely.

Naturally, the men too wanted to forget, so both sexes proceeded to do just that. They resumed their prewar habits along with their prewar confidence that the future would be better than the past. And they resumed their prewar sex roles—women staying home and men setting forth each morning for factories and offices. For hadn't men always been the breadwinners and sole supporters of their families? Only during national emergencies could women assume men's jobs. Neither war nor advanced technology could disrupt culturally imprinted behavior. So now, in 1945, many women dutifully gave up their jobs to men. Those who continued working fell back into low-paid, inferior positions. Those who returned to the home quickly became pregnant and lauded motherhood as the true destiny of women.

The postwar baby boom reflected Americans' uncritical commitment to family and domesticity. The war's survivors never doubted the validity of creating life only to have it destroyed in another war. While the power of destruction had increased dramatically in the twentieth century, the power of the home remained intact. In a changing world, threatened by the atom bomb, the home was the only constant, unchanging institution of society—the only dependable refuge in a confusing, unpredictable world. Within this context, then, the role of women also had to be solid and unchanging.

Thus, women's position in American society did not alter greatly after 1945. More of them worked, but in insignificant jobs; indeed, the large increase of women workers took place in the clerical area. Professional women—that is, the women who dared to endure and overcome the prejudices of men in order to practice a profession—remained in the minority. The medical, legal, and scientific establishments, as we have seen, had always been unwilling to admit women to their ranks. Hence each generation of women who aspired to careers in law, medicine, and the physical sciences had to break down the same barriers. It was no easier in 1945 than it had been in the past. The elite professions continued to discriminate against women, blacks, and other minority groups until well into the 1960s.

A WORKING MOTHER'S SCHEDULE

6:30 A.M. Rise and shine (?).

7:00 A.M. Prepare breakfast for the children and their school lunches.

7:30 A.M. Waken any children still sleeping. Supervise their dressing, and comb their hair.

8:00 A.M. Put breakfast on the table. Drink a cup of coffee.

8:30 A.M. Leave the house for work along with the children who are walking to school.

9:00 A.M. Arrive at the office.

9:00 A.M.–5:00 P.M. Work.

5:30 P.M. Arrive home. Listen to the children's reports about what has happened during the day.

5:45 P.M. Prepare dinner.

6:00 P.M. Greet husband. Serve dinner to the family.

6:30 P.M. Send the children off to play. Talk with husband over a cup of coffee.

6:45 P.M. Do the dishes while husband watches TV with the children.

8:00 P.M. Put children to bed.

8:30 P.M. Free time.

The Holy Home

American society was organized around a belief in the holiness of the family, motherhood, and the private home. Witness the suburbs built to accommodate the growing middle class, all made up largely of single-family homes rather than apartment houses. Along with the commitment to private property and family privacy, this belief enforced the traditional life style of women in the 1950s. Every wife and mother was held responsible for maintaining her home and caring for her children. In the suburbs, women also engaged in community activities but spent much more time driving their husbands to commuter train stations and their children to school. As one contemporary commentator noted, women became the "telephoners, organizers, the arrangers of community organizational life." Thanks to the fact that the powers-that-be preferred highways to cheap, efficient public transporation, the housewife became an unpaid chauffeur for other members of her family—unless they had two cars, which was uncommon at the time. The privatized, auto-oriented suburban way of life took growing numbers of middle-class women out of the city and away from its broader, more varied experiences. The suburban population tended to be homogeneous and often isolated from national concerns.

A SUBURBAN WIFE-MOTHER'S SCHEDULE

7:00 A.M. Rise and shine (?).
7:30 A.M. Waken any children who are still in bed.
7:35 A.M. Prepare breakfast.
7:45 A.M. Make school lunches.
8:00 A.M. Supervise breakfast. Drink a cup of coffee.
8:15 A.M. Walk the children to the school bus stop.
8:20 A.M. Drive husband to train station.
8:30 A.M. Sit down and have another cup of coffee.
9:00 A.M. Go to a P.T.A. board meeting.
11:00 A.M. Return home, and await arrival of nursery school child who attends school only in the mornings.
12:00 P.M. Prepare lunch for herself and the child.
12:30 P.M. Put the child to bed for a two-hour nap.
12:30 P.M.–2:30 P.M. Free time—for housework.
3:00 P.M. Await arrival of other children from school.

356

3:30 P.M. Take the two older children to their piano teacher for lessons (once a week).
4:30 P.M. Return home. Begin to prepare dinner.
6:30 P.M. Pick up husband at train station.
7:00 P.M. Serve dinner to family.
7:45 P.M. Get children ready for bed; bathe them, play games with them, tuck them in.
8:30 P.M. Do the dinner dishes.
9:15 P.M. Free time.

If the belief in the home as a sacred institution that housed one nuclear family could have been abandoned, or at least modified, then myriad possibilities for new life patterns would have been open to women. Charlotte Perkins Gilman's cooperative system for maintaining a whole group of households and caring for a whole group of preschool children (see page 221) would have freed wives from household duties and permitted them to pursue careers or creative interests. Women, who after all were natural resources worth developing, would have had many chances to realize their potentialities. But in a private-property, single-family-oriented society, all women were tied to the same domestic tasks—the educated and the uneducated, the enthusiastic housekeepers and the reluctant ones. Similarly, if the society were dedicated to developing all human talent, men too would be free to pursue a variety of interests. Those who enjoyed gardening, cooking, and child care could do these things to their heart's content. Since increased mechanization means that fewer people are needed to produce essential goods, the collectivizing of home functions could liberate both sexes from the traditional definitions of women's and men's work.

In the postwar period, few social commentators thought about these possibilities. Journalist Dorothy Thompson occasionally asked her *Ladies' Home Journal* readers why working women did not demand child-care facilities and flexible working schedules from the factories and offices of America, but she never got a response. After reading Simone de Beauvoir's *The Second Sex* and Ashley Montagu's *The Superiority of Women* in 1953, she became an enthusiastic feminist and began asking other questions: Why didn't women use their political and economic power for their own advantage? Why didn't they agitate in Washington for women's rights? These were impor-

357

tant, intelligent questions, but she could never answer them to her own satisfaction. Her challenging words, however, were as fresh and exciting as wind-stirred ripples on a dead-calm sea.

A popular movie of 1949, *Adam's Rib*, starring Katharine Hepburn and Spencer Tracy, presented an unusual view of marriage and man-woman relations. But its theme was never taken seriously. Rather, the husband-and-wife lawyers, Adam and Amanda Bonner, remained witty exceptions to the general run of married couples. Few people did anything but smile at Amanda's opinions on marriage:

> Balance. Equality. Mutual everything! There's no room in a marriage for what they used to call "the little woman." She's got to be as big as the man is. . . . Sharing! That's what it takes to keep a marriage from getting sick. . . . No part of life is the exclusive province of any one sex.

The words were spoken by a real feminist, Katharine Hepburn, in the role of an attorney—a rare woman playing a rare part in an American film. Her sentiments, fine as they were, hardly represented prevailing American attitudes.

Progress?

Outward changes in postwar society created a semblance of progress. Automobile production increased dramatically, and new highways were built to accommodate the vast numbers of cars. Although the thoughtful minority advocated public rather than private transportation, the government went on supporting the automobile industry. While the railroads steadily deteriorated in quality and service, the Eisenhower administration gave financial incentives to the thriving airline industry. Airports were built with federal funds as railroad companies languished. Streetcars were replaced by buses, but the great American goal was a car of one's own. Each family driving along the new interstate highways was exemplifying the current ideal way of life.

More Americans were going to school longer than ever before, another indication of social change. Educators had always claimed that education made all the difference in a society because it produced intelligent, responsible, and enlightened citizens. Logically, then, if more Americans went to high school and college and professional school, the quality of the society would improve. Yet what may be true in logic is not necessarily true in human experience. Educated middle-class Americans in the 1950s, escaping to their new suburban homes, chose to ignore social problems, not confront them. The new highways conveniently avoided the racial ghettos of the big cities, and residential segregation hid the poverty of blacks and whites from the fastidious eyes of middle- and upper-class Americans.

Once the war was over, technologists turned their attention to developing new consumer products. True, the armament and defense plants continued to prosper, but American industry had to find alluring new ways to interest the growing population. During wartime, few luxuries were available, and people saved their money out of necessity. Now product designers could devote themselves to enticing Americans back into their consumer roles. Hence the 1950s became consumer oriented much as the 1920s were, but with a difference: there was a far greater choice of products in the fifties. Advertisements lured women into retail stores to see the latest kitchen gadgets, house furnishings, and clothes. Buying on credit and installment plans was encouraged. Women as consumers, as major purchasers of all household goods, clothing, and foods, were the targets of the burgeoning Madison Avenue advertising industry.

Women as Puppets of Fashion

Gaudy Cadillac cars with fins, electric toothbrushes, and aqua-colored kitchens tempted the middle class and the lower class as well. Possessions, after all, had always been the measure of a person's status in society, separating the well-off from the less well-off. In agricultural America, the size of one's farm and the livestock one owned supplied the criterion. In industrial America, the size of one's house, its furnishings, one's car, and the clothes one wore were the gauge of a person's worth. Women basked in the glory of their husbands' economic success, displaying it on their backs and in their homes. Accepting the fact that consumer buying depended on constantly changing fashion tastes, women bought new wardrobes every year, and obediently changed their shoe styles and hairdos according to the dictates of stylists and industrialists.

There was a serious reason for these annual fashion changes. Textile manufacturers, dress designers, garment-makers, and retailers simply could not survive if women did not regularly discard last year's wardrobe and replace it with this year's. But instead of being grateful for their passive submissiveness to this economic necessity, the fashion industry arrogantly decreed dramatic shifts in style from one year to the next. Hemlines were steadily up in the fifties, reaching the upper thigh by the sixties. The narrow two-inch heels of the fifties gave way to three-inch heels in the early sixties and then to thick, cloggish heels at the end of the decade. Pointed-toe and round-toe shoe styles prevailed alternately with the whims of designers.

All this slavish devotion to styles of dress prompted a small number of historically minded people to recall the failure of Amelia Bloomer's crusade for dress reform a hundred years before. Women then and now dressed to please men—both their husbands and the male fashion designers. For the standard of taste in dress was created largely by males. Other people, therefore, determined whether a woman should wear a low-back or a low-front evening dress, and neither comfort, nor good sense, nor her own wishes entered into that determination.

Women accepted all these despotic fashion decrees as they accepted male domination in other areas of their lives, never rebelling at the rapidly changing styles. Then in the 1960s a miracle occurred. The designers went too far. Within one year, they expected young women to switch from the shortest skirts ever made into long ones. If the designers had lowered hemlines gradually over a five-year period, they probably would have succeeded, but by trying to accomplish the change in a single year, they failed.

Still, on the whole, women rebelled too infrequently, and they acted together too infrequently. Few agreed with Dorothy Thompson that since women shared so many problems as a sex, they should unite as a sex to solve them. Their meek acceptance of changing fashions is a telling example of their peculiar lassitude. But why fault women for following the cultural norms? What choice did they have? Rebels always live precariously, and most people prefer comfort and security to instability.

360

In the 1950s, the middle-class housewife was surrounded by labor-saving and time-saving devices. Cooking was simplified by her General Electric oven and the new already-frozen foods. Her washing machine was (supposedly) made even more efficient when supplied with well-advertised cleansing powders. (Procter and Gamble alone offered over a dozen detergents.) A continuing problem for the woman, then, was still what to do with her leisure time. The wife-mother role required her to stay home with her preschool children or be on hand when the school-agers came home for lunch and after school. To help her fill empty hours, the product-pushers advocated do-it-yourself projects —knitting and sewing, making rugs, and elaborate gourmet cooking ideas. Television, of course, became a popular medium in the 1950s, and in middle-class homes the large, bulky living-room radio was replaced by a television set with an eight-inch screen.

True to tradition, most women spent their time in passive diversions rather than creative or socially productive activities. Instead of reading popular romances, like the women of earlier periods, or listening to their favorite radio soap operas, they were now absorbed in essentially the same material on television. In the evening, rather than go out to a movie theater, husbands and wives alike stayed home and watched *I Love Lucy*, the *Ed Sullivan Show*, or the *Show of Shows*. While men were required to work for a living, women were assumed to be the beneficiaries of their labors. The harder a man worked to provide material goods for his family, the more time his wife had for leisurely pursuits. It seemed that woman's goal in a work-oriented culture was to be practically functionless.

Women Volunteers

A lot of women rejected this image and filled their days with important activities. They chauffeured their children and attended local meetings associated with school and community, did unpaid volunteer work in local hospitals, organized support for school bond referendums, worked for the League of Women Voters, campaigned for male candidates, and in general pricked the conscience of the community. (When asked why she did not appear on the platform with important legislators, a League of

361

Women Voters president replied, "I don't mind if they take the glory; I have the pleasure of knowing that the good law has been passed.") Actually they had played these same essential roles for many decades. Nineteenth-century women had been the back-bone of every social reform organization, every charitable effort, and every religious society. Mid-twentieth-century women were equally indispensable. No big-city hospital could operate with-out its women volunteers; no local charity could raise a dime without its women workers.

American society, which assumes that the only worthwhile work is paid work, has never given deserved recognition to its women volunteers. Perhaps this is because employed men and women believe that only non-working people have the time for humane community efforts. Women who work for pay, so the argument might go, must think first of their homes and families rather than the needy in society. In other words, volunteer work, because it is unpaid, is regarded as something extra and superfluous, engaged in by amateurs with time on their hands. Only professionals in the fields of human service—doctors, nurses, teachers, counselors, social workers—receive pay and recognition for helping others. Women volunteers go unre-warded in a mercenary culture.

Women Workers

Many women, of course, took part-time or full-time jobs just to be able to afford the delectable new consumer products. Many comfortable middle-class families now needed two incomes to make ends meet—a new phenomenon of the period. Labor Department statistics showed a constant increase in the number of employed women in the United States (21 million working women in a labor force of 64 million by the mid-1950's), but attitudes toward "proper" jobs for women did not change. Nor did women's own views regarding their work: it was still a secondary, though necessary, part of their lives. Married career women could have rebelled against this traditional assumption, but more often than not they accepted it. Being a good wife and mother came first. If they could not manage a home, a family, and a career, they gave up the career.

Even though machines were now replacing much unskilled labor, many working-class and untrained middle-class women

362

were limited to dull, dismal, repetitive jobs. More and more of them went into personal-service occupations, which on the surface might appear to fit in with women's experience in serving others. But because the higher echelon jobs in human service (medicine) and human relations (social welfare work) were held by males, women got less pay, less recognition, fewer responsibilities and fewer promotions. Particularly during the Eisenhower years, unemployment was high, and women, blacks, and teenagers were (as in the past) the last to be hired and the first to be fired. Moreover, the Eisenhower administration did not make any strong effort to increase welfare spending or to train chronic unemployables.

Thanks to technology, the whole concept of work had deteriorated significantly since the early settlers came to America. Work was no longer dignified and glorified as a Christian virtue. In the past, no one questioned its necessity; few doubted its positive contribution to an individual's well-being and to the social good. But by the 1950s, work was no longer considered important in itself. Work was a way of earning one's living, that was all. It afforded little gratification, either personal or social, to male or female employees. By the 1960s, people had begun to protest their dull, often meaningless, jobs. Auto workers in Detroit sabotaged the assembly lines in their factories, and alcoholism, always a problem, became publicly acknowledged as one manifestation of unhappy workers.

Because work was deemed a necessity, if an inglorious one, people assumed that poverty was an avoidable evil. If the poor would get jobs instead of living on relief, poverty would automatically be eliminated. The poor as a class whose children would repeat the same life pattern did not exist in the public mind, and Michael Harrington's *The Other America* was still in the future. The Americans of the 1950s looked inward, not outward. They did not challenge traditional values. Women belonged in the home, if their husbands could afford to keep them there, and men were the natural leaders in government and the business world. And that was that.

Popular Arts

The popular songs of an era, like best-selling novels, not only reflect the public taste but enforce accepted cultural values.

Even when their music departs from traditional harmonies and rhythms, their words usually express people's current feelings and attitudes. So it was in the 1950s, with the spectacular rise and success of entertainer Elvis Presley (1934–   ). Bumping and grinding to a new musical beat, he captivated the nation's young people. They attended his concerts in droves, squealed with delight, and bought his records by the millions. But although the sound and the sight of Presley gave rise to rapturous frenzy, the lyrics of his songs (such as "Don't Step on My Blue Suede Shoes") did nothing to challenge established attitudes. His style of delivery was novel, but his message was not. As he sang of love and marriage, virtuous love, and loyalty, he gave his youthful audiences a chance to release their tensions and work off excess energy. Thus, young people who behaved convention-ally during the day became hysterical during a Presley concert, yet otherwise were unaffected by his music. In this sense, Elvis Presley's influence was negligible, despite the hue and cry of conservatives who feared that his gyrations would somehow corrupt youth.

The movies of the late forties and fifties also upheld tradi-tional values, particularly the image of women. Pop music had no women singers of the stature of Elvis Presley, and Hollywood had no women movie stars of the caliber of those of the thirties: Katharine Hepburn, Bette Davis, Barbara Stanwyck, and Joan Crawford. Movie-makers abandoned films portraying career women, women lawyers, women athletes in favor of those portraying an age-old female figure, the sex goddess. The women stars of the postwar era—among them Ann Sheridan, Rita Hayworth, Lana Turner, and Betty Grable—all played, over and over, the role of glamorous seductress whose only purpose was to look beautiful and allure men. If they were virtuous, they would receive a marriage proposal from the most charming of these men; if they were shady ladies, they would receive a different kind of proposal.

Of this new crop of women movie stars in the late forties and fifties, Elizabeth Taylor ranks as one of the most important. Born in February 1932, she was ten years old when she became a child star in a Lassie film. Two years later, she won fame in *National Velvet*. By the late forties, she was a mature-looking teenager who played sexy roles opposite such male leads as Robert Taylor. Then, after shedding the sweet-girl image, she became

Actress Elizabeth Taylor,
from child star
to sex goddess.
(Brown Bros.)

the temptress par excellence, known throughout the movie-going world for her flashing green eyes and dark hair, her low sultry voice, and her voluptuous body. Movie magazines reported her every movement, and eager youth reveled in stories of her teenage romance and marriage to hotel heir Nicky Hilton (1950), her subsequent divorce from him (1952), her marriage to father-figure actor Michael Wilding (1952) followed by divorce (1957), and her marriage to Mike Todd that same year. Todd's tragic death in a plane crash was another in a series of romantic tragedies that highlighted her life.

Elizabeth Taylor's portrayal of Maggie the Cat in *Cat on a Hot Tin Roof* (1958) marked her twenty-fifth film appearance and her first significant dramatic role. More important, it established her as a sex goddess of current American films. Her characterization of restless, sensuous Maggie convinced many movie-goers, and many critics, that she was a serious actress as well as a beautiful woman. Marilyn Monroe (1926–1963), who achieved fame during the same period as the most seductive sex goddess, was never taken seriously as an actress. She invariably represented pure sensuality, though sometimes with a touch of comedy *(Some Like It Hot).* Yet both these strikingly

365

Marilyn Monroe entertaining the troops in Korea, 1954.
(Wide World)

beautiful women stars projected the same essential image—
of a sexually alluring temptress.

From the point of view of cultural attitudes, Elizabeth Taylor
and Marilyn Monroe symbolized the significant change in
women's movie roles from the sturdy, independent heroines of
the thirties to the charmers of the fifties. But why did this change
come about? Perhaps because the wife who had worked during
the war and returned to housekeeping afterward may have been
comforted by a roughly corresponding shift in movie plots
—although the beauty of Elizabeth Taylor and Marilyn Monroe
could have aroused pangs of envy and resentment. Perhaps
because those stars brought pure delight to the men of the
audience, the embodiment of their private dreams. Film-makers,
for their part, seemed convinced that the strong, confident
women played by Bette Davis and Katharine Hepburn were no
longer desirable for audiences of the postwar era. During the
depression and the war, strong female symbols were needed in

films, but now that domesticity was being lauded once again, and women were encouraged to forget career ambitions, sex symbols like Elizabeth Taylor and Marilyn Monroe were more appropriate.

The old definition of woman's nature and place had not changed basically, despite the temporary expansion of her role during the war. As we have seen, in every war women have worked outside the home in male-defined jobs and have assumed positions of responsibility. They have shown themselves wholly capable of tackling men's jobs under stress, but these roles have been transient. So after World War II, women resumed their old image—as wife and mother in reality, and as sex goddess in fantasy. Men and women alike wanted to believe that all women were alluring, attractive, and seductive, and every woman wanted to be a combination of wife, mother, Eve, and the Virgin Mary. The sex-goddess stars have always represented Eve in that combination, and the appeal of Mae West, Marlene Dietrich, Elizabeth Taylor, and Marilyn Monroe is as old as human history. But real women had other roles to play and although men admired the sexually free women whom they saw on the screen, they did not expect or want their wives to behave that way.

Doris Day's (1924–   ) success during the 1950s symbolized the appeal of another part of woman's image—that of the healthy American girl, the girl next door, who used her womanly wiles to capture a husband. She embodied the wife-mother rather than the temptress. Her broad smile, blonde hair, and freckles, plus her well-guarded virginity, made her a favorite with family audiences. (Oscar Levant once recalled that he had played in her first picture; "that was before she became a virgin.") Women could relate to her pleasant wholesomeness while men saw her as a desirable girl to marry. Rock Hudson was Doris Day's romantic lead on the screen, and together—first in *Pillow Talk* (1959) and then in subsequent films—they worked and reworked the theme of a sweet girl resisting a man's advances until he married her.

Doris Day, then, became the counterpoint to Elizabeth Taylor and Marilyn Monroe in the films of the 1950s. All three dramatized the old, demeaning, limiting definition of woman that precluded any return to the roles immortalized earlier by Katharine Hepburn, Bette Davis, and Joan Crawford.

367

Doris Day, the girl
next door. (Brown Bros.)

In the 1950s, television became the most popular new form of entertainment. Whereas in 1947 there were 10,000 television sets in American homes, ten years later the figure was 40 million! By 1970, it was estimated that there was at least one television set in every American home, regardless of its economic status. The radio, record, and movie businesses all suffered from competition with television. Each had to change its format, adapt to the new entertainment medium, and carve out a new market. Radio became music and news oriented, abandoning serial soap operas and situation comedies. Record companies worked furiously to discover new popular recording artists. Movies unsuccessfully experimented with new techniques such as three-dimensional screens and wide-angle screens such as Cinemascope and Cinerama.

Television changed the leisure-time habits of Americans. People stayed home more and sat in hushed silence during prime-time TV programs. The art of conversation languished; no one talked while the television set was on. The "TV dinner" was invented in 1954, and the family could now eat an easily heated-up dinner in silence—while watching TV. Americans adored *Gunsmoke,* a typical Western program that was a direct descendant of the dime novels of the 1890s, the silent-screen cowboy thrillers, and decades of John Wayne movies. People watched Lucille Ball, of *I Love Lucy,* as she grimaced, slipped on a banana peel, and made fun of her husband Desi's Cuban accent. Both shows have survived the fifties and continue to amuse vast numbers of TV watchers.

Child Care

As early as the 1790s, parents sought expert help with child-raising problems. In manuals written by doctors and midwives, they read about how to care for their infants, how to treat them when they were ill, and how to discipline them. As the period of childhood lengthened, the experts extended their advice to include older children and, by the end of the nineteenth century, teenagers. Until World War I, most of them recommended regular schedules, strict discipline, and physical punishment when necessary. The new psychology, along with the child-centered educational studies of John Dewey, brought a change in these approaches. The needs and wishes of the children themselves, and their particular stages of development, said the modernists, must be considered in all phases of child guidance.

Parents were advised that, rather than imposing social rules on children too young to assimilate them, they should adjust their training to each child's age and personality. In 1946, the most popular book on child care—indeed, one of the most popular books ever printed in the United States—was published: Dr. Benjamin Spock's *Common Sense Book of Baby and Child Care* (later changed to *Baby and Child Care*). By 1964, it had gone through 130 printings. New mothers, during the postwar baby-boom years, gobbled up the advice of Dr. Spock. He became their mentor and bedside consultant, and the most famous pediatrician in the country. Whatever he told them to do for their children, they did—or so claimed thousands upon thousands of mothers.

In simple, direct language, Dr. Spock talked to parents on specific and general subjects: infant feeding, the myriad of childhood illnesses, how to bathe a baby, how to determine a feeding schedule, and so on. His general point of view, as

369

suggested by the book's title, was plain common sense. He told parents that their guiding principle should be kindheartedness and love. When they punished a child out of love and concern, and not out of resentment or hatred, the child would understand that the punishment was for his/her own benefit. Dr. Spock frequently reminded his readers that they should always balance their own wishes and needs against those of their children, and that the needs of infants and young children should come first.

In a brief section on "The Working Mother," Dr. Spock recognized that some mothers have to work out of economic need and also that others, the professionally trained, wanted to work. But he frowned on mothers who went to work just because they didn't wish to stay home.

> The important thing for a mother to realize is that the younger the child the more necessary it is for him to have a steady, loving person taking care of him. In most cases, the mother is the best one to give him this feeling of "belonging," safely and surely.

This applied, he explained, to the child under three years old. After that it would be all right to send him to a good nursery school. If no good school was available, however, the mother should stay at home until the child was ready for first grade.

Dr. Spock considered that proper maternal care was essential for bringing up healthy, well-adjusted children. Thus he reinforced an idea that became tantamount to a holy law in this century: good children were the result of their mothers' constant presence and absent mothers could only produce bad children. This simple-minded equation has served to keep mothers in the home and away from jobs for most of the twentieth century—and to place a heavy burden of guilt on mothers who must work. In earlier generations, when America was made up of agricultural communities and all mothers helped with work on the farm, they certainly could not spend every waking hour tending their young. But now it was the edict of Dr. Spock and other experts that mothers must personally care for their children and that few other adults could fulfill such a responsibility. For Dr. Spock's elaborate and detailed descriptions of a child's crying, eating, and defecating patterns suggested that child-raising was a serious, full-time, and difficult task.

Most mothers, it is true, never bothered to read child-raising

370

manuals, relying on their natural instincts instead. But Dr. Spock's book gave doubtful parents the self-confidence and specific guidance they seemed to need. Further, the trend toward the specializing and fragmenting of many human tasks gave people the idea that child-raising was a professional art and only the experts knew its secrets. Because Dr. Spock was willing to share those secrets, he won the gratitude of literally millions of mothers.

If we look at this period of history from the child's point of view, we may gain some additional insight into the problems that complicated the business of child-raising in an urban technological society. In previous periods, children usually lived in small agricultural communities and were acquainted with many different adults. They listened to and spoke with adult relatives, neighbors, family friends. They felt comfortable with a variety of people of all ages, from whom they learned a great deal.

Then, as America became urban-centered and as public education kept children in school for ever longer periods, much of this easy mingling disappeared. Children's relations with adult authority figures—teachers, parents, the family minister —became rigid and formalized. There were fewer opportunities for children to exchange ideas with adults, and often only under clearly defined conditions such as at the dinner table, in the classroom, or in Sunday school. The result was a serious loss to both children and adults: informal learning from and about one another decreased, along with conviviality and spontaneity. The two groups were segregated according to age. Youth mingled largely with other youth, and adults with adults, instead of freely mixing together. The consequences of these human role changes continue to be felt in the latter part of the twentieth century.

Black Americans

Discrimination and prejudice continued to characterize white Americans' behavior toward black Americans. Nothing occurred to alter that basic posture. There was no moral awakening or threat of violent revolution—seemingly the only two possible ways to change the situation. But within this framework of bias, a black middle class developed in the 1950s, and the small black elite grew larger as the number of black college graduates increased. Yet the majority of black Americans were poor, unskilled marginal farmers and workers.

President Truman desegregated the armed forces in time for the Korean War in 1950, and in so doing broke down racial barriers in one significant governmental structure. For the first time, blacks and whites attended military training camps together and served in combat together. This experience created neither immediate interracial warmth and harmony nor chaos and upheaval. But it demonstrated that the government could live up to its own principles.

The Supreme Court also showed its concern for black civil liberties in the famous *Brown v. Board of Education* case in 1954. The Court's decision that separate educational facilities for American blacks were inherently unequal overturned the 1896 *Plessy v. Ferguson* decision that separate but equal facilities were acceptable. The *Brown v. Board of Education* ruling, though specifically pertaining to educational facilities, opened up the whole issue of segregation. Southern cities with separate public washrooms for each race, separate parks, and separate seating in transportation vehicles could not claim to be providing equal resources for both races.

The Supreme Court ordered school systems to desegregate "with all deliberate speed"—a vague directive that allowed many unwilling governors and school administrators to ignore the edict for years. Indeed, a whole generation later, many school systems in both North and South are still segregated.

The Eisenhower administration chose to follow the nation's established social attitudes rather than lead the way to new ones. President Eisenhower believed that Americans wanted continuity, not change, after the damaging years of war. Projecting a grandfatherly image, he encouraged them to pursue their own careers, hobbies, and daily lives instead of crusading for new causes. Although he sent federal troops to Little Rock, Arkansas, in 1956 to aid in high school desegregation, he made little further effort to support the Supreme Court's decision. Then, too, the U.S. Congress, dominated by Southern Democrats dedicated to preserving the status quo, was unwilling to consider any important new laws in behalf of black Americans. Like women, blacks have had a long, hard struggle to achieve equal rights in the United States. In every generation, they have tried to change attitudes, pass new laws, and persuade officials to enforce those already in existence. Their efforts have not yet produced the desired results.

Blacks were particularly hurt by the 1950 recession; their median income, always low, fell even lower. Black union workers, the elite of the black working population, found labor unions as unresponsive to their plea for civil liberties as was the society at large. In the early 1950s, there were 1.5 million black union members out of a total union membership of 15 million. Yet the American Federation of Labor (AFL) did nothing to prevent its local unions from discriminating against blacks or from barring black apprentices in key unions, notably the building trades unions. When the AFL merged with the more liberal Congress of Industrial Organizations (CIO) in 1955, two black vice-presidents were elected to the new organization, A. Philip Randolph and Willard Townsend. But their presence alongside 27 white vice-presidents did not affect basic union policies.

At the 1959 NAACP convention, when A. Philip Randolph spoke on "The Civil Rights Revolution and Labor," he complained of the continued discrimination against black workers. Labor, he told his audience, "must project a massive revolution within its house to effect a transition of the Negro worker from the status of second-class to first-class economic citizenship." His dissatisfaction with organized labor's response to black workers led to the organization of the Negro American Labor Council, an organization designed to articulate to the public the particular problems of black workers. Black union members, for example, had specific grievances against the white-dominated unions. Non-union black workers, on the other hand, had unending grievances against the whole white employment system.

Two black women writers of the late forties and fifties described the lives of black women with poignancy and dignity. Gwendolyn Brooks (1917–   ), named the poet laureate of Illinois in 1968, was born in Topeka, Kansas. She came to Chicago as a young woman, attended Wilson Junior College, and spent much of her time writing poetry. She married Henry Blakely in 1939, had two children, and continued to write about the subject she knew best—being black in America.

In 1950 she won a Pulitzer Prize, and has received numerous fellowships and poetry awards. In addition to her books of verse,

Pulitzer Prize
winning poet
Gwendolyn Brooks.

she has written children's books and a short, powerful piece,
Maud Martha (1953). The protagonist is a brave, hopeful woman
who endures the everyday hardships of being black in America
with a noble serenity and lovingkindness.

Ann Petry (1911–   ), the second of these two outstanding
black women writers, was born in Old Saybrook, Connecticut.
Her father was a pharmacist, and Ann followed in his footsteps
by graduating from the College of Pharmacy of the University
of Connecticut. However, she disappointed her parents by leaving Old Saybrook for New York City and a life of newspaper
reporting and story writing. She published many short stories
in *Crisis* and other magazines. *The Street* (1946) was her first
popular success. *Country Place* (1947) was highly praised as
a worthy successor to the realistic prose of Richard Wright.

Ann Petry's novels and short stories poignantly describe the
crippling effects of a poor and racist environment on black
people. *The Street* was a best-selling novel about a Harlem black
woman, Lutie Johnson, who finds the boundaries erected by
discrimination, and by being both black and poor, insurmounta-

374

Novelist,
short story writer
Ann Petry.
(Wide World)

ble. Hard-working, earnest, and honest, she abides by the rules of American society and hopes to succeed by them. At one point in the story, she muses that she and Ben Franklin had something in common: they both had to work their way up the socioeconomic ladder. But she reminds herself that "you're in Harlem and he was in Philadelphia a pretty long number of years ago." Since Lutie Johnson is a poorly educated black in race-conscious New York, her chances for success are minimal. At the novel's end, she has murdered a man in desperation. Yet Lutie began with the same optimism and faith as Maud Martha—and Ben Franklin. Anyone who read those two books would conclude, with sadness, that the United States was failing its black citizens badly.

The Environment: The Same Old Story

Experts in any field often anticipate a problem before the public perceives it. Ecologists in the 1950s, for example, understood the

375

limited nature of this continent's resources and tried to warn legislators and laymen alike of the need to redirect resources, conserve natural sources of energy, and control the population. Aldo Leopold's *A Sand County Almanac* (1949), Fairfield Osborn's *Our Plundered Planet* (1948), and Harrison Brown's *The Challenge of Man's Future* (1954) were only a few of the many fine professional books of the period.

Aldo Leopold wrote of mankind's relationship with all other living things, as well as mankind's moral obligation to respect that relationship. He proposed a "land ethic," which would recognize that each person has a responsibility to preserve and work for the healthfulness of the land. Everyone's future, including all living things, required it. Fairfield Osborn's book also stressed the urgent need to use natural resources intelligently, advocating an international level of cooperation to stem the tide of environmental destruction. Harrison Brown focused on the unpopular subject of population control in a decade when most people still believed optimistically that Planet Earth afforded infinite space and an infinite food supply. Even though the Catholic Church was opposed to birth control, Brown pointed out, the time had come when a concerted, world-wide effort was necessary to prevent widespread starvation.

All three writers sounded their warnings with eloquent discussions of ecological realities and grim forecasts of the future. But most people, including government officials, were not listening.

War and Peace

The 1950s had their war too: the Korean War. Begun inauspiciously in the summer of 1950, in a remote Asian region called Korea, it was accepted by Americans as the latest enactment of the drama between "democratic" and Communist nations. The war dragged on inconclusively for two years, with occasional excitement, such as President Truman's firing of General Douglas MacArthur for disobedience. It became a political issue during the presidential campaign of 1952, in which General Eisenhower benefited from his promise to end the war.

Unlike World War II, however, the Korean War did not engage the emotional energies of the American people, perhaps

376

because they did not feel directly threatened by it. They could, and would, pursue their personal lives in the same unvarying pattern while their troops fought overseas. Sons and husbands died in Korea as they had in previous wars, but the domestic economy and domestic attitudes were unaffected. The rush to attain material success—to own a home in the suburbs, to buy a new car, and to take a vacation trip—remained the dominant concern of most white Americans and fewer black Americans—except for the unfortunate few who served in Korea and whose families waited for news at home.

Suggestions for Further Reading

James Baldwin. *Go Tell It on the Mountain* (New York, 1954).
Simone de Beauvoir. *The Second Sex* (New York, 1953).
Ralph Ellison. *The Invisible Man* (New York, 1952).
Betty Friedan. *The Feminine Mystique* (New York, 1963).
Eric Goldman. *The Crucial Decade—and After, 1945–1960* (New York, 1960; paperback).
Alfred Kinsey. *Sexual Behavior in the Human Female* (New York, 1953).
Mirra Komarovsky. *Women in the Modern World* (New York, 1953).
Gunnar Myrdal. *An American Dilemma* (New York, 1964; paperback).
Richard Wright. *Black Boy* (New York, 1951).
Richard Wright. *Native Son* (New York, 1940).

CHAPTER FOURTEEN

The New Frontier?
1960–1973

As man proceeds toward his announced goal of the conquest of nature, he has written a depressing record of destruction, directed not only against the earth he inhabits but against the life that shares it with him.

—Rachel Carson, *Silent Spring*, 1962

All right, nobody's disputing it. Women are free. At least, they *look* free. They even feel free. But in reality women in the Western, industrialized world today are like the animals in a modern zoo.

—Brigid Brophy, *Women Are Prisoners of Their Sex*, 1963

The problems of ". . . unfulfilled and underutilized American women are at least as urgent public concerns as are the problems of our highways, our food surpluses, and our water shortages."

—Harvey Swados, *The Dilemma of the Educated Woman*, 1962

> I am locked in the kitchen, let me out.
> Burning in the toaster,
> Sizzling in the pan,
> Choked in the gas range,
> Iced in the kitchen glass,
> Broken in the bowl,
> I jump out of the cup.
> Throw dish rags over my anger,
> Crumbs over my head, anoint
> Me for the marriage bed.
> The bride is buttered, eaten when she's charred.
> Her tiger falls into a tub of lard.
>
> —Sandra Hochman, *Ivory and Horn*, 1963

379

*T*he sixties did not begin auspiciously. The presidential candidates, Richard M. Nixon and John F. Kennedy, were both younger men, but whether the new President would be progressive was uncertain. Nixon, the more experienced politician of the two and the incumbent Vice-President, seemed to have an edge; but the younger, handsomer, wealthier John F. Kennedy, with his attractive wife and two young children, promised a new energy, a new commitment, a new and vigorous leadership for the country. The closeness of Kennedy's election victory revealed the American voters' belief that the two candidates were more alike than different.

Kennedy's inaugural address, however, built upon the theme of newness. He promised Americans a new frontier and invited them, especially youth, to participate in social adventures and in conquering social problems. To the liberals who had despaired during the Eisenhower years of inactivity, Kennedy symbolized a break with the past and a hope for positive government action on many fronts.

In some senses, J.F.K. fulfilled the projected image. He originated the Peace Corps, an updated version of a New Deal program for youth; he publicized the new space program and gave it needed encouragement; he commissioned a prestigious group of men and women to investigate the status of women; and he worked for the passage of a vigorous civil rights bill that would aid black Americans. Yet at the same time Kennedy revived the Green Berets, a semi-secret corps of trained military men who engaged in guerrilla activities. He accepted the now traditional idea that Communism had to be contained wherever and whenever it reared its head, and that American troops, equipment, and money should be used in such an effort.

Presidents, Women, and First Ladies

Kennedy's years in office, tragically cut off by his assassination, were all too brief—so brief that it is difficult to evaluate his accomplishments in behalf of women and minority groups. Kennedy promised to be a vigorous leader, to bring creative energy back to Washington, and to regain a central focus for national life. Whereas the Eisenhower administration encouraged decentralization—that is, local control rather than federal control—President Kennedy reversed that process, giving the country notice that he enjoyed the presidency and believed in a strong President. Modeling himself after the Roosevelts (as did his successor, Lyndon B. Johnson), he hoped to bridge the gap between America's promises to its citizenry and its performance. He buoyed the spirits of black Americans, other minority groups, and women. He became a master of the rhetoric of positive change. Unfortunately, his deeds, up to the time of his death, did not always equal his rhetoric.

The Commission on the Status of Women, which he created, became one of President Kennedy's few positive contributions to the cause of women's rights. The findings in the Commission's report, issued in 1963, confirmed feminists' judgments: Americans discriminated against women in both overt and subtle ways. The professions did not admit them, the graduate schools did not encourage them, and indeed even the elementary schools discouraged girls from seeking advanced education, programing them early to accept their cultural role. The Commission recommended a number of specific actions to remedy the situation:

More flexible admission requirements on the part of colleges.

Government-sponsored day-care centers.

Adequate job-counseling services for women.

An end to discrimination in hiring and employment practices within the federal government.

For the most part, these very reasonable recommendations went unheeded. The President issued a memo asking his department heads to review employment criteria and to eliminate discrimination against women; the Congress funded a modest program to investigate local day-care-facilities; and the President created an interdepartmental bureau to oversee hiring within government agencies. The Equal Pay Act of 1963 and the providing of funds to state welfare agencies to expand their day-care centers completed the Kennedy administration's efforts in behalf of women.

Women, then, did not receive top priority in the President's scheme of values. Though he spoke occasionally about the need to utilize all human talent, which presumably included women's talent, President Kennedy did not regard the American woman's status as a social problem of the dimensions of civil rights for black Americans or poverty. On numerous occasions during his press conferences, he joked with reporter May Craig on a variety of subjects. When Mrs. Craig asked the President why his administration failed to fulfill the Democratic party's pledge of equal rights for women, he lightly answered, "I think that we ought to do better than we're doing and I'm glad that you reminded me of it, Mrs. Craig." But he did not propose an ambitious and vigorous program to fulfill that promise. Women still, as in the past, had to organize on their own behalf.

The feminists in the 1960s, like their sisters who worked for abolition in the 1850s, were slow to discover that working for the civil rights of blacks would not assure women their own rights. Unlike their predecessors, however, many women activists did not even perceive that their own status was akin to that of blacks. After a few years' work in the civil rights and the later anti-war movements, many younger women realized that their participation in another reform group's struggle did not guarantee their own liberation. During the first three years of the 1960s, however, there was no serious protest by organized womanhood, either the over-thirty middle-class organization women or women college students.

Jacqueline Kennedy did nothing for the cause, either as an individual or as the nation's leading lady. Whereas Eleanor Roosevelt had been a living example of an authentic, fully realized human being, Mamie Eisenhower had receded into the traditional image of a self-effacing, almost nonexistent First Lady. Jacqueline Kennedy, in contrast to Mrs. Eisenhower, had visibility; her youthfulness, her athletic interests, her clothes, and her interest in refurbishing the White House gained her a great deal of publicity. The novelty of having such an attractive young couple in the White House drew a constant procession of photographers and reporters into its inner sanctums. But Jacqueline Kennedy had no interest in social welfare, only in social taste. She never discussed public matters and seemed generally uninterested in affairs of state. She did not become a desirable role-model for American women or a cultural heroine. Rather, she reinforced the established cultural view that woman's predominant interests—especially the upper-class woman's—are taste, fashion, superficial culture, and ceremony. Jacqueline Kennedy set the style for bouffant hairdos and pillbox hats, but she demonstrated no new roles for women, no new frontier for women's rights.

Lyndon and Lady Bird Johnson, on the other hand, displayed a positive commitment to women's rights as well as a great respect for women's accomplishments. Despite their Southern background, both Johnsons believed that women should participate actively in all areas of life.

Claudia (Lady Bird) Taylor Johnson (1912–) was born in Marshall, Texas, and as a little girl was said to be "pretty as a ladybird." From childhood on, therefore, she was called Lady Bird. Her mother died when she was five and Lady Bird Taylor traveled with her rancher-father, learned to love the flowers and the land of Texas, and became an astute businesswoman as well. For example, using an inheritance from her mother, she built a broadcasting company from modest beginnings to an impressive multi-station company.

She met and married young politician Lyndon Baines Johnson in 1934. Subsequently, they had two daughters, and Mrs. Johnson accompanied her husband to the U.S. Senate and eventually to the White House. As First Lady, she traveled around the country supporting the President's domestic programs, particularly the War on Poverty, VISTA (a domestic version of the Peace Corps), and environmental beautification projects.

President Johnson recruited more women to high administrative positions in Washington than any previous President. He vigorously appointed women to agencies that had never before had women members—for example, the Atomic Energy Commission (Mary I. Bunting), the Interstate Commerce Commission (Virginia Mae Brown), and the Equal Employment Opportunities Commission (Aileen Hernandez). Women lawyers be-

Supporters of women's rights: President and Mrs. Johnson. (Wide World)

came valuable government assets. He boosted the salaries of thousands of women civil servants and ordered his staff to hire more women. Lyndon Johnson improved the status of women through his appointments, through Executive Order 11246, and through the passage of the Civil Rights Act of 1964. This bill, designed to grant black Americans equal rights, also contained an article (number seven) that eliminated sex discrimination in employment. During the late sixties, this article served as an important legal tool for women fighting job discrimination.

Indeed, Johnson's awe-inspiring legislative skills—perfected while he was majority leader in the U.S. Senate throughout most of the 1950s—contributed to major legislative victories for black Americans, women, chicanos, and the poor. The Civil Rights Acts of 1964 and 1965 removed most forms of discrimination against blacks and effectively challenged the racist attitudes of many white Americans. Federal agents supervised registration drives in Southern counties where black voter registration had

385

been the lowest; by the end of the decade, black Southerners who had never voted were voting regularly. Black citizens elected black men and women to local, state, and national offices.

President Johnson's Great Society program aimed to gather neglected Americans into the fold. He hoped not only to end poverty, but to end discrimination against women, black Americans, and Mexican Americans, a group whom he had known intimately during his youth in Texas. That he did not accomplish this ambitious domestic program is partially due to the Vietnam War and partially to the overly optimistic conviction that all complex social problems could be conquered within a short span of time.

His optimism, which may have bordered on arrogance, was a typically American trait based on a familiar assumption: all attitudes will change once the laws have been changed. Unfortunately, it is not as easy as all that. Proper laws properly enforced are surely essential to an egalitarian society. But a great deal of time is then needed for people to adjust to the new realities. Southern whites did not alter their views toward blacks immediately upon the passage of a new civil rights law. American men did not encourage their wives to go to law school because EEOC Commissioner Aileen Hernandez had.

In 1968, Richard M. Nixon was elected President. He promised to end the war in Vietnam and bring social stability to the domestic scene. Though it took him five years to accomplish the former goal, by 1970 quiet had settled upon the cities—except for the college protests during the spring of 1970 when the President ordered the invasion of Cambodia. (That was when four students were killed at Kent State University after National Guardsmen fired into a crowd.)

President Nixon did not view women or minority groups as serious social problems. He made no effective effort to hire or appoint women or blacks to key positions. When he had the opportunity to nominate four new Supreme Court justices, he chose four men, though the National Organization for Women (NOW) and many other women's groups recommended numerous able women lawyers for consideration.

Mrs. Nixon and her daughters played unobtrusive, passive roles. Pat Nixon did not establish an independent identity. She neither became an admired fashion plate like Jacqueline Ken-

386

nedy nor a social activist like Lady Bird Johnson or Eleanor Roosevelt. She remained in the background. And the Nixon administration did not distinguish itself in its actions toward the needy.

Women Organize

Women activists who read the recommendations of President Kennedy's Commission on the Status of Women and applauded President Johnson's active support of women's rights were encouraged by these positive signs but realized how much remained to be done. In 1966, a group of educated women led by author Betty Friedan organized the National Organization for Women. NOW's members publicized the urgent need for ending sex discrimination in employment, for equalizing Social Security benefits to both sexes, and for opening up educational opportunites to all women. They behaved in much the same way as the NAACP had done, using propaganda, legal battles, and educational tools to convince legislators and the public of the rightness of their cause. (See Appendix III for NOW platform.)

Within a year, more militant women began organizing a women's liberation movement in which college students, housewives, and other women began forming discussion groups, planning meetings, and holding consciousness-raising sessions in which they talked about the many ways in which American culture determined their life roles. Who were these women? How did they achieve this new (or old) awareness? Many were women students, activists in the social movements of the period, who had become painfully aware that many male radicals shared the traditional view of woman's role. (Women radicals, for example, were expected to make the coffee and run the mimeograph machine.)

Rebellion against this form of male domination produced many young women liberationists. Robin Morgan had been active in the peace movement as well as the student uprising at Columbia University in 1968. As time went on she discovered that to most radical men a "liberated" woman meant a woman "who is indiscriminate about whom she sleeps with," with no realization that "women don't want to be objects." And Jo Freeman, who organized the first women's consciousness-raising

387

group in Chicago in 1967, became a feminist after finding that her male colleagues in the civil rights movement discriminated against her because of her sex. "I had to face getting turned down simply for being a woman. It changed my life. I became a raging gut feminist."

The women's liberation movement remained loosely organized, with no hierarchy or chain of command, perhaps because women's liberation groups rejected the traditional power structures of male-dominated society. In style, tone, and goals, these younger liberationists differed markedly from the older, educated, professional members of NOW. While NOW committed itself to evolutionary change within the system, women's liberation spoke for revolutionary changes throughout American society. NOW did not challenge the family structure or the basic capitalistic system; women's liberation did. Some women liberationists, those who also considered themselves Marxists, spoke in terms of the sex and class struggle, of an end to capitalism, and the collectivization of all aspects of life.

By 1969, the NOW platform included a plank on woman's right to an abortion, thus showing its awareness of the need to deal with delicate but important sexual issues. This organization did not adopt the language nor the goals of Marxism, but steadily supported basic women's issues. Whereas members of the most militant wing of the women's liberation movement shared a positive hatred of men, NOW invited both sexes to join the organization and welcomed men's participation. Indeed NOW looked forward to a society made up of healthy, heterosexual relationships, a goal shared by many liberationists as well.

As the radical Redstockings Manifesto expressed it in 1969: "Women are an oppressed class. Our oppression is total, affecting every facet of our lives. We are exploited as sex objects, breeders, domestic servants, and cheap labor. We are considered inferior beings, whose only purpose is to enhance men's lives. Our humanity is denied." It must be said, however, that only a fraction of women liberationists rejected men totally, arguing that mutually responsive love between a man and a woman could not exist in capitalistic America.

Rage and hostility seethed through the outpourings of women activists by the end of the decade—a decade that began in hope and ended in frustration. Women were still victimized in egalitarian America, just as they had been ever since the days of

388

A women's liberation march, 1970. (Wide World)

the white English settlers. Youthful activist-reformers (a minority blown up to a majority by the news media) expressed their outrage in shocking language, wild demonstrations, and legitimate angry protests. Radical groups, both men and women, had not succeeded in eliminating racial prejudice, and they still had a long road to travel before they could change outdated man-woman roles.

Interestingly enough, the formation of separate women's liberation groups recalls the split, one hundred years earlier, between the abolitionist and feminist movements. At that time, Elizabeth Cady Stanton and her supporters, perceiving that women's rights would not receive due attention within the black freedom movement, formed a separate woman's suffrage organization. Similarly, young women students in the 1960s learned from personal experience that the white male radicals in Students for a Democratic Society (SDS) treated women as subservient beings, much as the larger society did. By the later sixties, black militants also rejected white support for their movement, so that white radicals, male and female alike, had to find other allegiances.

Again let it be said that despite their visibility, only a minority of college young people participated in these organizational efforts to change society. The majority of college students—and the number had grown to seven million by the end of the sixties—remained essentially conservative and apathetic to social causes.

The Feminine Mystique *and* Sexual Politics

Among the many popular books that dealt with the status of women in the United States, two of the most important and influential were Betty Friedan's *The Feminine Mystique* (1963) and Kate Millett's *Sexual Politics* (1970). Both books expressed the educated woman's discontent with her lot in a country that preached equality while practicing inequality, but there were significant differences between them.

Betty Friedan (1921–) based her material on interviews with educated women of the upper-middle class who believed they had been overeducated (at Smith College) for the conventional role of wife and mother. Their superior education had promised them intellectual excitement and full use of their mental abilities. Instead, they married, had children, and for hours each day were utterly bored by busywork. Mrs. Friedan blamed advertisers, women's magazine editors, and the general mystique of the culture for women's unhappiness. Women had been promised that marriage and the products of affluence would compose a good life—they discovered otherwise. The image of woman as buyers and consumers satisfied Madison Avenue and manufacturers but not American women. In essence, Betty Friedan's solution to the woman's dilemma was to find stimulating, personally rewarding work outside the home—either a career that could be interrupted for childbearing or an interesting part-time job.

Kate Millett (1934–), writing at the end of the decade, viewed the problem from a broader perspective. Her *Sexual Politics* began as a doctoral thesis in comparative literature and ended as a critique of Western man's views and treatment of women. Writing in a far angrier tone than Betty Friedan, Kate

390

The Feminine Mystique *and* Sexual Politics

Millett called for a total revolution in attitudes toward women; nothing less could assure their liberation. Jobs for women, she maintained, could not possibly solve such a complex and far-reaching problem. In her many-sided survey, she attacked male writers like D. H. Lawrence, Henry Miller, and Norman Mailer for their contributions to sexism (a new term coined in the late 1960s meaning discrimination on the basis of sex; analogous to racism). She described the inhumanity toward women exhibited in Nazi Germany, and discussed the unfulfilled hopes for women's liberation in the Soviet Union. Her accusations fell selectively on different representatives of Western culture as well as different time periods. While Betty Friedan concentrated on twentieth-century America, and particularly after World War II, Kate Millett ranged through the realm of mythology and all Western history for examples of discrimination against women.

But both writers indicted Western culture. Both revealed the culture's deep antipathy toward women, as well as the consistent

Leaders of the National Women's Political Caucus, 1972:
Seated from left to right: Gloria Steinem, Rep. Shirley
Chisholm, and Betty Friedan. Standing is Rep. Bella Abzug.
(Wide World)

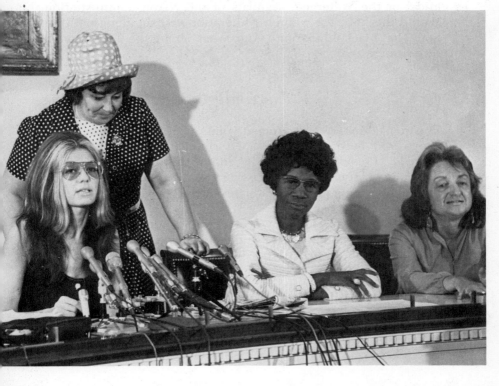

practice of keeping women in highly restricted roles. Both pointed out that men, who occupy the positions of power in society, strive at all costs to preserve the status quo. Whereas Betty Friedan hoped that substantial change in attitudes toward women would occur within the political, economic, and social structure of society, Kate Millett predicted that patchwork legislation alone could not cure such a pervasive disease as discrimination against the female sex. No less than a total revolution in beliefs and practices would be necessary to give women their desired and deserved place in society. Both Betty Friedan, an evolutionist, and Kate Millett, a revolutionist, hoped for a feminist Utopia but differed on the means of achieving it. Kate Millett envisioned a restructuring of the family, the economy, and all other institutions on order to accomplish it. Betty Friedan remained faithful to the accepted American methods of reform.

Which scenario would be acted out in the 1970s? Or was there at least one other possibility—that neither evolutionary nor revolutionary change would occur? By the early 1970s, the status quo seemed to have been reestablished in many areas. Youth no longer protested or demonstrated against war, against racism or sexism, or against environmental pollution. The last vestige of the promised Great Society of the mid-sixties evaporated in the midst of the Watergate scandals of the Nixon administration. Would the hope for women's liberation vanish, along with the hope for black liberation? And what about the liberation of American youth?

The Youth Culture: A Mixed Bag

President Kennedy encouraged young people to join the Peace Corps and help underdeveloped countries develop their resources. President Johnson's administration encouraged a domestic version of the Peace Corps called VISTA. Yet at that time, most young college graduates chose to commit themselves to their personal careers.

In this same period, however, a well-publicized minority of undergraduate and graduate students became politically and socially active in a way unprecedented in American history. The 1968 Democratic presidential primary elections, for example, will long be remembered for the huge numbers of youth who worked to get Senator Eugene McCarthy nominated as the Democratic party's candidate. Young people dropped out of college, law school, and graduate school to ring doorbells, answer telephones, and canvass voters. Others worked in the campaign of Governor George C. Wallace, the third-party presidential candidate. Of course, Wallace represented traditional and reactionary Amerian values, while McCarthy stood for progressive values. But youth's participation in both campaigns demonstrated that the eighteen- to thirty-year-olds were not a philosophically homogeneous group.

In the early 1970s, when eighteen-year-olds were given the vote, the progressives hopefully assumed, and conservatives feared, that young voters would support liberal candidates and issues. Both groups turned out to be wrong. The fact that the eighteen-year-olds had been given the franchise changed nothing. Like the new women voters in 1920, not all of them voted. And just as the women followed the political choices of their husbands, so eighteen-year-old voters in 1972 seldom departed from family political behavior.

By the 1960s, as we have seen, young people were staying in school longer, were remaining financially dependent upon their parents longer, and were defined as "youth" much longer, often until their mid-twenties. "Adolescence," "teenage," and "young adulthood" were terms applied to them in twentieth-century urban-industrial America. We must not forget, however, that the economy itself was demanding more and more education from its young citizens. Industrial enterprises insisted upon better schooled employees, the professions required years of postgraduate education, and a blue-collar worker had to have a high school diploma.

During this prolonged period of preparation, youth became a new consumer market. Financed by allowances from their parents and/or by wages from part-time jobs, young people had plenty of money to spend. New industries grew up to serve the tastes and desires of the new consumers. Records, tapes, cassettes, electrical musical instruments, youth-oriented clothes, motorcycles, and bicycles were only a few of the products that catered to the new market. Just as women had been, and continued to be, important purchasers of consumer goods, so teenagers and young adults now received attention from the product-pushers.

393

The New Frontier? 1960–1973

Though superficially, young people's style of dress and style of life seemed radically unlike those of their parents, their basic values did not differ significantly. In this respect, the 1960s and 1970s resembled the 1920s. The flapper *appeared* to be different from her mother. She dressed differently, spoke differently, and danced to different tunes. But she married, had children (though fewer), and proceeded to repeat her mother's life pattern. Similarly, the flapper's male companions got jobs, married, and entered the world of middle-class respectability.

As in the flapper era, youth got a lot of publicity for its apparent breakthroughs in fashion and behavior. Young men in the late 1960s grew their hair longer, wore colorful shirts that resembled women's blouses, wore cologne and hair spray and strings of beads, and danced with their girl friends to frenetic new musical sounds. Young girls adopted the unisex look, deemphasizing their sexuality by wearing slacks, clumpy shoes, and man's shirts. Both sexes wore their hair long. (In the twenties, girls shingled their hair to resemble men's short hair styles.) Flat-chested girls (and some others) went without bras. And while the Charleston kept the girls dancing all night in the twenties, the monkey, squirrel, and the frug absorbed youth's dancing energies in the sixties. Young people listened rapturously to popular music in both eras. The big dance bands attracted them in the twenties, rock concerts in the sixties. Four hundred thousand young people congregated at Woodstock, New York, in August 1969 for a weekend rock festival, the largest gathering of its kind in history.

Each summer in the mid-sixties, citizens could look forward, with trepidation or anticipation, to demonstrations for civil rights (1963, 1964) and/or marches against the war in Vietnam (1968, 1969, 1970). Local and national marches became commonplace. Race riots, unfortunately, also occurred in Southern cities as well as in Chicago (1965), Los Angeles (1965), and Detroit (1967). With the media reporting every event, with great distances easy to travel, and with activist organizations better prepared, large numbers of people could be mobilized for a particular cause. Woodstock symbolized a pinnacle of personal pleasure for youth of the sixties, while the March on Washington marked a high point in the movement toward social awareness.

Another form of activism during the sixties was the series of eruptions and demonstrations on college campuses. The two most significant occurred on the Berkeley campus of the University of California (1964) and at Columbia University (1968), but for a time even students at small colleges joined the activist outbreaks. Though the issues were often blurred, students' right to participate in college decisions was one primary concern. Using the model of the civil rights and anti-war movements, campus radicals staged marches and drafted lists of demands. And under male leaders such as Mario Savio at Berkeley, female participants learned, often by painful experience, that only through separation and self-assertion could they hope to call attention to their own sex's problems.

War and peace, black and white, young and old, male and female became the dual alignments in many of the struggles of the sixties. Young men argued that manliness and war no longer went together, and though the number of anti-war activists was small in 1965, by the end of the decade they had won the support of the American people. Civil rights activists led by the Reverend Martin Luther King, Jr., aroused the moral conscience of white America and publicized the continued grievances of black people. Abbie Hoffman of the Yippies glorified youth and questioned the values of the over-thirty generation. Women liberationists declared their emancipation from cultural definitions of themselves. True, most of the social problems articulated by these groups remained with the nation in the 1970s, but they received eloquent expression during the turbulent sixties.

Women in the 1960s

Young women went to college in greater numbers, they worked before and during marriage, and they participated in the social protest movements on their college campuses. On the surface, their lives seemed significantly different from their mothers'; but once again, like their sisters in the 1920s, their life goals remained essentially traditional. Few defined themselves in terms of their own achievements and aspirations. On the statistical level, these changes could be recorded:

1920	20 out of every 100 girls graduated from high school
1970	78 out of every 100 girls graduated from high school
1920	2 out of every 100 young women graduated from college
1970	19 out of every 100 young women graduated from college

1920	23% of all women were in the labor force
1970	43% of all women were in the labor force

1920	The average woman worker was single and 28 years old
1970	The average woman worker was married and 39 years old

Young women married younger in the 1960s than they had in the preceding eighty years. Whereas their median age of marriage in 1890 was 22, young women in 1960 were marrying at a median age of 20.3 years of age. However, the picture may be changing in the 1970s. Young women seemed to be delaying marriage longer, and to the surprise of many demographers, the birthrate began a significant decline. One reason was that women were now able to control conception much more effectively than ever before because of the birth control pill. Thus an old feminist dream had finally become a reality. But, as with most reforms, the pill was developed not because of the strength of the feminists' argument but rather because world population had reached astounding proportions and many people feared mass starvation in the future.

American women, better educated and financially better off than most women in the world, were the first major beneficiaries of this new invention. By 1970, millions of them were taking the pill. For the first time in history, women could be wives without also, and inevitably, becoming mothers. They could choose whether to have children and could plan the size of their families. True, some medical scientists considered the pill's side effects more serious than the advocates admitted. Yet the pill, combined with the less-than-perfect intrauterine device and the diaphragm, gave women greater control over their reproductive organs than ever before.

Women won another victory for personal freedom in January 1973, when the Supreme Court ruled that all state laws that prohibit or restrict a woman's right to have an abortion in the first trimester of pregnancy are unconstitutional; the matter is to be decided by the woman and her physician. Under this ruling, the states could develop guidelines for performing second-trimester abortions and could proscribe the performance of third-trimester abortions except when a woman's life was endangered. Opponents of abortion, most notably the Roman Catholic Church,

396

have continued to lobby against this ruling, and the issue remains a highly explosive one.

At the opening of the sixties, 19 percent of mothers with children under six were working; ten years later, the figure had jumped to 30 per cent. Women remained in the work force for longer periods than ever before. But they continued to hold the lowest paid jobs. When their work was comparable to men's, they still earned 30 to 60 per cent less than the men.

WOMEN MAKE UP A GROWING SHARE OF THE WORK FORCE

	Male Workers	Female Workers	Women as a Percentage of Labor Force
1955	44.5 mil.	20.5 mil.	32%
1960	46.4 mil.	23.2 mil.	33%
1965	48.3 mil.	26.2 mil.	35%
1970	51.2 mil.	31.5 mil.	38%
1972	54.1 mil.	34.1 mil.	39%

... BUT FALL FURTHER BEHIND MEN IN PAY

Median Earnings of Full-Time Workers

	Men	Women	$ Difference
1955	$4,252	$2,719	$1,533
1960	$5,417	$3,293	$2,124
1965	$6,375	$3,823	$2,552
1971	$9,399	$5,593	$3,806

... AND EARN LESS IN ALL KINDS OF JOBS

Median Annual Earnings of Full-Time Workers

1972

	Men	Women
Professional, technical	$12,518	$8,312
Schoolteachers	$ 9,913	$8,126
Managerial	$12,721	$6,738
Clerks	$ 9,124	$5,696
Salesmen	$10,650	$4,485
Craftsmen	$ 9,627	$5,425

Factory hands	$ 7,915	$4,789
Laborers	$ 6,866	$4,548
Service workers	$ 7,111	$4,159

Source: U.S. Dept. of Commerce

More and more women were the sole supporting heads of families—in one family in ten among whites and one in five in black communities. The same statistics show that eight million children under the age of eighteen were being cared for by single women. The popular image of Daddy as the breadwinner and Mommy staying at home surrounded by the children no longer describes reality in America. Yet in 1970, families headed by women had a median income of $4,000, in contrast to $11,600 for families headed by men.

The American family of 1970 does not have one definition or shape. It can consist of a working mother and her dependent children; a mother and father and their two children; a divorced mother with three children; a divorced or widowed father with four children. While women have always been paid less than men for the same work, their salaries were often adequate in the past because they were single or because their salary was a second income for their family. In the 1970s, when increasing numbers of women are supporting their families, the age-old discrimination against women can have serious social consequences.

New Cultural Heroines and Heroes

One significant occurrence of the 1960s was the rise of a new group of heroines and heroes for black Americans, women, and students. An impressive number of black, women, and student leaders received popular recognition as representatives of their special groups. Martin Luther King, Jr., emerged as an appealing spokesman for the rights of black people, as did Malcolm X. Gloria Steinem and Betty Friedan were widely known champions of women's rights. Student leaders Tom Hayden, Jerry Rubin, Rennie Davis, and others voiced the discontent of their peers. These are only a few of the many leaders who became well known to television and lecture audiences. Whitney Young,

398

the Reverend Jesse Jackson, and the Reverend Ralph Abernathy spoke before innumerable audiences, black and white, and provided admirable heroes for their people. Actress Jane Fonda, feminist Ti-Grace Atkinson, and feminist-writer Kate Millett galvanized women to unite on their own behalf.

In the 1930s, men and women had looked to President Roosevelt for one kind of leadership and to their favorite movie stars and sports figures for entertainment and vicarious pleasure. In the 1940s, the cultural heroes and heroines were movie stars, military heroes, popular singers, joined in the fifties by television personalities. The youth of the sixties also worshipped the same gods. In this period, however, while women could look up to the influential feminist leaders featured in the media, they could only be discouraged by the conspicuous lack of outstanding women in the popular arts. There were few movie stars and television personalities for women to admire. Although Jane Fonda, Barbra Streisand, Ali McGraw, and Liza Minnelli starred in popular films of the decade, they hardly qualified as stars of

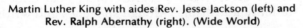

Martin Luther King with aides Rev. Jesse Jackson (left) and Rev. Ralph Abernathy (right). (Wide World)

the magnitude of Katharine Hepburn, Bette Davis, or Joan Crawford. And comedienne Lucille Ball, the most durable woman star on television, conveyed the impression of a silly, zany creature, as did Carol Burnett, the only other popular woman television star. One exception, however, is Barbara Walters, co-host of NBC's *Today* show, whose stature on television commands the respect of men and women alike. Though not outwardly an advocate of women's rights, she has, by example, expanded women's role on serious talk shows and news programs. Noted for her persistence and intelligence, she demonstrates these qualities on the *Today* show and on her own widely appealing show, *Not for Women Only*.

Modern heroes and heroines fall into two different categories: the persuaders and the entertainers. The persuaders present the grievances of the particular group they represent in a forceful and dramatic way. Martin Luther King, for example, was an effective persuader, speaking and writing of black Americans' demands for equality. Betty Friedan, in her book *The Feminine Mystique*, stated the case for feminism clearly and powerfully. Tom Hayden's Port Huron Statement (1962) spoke effectively for the new student radicalism. Through speeches and writings, the

Television personality
Barbara Walters. (Wide World)

persuaders argued the legitimacy of their cause. And all the while they presented images for their followers to respect and admire; they conveyed the dignity and self-confidence of committed people. Martin Luther King, Jr.'s famous "I Have a Dream" speech, delivered at the 1963 March on Washington, captured the mood of black America. The Reverend King was not only an inspired leader of his own people but one who could communicate brilliantly with whites. Feminist heroine Gloria Steinem has the same talent for reaching all kinds of people.

Entertainers are also cultural heroines and heroes. They provide fantasy outlets, pure entertainment, and vicarious experiences for their constituency. For young people, women, and blacks, their heroes and heroines are the successful and visible representatives of their particular group. The many take pride in the accomplishments of the few. The stars create enjoyable moments for their followers, and their followers repay them with devotion, the price of a ticket to a concert, and the purchase of a record album—if the star is a singer. Both sides receive gratification from the relationship.

The actors-actresses as entertainers can serve another function for their particular group: through their roles in movies and in television plays, they can suggest career possibilities to their audiences. If women see only men doctors on television, if black Americans see only persons with white faces in powerful positions, and if young people see only over-forty types portraying all important roles, these groups wonder where they belong. Whom should they imitate? Or emulate? If there are no visible heroines, white or black, for little girls to imitate, they conclude rightly that the only life option available to them will be the traditional wife-mother role. If women on television are the secretaries to male lawyers and detectives, young girls get the message.

Fortunately, another set of remarkable heroines began to be visible during the 1960s and gained tremendous influence in the 1970s—women athletes. Here are superb models for those little girls to adore and to imitate and perhaps to follow. Boys have long had their baseball heroes. Now their sisters can have comparable heroines.

Because there are so many amazing young women athletes who have not yet reached the height of their careers, let us consider only one of them as a symbol of future heroines in this field.

Billie Jean King is not only one of the greatest women tennis players in history but a leader in the cause of equal rights for women—especially, of course, women in sports.

Billie Jean was born in 1943 in Long Beach, California. She began playing tennis at the age of eleven when her parents encouraged her to develop her natural athletic ability. She astounded them by becoming totally devoted to the game. In addition to practicing constantly, she walked three and a half miles to school each day to strengthen her legs. It all paid off when, at eighteen, she upset Margaret Smith, the first-ranked Australian woman tennis player, in the first round of the amateur women's tournament at Wimbledon, England. From that point on, she developed into a star tennis player, though taking time out to attend California State College at Los Angeles. She married Larry King in 1965.

By 1974, Billie Jean King had won all major titles in women's tennis. Further, since 1967 she has been an outspoken advocate of equal treatment and equal earnings for women tennis players. She has probably done more than any other single person to make women's tennis an exciting, popular sport and to elevate the status of women tennis players. In 1973, she won *Sports Illustrated*'s award for the Woman Athlete of the Year. Perhaps this growing appreciation of women athletes has made it possible for a very few young girls to join in athletic events once completely male dominated. Jockeys, high school tennis teams, little league baseball, are a few such examples.

Women Politicians

One group who may become cultural heroines to the young women of today are the few but articulate women members of the U.S. Congress. In 1973, women occupied 16 of the 435 seats in the House of Representatives. While the Watergate affair of 1972–1973 besmirched politicians in general, the women legislators remained free of the scandal. Of the senior members of Congress, Edith Green (D., Oregon) and Martha Griffiths (D., Michigan) have each earned a solid but unpublicized reputation for their work in behalf of women, labor, and education. Representative Green, for example, sponsored the Equal Pay Act of 1963. In 1972, Representative Griffiths led the floor fight for the Equal

Tennis great and women's rights advocate Billie Jean King
allows herself to be congratulated by the loser, Sept. 1973.
(Wide World)

Rights Amendment, first introduced in 1923 by Alice Paul. The amendment finally received congressional approval and was sent to the states for ratification.

More likely candidates for popular adulation are recently elected Shirley Chisholm (D., New York), the first black woman in Congress, elected in 1968; Bella Abzug (D., New York), elected in 1970; Barbara Jordan (D., Texas), the first black woman from the South to be elected to Congress; Yvonne Burke (D., California), a black and the first woman to co-chair a Democratic convention (1972); and Elizabeth Holtzman (D., New York), who challenged the U.S. bombing of Cambodia in 1973. In 1972, Congresswoman Chisholm ran in the Democratic presidential primaries, and though her performance was modest at best, she gave the American public the opportunity to hear an articulate, informed woman politician speak on critical issues. Congresswoman Chisholm has said that "racism and anti-feminism are two of the prime traditions of this country," and her work is an effort to combat both traditions. Congresswoman Bella Abzug broke with congressional tradition in 1970 by requesting an appointment on the Armed Services Committee, which had never had a woman member. Her request was denied.

> One of the basic reasons I'm claiming a right to a seat on the Armed Services Committee is that I'm a woman. . . . Do you realize there are 42,000 women in the military? Do you realize that about half the civilian employees of the Defense Department are women— 290,000 of them at last count? And, as if that isn't enough, there are one and a half million wives of military personnel.

Women in Politics

Facts   Women have constituted 51 per cent of the electorate since the 1960s.

The percentage of women holding public office is 2.5.

In the late 1960s, there were 1,400 elective and appointive offices in federal, state, and municipal governments. Of these 1,400 posts, 40 were held by women.

First women to hold elected office:

404

Jeanette Rankin, Montana, first woman elected to the U.S. House of Representatives, 1916.

Rebecca Latimer Felton, Georgia, first woman appointed to serve in the U.S. Senate, *for one day,* 1922.

Hattie W. Carraway, Arkansas, first woman to serve a full term in the U.S. Senate, 1934–1940.

Nellie Tayloe Ross, Wyoming, first woman governor, 1925.

Women who ran for President of the United States:

Victoria Claflin Woodhull, 1872.
Shirley Chisholm, 1972.

In the early 1970s, the National Women's Political Caucus was formed to organize women politically. Like the feminists who worked for woman's suffrage from the pre–Civil War days until World War I, its supporters, among them Congresswomen Shirley Chisholm and Bella Abzug, are committed to the idea that women voters and women politicians together represent a powerful bloc. Once they are made aware of this, it is felt, they can bring about the legislative changes they desire. (See Appendix IV for the Caucus platform.)

Other Americans

During the 1960s, black Americans, especially those in the metropolitan areas of Northern and Western cities, had more opportunities for self-fulfillment than ever before. They went to school longer, got better jobs, and could afford a relatively high standard of living. In the South, however, black marginal farmers continued to be the poorest, the least educated, and the worst clothed and housed portion of the population. And in both North and South, all black Americans still experienced serious discrimination in housing, education, and jobs. White Americans moved to the suburbs, leaving the blighted areas of the central city to the blacks. Residential segregation left black Americans with no choice but to occupy the oldest and least desirable housing available. The schools in the inner cities were also the oldest and most poorly equipped. Employment was somewhat less of a problem. For the first time in American history, more than 50 per cent of black Americans held skilled, white-collar, and semi-skilled jobs.

Black Americans: Economic Status, 1972

Percentage of the black population below the poverty level 33
Percentage of the white population below the poverty level 9

The Income Gap

	Percent of Black to White	Median Income (Blacks)	Median Income (Whites)
1964	50%	$3,724	$ 6,858
1965	50%	3,886	7,251
1966	58%	4,507	7,792
1967	59%	4,875	8,234
1968	60%	5,360	8,937
1969	61%	5,999	9,794
1970	61%	6,279	10,236
1971	60%	6,440	10,672
1972	59%	6,864	11,549

Source: Bureau of the Census

Education

Black Americans	Educational Level
1967	370,000 black students were in college
	54% of all blacks (20–29 years old) were high school graduates
1972	727,000 black students were in college
	65% of all blacks (20–29 years old) were high school graduates

Source: The New York Times, July 23, 1973

But a 1968 Department of Labor report pointed out some sobering facts: "Compared to whites, Negroes still are more than

406

three times as likely to be in poverty, twice as likely to be unemployed, and three times as likely to die in infancy or childbirth." Thus, the positive gains won by black Americans had to be weighed against the still prevailing restrictions placed upon people of their skin color. Black women were the lowest paid group on the wage scale, although the number of families headed by black women were increasing at the end of the decade. These discrepancies cried out for attention from the federal government, from industry, and from all social and educational agencies. Would the government give black mothers who worked to support their families enough income so they could remain home with their children? (A similar suggestion was made by Crystal Eastman more than sixty years ago.) Would employers pay black women respectable wages, equal, at least, to those of white women? Would adequate child-care facilities be provided for working mothers? These important questions received less than satisfactory responses from the Nixon administration. President Nixon's social philosophy resembled Grover Cleveland's rather than Franklin Roosevelt's. He demanded that all citizens work and that an unemployed person submit evidence of attempts to obtain work before he could receive welfare payments. In the early 1970s, President Nixon vetoed funds for child-care facilities and cut back family welfare payments.

Fewer Southern blacks migrated to the North in the 1960s than in all previous years since 1914. Perhaps the Civil Rights Act of 1964 and the Voting Rights Act of 1965 gave them less reason to do so, now that they could vote and participate in electoral politics. From 1964 to 1968, a million new black voters registered to vote. And although in 1965 only 75 blacks held elective office in the South (out of a possible 70,000 offices), in 1973, there were 1,400 black officeholders. Many Southern blacks believed that they could deal with the overt racism of white Southerners more easily than with the more covert racists of the North. But the major concentrations of blacks continued to be in such Northern cities as New York, Boston, Philadelphia, Detroit, and Chicago, where they made up from 20 to 25 per cent of the population. Black Americans became synonymous with urban Americans in the 1960s and 1970s, and their problems were those of all city dwellers: inadequate housing, poor public transportation, and low-quality educational facilities.

The benefits of the new technology did not filter down to the inner-city ghettos. The poor black families who lived there may

407

have been better off than the poor of India, but their poverty in affluent, supposedly egalitarian America was inexcusable. In the richest country in the world, infants born to poor families still died in shocking numbers, malnutrition robbed youth of energy and the will to learn, and disease killed many more people than in middle-class communities. Hospital facilities, medical treatment, and preventive health care were out of reach except in crowded, understaffed clinics.

Of the American Indians who had once roamed the whole continent, less than one million remained—most of them still segregated on the reservations established for them in the last decades of the nineteenth century. So limited were the federal provisions for their education, health, and employment that they spent their lives barely subsisting, and so unconcerned was the American public for their welfare that they remained an invisible group. The best-selling book *Bury My Heart at Wounded Knee* (1971) by Dee Brown dramatized their tragic fate and aroused both the Indians and sympathetic white supporters to long-delayed action. Taking their cue from the civil rights, anti-war, and black militant movements, American Indians at the end of the decade organized on their own behalf. In 1972, they took over Alcatraz prison in San Francisco to publicize their shabby treatment at the hands of the federal government. A year later, they occupied Wounded Knee, the site of their last major military encounter with white America. No dramatic improvements resulted from these actions but they did have a positive psychological effect. More and more Indians took pride in their heritage and asserted their right to the respect and dignity they had so long been denied.

Facts About American Indians

Number: 792,730 in 1970—and increasing at a faster rate than the U.S. population.

Tribes: About a third are either Navajo, Cherokee, Sioux, or Chippewa. The Navajo tribe, making up 13 per cent of all Indians, is the biggest.

Location: About half live in the West, a fourth in the South. Oklahoma, Arizona, California, New Mexico, and North Carolina have the largest Indian populations. More than half—55 per cent—live in rural areas, largely on reservations. One in 5 lives in central cities, 1 in 4 in suburbs or smaller cities.

Annual income: $1,115 per person on reservations, about a third of the U.S. average. Counting all Indians, median family income is about half the U.S. average of $11,200, about four-fifths as large as the average of black families.

Life expectancy: 64 years at birth, compared with 70.5 years for all Americans.

Infant mortality: About 24 per cent higher than the U.S. average.

Unemployment: 40 per cent of all Indians on reservations above age 16.

Source: Census Bureau, Dept. of Interior, Office of Management and Budget

The Environment

As in past decades, a minority of experts and critics looked at Americans' abuse of their environment and lamented the results. Rachel Carson's *Silent Spring* (1962) warned of the devastating effects of pesticides upon people and wildlife. Population experts warned of imminent food shortages. Secretary of the Interior Stewart Udall tried to publicize the need for conservation of natural resources. Lady Bird Johnson lobbied for the Highway Beautification Act of 1965, urged citizens to create community groups for cleaning up and beautifying their surroundings, and spoke vigorously against strip mining and the dumping of industrial wastes into rivers. By the end of the decade, the word "ecology" had become popular (though its original meaning was pretty well lost), and prophets of doom like Paul Ehrlich wrote dramatically about how Americans would pollute themselves into oblivion.

In 1969, the U.S. Congress passed the National Environmental Policy Act, which established a Council on Environmental Quality to provide national guidelines on the environment. The Council was to examine all aspects of the problem: the population, the air, water, and all other natural resources. Industrialists were to be prosecuted if they violated federal pollution stand-

409

ards. Automobile manufacturers were told to devise ways of preventing exhaust fumes from polluting the atmosphere. In 1970, a new national holiday was declared—Earth Day. All this quickly alerted the public to the dangers of pollution, but most people still comfortably believed that the very technology which had created the problem would assuredly conquer it.

The Environmental Protection Agency also became a national watchdog, but although it issued numerous statements on pollution, the agency prosecuted very few polluters. Two firmly rooted but outmoded American convictions have blocked environmental programs in general: the belief in inevitable progress and the belief in the infinite resources of the country. Americans consume, waste, and discard an incredibly high quantity of those resources. They continue to travel in their own cars rather than insist upon efficient public transportation, and their internal combustion engines throw a cloud of polluted fumes across the overcrowded highways. But there are hopeful signs that they are slowly becoming aware of imminent dangers to their environment, dangers ranging from overpopulation to the disappearance of wildlife.

For one thing, the U.S. population in 1970 reflected a decided decrease in size, suggesting that Americans, thanks to effective birth control methods and an inflationary economy, are limiting the size of their families. For another, constructive efforts are under way to clean up the nation's rivers. Then, too, the federal government is protecting the animals labeled endangered species. Finally, agriculturists have succeeded in replacing the most destructive pesticides with harmless substitutes.

But the environmental problem, still a long way from solution, is not limited to America; it is world wide. Consequently, a mammoth, coordinated effort is needed in all countries—an effort that has not yet occurred. But the United States is still the world's number-one polluter. While Americans now use recyclable paper, grocery bags, and beer cans, they are only now starting to cut down on their use of electricity and other precious resources. It will be hard for them to give up the technological devices that make them more comfortable and relieve their lives of drudgery. Air-conditioning, for example, is a luxury that has become a necessity for many Americans. Freezers filled with frozen foods are another benefit of the new technology, as are the foods themselves.

Indeed, the whole buy-buy-buy syndrome, which began in the 1920s, has accelerated to such an extent that Americans have accepted the built-in obsolescence of their appliances, have bought a new car every few years, and have discarded still new clothes in favor of the latest fashions. The gasoline shortage of 1974 created a new awareness of how far Americans are from self-sufficiency in terms of energy sources. But most people have not yet seen the connection between their private consumption patterns and the despoliation of the environment. That must come—along with important changes in human thinking and behavior. For these changes may be essential to the survival of all life on this planet.

Change as Paradox

As the 1960s ended, the multiple paradoxes and blatant contradictions of the decade glared in the face of any interested observer. The sixties produced more public interest in the problems of the poor, of black Americans, of women, and of the victims of war than ever before. At the same time, death through violence ended the lives of civil rights workers and of student protestors. Assassins took the lives of President John F. Kennedy, Reverend Martin Luther King, Jr., and Senator Robert F. Kennedy. While youth proclaimed their liberation from traditional values, the Rolling Stones, a most spectacular and successful rock group, sang of women as "yesterday's newspaper"—as objects to be used and rejected afterward. Rock singers sang lyrics that demanded woman's complete fidelity but lauded infidelity among men, the old double standard of Western civilization. Women singers often contributed to the same negative stereotype of women. Brenda Lee sang "I'm Sorry, So Sorry That I Was Such a Fool," while Joni Summers belted out "I Want a Brave Man, a Cave Man. . . ."

Youth declared their desire to be free and conscious of life's full possibilities, and then took LSD or heroin, which turned them into "freaks"—human beings who lost control and often consciousness as well. Youth criticized their elders for apathy and lack of interest in social affairs and then proceeded to "drop out" themselves. The older generation clung to its age-old beliefs in individual will and achievement while demanding greater Social Security and pension benefits. Labor unions, which had achieved a measure of affluence since the 1930s, protected their own and turned a deaf ear to the demands of minority groups who wanted access to union positions. The promise of America continued to be a promise, not a reality, as the sixties slid into the seventies.

Indeed, the most significant outcome of the liberation movements of the sixties might well have been the sense of personal liberation gained by individual participants. On the surface, not much was accomplished by the activists of any group. There were no signs that the general public, the WASM, had altered their attitudes toward women, blacks, or Indians. Yet many youthful workers in these movements developed self-confidence and a clear set of life values. Women liberationists came to understand their own status and role in history. Black Americans and American Indians began to see themselves as independent, self-respecting human beings.

This process of self-discovery led some people to continue crusading for causes, while others now defined their goals as personal and private. Whether the younger activists of the sixties will become socially responsible leaders of the seventies remains to be seen. There are several hopeful signs, such as the trend toward young lawyers and doctors devoting themselves to public law and public medicine and the increasing numbers of young people engaging in elective politics. (The youthful mayor of Madison, Wisconsin in 1973 had been a student activist at the University a few years earlier.)

The youth culture has indeed been a mixed bag—a colorful assortment of positive and negative actions. Its consequences remain to be seen.

Suggestions for Further Reading

Bella Abzug. *Bella!* (New York, 1971).
Caroline Bird. *Born Female* (New York, 1968).
Shirley Chisholm. *Unbought and Unbossed* (Boston, 1970).
Mary Ellmann. *Thinking About Women* (New York, 1969).
Shulamith Firestone and Anne Koedt, editors. *Notes from the Second Year: Major Writings of the Radical Feminists* (Boston, 1970).
Martin Luther King, Jr. *Why We Can't Wait* (New York, 1964).
Robert J. Lifton, *The Woman in America* (Boston, 1965).

Suggestions for Further Reading

Malcolm X. *The Autobiography of Malcolm X* (New York, 1966).

Robin Morgan, editor. *Sisterhood Is Powerful* (New York, 1970).

William L. O'Neill. *Coming Apart: An Informal History of America in the 1960s* (Chicago, 1971).

June Sochen. *Movers and Shakers: American Women Thinkers and Activists, 1900–1970* (New York, 1973).

Arthur I. Waskow. *From Race Riot to Sit-In: 1919 and the 1960s* (New York, 1966).

Howard Zinn. *SNCC: The New Abolitionists* (Boston, 1964).

Suggestions for Further Reading

CHAPTER FIFTEEN

The Future Is Now

> One often advises rulers, statesmen, and peoples to learn from the experiences of history. But what experience and history teach is that peoples and governments have never yet learned from history, let alone acted according to its lessons.
> —Hegel

> Those who do not know the past are doomed to repeat it.
> —Santayana

A history book is made up of fragile facts whose worth is largely determined by the historian who presents them. American history—or herstory from my point of view—is not a record of steady progress. Rather it has been one of jagged change, uneven administration of justice, and often blind disregard for the rights of human beings. Positive improvements for certain groups have frequently been gained at the cost of cruelty, violence, and discrimination toward others. Extending the right to vote to all white American males in the 1820s certainly benefited them, but it did nothing for women, slaves, and Indians. Clearing the wilderness for white human settlement aided the pioneers but robbed the Indians of their territory and often despoiled the natural environment. In human history, people have made decisions they believed were inevitable and essential, though in fact they were cultural, value-laden, and debatable. Whenever any far-reaching change has taken place, some people have gained by it and some have lost. Rarely, if ever, does everyone win. Most Americans, however, insist on seeing all change as progress, as betterment.

To seventeenth-century Puritans, the environment was

415

infinite—a huge continent of virgin soil—and this attitude would have important and disastrous consequences for future generations. Farmers ignored nineteenth-century expert advice on how to conserve the land. As long as there was more land to the west, they could always move on to more fertile fields when their present soil was exhausted. Such optimism, combined with a supreme confidence in the rightness of their thoughts and actions, enabled the early New Englanders and Virginians to exert tremendous energy in pursuing their goals. Though our seventeenth-century ancestors experienced self-doubt, guilt, and anxiety, they were not paralyzed by it. They knew the right thing to do, according to their beliefs, and they did it. Their world-view embraced all aspects of human life: attitudes toward women, blacks, children, and Indians fitted neatly into their view of the natural world, their purpose on earth, and their life-goals. In this sense, our cultural forebears created a coherent whole, a fabric that could, and did, endure beyond their generation.

Self-confidence, of course, is an important and valuable trait, but it can lead to a total disregard for those who do not share one's own philosophy. Anne Hutchinson and Roger Williams, for example, were exiled because their views were different from their contemporaries, and threatened the hegemony of the existing power-holders. Tolerance has always rested on shaky ground in America. Puritans "tolerated" Unitarians and Quakers when they found they could not dispose of them all and when they could no longer hold their own brethren in check. But, as the ministers frequently reminded their congregations, tolerance was a dangerous proposition. It meant admitting the possible legitimacy of other points of view, and that would never do. Tolerance as an ideological principle, rather than simply a pragmatic necessity, can only occur in a culture that admits multiple paths to truth, a situation that has not existed anywhere in human history; a homogenous society can effectively ignore other views and a heterogeneous one has to learn, reluctantly, how to get along with differences.

Whether new settlers arrived on the *Mayflower*, or on a dingy freighter from Ireland in the 1840s, or on still another crowded, unsanitary vessel from Italy at the turn of the last century, they absorbed the WASM values: the importance of work, the rightness of the WASM power structure, the superiority of the white race, the place of women, and the proud conviction that America was the land of opportunity. America, they came to believe, could do no wrong and was never guilty of crude imperialism or human exploitation. There are elements of truth in this creed, just as there are serious distortions. That is what makes human history so perplexing, frustrating, and exciting; it is rarely a simple either/or proposition. America has provided more opportunities for economic success and social mobility than has any other country. Many immigrants who lived and worked according to the American creed did succeed. But many others who dutifully followed the same rules did not. Consider the Welsh coal miners in Pennsylvania, who almost never saw the light of day, never realized their dreams, and died of tuberculosis at the age of forty. Most women, as I have said repeatedly, never enjoyed the personal fulfillment promised by America to its menfolk. No black American or American Indian in this country has lived without being acutely aware that he was different from, and hence judged inferior to, white Americans. Yet the rhetoric of natural rights, articulated so dramatically in the eighteenth-century, gave hope and encouragement to deprived groups of Americans for each successive generation.

*   *   *

Humanists and feminists of every generation have worked for human rights. From this perspective, they view American history and are appalled. They feel that the Puritans' behavior toward the Indians, and all subsequent WASM actions against blacks, Indians, and women, should be condemned. They may, however, applaud the theory of natural rights and the thinking of James Madison, who, while discussing the new Constitution, analyzed the problem of how a society could be organized to respect the multiple groups it represented. True, Madison did not consider women or blacks as interest groups deserving of inclusion, but his theory of a pluralistic society responsive to the needs of varying interests could and would become the twentieth-century rallying cry of these groups. Nineteenth- and twentieth-century feminists have searched for kindred spirits, for thinkers who supported their views, and for energetic sisters and brothers who would work with them to achieve their goals.

Each generation's critics of established values and behavior patterns sought out sympathetic people with whom they could discuss both the ills of American society and the possible solutions. Their schemes for reform were sometimes wild and eccentric, sometimes valid, perceptive, and intelligent. Their success depended heavily upon their ability to present their reforms in convincing ways to the power-holders. Advocates of sanitary conditions in the meat-packing industry succeeded only when they gained the support of the leading meat packers.

Until the recent past, most reform interest groups—including students, blacks, and Indians—operated within the accepted rules of our society. They wrote letters to their congressmen, collected names on petitions, spoke before influential groups, and tried to convince rich, sympathetic listeners of the rightness of their cause. Sometimes they worked long and hard before receiving a respectful hearing; often they failed. When they succeeded, their success was usually diluted and incomplete. Even after black slaves gained their freedom, they found that their lives were as hard, as unpredictable, and as dependent on the good graces of white men as before. Interest groups in the 1960s and 1970s who expressed their grievances by bombing university laboratories and taking professors as hostages ultimately had as little success as the nonviolent protesters of previous generations.

The problem of contructive change is complex and multi-dimensional. The arrogance of reformers often forms a counterpoint to the arrogance of power-holders. No one wants to be told that he is prejudiced and blind and in the wrong. Everybody thinks he is right and needs subtle persuasion to be convinced otherwise. The most bigoted slave owners were often faithful church-goers, liberally interpreting the words of the Lord. Most everyone develops a simple or elaborate explanation for his own behavior; in order to convince most people of the need for change, some crack must be made in their defensive armor. Reformers, the agents for change, face innumerable obstacles. Frequently, the changes they desire may be too limited (woman's suffrage), while on other occasions they may strive for too much in too short a time (abolition of slavery and feminism); when the claims are too comprehensive, reformers usually fail to achieve all they desire. Furthermore, when a proposed reform is at first considered outrageous by the public (such as woman's suffrage) it cannot be accomplished in one generation. Finally, and perhaps most importantly, the result rarely fulfills the promise. Reformers always overstate their case because they think that is the only way to attain their goal. Education advocates, for example, have always promised American taxpayers that more schooling for more children will create an educated, peaceful citizenry. The goal has yet to be accomplished. Thus, reformers and everyone else, are always disappointed with the incomplete results of their crusades.

In reality, then, the achievement of any reform may bring frustration and failure in its wake. For this sad outcome, both reformers and their audiences must share responsibility. Both must continue to work for a cause after the desired legislation is passed. Both must supervise its enforcement and evaluate its results. Reformers tire, become discouraged, and eventually leave their work to others. And finally, one generation's success may be inadequate for the next generation. To complicate matters still further, new dilemmas have an unpleasant way of cropping up. But the most difficult, and continuous, problems of man-woman, adult-child, and black-white relationships are never completely resolved; they exist as long as life exists.

Each generation must face and try to solve both its old and new problems while knowing that all solutions are temporary, tentative, and subject to re-evaluation. Treating all human beings with respect and learning to live harmoniously in the natural environment are constant problems that will never disappear and never be entirely solved. Ultimately, human responsibility is a shared responsibility, with each individual participating in decisions and consequences. Women must unite with other women to achieve their common goals as other groups have done, and will continue to do. All of us, as individuals and members of groups, have some control and responsibility over our lives; if we do not use that responsibility wisely, then we are doomed to powerlessness.

Modest reforms of small injustices never have led to major social changes. The uneven patchwork of minor improvements that emerged by the 1880s did not begin to affect the basic problems facing America. A society that had all but destroyed its native Indian population, discriminated cruelly against its black people, and excluded its women from equal consideration needed serious revising. But the revisions had to be made in attitudes and values. Before WASMs and their male counterparts in other religions and ethnic groups could change their behavior, they had to change their attitudes. Attitudes determine action; it does not work the other way around. The few times in American history when the "right" laws were passed before attitudes changed, those laws were ignored, manipulated, or violated by the whites. The civil rights laws for black Americans after the Civil War did not change white attitudes or behavior. Passing a national temperance law (Prohibition) when people still liked to drink resulted in the rise of organized crime—that is, of a powerful group of criminal entrepreneurs who went into business to satisfy the population's desire for liquor.

But how do you change people's minds about something as important and far-reaching as the treatment of women, blacks, and Indians? How do you get people to stop wasting all-too-limited resources? Changing minds on important issues would require major shifts in thinking and mammoth changes in behavior. All human roles would have to be redefined and the result would truly be revolutionary. If all human beings were given equal opportunities to develop their minds and talents, to enjoy the fruits of industrialization and the right to free expression, new, unexpected behavior patterns might arise. Children of both sexes and of all colors and creeds might study together, love together, play together, and work together. Adults of both sexes and of all colors and creeds might share responsibilities formerly designated as male or female. Yet each human being would be regarded as unique and different from all others, and innate talents and personality traits would not be stifled by institutional and cultural discrimination.

Moving away from a pattern of fixed attitudes and prejudices to one of human consideration is not an easy task. People are basically conservative in their attitudes; they change their minds reluctantly. Fearing the unknown, they are content to remain with the known. Those in power do not want to lose their advantage, and most of the powerless believe that their lives today are better than their parents' were. They have a feeling of superiority because they can look down on those who have fewer material possessions and a lower socioeconomic status. Moreover, the deprived groups have tended to identify with the ideology of the powerful. In the past, women, blacks, and Indians (except for a minority of reformers within their respective groups) accepted their position in the society. They agreed with the taste-makers that woman's place was in the home and that blacks and Indians who did not succeed according to the American formula were responsible for their own failure. Even if they did not agree with the views of the majority, most of them did not become activist-reformers. Instead, they resigned themselves to their fate, hoping and praying that some day justice would be done and the wrongdoers would see the evil of their ways. Some day the American Dream would include them too.

We human beings tend to simplify and reduce experience to its lowest common denominator. To the Puritans, all non-Puritans were heathens. To many Americans, all blacks are born inferior to whites. Surely it is easy to deal with diverse peoples and problems in this way. Arriving at these simplistic conclusions does not require analysis, examination, or knowledge of other people. Similarly, when one looks at human beings, it is easy to assign them the simplest and most convenient label. Women bear children; this is a biological fact. From there, it is a quick leap to the conclusion that because women are natural mothers, motherhood is their natural role. Once this syllogism is completed, any other reasoning becomes unnecessary. Biology and culture unite to force the same role on all womankind.

Men are physically larger than women and supposedly stronger. Thus, as they were once the hunters and providers, they are required to be the breadwinners. In order for the society to operate on predictable lines, no one should violate these role definitions. Everyone must conform to the "natural" biological-cultural concept of how human beings function. Women may cultivate the fields and milk the cows, but these are secondary, supplementary roles, never primary ones. Men may nurture their young temporarily or under special circumstances, but for them the nurturing role can never be the major one. Both sexes have become locked into these early role definitions.

Novelists, poets, statemen, preachers, and musicians have all contributed to this definition of the sexes. They have lauded woman's domesticity while praising man's thirst for adventure. Songs have been written about the nobility of warfare and the virtues of motherhood. Plays, films, books, even children's books, confirm the traditional role definitions. Men are denied the right to shed tears, for tears are not manly. They are burdened with the lifelong responsiblity of earning a living to support their dependent families. Girls can cry, dictates tradition, boys cannot. Girls can play with dolls; boys cannot. Boys can play baseball; girls cannot. Boys can become engineers; girls cannot. Throughout American history, most people have lived

421

out their lives according to these age-old patterns and attitudes. They have experienced most of their joys and sorrows within the family circle. Their horizons have been limited, not unlimited; their human possibilities finite, not infinite. Even their hopes have usually had to be restricted, modestly nourished by the environment of their lives.

Despite the constant changes that have taken place in America over the last three centuries, these restraints on individual lives have persisted. Change within continuity, the blending of the new into the old, has been the motif. In the 1870s a Wisconsin farmer learned how to use the new International Harvester threshing machine while teaching his daughters to be obedient and dutiful. People in the 1880s looked wonderingly at the new bridges spanning broad rivers and went to church on Sunday to hear the same sermons they and their ancestors had heard countless times before. The old and the new, an unstable mixture at first, gradually became integrated in the minds of most Americans.

Material progress and human progress are two very different things. Human progress means learning how to live without war and how to respect individual and cultural differences. Material progress means replacing forests with factories, building bigger cities, and producing new consumer goods each year. Supposedly, material progress serves human progress, but unfortunately it often seems to be the other way around. Human beings become servants to material possessions and slaves of the machines and products they create. The future is unclear, though some progress has been made in granting equal rights to women and black Americans. Human attitudes and behavior are beginning to change. The liberation movements of the 1960s and 1970s have expressed the needs as well as the goals still to be achieved. Crystal Eastman, one of the great feminists of the 1910s, envisioned a world in which men and women work and play together as equals. She died too soon and never saw her dream realized. Will this generation see the fulfillment of that dream? Much has been done; much remains undone.

Suggestions for Further Reading

Paul Goodman. *Growing Up Absurd* (New York, 1960).
Oscar and Mary Handlin. *Facing Life: Youth and the Family in American History* (Boston, 1971).

Suggestions for Further Reading

Max Lerner. *America as a Civilization: Life and Thought in the United States Today* (New York, 1957).

Herbert Marcuse. *An Essay on Liberation* (Boston, 1969).

Philip Slater. *The Pursuit of Loneliness* (Boston, 1970).

William Irwin Thompson. *At the Edge of History* (New York, 1971).

Alfred F. Young, editor. *Dissent: Explorations in the History of American Radicalism* (DeKalb, Illinois, 1968).

Declaration of Sentiments and Resolutions

When, in the course of human events, it becomes necessary for one portion of the family of man to assume among the people of the earth a position different from that which they have hitherto occupied, but one to which the laws of nature and of nature's God entitle them, a decent respect to the opinions of mankind requires that they should declare the causes that impel them to such a course.

We hold these truths to be self-evident: that all men and women are created equal; that they are endowed by their Creator with certain inalienable rights; that among these are life, liberty, and the pursuit of happiness; that to secure these rights governments are instituted, deriving their just powers from the consent of the governed. Whenever any form of government becomes destructive of these ends, it is the right of those who suffer from it to refuse allegiance to it, and to insist upon the institution of a new government, laying its foundation on such principles, and organizing its powers in such form, as to them shall seem most likely to effect their safety and happiness. Prudence, indeed, will dictate that governments long established should not be changed for light and transient causes; and accordingly all experience hath shown that mankind are more disposed to suffer, while evils are sufferable, than to

425

right themselves by abolishing the forms to which they were accustomed. But when a long train of abuses and usurpations, pursuing invariably the same object, evinces a design to reduce them under absolute despotism, it is their duty to throw off such government, and to provide new guards for their future security. Such has been the patient sufferance of the women under this government, and such is now the necessity which constrains them to demand the equal station to which they are entitled.

The history of mankind is a history of repeated injuries and usurpations on the part of man toward woman, having in direct object the establishment of an absolute tyranny over her. To prove this, let facts be submitted to a candid world.

He has never permitted her to exercise her inalienable right to the elective franchise.

He has compelled her to submit to laws, in the formation of which she had no voice.

He has withheld from her rights which are given to the most ignorant and degraded men—both natives and foreigners.

Having deprived her of this first right of a citizen, the elective franchise, thereby leaving her without representation in the halls of legislation, he has oppressed her on all sides.

He has made her, if married, in the eye of the law, civilly dead.

He has taken from her all right in property, even to the wages she earns.

He has made her, morally, an irresponsible being, as she can commit many crimes with impunity, provided they be done in the presence of her husband. In the covenant of marriage, she is compelled to promise obedience to her husband, he becoming, to all intents and purposes, her master—the law giving him power to deprive her of her liberty, and to administer chastisement.

He has so framed the laws of divorce, as to what shall be the proper causes, and in case of separation, to whom the guardianship of the children shall be given, as to be wholly regardless of the happiness of women—the law, in all cases, going upon the false supposition of the supremacy of man, and giving all power into his hands.

After depriving her of all rights as a married woman, if single, and the owner of property, he has taxed her to support a government which recognizes her only when her property can be made profitable to it.

He has monopolized nearly all the profitable employments, and from those she is permitted to follow, she receives but a scanty remuneration. He closes against her all the avenues to wealth and distinction which he considers most honorable to himself. As a teacher of theology, medicine, or law, she is not known.

He has denied her the facilities for obtaining a thorough education, all colleges being closed against her.

He allows her in Church, as well as State, but a subordinate position, claiming Apostolic authority for her exclusion from the ministry, and, with some exceptions, from any public participation in the affairs of the Church.

He has created a false public sentiment by giving to the world a different code of morals for men and women, by which moral delinquencies which exclude women from society, are not only tolerated, but deemed of little account in man.

He has usurped the prerogative of Jehovah himself, claiming it as his right to assign for her a sphere of action, when that belongs to her conscience and to her God.

He has endeavored, in every way that he could, to destroy her confidence in her own powers, to lessen her self-respect, and to make her willing to lead a dependent and abject life.

Now, in view of this entire disfranchisement of one-half the people of this country, their social and religious degradation—in view of the unjust laws above mentioned, and because women do feel themselves aggrieved, oppressed, and fraudulently deprived of their most sacred rights, we insist that they have immediate admission to all the rights and privileges which belong to them as citizens of the United States.

In entering upon the great work before us, we anticipate no small amount of misconception, misrepresentation, and ridicule; but we shall use every instrumentality within our power to effect our object. We shall employ agents, circulate tracts, petition the State and National legislatures, and endeavor to enlist the pulpit and the press in our behalf. We hope this Convention will be followed by a series of Conventions embracing every part of the country.

RESOLUTIONS

WHEREAS, The great precept of nature is conceded to be, that "man shall pursue his own true and substantial happiness." Blackstone in his Commentaries remarks, that this law of Nature being coeval with mankind, and dictated by God himself, is of course superior in obligation to any other. It is binding over all the globe, in all countries and at all times; no human laws are of any validity if contrary to this, and such of them as are valid, derive all their force, and all their validity, and all their authority, mediately and immediately, from this original; therefore,

Resolved, That such laws as conflict, in any way, with the true and substantial happiness of woman, are contrary to the great precept of nature and of no validity, for this is "superior in obligation to any other."

Resolved, That all laws which prevent woman from occupying such a station in society as her conscience shall dictate, or which place her in a position inferior to that of man, are contrary to the great precept of nature, and therefore of no force or authority.

Resolved, That woman is man's equal—was intended to be so by the Creator, and the highest good of the race demands that she should be recognized as such.

Resolved, That the women of this country ought to be enlightened in regard to the laws under which they live, that they may no longer publish their degradation by declaring themselves satisfied with their present position, nor their ignorance, by asserting that they have all the rights they want.

Resolved, That inasmuch as man, while claiming for himself intellectual superiority, does accord to woman moral superiority, it is pre-eminently his duty to encourage her to speak and teach, as she has an opportunity, in all religious assemblies.

Resolved, That the same amount of virtue, delicacy, and refinement of behavior that is required of woman in the social state, should also be required of man, and the same transgressions should be visited with equal severity on both man and woman.

Resolved, That the objection of indelicacy and impropriety, which is so often brought against woman when she addresses a public audience, comes with a very ill-grace from those who encourage, by their attendance, her appearance on the stage, in the concert, or in feats of the circus.

Resolved, That woman has too long rested satisfied in the circumscribed limits which corrupt customs and a perverted application of the criptures have marked out for her, and that it is time she should move in the enlarged sphere which her great Creator has assigned her.

Resolved, That it is the duty of the women of this country to secure to themselves their sacred right to the elective franchise.

Resolved, That the equality of human rights results necessarily from the fact of the identity of the race in capabilities and responsibilities.

Resolved, therefore, That, being invested by the Creator with the same capabilities, and the same consciousness of responsibility for their exercise, it is demonstrably the right and duty of woman, equally with man, to promote every righteous cause by every righteous means; and especially in regard to the great subjects of morals and religion, it is self evidently her right to participate with her brother in teaching them, both in private and in public, by writing and by speaking, by any instrumentalities proper to be used, and in any assemblies proper to be held; and this being a self-evident truth growing out of the divinely implanted principles of human nature, any custom or authority adverse to it, whether modern or wearing the hoary sanction of antiquity, is to be regarded as a self-evident falsehood, and at war with mankind.

Resolved, That the speedy success of our cause depends upon the zealous and untiring efforts of both men and women, for the overthrow of the monopoly of the pulpit, and for the securing to woman an equal participation with men in the various trades, professions, and commerce.

Seneca Falls, N.Y., 1848

From The Woman's Bible *by Elizabeth Cady Stanton (1895 and 1898)*

THE BOOK OF GENESIS

CHAPTER I.

Genesis i : 26, 27, 28.

26 ¶And God said, Let us make man in our image, after our likeness: and let them have dominion over the fish of the sea, and over the fowl of the air, and over the cattle, and over all the earth, and over every creeping thing that creepeth upon the earth.

27 So God created man in his *own* image, in the image of God created he him; male and female created he them.

28 And God blessed them, and God said unto them, Be fruitful, and multiply, and replenish the earth, and subdue it; and have dominion over the fish of the sea, and over the fowl of the air, and over every living thing that moveth upon the earth.

Here is the sacred historian's first account of the advent of woman; a simultaneous creation of both sexes, in the image of God. It is evident from the language that there was consultation in the Godhead, and that the masculine and feminine elements were equally represented. Scott in his commentaries says, "this consultation of the Gods is the origin of the doctrine of the trinity." But instead of three

431

male personages, as generally represented, a Heavenly Father, Mother, and Son would seem more rational.

The first step in the elevation of woman to her true position, as an equal factor in human progress, is the cultivation of the religious sentiment in regard to her dignity and equality, the recognition by the rising generation of an ideal Heavenly Mother, to whom their prayers should be addressed, as well as to a Father.

If language has any meaning, we have in these texts a plain declaration of the existence of the feminine element in the Godhead, equal in power and glory with the masculine. The Heavenly Mother and Father! "God created man in his *own image, male and female.*" Thus Scripture, as well as science and philosophy, declares the eternity and equality of sex—the philosophical fact, without which there could have been no perpetuation of creation, no growth or development in the animal, vegetable, or mineral kingdoms, no awakening nor progressing in the world of thought. The masculine and feminine elements, exactly equal and balancing each other, are as essential to the maintenance of the equilibrium of the universe as positive and negative electricity, the centripetal and centrifugal forces, the laws of attraction which bind together all we know of this planet whereon we dwell and of the system in which we revolve.

In the great work of creation the crowning glory was realized, when man and woman were evolved on the sixth day, the masculine and feminine forces in the image of God, that must have existed eternally, in all forms of matter and mind. All the persons in the Godhead are represented in the Elohim the divine plurality taking counsel in regard to this last and highest form of life. Who were the members of this high council, and whether a duality or a trinity? Verse 27 declares the image of God male and female. How then is it possible to make woman an afterthought? We find in verses 5–16 the pronoun "he" used. Should it not in harmony with verse 26 be "they," a dual pronoun? We may attribute this to the same cause as the use of "his" in verse 11 instead of "it." The fruit tree yielding fruit after "his" kind instead of after after "its" kind. The paucity of a language may give rise to many misunderstandings.

The above texts plainly show the simultaneous creation of man and woman, and their equal importance in the development of the race. All those theories based on the assumption that man was prior in the creation, have no foundation in Scripture.

As to woman's subjection, on which both the canon and the civil law delight to dwell, it is important to note that equal dominion is given to woman over every living thing, but not one word is said giving man dominion over woman.

Here is the first title deed to this green earth giving alike to the sons and daughters of God. No lesson of woman's subjection can be fairly drawn from the first chapter of the Old Testament.

CHAPTER II.

Genesis ii: 21–25.

21 And the Lord God caused a deep sleep to fall upon Adam, and he slept; and he took one of his ribs, and closed up the flesh thereof.

22 And the rib which the Lord God had taken from man, made he a woman, and brought her unto the man.

23 And Adam said, This *is* now bone of my bone, and flesh of my flesh: she shall be called Woman, because she was taken out of man.

24 Therefore shall a man leave his father and his mother, and shall cleave unto his wife; and they shall be one flesh.

25 And they were both naked, the man and his wife, and were not ashamed.

As the account of the creation in the first chapter is in harmony with science, common sense, and the experience of mankind in natural laws, the inquiry naturally arises, why should there be two contradictory accounts in the same book, of the same event? It is fair to infer that the second version, which is found in some form in the different religions of all nations, is a mere allegory, symbolizing some mysterious conception of a highly imaginative editor.

The first account dignifies woman as an important factor in the creation, equal in power and glory with man. The second makes her a mere afterthought. The world in good running order without her. The only reason for her advent being the solitude of man.

There is something sublime in bringing order out of chaos; light out of darkness; giving each planet its place in the solar system; oceans and lands their limits; wholly inconsistent with a petty surgical operation, to find material for the mother of the race. It is on this allegory that all the enemies of women rest their battering rams, to prove her inferiority. Accepting the view that man was prior in the creation, some Scriptural writers say that as the woman was of the man, therefore, her position should be one of subjection. Grant it, then as the historical fact is reversed in our day, and the man is now of the woman, shall his place be one of subjection?

The equal position declared in the first account must prove more satisfactory to both sexes; created alike in the image of God—The Heavenly Mother and Father.

433

Thus, the Old Testament, "in the beginning," proclaims the simultaneous creation of man and woman, the eternity and equality of sex; and the New Testament echoes back through the centuries the individual sovereignty of woman growing out of this natural fact. Paul, in speaking of equality as the very soul and essence of Christianity, said, "There is neither Jew nor Greek, there is neither bond nor free, there is neither male nor female; for ye are all one in Christ Jesus." With this recognition of the feminine element in the Godhead in the Old Testament, and this declaration of the equality of the sexes in the New, we may well wonder at the contemptible status woman occupies in the Christian Church of to-day.

All the commentators and publicists writing on woman's position, go through an immense amount of fine-spun metaphysical speculations, to prove her subordination in harmony with the Creator's original design.

It is evident that some wily writer, seeing the perfect equality of man and woman in the first chapter, felt it important for the dignity and dominion of man to effect woman's subordination in some way. To do this a spirit of evil must be introduced, which at once proved itself stronger than the spirit of good, and man's supremacy was based on the downfall of all that had just been pronounced very good. This spirit of evil evidently existed before the supposed fall of man, hence woman was not the origin of sin as so often asserted.

National Organization for Women (NOW) Bill of Rights for 1969

I. Equal Rights Constitutional Amendment
II. Enforce Law Banning Sex Discrimination in Employment
III. Maternity Leave Rights in Employment and in Social Security Benefits
IV. Tax Deduction for Home and Child Care Expenses for Working Parents
V. Child Care Day Centers
VI. Equal and Unsegregated Education
VII. The Right of Women to Control Their Reproductive Lives

We Demand:

I. That the United States Congress immediately pass the Equal Rights Amendment to the Constitution to provide that "Equality of rights under the law shall not be denied or abridged by the United States or by any State on account of sex," and that such then be immediately ratified by the several States.

II. That equal employment opportunity be guaranteed to all women, as well as men, by insisting that the Equal Employment Opportunity Commission enforces the prohibitions against sex dis-

435

crimination in employment under Title VII of the Civil Rights Act of 1964 with the same vigor as it enforces the prohibitions against racial discrimination.

III.   That women be protected by law to ensure their rights to return to their jobs within a reasonable time after childbirth without loss of seniority or other accrued benefits, and be paid maternity leave as a form of social security and/or employee benefit.

IV.   Immediate revision of tax laws to permit the deduction of home and child care expenses for working parents.

V.   That child care facilities be established by law on the same basis as parks, libraries, and public schools, adequate to the needs of children from the preschool years through adolescence, as a community resource to be used by all citizens from all income levels.

VI.   That the right of women to be educated to their full potential equally with men be secured by Federal and State legislation, eliminating all discrimination and segregation by sex, written and unwritten, at all levels of education, including colleges, graduate and professional schools, loans and fellowships, and Federal and State training programs such as the Job Corps.

VII.   The right of women in poverty to secure job training, housing, and family allowances on equal terms with men, but without prejudice to a parent's right to remain at home to care for his or her children; revision of welfare legislation and poverty programs which deny women dignity, privacy and self-respect.

VIII.   The right of women to control their own reproductive lives by removing from penal codes laws limiting access to contraceptive information and devices and laws governing abortion.

National Women's Political Caucus: Platform

CIVIL RIGHTS

1. A priority effort to ratify the Equal Rights Amendment.
2. Amendment of existing civil rights legislation to prohibit discrimination on the basis of sex. Such change to:
   — eliminate discrimination against women in public accommodations and public facilities;
   — eliminate discrimination against women in public education;
   — eliminate discrimination against women in all federally-assisted programs and federally-contracted employment;
   — extend the jurisdiction of the Civil Rights Commission to include denial of civil rights on the basis of sex.

HUMAN RIGHTS

1. Implementation of the recommendations of the Presidential Commission on Population Growth and the American Future. In consonance with this study, all laws that affect a woman's right to decide her own reproductive and sexual life should be repealed.
2. Passage of comprehensive child care legislation.

3. Comprehensive legislation to provide preventive health care for all Americans, including provisions for maternity, abortion, and birth control aid regardless of age or marital status.
4. An immediate and concerted effort to end hunger and malnutrition for all Americans.
5. Fair treatment in housing to assure adequate shelter for all Americans, giving special attention to the elimination of discriminatory practices against women and families headed by women.
6. Reform of the criminal justice system, especially in those areas directly concerned with women.

ECONOMIC RIGHTS

1. Elimination of all tax inequities that affect women and children, such as higher taxes for single women.
2. Amendment of the Social Security Act to provide equitable retirement benefits for families with working wives, widows, women heads of households, and their children.
3. Extension of temporary disability benefits to cover pregnancy, childbirth, miscarriage, abortion and recovery.
4. Extension of equal pay, minimum wage, overtime and unemployment insurance to cover all workers.
5. Amendment of the Internal Revenue Code to permit families to deduct from gross income as a business expense reasonable amounts paid for a housekeeper, nurse, or related service for care of children or disabled dependents.
6. A guaranteed adequate income for all Americans.

NATIONAL COMMITMENT TO WOMEN

1. Appointment of women to positions of top responsibility in all branches of the Federal government to achieve an equitable ratio of women and men. Such positions include Cabinet members, agency heads, and Supreme Court justices.
2. Inclusion of women advisors in equitable ratios on all government studies, commissions and hearings.
3. Passage of the Women's Equality Act to implement the recommendations of the President's Task Force on Women's Rights and Responsibilities.
4. Passage of the Women's Education Act of 1973 which authorizes the Secretary of HEW to make grants to conduct special educational programs and activities concerning women.
5. Enactment of legislation authorizing Federal grants on a matching basis for financing State Commissions on the Status of Women.

438

Index

Index

440

Index

442

Index

Index

446